BROOKLANDS COLLEGE LIBRARY
HEATH ROAD, WEYBRIDGE, SURREY KT13 8TT
Tel: (01932) 797906

This item must be returned on or bef...
entered below. Subject to certain con...
period may be extended upon applicatio...

D0625146

Newslett...

Follow these tips ...

- ✔ Do lay out yo... headers, sub... illustrations.

- ✔ Don't invest i... use desktop publishing, web distribution or photocopying unless you have a large, paid-for circulation.

- ✔ Do build and nurture your own in-house list of customers, leads and referrals.

- ✔ Do understand the difference between an e-newsletter that annoys the recipient and a valuable e-newsletter people look forward to receiving.

- ✔ Do send your newsletter to a media list to generate publicity.

- ✔ Don't charge money for your newsletter unless you want to make it a serious product on its own rather than a publicity piece for your business.

- ✔ Do provide useful information, tips and news about your industry in every issue.

- ✔ Don't go into your own products in too much detail, otherwise readers won't value the news-letter as an objective source of information.

... ...ple to ask about your offerings, ...ke sure you have plenty of lead-generating communications out in the market at all times.

Here are some of the best all-around options:

- ✔ Freephone telephone numbers
- ✔ Directory listings
- ✔ Website address (in all your materials and ads)
- ✔ Fax numbers (on all your catalogues, brochures and ads)
- ✔ Sponsored links on Google when people search for terms associated with your product or brand
- ✔ Offers of free catalogues (through ads, brochures, directories and websites)
- ✔ Coupons
- ✔ Publicity (any media coverage tends to generate leads)

If you turn one in three leads into a sale, then all you need to do to get 50 more sales is generate 150 new leads. Not so hard when you look at it that way, is it?

Making Sure Your Business Card Brings You Business

Your business card leaves a lasting impression. Consider the following:

- ✔ Print custom business cards for specific events (your local printing shop can do short runs for you on the cheap).

- ✔ Design a two-fold, triple-sized business card. Its face looks like a normal card, but when you open it up, you get a mini-catalogue or brochure.

- ✔ Include customer quotes or testimonials on the back of your business card.

- ✔ Put a beautiful landscape photo on your card to make it appealing and memorable.

- ✔ Include a tagline emphasising your benefits to customers or your mission statement.

- ✔ Use unusual, high-quality paper to give your card a unique feel in the hand.

- ✔ Always have a business card with you and don't be afraid to ask for referrals. People are usually more than happy to help.

- ✔ Update your logo an... ...ed than competitors' cards.

BROOKLANDS COLLEGE LIBRARY

111112

WITHDRAWN FROM STO...
Brooklands College Library

For Dumm... ...s for Beginners

Marketing Kit For Dummies®

Ways to Simplify Your Planning

Follow these tips to save yourself valuable time when getting a marketing plan together:

- Figure out what you do best and what your customers like most. Let this strength form the foundation of your plan. Invest in making it even better, and in communicating it to customers and prospects.

- Find out where new customers come from. In your new plan, invest in these productive marketing activities and cut others.

- Use a template! There are templates and outlines you can use (see the CD that comes with this book for multiple templates), so don't try and reinvent the wheel.

- Write a paragraph for each line in your budget. The text and spreadsheet parts of the plan should correspond closely.

Planning with the Five Ps

When in doubt about how to improve your sales and marketing performance, stop and think about whether you can take some action in one of the 'P' areas:

- **Product:** Improve quality? Add new products or upgrades? Provide better service and support? Add a warranty? Bundle products?

- **Price:** Cut costs? Reduce prices? Offer discounts for quantity? Offer discounts for loyalty? Offer discounts for timely purchases? Offer better terms? Guarantee a refund for dissatisfied customers?

- **Placement:** Increase the availability of your product(s) by adding more distributors, retailers, or salespeople? Expand your target market to new geographic areas? To new groups of customers? Sell product over the Internet?

- **Promotion:** Improve the quantity or quality of sales leads through direct-response ads, trade shows, a website or e-newsletter, direct mail, better brochures and letters or a catalogue? Polish your visual image by upgrading your business cards, letterhead, web brochure or other materials? Raise the stopping power of your ads or marketing materials? Write letters that create high involvement? Close more sales by diagnosing style issues behind tough customers? Use promotions more effectively?

- **People:** Improve service? Train sales or service people better? Replace the computer voice on your telephones with helpful people? Work on motivating employees or distributors?

Different Sales Closing Techniques to Try

If you're having trouble getting someone to sign on the dotted line, try using a different closing technique than your usual one. Here are some options:

- **Direct close:** Ask your prospect whether he's ready to place his order.

- **Trial close:** Ask him to make small decisions that may eventually add up to a completed order.

- **Wrap-up close:** Summarise your presentation and his needs to set the stage for order-taking.

- **Process close:** Take him to the next steps as if he were going to order (for example, write down specifics of what he needs).

- **Analytical close:** Examine the pros and cons of different options or otherwise analyse the prospect's decision, leading him to a logical purchase option.

- **Sales promotion close:** Offer a discount, time-sensitive extra, or other incentive to get him to make the purchase.

Wiley, the Wiley Publishing logo, For Dummies, the Dummies Man logo, the For Dummies Bestselling Book Series logo and all related trade dress are trademarks or registered trademarks of John Wiley & Sons, Inc., and/or its affiliates. All other trademarks are property of their respective owners.

Copyright © 2009 John Wiley & Sons, Ltd. All rights reserved. Item 4490-1. For more information about John Wiley & Sons, call (+44) 1234 779777.

For Dummies: Bestselling Book Series for Beginners

Marketing Kit

FOR

DUMMIES®

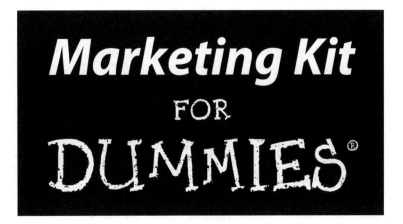

Marketing Kit
FOR
DUMMIES®

by Ruth Mortimer, Greg Brooks and
Alexander Hiam

WILEY

A John Wiley and Sons, Ltd, Publication

Marketing Kit For Dummies®

Published by
John Wiley & Sons, Ltd
The Atrium
Southern Gate
Chichester
West Sussex
PO19 8SQ
England

Email (for orders and customer service enquires): cs-books@wiley.co.uk

Visit our Home Page on www.wiley.com

Copyright © 2009 John Wiley & Sons, Ltd, Chichester, West Sussex, England

Published by John Wiley & Sons, Ltd, Chichester, West Sussex

All Rights Reserved. No part of this publication may be reproduced, stored in a retrieval system or
transmitted in any form or by any means, electronic, mechanical, photocopying, recording, scanning or
otherwise, except under the terms of the Copyright, Designs and Patents Act 1988 or under the terms of
a licence issued by the Copyright Licensing Agency Ltd, Saffron House, 6-10 Kirby Street, London
EC1N 8TS, UK, without the permission in writing of the Publisher. Requests to the Publisher for permission should be addressed to the Permissions Department, John Wiley & Sons, Ltd, The Atrium, Southern
Gate, Chichester, West Sussex, PO19 8SQ, England, or emailed to permreq@wiley.co.uk, or faxed to
(44) 1243 770620.

Trademarks: Wiley, the Wiley Publishing logo, For Dummies, the Dummies Man logo, A Reference for the
Rest of Us!, The Dummies Way, Dummies Daily, The Fun and Easy Way, Dummies.com and related trade
dress are trademarks or registered trademarks of John Wiley & Sons, Inc. and/or its affiliates in the United
States and other countries, and may not be used without written permission. All other trademarks are the
property of their respective owners. Wiley Publishing, Inc., is not associated with any product or vendor
mentioned in this book.

LIMIT OF LIABILITY/DISCLAIMER OF WARRANTY: THE PUBLISHER, THE AUTHOR, AND ANYONE
ELSE INVOLVED IN PREPARING THIS WORK MAKE NO REPRESENTATIONS OR WARRANTIES WITH
RESPECT TO THE ACCURACY OR COMPLETENESS OF THE CONTENTS OF THIS WORK AND SPECIFI-
CALLY DISCLAIM ALL WARRANTIES, INCLUDING WITHOUT LIMITATION WARRANTIES OF FITNESS
FOR A PARTICULAR PURPOSE. NO WARRANTY MAY BE CREATED OR EXTENDED BY SALES OR PRO-
MOTIONAL MATERIALS. THE ADVICE AND STRATEGIES CONTAINED HEREIN MAY NOT BE SUITABLE
FOR EVERY SITUATION. THIS WORK IS SOLD WITH THE UNDERSTANDING THAT THE PUBLISHER IS
NOT ENGAGED IN RENDERING LEGAL, ACCOUNTING, OR OTHER PROFESSIONAL SERVICES. IF PRO-
FESSIONAL ASSISTANCE IS REQUIRED, THE SERVICES OF A COMPETENT PROFESSIONAL PERSON
SHOULD BE SOUGHT. NEITHER THE PUBLISHER NOR THE AUTHOR SHALL BE LIABLE FOR DAMAGES
ARISING HEREFROM. THE FACT THAT AN ORGANIZATION OR WEBSITE IS REFERRED TO IN THIS
WORK AS A CITATION AND/OR A POTENTIAL SOURCE OF FURTHER INFORMATION DOES NOT MEAN
THAT THE AUTHOR OR THE PUBLISHER ENDORSES THE INFORMATION THE ORGANIZATION OR
WEBSITE MAY PROVIDE OR RECOMMENDATIONS IT MAY MAKE. FURTHER, READERS SHOULD BE
AWARE THAT INTERNET WEBSITES LISTED IN THIS WORK MAY HAVE CHANGED OR DISAPPEARED
BETWEEN WHEN THIS WORK WAS WRITTEN AND WHEN IT IS READ.

For general information on our other products and services, please contact our Customer Care
Department within the U.S. at 877-762-2974, outside the U.S. at 317-572-3993, or fax 317-572-4002.

For technical support, please visit www.wiley.com/techsupport.

Wiley also publishes its books in a variety of electronic formats. Some content that appears in print may
not be available in electronic books.

British Library Cataloguing in Publication Data: A catalogue record for this book is available from the
British Library

ISBN: 978-0-470-74490-1

Printed and bound in Great Britain by Bell & Bain Ltd, Glasgow

10 9 8 7 6 5 4 3 2 1

WILEY

About the Authors

Ruth Mortimer is associate editor for *Marketing Week* magazine. In charge of a team of dedicated features writers at the publication, she appears regularly in national press such as *The Independent* and the *Daily Express* discussing issues relating to business, marketing and branding. She also appears on TV and radio as an expert commentator in this field for multiple programmes, including those on the BBC and Sky.

Previous to joining *Marketing Week*, Ruth was editor of global business title *Brand Strategy*, as well as writing for Channel 4's *4talent* service to let young people know about new talents in music, design, arts and digital techniques. At *Brand Strategy*, she took the magazine through a full redesign and repositioning, introducing a new range of supplements and a conference programme, while contributing articles to sister titles *Design Week* and *New Media Age*. Before writing about marketing for a living, Ruth was an archaeologist, working mainly in the Middle East.

Greg Brooks is Content Strategy Director at C Squared, publisher of *M&M* magazine, creative information service www.creamglobal.com and producer of the Festival of Media. He is also a freelance journalist and digital media consultant with ten years experience covering the global digital industry. He has been a regular contributor to UK national titles such as *Marketing*, *New Media Age*, *Brand Strategy*, *Broadcast*, *Future Media*, *The Guardian* and Channel 4's *4Talent* online portal. He is also co-author of *Digital Marketing For Dummies* and *Marketing For Dummies.* In a consultancy role he has worked with Sky, McDonald's, News International, BT, Red Bull, Camelot (the UK Lottery operator), EnergyWatch, Visit Britain and OfCOM (the UK communications regulator), advising on the future strategic use of digital media.

Alex Hiam is the bestselling co-author of *Marketing For Dummies* and *The Portable MBA in Marketing*, as well as numerous books on management and leadership. He is the founder of INSIGHTS for Training & Development, which provides management, customer service, and sales force training to client companies throughout the world. He also designs and publishes training materials and curricula used by the in-house training departments of many companies and government agencies. You can find descriptions of his firm's marketing and sales products and services at www.insightsformarketing.com.

Dedications

To all my friends, family and workmates who have put up with me spreading myself too thinly over the last year, thank you all. Also to Greg, who is always an excellent partner in crime (and writing books).

– RM

To Ruth, the perfect partner.

– GB

There are so many wonderful people in my life, it is hard not to overflow the dedication page with their names. But as I worked on this book, my mind kept returning to my Dad, who passed away about the same time we were negotiating the contract to do this second edition. A quiet leader and generoushearted grandfather, friend, and philanthropist, he set an example for business and personal success that inspired his family and friends. He never boasted about his many accomplishments, so I won't here. Suffice it to say that his warm support and fine example are with us still.

– AH

Authors' Acknowledgements

My first thanks must go to my co-author Greg Brooks. Despite both of us changing jobs during the writing process and a tumultuous economic situation requiring regular updates to all our work, this turned into an interesting and worthwhile project. Much of that is down to your clear thinking and abilities as a writer so it has been a pleasure working with you.

This book would not have been possible without the hard work of the team at Wiley, so thank you very much for taking our words and making sure they made sense to people outside the bubble of the marketing world. The *Marketing Kit For Dummies* team have constantly improved and enhanced our work at every turn, so many thanks.

Last but most definitely not least, thank you to the people (and the brands where they work) who gave up their time and ideas to make sure that *Marketing Kit For Dummies* could be of use to people, no matter the size of the organisation or marketing budget.

– RM

Marketing Kit For Dummies would not be the useful and relevant book that it is without the steadying hand, eagle-eye and encouraging words of my partner in crime, Ruth. It's been a hectic few months and thanks to your drive and enthusiasm, the finished article is every bit as good as we wanted it to be. That is down to you.

Thanks also go to the Wiley team, never slow to help us along the way if we needed a helping hand (or the occasional prod).

Lastly, thanks to everyone for their input on this project, be you a creative, online or media agency, a brand, social network, research company or one of our valuable contacts. This book wouldn't exist without your help.

– GB

Thanks to my able staff and associates for all their contributions to this book, especially to Stephanie Sousbies, Eric Riess, Angela Pablo, Chrissy Guthrie and Celia Rocks.

– AH

Publisher's Acknowledgements

We're proud of this book; please send us your comments through our Dummies online registration form located at www.dummies.com/register/.

Some of the people who helped bring this book to market include the following:

Acquisitions, Editorial, and Media Development

Project Editor: Rachael Chilvers

Content Editor: Jo Theedom

Commissioning Editor: Wejdan Ismail

Assistant Editor: Jennifer Prytherch

Development Editor: Andy Finch

Proofreader: Kelly Cattermole

Production Manager: Daniel Mersey

Cover Photos: © joSon/Getty Images

Cartoons: Ed McLachlan

Composition Services

Project Coordinator: Lynsey Stanford

Layout and Graphics: SDJumper

Proofreaders: Melissa Cossell

Indexer: Ty Koontz

Contents at a Glance

Table of Contents

Part II: Advertising Management and Design 89

Chapter 5: Planning and Budgeting Ad Campaigns 91

Chapter 6: Shortcuts to Great Ads 105

Introduction

. . . .

*W*hat can you do today to boost sales, attract new customers and retain old customers? Well, for starters, you can read this book and make a commitment to work on your marketing programme! In *Marketing Kit For Dummies*, we provide information, resources and tools for the active marketer, salesperson or manager. Furthermore, you get the benefit of an accompanying CD-ROM that's chock-full of templates for making plans, sales projections, surveys and coupon profitability analysis, to name just a few of the goodies we've put on there for you.

About This Book

Marketing Kit For Dummies offers a lot of help to anyone in business and covers a wide range of subjects, including:

- ✔ Simple, powerful templates and general rules for writing a marketing plan or ad campaign and budgeting your expenses.

- ✔ A collection of advertising templates, brochure templates, and even templates for letterheads and business cards.

- ✔ Insights on how to close the sale successfully through improved sales or marketing techniques.

- ✔ Plenty of ideas, examples, tips and templates to make your sales and marketing materials look great – and function well, too.

- ✔ Neat marketing software to help you do the chores of good marketing quickly *and* well.

- ✔ Plenty of hands-on tools and activities to help you boost your own performance in sales and marketing.

We wrote *Marketing Kit For Dummies* for all of you who want to take responsibility for any aspect of sales or marketing in your organisation – whether that organisation is a small one-person operation, a large multinational corporation, or a public sector or non-profit organisation.

Marketing Kit For Dummies focuses on helping readers communicate better with customers. Whether person-to-person, through a letter, the telephone, a brochure, a website or any other medium, your customer communications play a vital role in the success of your business. We've cued up an immense amount of information, resources and templates to help you improve your customer communications and your overall business image. Have a peek at the contents of the CD to see what we mean! (But be sure to use this valuable CD – just a peek won't do – because using it correctly can make the difference between a profitable business and no business.)

Conventions Used in This Book

When reading this book, be aware of the following conventions:

- ✔ Websites and email addresses appear in `monofont` to help them stand out.
- ✔ Any information that's helpful or interesting but not essential appears in sidebars, which are the grey-shaded boxes sprinkled throughout the book.
- ✔ Whenever we introduce a new term, we *italicise* it.
- ✔ CD files are numbered, with the first two digits designating the chapter they support and the next two digits indicating the order in which we refer to them in the chapter.

Foolish Assumptions

We hate to make assumptions about people we don't know, but, dear reader, we did have to assume a few things about you when writing this book. Hopefully at least one of these assumptions applies to you:

- ✔ You're a marketer, salesperson or at least someone interested in marketing.
- ✔ Your business isn't as successful as you'd like it to be, and you want to know how you can fix that.
- ✔ You know what you need to do to improve your marketing programme, but you want someone to walk you through the necessary planning and actions.
- ✔ Or maybe you aren't sure what to do; you need to do some planning or develop a winning strategy.

How This Book Is Organised

Marketing Kit For Dummies consists of 22 chapters and a CD-ROM that has examples, templates, forms and software organised to support and extend each chapter's coverage. Here's how we organised all this great information.

Part I: Tools for Designing Great Marketing Programmes

Things go better when you have a plan in mind. In marketing, this plan can be as simple as a back-of-the-envelope programme using the Five Ps (product, pricing, placement, promotions and people), which we cover in Chapter 2. Or it can be as complex as a detailed, systematic audit of all marketing activities, followed by a carefully written plan and a spreadsheet-based budget to go with it. We cover all these options in Part I, and we include the templates needed to take the sting out of designing a good programme that boosts sales and profits.

Part II: Advertising Management and Design

Ads are often the key element of a marketing programme, and in this part, we share insights, how-to tips and tools to help you design winning ads for your campaign. Advertising needs to start with a good plan and an affordable budget, which we cover in Chapter 5. Then you have to actually design hard-hitting ads that draw attention to your message and produce leads and sales. These challenges are covered in Chapter 6.

Part III: Power Marketing Alternatives to Advertising

Advertising is costly. In this part, we show you how to get your message across and generate leads and sales in creative ways that cost less than traditional advertising. Sometimes something as simple as a really well-designed business card is the secret to winning business and boosting sales.

Newsletters, publicity, catalogues, logos and letterheads and other marketing elements may also boost your sales. Check out this part if you want to save money on expensive advertising or just to make sure that you're doing these essentials as well as you can.

Part IV: Honing Your Marketing Skills

Some important skills are involved in doing good marketing. For example, you need to do market research to find out what customers want and how to sell better than your competitors do. And communicating well is obviously important in marketing, so we cover writing in this part as well. The star of this section is that secret ingredient that transforms ordinary marketing into the stuff of brilliant breakthroughs: creativity. We include a chapter specifically on this subject to help you to develop creative thinking through simple tools and workshop exercises.

Part V: Sales and Service Success

Sales and marketing: that's what people usually say, separating these two intertwined activities in an artificial way. We don't really know where selling stops and marketing begins. In every successful business we've seen, the two activities work hand in glove to signal new customers to the door, serve current customers and thank past customers for their business in such a way that they feel good about coming back again. So this part on how to do great sales is an important complement to the other parts of the book. Use it to make sure that you're finding and closing as many good leads as you possibly can, or use it to diagnose or improve any sales process for improved performance.

Part VI: The Part of Tens

This part covers several topics that may give you winning ideas for your marketing programme. Take a look at the collection of winning marketing strategies in Chapter 20 – maybe one of them will work for you! We also cover ways to cut costs and increase the return of your marketing investment in this part. And last but definitely not least, we've collected simple ideas for using the Internet to boost sales and leverage your marketing programme.

And don't overlook the Appendix, which explains how to use the CD, or the CD itself. It's attached to the inside back cover of this book.

Icons Used in This Book

We occasionally use icons to flag certain passages. Here's what the icons mean:

This icon points out good ideas and shortcuts to make your life as a marketer easier.

Any information that's especially important and worth remembering gets this icon.

This icon indicates mistakes and pitfalls to avoid. Whatever you do, don't skip these paragraphs!

This icon highlights a method or approach that's been used successfully in real life, or highlights an example to illustrate a point.

When you see this icon, you know that an accompanying example, form or spreadsheet is available on the CD that comes with this book.

Where to Go from Here

The beauty of this book is that you can skip to any section or chapter as you desire. You can certainly read the book from cover to cover, but you don't have to. Start with whatever topic is most important to you and don't forget to use the accompanying tools on the CD.

We encourage you to start using the ideas and tools from this book right away to improve your marketing and boost your sales.

And if you want even more information and advice about marketing principles, check out other useful books such as *Marketing For Dummies,* (Wiley) and *Digital Marketing For Dummies* (Wiley). You certainly don't *need* all of these books, but they do complement one another nicely.

Part I
Tools for Designing Great Marketing Programmes

'Are you sure this stunt is going to sell our
custard pies, Colin?'

In this part . . .

We equip you with tools and ideas for improving your marketing and boosting your sales. We also share the secret of successful marketers – how they find their marketing zone, the formula that makes producing growth and controlling marketing costs easy.

Need a marketing plan? Honestly, everybody does, but most people dread the challenge of creating one. Probably the best feature in this part is the template and instructions for preparing your own marketing plan in Chapter 3. We include a really cool set of templates: a Word file that you can customise for the text portion of your plan and Excel spreadsheet templates that you can use for your sales projections and marketing budget. These tools usually cost hundreds of pounds from consultants and will prove invaluable to you as you grow your business, so take advantage of our generosity.

Chapter 1

The Art of Marketing

In This Chapter

▶ Creating successful marketing programmes

▶ Using advertising effectively

▶ Exploiting all the available media

▶ Discovering your marketing imagination

Marketing is all pervasive. The chances are that you already do quite a bit of marketing. You may not even realise that you're doing it, but if you have a product or service that's selling, know who your best customers are and what they want, and you have plans to develop new products for them or to find more customers, you're already addressing some of the fundamentals of marketing.

In this chapter, we introduce you to the basics of successful marketing and encourage you to expand your ideas of what marketing is. We show you that marketing consists of more than just advertising and doesn't have to be restricted to traditional media, and we also help you develop one vital ingredient: your own marketing imagination.

We walk you through the tools of the marketing trade so that you can begin to lay the foundations of a successful marketing career, including helping you to develop a marketing programme.

This chapter serves as an important foundation to topics that we cover in much more depth throughout this book.

Developing Great Marketing Programmes

The most common mistake made by organisations is believing that marketing means advertising. Not so. Advertising, or promotion, is just one discipline within the broader church of marketing. Many other parts of the marketing programme may be things that you think of as everyday parts of doing your business: setting the right price for your products and services; thinking about your distribution and how your customers find your products and services; offering the right kind of after-care; and even giving your customers the chance to complain if they're unhappy.

Great marketing programmes can make or break an organisation. Think about those brands that give you a good experience. Is this success down to one individual element or a combination of elements all working together to create the perfect customer environment? The chances are it's down to the overall marketing programme rather than any one aspect of the brand's operations.

The key to successful marketing is to bring all these elements together under a formal marketing framework. Without this framework, your separate efforts aren't nearly as efficient or effective as they can be.

Your marketing activity (by which we mean everything about your organisation that makes a difference to your customers) is crucial because it's what gets your business from where it is now to where you want it to be. In purchasing this book, you've taken the first step towards great marketing. We give you lots of simple, quick steps you can take to make progress with your marketing activities and back these up with practical exercises and examples on the accompanying CD-ROM.

Marketing, however, is more than just a group of formulas and processes. We do provide step-by-step guides, but the final ingredient, marketing magic, needs to come from you. We can give you a guide to the practical side of marketing, but you need to supply the imagination and experimentation that complements the know-how. Together all these elements work together, and we help you to develop your own programme for marketing success.

Understanding your customers and market

The first step towards success is understanding who your customer is and the market you operate in. You need to find your own Marketing Zone: your individual blueprint for marketing. We tackle this subject for you in Chapter 2.

But before you can get down to the business of finding your Marketing Zone, we're going to go through some of the most important things you discover in this book and why they matter. Whether you're product or customer-orientated, you need to understand how customers think and what they like in order to market to them effectively. Only then can you develop products or services that meet those needs and come up with appropriate and appealing ways to communicate them.

This may sound simple, but like everything in life, it's a bit more complicated. You need to understand your customers on two levels: the rational, functional dimension of making a purchase decision; and the irrational, emotional dimension that people use to choose what they buy.

Every purchase – whether it's a fizzy drink, a software program, a consulting service, a book or a manufacturing part – has both rational and emotional elements. So to truly know your customer, you must explore two primary questions:

- ✔ **What do customers think about your product?** Do they understand it? Do they think its features and benefits are superior to the competition and can meet their needs? Do they think that your product is good value, given its benefits and costs? In other words, how do your customers respond rationally to your product?

- ✔ **How do customers feel about your product?** Does it make them feel good? Do they like its personality? Do they like how your product makes them feel about themselves? In other words, how do your customers respond emotionally to your product?

If you decide that one of these dimensions dominates the other, you have uncovered some important information, which can inform your marketing programme. If rationality is the most important area, you may need to think more about the rational promises you make in any marketing; if emotion has more relevance to your buyers, you may need to appeal more to their hearts than their heads.

In most cases, depending on your customers, you need to take one of the three following approaches in your marketing programme:

- ✔ **Informational approach.** You use this approach when your customers buy in a rational manner. This approach involves showing off the product and talking about its benefits. Demonstrating how your products or services are better than any alternatives is important when using an informational approach. Use this approach when you think buyers are going to make a careful, thoughtful, informed purchase decision led by their heads, not just their hearts.

- ✔ **Emotional approach.** This approach pushes emotional rather than rational buttons. For example, a marketer of virus-scanning software may try to scare computer users by asking them in a headline: 'What would it cost you if a virus destroyed everything on your computer right now?' That emotional appeal can be much more powerful than a pile of statistics about the frequency and type of viruses on the Internet, which may just bore people. Use an emotional approach when your customers have strong feelings that you can tap into and relate to your product or service.

> ✔ **Balanced mix.** This approach uses a combination of both informational and emotional appeals. For example, after a scare-tactic (emotional) headline asking: 'How much would it cost you if a virus destroyed everything on your computer?', we would follow it up with a few statistics such as: 'One out of every ten computer users suffers a catastrophic virus attack each year.' The use of facts helps reinforce the nervous feelings the initial headline evoked.

You need to decide which of these three approaches to use and use it consistently in all your communications. When in doubt, use the balanced mix to hedge your bets.

Creating a marketing plan

You're not going to believe all the great tools on the CD for this book to help you create a winning marketing plan! We can hardly believe them ourselves. The CD contains dozens of pages of templates, audit forms, interactive forecasting, planning and budgeting tools for you to use. Many readers wrestle with how to write a marketing plan and prepare a good budget. How to improve a marketing programme isn't always obvious. These tasks are difficult. The only way to make it relatively easy is to have someone walk you through the process, which is what we do through this book.

You don't have to write a marketing plan to use this book or even to benefit from it, but you may want to, because doing so isn't as hard as you may think and, most importantly, a good plan increases your odds of success. In fact, most of the really successful businesses we know – small or large, new or old – write a careful marketing plan at least once a year.

Marketing combines lots of activities and expenditures in the hope of generating or increasing sales and maintaining or increasing market share. You don't see those sales numbers rise without a coherent plan that finds a way of using the strengths of your position to create marketing and sales activities that can convince the right customers to buy.

A single plan is fine if all your marketing activities are consistent and clearly of one kind. If you operate a more complex business – offering both services and products, for example – you may find that you need to work up one plan for selling products and another plan for convincing product buyers to use your services. We give you help with both these tasks in Chapter 3, but the general rule is that if the plan seems too complicated – divide and conquer! Then add everything up to get the big picture with its overall projections and budgets.

Getting to Grips with Advertising Management and Design

Advertising can be a potent weapon in the armoury of a marketer. It can bring great rewards, but use it badly and it can backfire. Although the creation of a great programme and careful planning are vital to the success of your marketing, if the resulting advertising isn't up to scratch, you can kiss goodbye to any benefits that you may hope to gain.

Ads need to look good, read well, sound great, catch the eye, make a lasting impression and be the stuff of dinner conversation – and that's what we show you how to achieve in Chapter 6. However, before you start designing specific ads, you need to create an advertising plan, as we show you in Chapter 5.

 The importance of advertising management can be very simply put: with advertising, you can easily spend more money than you ever imagined in your wildest dreams! Even in the midst of a global economic downturn in 2008, a company such as Procter & Gamble, which owns Ariel washing powder and Olay skincare, reportedly spent nearly £7 billion worldwide on advertising its products. However, because most of us don't have billions to work with, you're sensible to put practical limits on your advertising, which still allow you to gain all the benefits you need within a workable budget.

Planning and budgeting

When you're reading about planning and budgeting for advertising, bear in mind that most of the conventional wisdom applied to this particular discipline is derived from what the world's biggest brands do. People look at what is done at big companies such as Procter & Gamble and then try to apply it to their own businesses.

But large organisations are working with huge budgets, which if you're a small or medium-sized business, may not apply to you. The most important rule for practical small-business advertising is *use cheap ads so that you can run them frequently without going broke!*

For example, imagine that you're the owner of a local restaurant. Before you consider setting down an advertising plan to start spending your hard-earned cash on promoting your food, atmosphere and style to potential customers, you need to make sure that you've considered your plan in the context of the overall budget available. You need to take into account elements such as rent, payroll and other costs before you start thinking about whether you want to appear on TV or in a local newspaper. We cover the vital topic of planning advertising thoroughly in Chapter 5.

Advertising is a fantastic thing that can bring you great success if carried out properly. But it can also be a millstone around your neck if you don't plan it carefully.

If you're going to spend money on marketing, make sure that you're spending it in the right places and on the right elements. The last thing we want you to do is launch an unbudgeted advertising campaign that does your business more harm than good!

Creating advertising campaigns

With the warning about keeping your advertising within budget still ringing in your ears, we move on to the fun part of advertising: coming up with fantastic, widely-admired ideas and creating memorable ads.

For most small and mid-sized businesses, most advertising isn't a 30-second ad in the middle of *Coronation Street*. Simple, inexpensive approaches to ad design are best for most marketing plans, because the goal is to keep your design or creation costs low in order to ensure that most of your advertising budget is spent on actually getting those ads out in front of potential buyers.

Most adverts from small businesses don't have to be award-winners. Creating an ad with awards in mind is a luxury most businesses can't afford; but a healthy dose of imagination can be very, very useful. For those of us who can't come up with million-pound ideas at the flick of a switch, just make sure that your ads are professional and simple enough that the message gets through loud and clear. And make them visually appealing because that's usually the secret to noticeable, memorable ads.

Chapter 6 gives you some information about different styles of ad design, including using imagery and different concepts, as well as some very useful ad templates on the CD-ROM.

Exploring Alternatives to Advertising

Advertising is only one piece of the marketing puzzle, and you can do lots of other things to drive sales that aren't classified as traditional advertising. Your brand should speak to its potential customers no matter what environment it is seen or heard in – radio, TV, packaging, in shops, in a newsletter, in a newspaper article, on a business card and so on.

In Part III of this book, we show you how you can take advantage of every opportunity to promote your brand. These opportunities start with the basics of business cards, letterheads, emails and faxes all the way through to the importance of presenting your brand on the Internet. We even give some practical advice on the stalwarts of small business promotion – brochures, blogs and press releases.

Using business cards, brochures and PR

Chapter 7 covers the basics of branding, which includes areas such as clarifying your brand identity – including designing your business name and logo – all the way through to creating successful marketing collateral such as business cards, letterheads, envelopes and emails.

You'd be surprised how little attention people pay to these areas, even if they have great advertising. When your business is running eye-catching ads on the TV or radio, forgetting the more basic areas is all too easy.

For small businesses, these elements are possibly even more important. As a small firm, you rely more on customer recommendations to build business and make first impressions count. A good-looking business card, brochure or letterhead can set you up in someone's mind as a well-run, professional organisation while a bad one can create the impression of a shoddy firm that doesn't really pay attention to detail.

Would you trust a dentist who has bad teeth? Probably not. That same snap judgement is what people make when assessing your business through any of its marketing elements. Throughout Chapter 7, we show you how to take a close look at how your business looks to the outside world, starting with an examination of the brand identity and then making sure that your business cards, stationery, labels, envelopes or boxes, faxes and emails convey your identity clearly and well.

Exploiting the power of the Internet

The Internet is the single greatest marketing invention of the last century. Why? Well, the TV is a fantastic medium for large firms to reach mass audiences with their big brand messages, but it isn't very accessible for most small and medium-sized businesses.

Online, however, the playing field is level. Good web marketers use the Internet to their advantage by ensuring that their businesses are seen in the relevant places. And do you know what's even better about the Internet? If you make sure that your brand is in the right place, that place can be filled with *pre-qualified eyeballs* – people who already want to know about your firm or product.

Imagine that you run a small restaurant. If you're based in Camden, London, you can advertise on websites for your local area, ensuring that most people who see your restaurant on that site on a regular basis may often pass it on the street too and become potential customers.

You can also make sure that you get listed on a restaurant review website for Camden restaurants. Most people looking at that website are looking very specifically for a restaurant to eat in within Camden. You can't say the same for advertising on TV or radio, because the broadcasting areas for local TV and radio stations are much wider than the targeted offerings online.

If you think targeted Internet marketing may become the most important part of your business promotion activities, pick up a copy of *Digital Marketing For Dummies* by Ben Carter, Gregory Brooks, Frank Catalano and Bud E. Smith (Wiley) to find out more about the available opportunities.

Another great development offered by digital technology (Internet, mobile phone and email) is the ability to communicate with your customers very cost efficiently, very quickly and on a tightly targeted basis. Chapter 10 takes you through the opportunities presented by email and online newsletters, which are great tools for the small business and can be powerful when used as part of a word-of-mouth marketing programme.

Don't fall into the trap of thinking that websites aren't for your business. The Internet offers huge opportunities for imaginative marketers. No successful marketers can afford to ignore the Internet!

Writing Effectively for Marketing

No matter what channels you decide to use in your marketing, you have to develop the skill of effective copywriting. This skill – the ability to write short, snappy and to-the-point text that gets your message across – is a lot harder to hone that you may first imagine.

We can't recall an ad in any medium that doesn't have some writing in it, and many ads are dominated by writing.

This fact is especially relevant in business advertising and when trying to explain the benefits of a complicated product or service. Other types of marketing, such as coupons (covered in Chapter 9), also need clear writing to communicate their benefits and rules to customers.

Businesses ask a lot of their marketing communications, whether they're ads, flyers, web pages, catalogues, brochures or other forms of communication with customers and potential buyers. So you need to do quite a bit of thinking in order to come up with ideas that really work.

Due to the number of marketing messages that we all see every day, you need to stay away from clichés, find ways to persuade your audience to part with their money and ensure that your messages get *cut-through* (a marketing term that means that people actually pay attention to your efforts). Chapter 14 helps you to hone these skills.

Enjoying Successful Sales and Service

Part V of this book covers the biggest puzzle faced by the marketer: how to sell, sell, sell on the back of your efforts. We can't stress enough how important it is to take advantage of all the work you've done to get to this point. Many people don't think about selling as being part of the marketing plan, but it's an absolutely vital element. In many respects, your whole marketing programme has been all about getting to the eventual sale.

Sales skills are important, whatever business you're in and whatever job you're doing, even if you're not in a formal sales role.

Just think about this issue for a moment. If you're a member of shop staff, for example, you interact with customers to help them find what they want and make them feel good about spending their money there. Construction contractors discuss a project with a prospective customer and then prepare and present (in other words – sell) the proposal they think is going to win them the job. Marketers selling services from one business to another contact their prospects in person, by email and telephone to generate business.

Even businesses that don't use people to sell have the occasional need for this skill. For example, the owner of a web-based business may need to make a pitch to a bank loan officer or investor in order to fund an expansion plan. Personal selling is an incredibly important part of marketing. In the final section of this book, we look at how the sales process works and how to maximise its effectiveness in your business.

Selling effectively

Every expert has a different model of the sales process. Some models are simple; many are highly elaborate. And, to be honest, few of them really give you much help in improving your sales success because they're rarely realistic or tailored to your exact circumstances. We favour a model that reflects reality: you need to do some work to figure out what the prospect needs, and then you present your offerings to meet that need. We also favour a model that suggests what to do and how and when to do it to optimise your sales efficiency.

In Chapter 18, we cover topics including understanding the importance of great sales leads, discovering how to be flexible in your sales approach and – the most important element of all – staying positive in the face of failure.

When we talk about failure we mean the time when you've seemingly done everything right, but are still rejected and the sale doesn't happen. How you respond to this setback is just as important as the fact that you got the sales opportunity in the first place. Responding with the right attitude and tools can make all the difference to making sure that your next sale ends in success.

Good selling is about having quality leads, making a good impression, having a flexible approach and the all-important positive attitude towards both success and failure. We cover all these aspects in more detail in Chapters 16 to 19.

Closing the deal

Within the sales process itself, the vital point is the *close*. That's when the sale is agreed, the contracts are signed and you're assured of getting your hands on the cash. In Chapter 17, you can investigate the many different ways of sealing the deal, how to use sales in all your marketing materials and methods, and passing the prospect's smell test.

The *smell test* is the crucial need for you to be professional in all your sales dealings. The rest of your marketing communications may be fantastic, but if the customer has a few questions at the moment of purchase and the sales-person can't answer them, the customer may get nervous, smell that some-thing isn't quite right and back out of the deal.

Some salespeople say not to accept a 'No' until you've tried to close the deal at least three times, whereas others never accept a 'No' when they sense an opportunity for a 'Yes'. We believe that the truth lies somewhere in between and that if you study and understand closing techniques, you'll be accepting far fewer rejections

How you ask for the business often determines if you get the business and how much of it you get.

In Chapter 17, we take you through this process so that by taking on what we have to say throughout this book, you can become not only a seasoned marketer, but also an expert salesperson. We also challenge one of the longest-held myths in marketing: that top-performing salespeople are born, not made. Anyone can sell if they have the right tools, techniques and enthusiasm.

The truth is that training and motivation are more important than talent. Big companies get good results when they train and support their sales forces. If you train and support yourself, you too can be a high-performing salesperson. And discovering and practising closing techniques is, in our opinion, the most important thing you can do to boost your sales performance.

Becoming a Marketing Expert

You're likely to be carrying out some form of marketing already, perhaps without even realising it. In this book we bring you the processes and formulas that help you to create great marketing, but you have to bring the imagination yourself to make it all work.

By working through this book and paying attention to the advice we offer, the lessons we explain and the practical tools we give you on the CD-ROM, we guarantee that you have all the elements required to plan, create and execute a successful marketing programme.

Imagination is something that is much harder for us to help you with. In Chapter 13, we try to help you with this area by giving you tools and techniques for generating creative concepts. But this is somewhere that your ideas, enthusiasm and commitment make all the difference to the end result.

We use the term *marketing imagination* throughout this book, and this concept is probably the most important factor in marketing success or failure.

Your ability to imagine new approaches is vital to your success as a marketer. The salesperson who invents a really convincing opener or comes up with a new strategy for generating leads is the one who sells the most products. The distributor who finds creative ways to serve customers through the Internet is the one who beats the competition with ease. Advertisers who come up with intriguing and beguiling ideas that capture consumer attention interest more people in their businesses. And the small firm that seeks new ways to promote its products and services makes a bigger impact than its rivals at a lower cost.

Using this book and the tools on the CD helps you unlock your creative potential, find success and become an expert marketer. No single simple secret exists to conjure up marketing success, but use this book carefully and you've started using the kind of techniques and ideas that can lead to that elusive marketing magic.

Chapter 2

Boosting Your Business with Great Marketing

*Y*our marketing – the specific methods *you* develop to boost *your* sales and improve *your* profits – eventually crystallises into a tried-and-true formula that works for you. But this formula is unique to your business and you can't copy it from anyone else. In this chapter, we help you work on the formula that puts you in your marketing zone, with reliable results from an efficient, effective marketing programme.

Finding Your Marketing Zone

Your *marketing zone* is the right combination of strategies and tactics to bring you all the business you need (see Figure 2-1). Finding your zone means exploring marketing options until you develop a formula that really works and that you can rely on with only minor adjustments from time to time.

Imagine that you're a dentist with your own practice. Over several years of experimentation, you work out a marketing formula based on three elements: a friendly service from all employees (from the receptionist to the nurse); a good location where plenty of people can find the practice; and regular customer contact via phone calls and postcards.

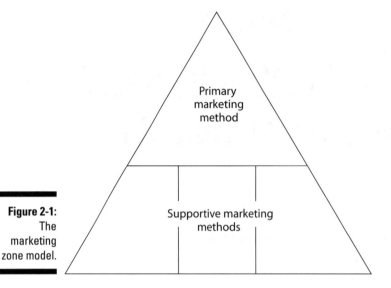

Figure 2-1:
The
marketing
zone model.

These three components form your marketing programme. Within this pro-gramme, the primary element of the marketing is the friendly staff and great service; the location, calls and postcards form the secondary element. You know how much your practice needs to spend to sustain the programme and get consistent results.

When you're profitable and successful, you may think about opening a branch office, adding another dentist, expanding into orthodontics or any number of ideas that can grow the business beyond its current base. But until you work out the basic marketing formula and enter your marketing zone, starting any new initiatives would be foolish. So how do you know you're in the zone? Well, when you're in the marketing zone, you find that:

- ✔ **You get reasonably consistent results every time you use a marketing tool.** For example, if you do a mailing, you should be able to predict within 10 per cent how many responses you're going to get.

- ✔ **You operate in the black.** Your marketing activities should return a profit. Successful marketing can be defined as any marketing that reliably returns more in profits than it costs to carry out.

- ✔ **You know what your top three to five marketing activities are and how to do them well.** And you should probably be investing close to half of your marketing spending in the single most effective marketing activity.

When you've satisfied these three requirements, you know that you've found your marketing zone. The search is over! Now you just need to work on repeating the formula with small improvements and watch your sales and profits grow.

No formula works forever. Eventually, you may begin to find that results are slipping or profits are shrinking. If performance deteriorates, you need to search for the zone again. Perhaps you need to alter your formula and update your plans. Ask yourself whether a new lead marketing method should replace your old one or whether you need to make a major change in one or more of your top three to five marketing activities. Take a close look and be prepared to spend time and effort revitalising your zone if performance slips and you can no longer say 'yes' to the three indicators described in the preceding checklist.

Enjoying the Benefits of Your Marketing Zone

When your business is in its marketing zone, you can count on a healthy flow of sales and spend more time thinking about the future. When you have the basics covered, you can focus on what exciting new things to do next.

Operating in your zone should be your standard business mode. Think of it as the equivalent of making sure that your car has had its MOT service and is ticking over nicely.

When your business is purring like a well-oiled engine, you can spend more time on other, more exciting parts of the business – just imagine turning your reliable family business into a super Hot Rod by adding in new offices, new product developments and so on.

Each of these new areas requires you to revisit your zone to ensure that everything you do adheres to your basic marketing principles; the same applies if you want to reinvent your brand and update its image.

For example, organic chocolate brand Green & Black's (now owned by Cadbury) started life with packaging proudly proclaiming its organic roots and detailing the principles of fair trading on which the business was based. For a while, this strategy worked because Green & Black's ethical values and worthy look helped it stand out from other chocolate brands. But as more fairly traded confectionery bars flooded onto the market, the ethical story no longer worked as its primary marketing tool. To address this issue, Green & Black's redesigned its packaging and changed all its marketing to advertise itself as better tasting and more luxurious than other chocolate. After emphasising the taste of the chocolate as its lead marketing focus rather than the brand's ethics, the company was quickly snapped up by mainstream confectioner Cadbury and has now expanded to North America.

The other benefits of finding your zone include:

- ✔ The ability to focus on scaling your business (making it bigger).
- ✔ More knowledge about your core customers (as you identified them in order to reach them in your zone).
- ✔ A great benchmark from which to try different marketing techniques and measure their performance.
- ✔ A strong, consistent brand message that helps to generate loyalty.
- ✔ The knowledge of what works best if times get tough and you need to batten down the hatches (in a tough economic climate).

Pinpointing Your Top Three Sales and Marketing Tools

If your business has been operating for a year or more, you're probably doing one or more marketing activities that work fairly well. Start by examining the three methods that have been most productive for you so far and see if you can refine them to make them work even better.

Your past experience is your most powerful source of information about what your top marketing tools should be.

Next, take a calculated look at other businesses. Start with your most successful competitors (but don't try to copy companies that are more than three times your size, because their budget puts them in a different marketing class and you probably can't afford to use their formulas right now). A good idea is to search for a successful similar company in another region and then study what it does. This approach isn't out and out copying; it's *benchmarking* (or learning from others' successful examples), which takes advantage of the fact that ideas are free and anyone can try them.

Don't copy the text or art of any other company's marketing materials directly – those are copyrighted. Only benchmark general ideas or themes – for example, if another business uses a large display ad in the Yellow Pages, try the same strategy with an ad of your own.

After you've examined similar companies for marketing ideas, take a look at dissimilar ones. Sometimes the best ideas come from outside your industry.

You're the owner of a small company making fishing equipment. You're talking to a couple of friends and discover that they write an Internet blog (or online diary) all about business insurance and how to buy and use it. Realising that no-one in the fishing equipment field is writing blogs, you follow their lead and start blogging. You write about your experiences fishing, what equipment you're using and what results you're getting. Over time, people who love fishing start to read regularly, and gradually the blog becomes your lead marketing tool. Then you support it with a website, traditional printed catalogue and a freephone number for people wanting to call and order.

Well done! You've found your marketing zone without using high-cost advertising. Whereas more traditional competitors run ads in magazines, your formula works just as well and costs much less. (See Chapter 10 for advice on using newsletters and blogs to grow your business.)

Experiment with your marketing mix until you get a predictable and highly profitable formula. Often, when we look at marketing plans, we find ourselves suggesting that the current lead marketing tool be demoted to secondary status and a new tool put in top place. Be willing to try a few variations until you find a lead marketing method that really pulls its weight.

Here's a great example of the search for a successful marketing formula. A friend of ours who owns a landscape gardening firm was doing a mix of residential and commercial work for office buildings and stores. Her business was struggling with marginal profits until a large, profitable contract with a big office building pointed the way toward a lucrative marketing zone. Now she avoids smaller scale residential customers and instead focuses on making sales calls to commercial property owners and managers who can commit to large annual contracts.

These days she puts her marketing material inside a professional-looking sales binder with testimonial letters from customers and a detailed listing of service and price options, which sets her apart from less organised competitors. Gone are the small low-profit accounts.

Now she has a dozen annual contracts that support a staff of ten and provide a healthy profit. She pays her staff well and hires reliable people who deliver a professional, consistent service. Trucks displaying her signs are often parked in front of upscale professional buildings, helping to build her brand and spread awareness of her business. She follows up all leads personally with a well-rehearsed office visit that often produces a new contract. Her goal is to add one to three new accounts each year – and so far, her simple marketing formula has met or exceeded that goal.

Adjusting for the Economic Cycle

It would be wonderful if the marketing formula that worked last year also worked perfectly this year. However, even a great marketing formula needs improvement. New competitors, new tastes and new technologies can out-date your products or antiquate your marketing message, pushing you out of your zone. Marketing is inherently creative for this reason (that's what we love about it!). So you should anticipate and welcome changes.

But if the economic cycle is shifting, you *really* have to be on your guard because your marketing formula probably needs to change dramatically in order to keep ahead of the economy. Think of the economic cycle as the key to whether you should be playing defensively or offensively as you formulate your marketing game plan.

Economic cycles are inevitable. If you adjust your marketing-zone formula accordingly, you can survive the tough times and grow in the good times. Marketers who adopt this approach create faster growth and higher profits than typical marketers who fail to adjust rapidly to changing economic conditions.

Tightening up for tough times

Look back at the situation in 2008. The rise in energy and food prices created a lot of cost and price pressures on businesses. Restaurants found the cost of ingredients going up by 30 per cent at the same time that customers were trying to cut their fuel use by avoiding long drives to distant restaurants. Hotels and other travel businesses also suffered from the rising cost of travel by car or plane. Book sales, casino revenues, movie ticket sales and many other categories declined. And because banks had hugely over-extended their credit-card and home mortgage lending in the earlier boom period, loans became extremely tight that year, too – which meant that consumers were cutting back on spending across the board, not just in areas affected by energy and food prices.

What do you need to do in this situation? The following three steps help smart marketers get through tough periods and emerge stronger:

1. **Control your own costs.**

   Sales fall because your customers are trying to control their spending. If you don't cut your costs more aggressively than they do, your profits are going to be squeezed. Renegotiate contracts whenever possible. Switch to lower-cost suppliers or ingredients. Lay off idle workers. Find ways to reduce your use of energy, even if it means closing off part of your work-space and not heating it. Be a miser. Don't make the mistake of waiting to see what happens. Take the lead in changing the rules of your business.

2. Change your offerings.

The things people buy in good economic times are different from the things they buy in bad times, but people still need to buy. Figure out what you should be selling in a depressed economy by imagining that you're starting a new business specifically for this economy, using the assets of your old business as building blocks. For example, if you own a luxury restaurant, think about how you can convert it to a profitable establishment with a menu based on lower-priced ingredients, a smaller, less highly trained kitchen staff and fewer wait-staff. As soon as you've worked out the details, print a new menu and make the changes.

To hesitate is to lose money, so make changes right away. You can always go back to the old formula next year or whenever the economy turns around. Ideas for adjusting your offer (if you're a restaurant adjusting for a depressed economy) include smaller portions, less expensive ingredients or components, shorter-term contracts for staff and anything that reduces the price, risk or upfront investment for your customers. Scaled-back offerings are considerate and appropriate in harder times.

3. Keep marketing!

Don't disappear from potential customers' radar screens. When you've controlled your costs and adjusted your offerings for the current situation, get back out there with modest short-term investments. What about new signs, local newspaper ads, listings in web directories, radio ads, a mailer or whatever you think may work to reach consumers.

Increase your use of paid-search advertising (pay-per-click advertising) on Google and Yahoo! because these search engines target only those customers who are still shopping in spite of the bad economy. Even though sales are down, some people continue to buy. Be the visible, realistic option for them, and you may even grow your business in the bad times – and emerge a stronger leader come the next economic boom. (See Chapter 4 for more ways to market on the Internet.)

These three simple steps work pretty well for any business, as long as you're capable of controlling costs and avoiding large losses. However, if you find your spending is out of control and you're bleeding money, consider a more radical response: shut down, sell or convert your business into something that can make money. Never go down with the ship. In every economic downturn, many businesses are too poorly prepared or weak to survive. You can tell if yours is one of them if you find that controlling your costs is impossible despite a month or two of hard effort. If that happens, stop bailing and bail out. But do bear in mind that most businesses with a really enduring offer at their core can be adjusted to survive the downturn and emerge stronger (although perhaps smaller) when the economy recovers.

Another word of warning: you have to use the three steps above *in order.* If you try to fix all your problems with a new advertising campaign or other marketing gimmick (Step 3) before you control costs (Step 1) and adjust your offering for the current economy (Step 2), your marketing initiative is sure to lose money and put you further behind. Don't say we didn't warn you!

Taking advantage of a growth economy

What about when the pendulum swings the other way, and the economy starts to grow at an accelerated rate? This situation also requires adjustment. Marketers who continue to be conservative get passed by flashy new competitors.

Here's how to adjust to a growth economy after you've survived the downturn:

1. **Pick your fastest-growing product or service and invest in it.**

   Promote aggressively whatever seems to be sharing in the economic momentum. Find new customers. Do more sales and marketing. Run more ads. Expand your territory. You need to grow sales in the easiest way possible, in order to start bringing in extra profits right away. Otherwise, you don't accumulate the cash needed to invest in growing your business rapidly during the upturn.

2. **Redesign your product line and pricing with the single-minded goal of raising the size of the average purchase.**

   Add options and extras. Cross-sell products with a special two-for-one or trial offer. Increase the size of your packages and offer a quantity incentive. Ideally, aim to at least double the average sale during an economic boom.

3. **Look for new products and/or customers.**

   Expanding into new categories and territories is your next source of growth, after you successfully leverage your most promising product and double the size of the average purchase. Now is the time to innovate. Pick up a new line of products that seems exciting and different. Go after an emerging group of customers with new tastes or needs. But don't forget to keep your core business healthy and profitable (see Steps 1 and 2) because a thriving core business gives you the capacity to try exciting new growth ideas.

Avoiding Costs and Risks with Smart Marketing

Marketing can be a dangerous game. We've seen many businesses commit to a marketing plan, only to find that the expected sales don't materialise and they run out of cash. What happens if you use most of your marketing budget to buy a mailing list and print and send out a new catalogue, but hardly any orders come in? This event happens all too often.

Here are some rules to keep you from blowing your marketing budget on things that don't bring in a good return:

- **Spend no more than 10 per cent of your marketing budget on unproven ideas.** If an idea hasn't worked several times for you already, it's unproven for you, no matter what others may say. You have to test it for your business before admitting it into your marketing zone.

- **Test each marketing idea several times on a small scale before committing to a big buy or large run.** You don't know enough to draw firm conclusions until you see what happens with repetition. (A small website needs to bring in orders before you invest in a big expensive one.)

- **Make sure that your ad, mailing, web directory or other marketing tool reaches *your* customers.** Many media buys sound great because they promise a big reach – otherwise known as a large audience – but who cares? What matters is whether your target customers and prospects are in that audience. For example, if your customers don't listen to radio, avoid the temptation of sponsoring your local radio station, even though it's cheaper than buying ad time on TV; it's a pointless exercise.

- **Don't try to imitate the big spenders.** The Coca-Cola brand is maintained in people's minds through millions of pounds of TV and outdoor advertising every day. Obviously, most businesses can't afford to flood the world with their brand identity. Nor can they print glossy catalogues every month. These highly visible marketing role models are completely useless for 99.9 per cent of businesses. Look for successful *local* marketing and advertising case studies because thriving small and mid-sized businesses offer the most practical and affordable benchmarks.

- **Collect junk mail.** One person's rubbish is another's treasure. Many of the best marketing talents are busy writing postcards and pitch letters, designing coupons and special offers or brainstorming new ways of making the outside of a mailing so intriguing that it actually gets read before being recycled. Discover what works from their ads. You'll find that a lot of your junk mail is from local and small-scale marketers and they're your best sources of good ideas if you're a small to mid-sized marketer, too. Try keeping a file of the latest junk mail that catches your eye or bookmark interesting links on your web browser. Just make sure that plenty of these ideas are low-cost and that they do the trick at a modest price.

In addition to these risk-reducing marketing tips, we strongly recommend that you keep a close eye on cash flow. Sometimes marketers get new-idea fever: they get so excited about a new marketing concept that they gamble too much on its success. Don't overspend on marketing! The best marketing budget is the one that you can afford to lose if nothing goes the way you hoped and planned. Yes, that is a pessimistic statement, but it's born of reality.

For example, an expensive ad campaign may or may not work. If it produces few or no sales, you better make sure that you can survive to try another idea. Our recommendation is that you spend your *extra* cash on your marketing. Don't spend money that you have to earn back by the end of the month to pay the rent and electric bill. Nothing in marketing is guaranteed. Everything is a gamble. As you refine your formula and find your marketing zone, the risk goes down – but it never goes away completely.

Strengthening Your Marketing Skills

Some people are much better at marketing than others. You can continue to feel challenged in this area or you can commit to strengthening your skill-set and becoming one of those all-too-rare expert marketers.

Skilled marketers are rare because marketing requires such a wide range of skills. Here are just some of the most important attributes:

- ✔ Ability to work with the Internet
- ✔ Budgeting
- ✔ Communication
- ✔ Creativity
- ✔ Database management
- ✔ Forecasting
- ✔ Pricing knowledge
- ✔ Problem-solving
- ✔ Research
- ✔ Salesmanship
- ✔ Technical understanding of printing

And this list doesn't even mention presentation skills, customer service and service recovery abilities, and the tenacity needed to shift rapidly from one of these skills to another . . . and another . . . and another. We think marketing is incredibly challenging and difficult, and we rarely meet anyone who's truly great at it.

However, we do meet a lot of successful businesspeople with one thing in common: an enthusiasm for strengthening their marketing skills. Gradually, with practice, they get pretty good at the majority of these skills. To follow in their footsteps, you need to be willing to be an adult pupil. Pick up a good book, find out about a new software program and talk to someone who knows all about something you know nothing about – be open and interested and you can expand your skills, too.

Design, copywriting, creativity and more

In this book, we help you work on a variety of marketing skills. Graphic design comes to the forefront in ad and business card design (see Chapters 6 and 7). Copywriting surfaces in Chapter 10 when we address blogging and newsletters and again in Chapter 11 when we address publicity. Communication is so essential to good marketing that we cover the basics of persuasive writing in Chapter 14.

Research skills are invaluable to the marketer, and we share some of them (along with tools for your customer research) in Chapter 12. Creative thinking is one of the most important marketing skills as regards advertising, and we hope that the examples and ideas in every chapter of this book help you power up your marketing imagination – but to be doubly sure, we include skill-building information in a mini workshop on creativity in Chapter 13.

Artful persuasion: Sales skills to the fore

What is the most important marketing skill? Is it communicating? Thinking creatively? Researching new opportunities? Planning? Pricing? It's pretty hard to decide, because so many skills are important. Some people, though, would say that the single most important marketing skill is salesmanship.

We know a lot of excellent salespeople and also a lot of business owners and managers, but honestly, the two lists don't really overlap. Most of the people who read marketing books don't feel very confident when they have to do sales. That's why we recommend studying Part V carefully. You have so many opportunities to use a little salesmanship – make sure that you have the skills needed to take advantage of every opportunity!

Quick skill-building tricks and tips

You have plenty of time to refine your skills, so we don't go into depth on the topic here (Part IV goes into skill-development in depth). However, we do want to pass on several skill-building tips that you can begin to practise right away, and that help to improve your marketing performance:

- ✔ **Say what is necessary in half the words.** This advice means cutting the other half. Almost every letter, slogan, email, ad headline, blog, product description, sales pitch or web page is too long. Discipline yourself to communicate succinctly. You'll be amazed at the impact.

- ✔ **Be concrete.** Give examples. Quote satisfied customers. Give specific information (statistics, specifications). Let the facts do the selling for you.

- ✔ **Know your customer.** If you can describe your target customer very clearly, you're probably ready to grow your sales. Too often, marketers have only a vague concept of who they need to reach and make a sale to. A lack of clarity about your target customer makes your entire marketing programme poorly focused, which dooms it to low response rates and low profitability.

- ✔ **Give your brand a winning personality and make everything consistent with it.** Customers need to *like* your brand, so try to imagine it as a person and make sure that it goes to work each day with a cheerful demeanour and appropriate attire. Inconsistent, unappealing presentation is the bane of good marketing. Make sure that everything the customer sees (from an invoice to a shop front) is appealing and consistent with the image you want to project.

If you're not already doing these four things well (and most marketers aren't), get to work on them right now. There's no time like the present for boosting your skills – and your marketing results!

Designing Your Marketing Programme

Your *marketing programme* is the co-ordinated, thoughtfully designed set of activities that put you in your marketing zone. (For more on that topic, see the earlier section 'Finding Your Marketing Zone'.) As you may recognise from Figure 2-1, also earlier in this chapter, good marketing programmes usually have a primary marketing method, supported by several strong secondary methods.

In addition, good programmes usually include a range of small activities that make up a foundation at the bottom of the pyramid: your tertiary options. All together, these small foundation blocks should not add up to more than 10 per cent of your budget. They include basics such as your business cards and telephones, as well as experiments with new marketing methods that may one day rise up to replace older methods farther up your marketing pyramid.

Your marketing programme may consist of any one of the hundreds of things that marketers do to spread the word about a brand or ask customers for a sale. Making a master list of all the possibilities is almost impossible. For example, think of how many options you have just for displaying an advertisement. You can place it in a consumer or trade magazine, a newspaper or newspaper insert, the phone book or other printed directories, web pages with high traffic, bus and bus stop signs, roadside billboards, airport posters and backlit displays, motorway signs and bumper stickers, sponsorship signs at sporting events and so on. Which of the many advertising options should be in your programme?

To make programme design even tougher, many alternatives compete with advertising. You can mail postcards, free samples, catalogues, direct response sales letters, emails or other communications directly to prospective customers. Hundreds of list brokers and printers are eager to design and deliver a direct response marketing piece for you, if you think this approach is a better use of your marketing pound than print advertising. Or what about the old adage that the three secrets of success in marketing are location, location, location? Maybe you need to emphasise having a shop front or accessible office or showroom in a good location, with plenty of appealing signage or window displays to draw customers in. Then again, perhaps all these marketing ideas are too costly and customers would rather you offer them a rock-bottom price instead. Speaking of price, what about coupons, discounts and other special offers? You have lots of options in this area, too.

No wonder that most marketers throw up their hands and just do the same thing they did last year! Changing their marketing mix and planning a new programme seems daunting. However, we promise you one thing: if you use the same marketing programme you did last year, you get worse results. Marketing programmes need to be studied and improved from year to year, taking new lessons from each effort.

The variety and complexity of the options makes getting organised and focused difficult. Fortunately, you can use what we call the Five Ps to organise your thinking, decide what to do and document and budget your programme.

The *Five Ps* stand for the five broad areas (product, price, placement, promotion and people) you can look to for ways to boost sales or accomplish other marketing goals. The Five Ps help build customer commitment to your brilliant products, services or brands. As you design your marketing programme, decide which of the Five Ps is most important for you right now. Rank all five by importance so that you know where to focus your efforts and spending.

For example, if you're the inventor of a hot new product, then product is probably your number one priority. You need to put the most resources into refining and producing the product because it's the star of your programme.

To sell it, you probably should focus on giving away samples and getting people to test it. Then your product can sell itself.

The following sections explore each of the Five Ps.

Product

To marketers, *product* is what you sell, whether it's a physical item or a service, idea or even another person (such as in politics) or yourself (just like when you search for a new job). When you think about ways of changing your product offering to boost sales, you can look at anything from new or upgraded products, to different packaging, to added extras such as services or warranties. And you can also think about ways to improve the quality of your product. After all, people want the best quality they can get, so any improvements in quality usually translate into gains in sales as well.

Price

To marketers, *price* is not only the list price or sticker price of a product, but also any adjustments to that price, such as discounts and other cost-oriented inducements to buy, including coupons, frequency rewards, quantity discounts and free samples. Any such offers adjust the price the customer pays, with the goal of boosting sales.

Price-based inducements to buy are generally termed *sales promotions* by marketers, just to confuse the issue hopelessly. We delve further into this subject in Chapter 9, where you also find out how to use price-based promotions to boost your sales and attract new customers. (We also cover pricing in depth in the companion book, *Marketing For Dummies,* by yours truly, published by Wiley.)

Placement

Placement is where and when you present your product to customers. You have many options as to how you place the product in both time and space. Whether you're dealing with retail stores, catalogues, sales calls, web pages or 24-hour-a-day telephone services that can process customer orders, you're dealing with that placement *P.*

If you want to get a feel of how important placement is to the marketing mix, just think about the value of shelf placement at your local supermarket to, say, Coke or Pepsi. Imagine what that placement is worth to the marketing of those products!

Oh, by the way, marketers stretch a point by calling this third *P* 'placement' when conventionally it's called distribution. But that starts with a *d*, and so doesn't sound as good. However, just remember that when people talk about distribution, they're talking about placement and vice versa.

You may also hear one more term that relates to placement: logistics. *Logistics* is the physical distribution of products – shipping, taking inventory and all the fancy transportation and information technologies that you can harness to improve the efficiency and effectiveness of your distribution processes. Logistics is another useful path to go down when you want to think about where products should be placed for easy purchase.

To elaborate on these terms: distribution concerns where and when products are offered for sale, whereas logistics addresses how they get there. These concerns are related, of course, so they both require consideration when you want to think hard about placement. You can play around with either one or both in your efforts to build a strong marketing programme. For example, if you add distributors and update your website to offer online ordering, you're boosting placement by enhancing both distribution and logistics to create more ways to get the product to customers. Some marketing programmes place distributors in the primary spot at the top of their marketing zone pyramid.

If you have something unique and can afford to sell at *wholesale* (at least 50 per cent off the list price), you should seriously consider finding distributors and letting them do the heavy lifting when it comes to tracking down customers and making sales. The more marketers, the better!

Promotion

Promotion is all the sales activities, advertising, publicity, special events, displays, signs, web pages and other communications designed to inform and persuade people about your product. We like to think of promotion as the face of marketing because it's the part that reaches out to ask customers for their business. Promotion ought to be a visible and friendly face, because you can't just tell people what to do and expect them to obey. Instead, promotion must find ways to attract prospective customers' attention long enough to communicate something appealing about the product.

The goal of all promotions is to stimulate people to want to buy. Promotions need to be motivational. They also need to move people closer to a purchase.

Sometimes a promotion's goal is to move people all the way to a purchase, such as with a so-called direct-response ad. A *direct-response ad* invites people to call, email, fax or mail in their orders right away. Many catalogues use this strategy. Readers are supposed to select some items, fill in their order forms and mail them in with their credit-card numbers.

Other promotions do less. For example, a 30-second television spot may be designed only to make people remember a brand so that they're a little more likely to buy it the next time they're in a shop where it's sold. But all promotions work towards that ultimate sale in some way, and when you think about all the creative options for communicating with prospective customers, you should always be clear about what part of the customer's movement toward purchase your promotion is supposed to accomplish.

People

In most businesses, people are responsible for many aspects of product or service quality. The personal connection between your people and your customers and clients may be a powerful influence on *referral marketing* – where your customers serve as a sort of mini sales force for you, often called *word-of-mouth marketing*. Your customers refer others to you because they've had a positive relationship with your people. In many businesses, employees are directly responsible for the customer contacts through personal sales and service. If your employees work directly with customers, add training, recognition and reward to your marketing programme, because it helps to make those people positive and enthusiastic.

You can find many connections between how employees feel and how customers feel. For example, we often work with companies where the salespeople or service people say that they're frustrated because they have to deal with angry, uninformed or otherwise difficult customers. Of course, when the employees feel this way about the customers, they tend to be negative (impatient and defensive) with customers, which makes the customers even more difficult. You can rectify this situation in different ways, often using techniques based on building the motivation of salespeople and other employees, improving communications with customers, and handling service problems and customer frustrations. (See Chapter 19 for some of the most important ways of improving customer service.)

To profit from the Five Ps, use the list as a mental tool to think about these five broad ways of growing your business and boosting your sales. The Five Ps are just a starting point – like the street signs along the road to a great marketing programme – and to benefit from them, you have to explore the roads that they mark.

Can I have five Ps, please Bob?

The Four Ps (yes, four) are the first things taught to students in a formal marketing class. The Four Ps are just like our list of the Five Ps except that 'people' is left out (a big mistake in real-world marketing, if not at business schools).

The people side of marketing is often the least visible side – which is why traditionally people aren't included in the list of marketing Ps. But we believe that adding people to the list offers you another powerful tool to achieve your sales and marketing goals.

Profiting from the Five Ps

One way you can profit from the Five Ps is to look systematically for weaknesses and strengths in each of the five areas: your product, pricing, placement, promotions and personal connections with customers. You can use File 2-1 on the CD (Your Five-Minute Marketing Plan) to do a quick planning exercise based on the Five Ps. Print a copy, sharpen your pencil and your wits and see if you can brainstorm some ideas for improving your marketing programme in one or more of the Five Ps' areas.

A good way to profit from your knowledge of the Five Ps is to do some creative thinking about each of the Five Ps every day. Stop and ask yourself these five simple, powerful questions and see if you can find ways to build your sales by doing something new and creative in at least one of these vital marketing areas. What can you do to make your:

- ✔ Product more appealing?
- ✔ Product more accessible?
- ✔ Prices more appealing?
- ✔ Promotions more visible and persuasive?
- ✔ Human interactions with customers more friendly and helpful?

Notice that these questions are open-ended. They don't have right answers. Instead, they invite exploration and experimentation. They're the kind of questions you can even ask your employees – and offer incentives for new ideas. These questions tease the imagination, because a considerable amount of imagination is necessary to grow any business or boost the sales of any product. You aren't going to find any silver bullet formulas that are guaranteed to work.

Marketing isn't like chemistry or algebra or accounting. Marketing has no right answers – only the solutions you invent, test and develop. After much thinking and trying, you develop new and better formulas for yourself and your business; formulas that give you pretty good results, at least for a time, and then you have to update or replace them in order to keep sales flowing and growing.

Exercising Your Marketing Imagination

Marketing imagination is the one term we want everyone to associate with marketing, because it's even more important than the Five Ps. (See the preceding section 'Designing Your Marketing Programme' for more on the Five Ps.) *Marketing imagination* is creative questioning about everything and anything that may help boost sales and make for more satisfied customers. Marketing imagination is ultimately what drives growth and development in your business.

Look at any successful company and you find that it's done innovative things and tried many new ideas. Business leaders are imaginative and willing, even eager, to try out new ideas and approaches. They have active marketing imaginations and are always looking to perfect all Five Ps.

Oddly, creativity is often left out of books and courses on marketing. People tend to think of advertising as creative, but they overlook the importance of creativity in all aspects of marketing. Yet a creative approach to your basic marketing strategy can also be very powerful – think about the success of eBay.com, the first company to offer online auctions that you can participate in from any computer in the world. Its founder took an idea that had existed for hundreds of years – auctions – and married it to a new technology – the Internet. By being creative enough to combine the two ideas, eBay.com, a business worth billions, was created.

We guarantee that you can innovate in any of your Five Ps, if you're willing to be open-minded and inquisitive about your options. (For more on marketing strategies, see Chapter 4.)

Plenty of examples of creativity exist in pricing and product offerings. Just think how many times a business succeeds by offering a new or different product selection.

Here's a simple example. Quite a few gyms in any local area compete for customers, but imagine that one of them makes two simple changes:

- ✓ **Product innovation:** They introduce a new class on capoeira – a blend of martial arts and dance to Brazilian drums – featuring a high-energy workout that appeals to younger people looking for something new and exciting to do.

- ✓ **Pricing:** They advertise a first-class-free policy for the new capoeira class because they feel that people would really like it if they just tried it. The result is that the gym's promotion attracts a whole bunch of curious people, many of whom like the free course so much that they sign up for ten more courses at full price. And some go on to become full members of the gym, using the weight machines and other services, too.

This example illustrates two important points about the exercise of marketing imagination. The first point is that you don't have to come up with something dramatically new. True, a patentable new invention may be a great product innovation. But in general, you can make plenty of progress simply by coming up with many small ideas. We're not talking rocket science here. Anyone in business has enough intelligence, imagination and funding to be a great marketer. The second point is that you have to go out and try your ideas; try them in simple, easy ways that don't expose you to excessive risk of failure. (For more on risks, see the section 'Avoiding Costs and Risks with Smart Marketing' earlier in this chapter.)

Great marketing arises from frequent cycles of thinking and trying out your ideas. Here's how it works. You have an insight or idea. You think of ways to try it out. You test it in the real world and see what happens. You discover things from how customers respond. Their responses fuel more ideas and planning, which then lead to more testing and trying. The process goes on in an endless loop, driven by your marketing imagination, but firmly rooted in the real world of customer opinion and action.

What you must remember is that marketing imagination is not only creative, it's also experimental. Great marketers wear two hats – the hat of the artist and the hat of the scientist. A great marketer may have an 'Ah ha!' experience in the shower one morning and show up at work thinking, 'Wouldn't it be cool to do such and such?' By lunchtime, she's changed hats and is carefully reviewing her options for trying out the idea. By the time she goes home, she's already said to herself, 'I think I've figured out how to safely test my cool new idea.'

Reframing Your Presentation

Every marketing programme has a common theme – communications that present the product offering in a persuasive manner. Whether you rely on advertising, packaging, a brochure, catalogues, websites, signs or even public relations, you're relying on the persuasive power of information.

A great use for your creativity is to rewrite your marketing communications. Bump them up. Make them more persuasive.

But before you start working on clever or humorous ad concepts like the expensive ads you see on national TV, we want to ask you to focus your creative communications more simply than that. Just try to get across a few compelling facts. Figure out what information you can share with prospects that helps convert them to purchasers. The better you support your information, the easier it is for people to take a chance and make a purchase.

The Five-Minute Marketing Zone Plan

This plan is a quick exercise that helps you design a winning marketing programme. Do it now or use it as the foundation for a more detailed planning process based on Chapter 3. It's the perfect transition into that topic and chapter. Oh, but what, exactly, is 'it'?

The persuasive power of information

To understand the vital importance of making your marketing work harder for you, have a look at the car market. A friend of ours who sells cars tells us that the number of people coming in to take multiple test drives has dropped. Ten years ago, someone looking for a car may have dropped by the dealership a few times and taken out different desired models for test drives to check their specifications before eventually buying one.

But now things have changed, according to our friend. These days, customers come along to the dealership twice or even just once. They've already researched every element of the cars they're interested in by using the Internet. They normally have a shortlist and know a lot about different models. Some people have even decided on the car brand they want without ever getting behind the wheel.

This demonstrates just how important information is to your marketing. The car companies with plenty of information on the Internet have already built up relationships with customers long before they ever get to the dealership. If, like the car companies, you can make a strong case for your products before people ever get to see or use them, you increase your sales.

Print copies of Files 2-2 and 2-3. The first is a worksheet for listing and analysing all the marketing activities that are candidates for your marketing programme. Use this form to focus your search on the most appropriate and powerful marketing activities for your particular business. The second form is another worksheet, this time a marketing zone pyramid. Use it to create a sketch of your marketing programme by filling in the blanks. This sketch helps you structure the plan by defining your primary marketing method or tool (which should receive roughly 40 per cent of your marketing budget), your several secondary tools (which together should receive no more than 50 per cent of your budget) and your tertiary options (which receive no more than 10 per cent of your budget).

You can decide – and sometimes it's necessary – to do more detailed and laborious planning. However, the results from these quick worksheet exercises are often fairly good and can improve your focus and clarity about how to market your product. If you think that these exercises have done the trick and you know enough now to forge ahead without more formal planning, go right ahead. You can skip to the later chapters that apply to your primary, secondary and tertiary marketing tools. Or if you want to be more thoughtful and careful about your planning, take your worksheet results and flip to Chapter 3.

Files on the CD

Check out the following items on the CD-ROM:

- ✔ **File 2-1:** Your Five-Minute Marketing Plan
- ✔ **File 2-2:** Your Marketing Zone Programme Worksheet
- ✔ **File 2-3:** Your Marketing Zone Planning Pyramid

Chapter 3

Crafting a Breakthrough Marketing Plan

In This Chapter

▶ Analysing your marketing activities

▶ Using a marketing audit to concentrate on problem areas

▶ Focusing and formatting your marketing plan

▶ Designing your plan using a standard outline or the CD template

▶ Selecting your winning marketing strategy

▶ Learning from experience

*T*he CD files for this chapter contain dozens of pages of templates, audit forms and interactive forecasting, planning and budgeting tools for you to use. The reason we put so many practical tools on the CD-ROM for marketing audits, plans and budgets is that we get more questions about these topics than any others. Many readers wrestle with how to audit and improve a marketing programme and how to write a marketing plan and prepare a good budget. These tasks are difficult. The only way to make these tasks relatively easy is to have someone walk you through the process, which is what we do in this chapter.

Auditing Your Marketing Activities

A *marketing audit* often identifies problems that are holding you back, reviewing everything that influences customer behaviour and helping you to identify hidden problems and opportunities. A *marketing plan* lays out your analysis of the situation in your market along with your strategies and how you plan to use the various elements of your marketing mix (such as advertising, your website and pricing) to execute the strategy. The plan also has sales projections and a budget for your marketing spending.

An audit is a quick way to find and work on weak areas in your marketing process. A marketing audit can also form the basis of your marketing plan. How?

Well, if you take the audit, which you can find on the CD as File 3-1, and then make a list of the items that you scored a No on, this information can become a starting agenda for what to do in your next plan to improve your marketing performance and results.

The editable Microsoft Word format marketing audit on your CD (File 3-1) is divided into nine areas, each with a list of a dozen or more specific questions. The questions have Yes/No answers, which makes the audit quick and easy to complete. In case you find opening this file difficult or you want a simpler, non-editable file format, you can print File 3-2, which is the same audit saved as a PDF file. You can then use the printout of File 3-2 to complete your audit on paper.

When you complete the audit (using File 3-1 or 3-2 depending on your preference for file formats), simply count the number of Yes answers in each section and divide by the number of questions to get your section scores. You can then use Table 3-1 to calculate your scores manually, or if you have access to Microsoft Excel, open File 3-3 and use the provided calculator.

Table 3-1	Marketing Audit Worksheet	
Activity Area	**Formula**	**Profile Score**
A. Marketing focus	# of yeses_____ ÷ 12 =	_____ %
B. Marketing scope	# of yeses_____ ÷ 11 =	_____ %
C. Customer acquisition activities	# of yeses_____ ÷ 17 =	_____ %
D. Information-gathering activities	# of yeses_____ ÷ 16 =	_____ %
E. Marketing planning activities	# of yeses_____ ÷ 18 =	_____ %
F. Communications activities	# of yeses_____ ÷ 37 =	_____ %
G. Customer service activities	# of yeses_____ ÷ 15 =	_____ %
H. Management and control	# of yeses_____ ÷ 12 =	_____ %
I. Creativity	# of yeses_____ ÷ 13 =	_____ %
Overall Score Calculation	Total # of yeses_____ ÷ 150 =	_____ %

Obviously, a 100 per cent score is the ideal. Any score less than 85 per cent for a section indicates a weakness in an area that probably deserves close attention. After you convert all your section scores into percentages, you can compare them and see which areas are lacking and deserve attention. Working on the one or two areas where your scores are lowest is a good idea because it gives you a helpful focus in your efforts and plans.

After you take the marketing audit, you can analyse your results in each of the nine areas.

You should make marketing decisions according to the Five Ps (that is, deciding what your product, pricing, placement, promotions and people should be), as we describe in Chapter 2. But you should also monitor ongoing actions across the Five Ps by looking at activities in the nine areas of the marketing audit.

You may notice that most of the sections of the marketing audit have questions about the Five Ps. That's because you really need to take actions to help implement your marketing programme across all the Ps. For example, any employees that gather information in their daily jobs need to keep you informed about competitor product development, customer reactions to your pricing and promotions and so on. If you like having everything integrated into one big model, you can think of the audit as cutting across the Five Ps, and you can even build a big grid out of the two lists, if you want to.

Evaluating your marketing focus

Part A of the marketing audit helps you evaluate your *focus*, which means working out how clearly and effectively your marketing takes aim based on your strengths and opportunities.

The following questions are just about the most important you can ask, and they need to have good, clear answers before you worry about any of the hundreds of details of your marketing programme:

  ✔ Do you have specific growth goals to motivate and focus your marketing efforts?
  ✔ Do you have a clear strategy to help you achieve those growth goals?

Don't take action until you have a clear strategic focus to give those actions purpose and direction. You want your marketing programme to be a wolf leaping forward, not a hundred scared rabbits hopping in all directions at once.

Although 85 per cent is a minimum score for passing the audit, you really want to get as close to 100 per cent as possible on the focus section.

Assessing your marketing scope

Think of the *scope* of marketing as how broadly and aggressively you pursue customers and try to make sales. To win the great game of marketing, you first have to show up. Auditing your scope helps you figure out if you're showing up and pursuing sales in the markets and with the customers who matter to your success. The scope should also indicate if you're doing this on a large enough scale to achieve your goals and realise your potential.

Don't even think of skipping this section of the marketing audit. We may seem to be stating the obvious when we say that your marketing needs to have enough scope to achieve the impact you want, but in almost every business that's having problems with sales or marketing, we can trace at least some of the problems to the issue of scope. Thinking big isn't enough – you have to act big, too.

For example, many businesses provide just one or a few products or services to their customers when offering a broader range would be easy and more useful to the customers. Don't limit your potential by offering just one product or service, or in any of the other ways covered in Part B of the marketing audit.

Take a look at the questions in this section of File 3-1 and, if you answer No more than once or twice, rethink the way you're approaching marketing. Ask yourself what you can do to think bigger and expand the scope of your marketing efforts. Maybe the solution is as simple as advertising to a larger geographic area or seeking new, more professional sales representatives or distributors. Aiming for the best customers in your market – the biggest purchasers or the ones who take the lead in buying trends and fashions – is important, too.

Thinking big is an important part of marketing success.

Appraising your marketing activities

Parts C through G of the marketing audit look at many of the specific activities that you ought to be doing or having competent people do in order to have a really good marketing programme. Depending on your business size and type, some activities may not be relevant to you, but most, if not all, are important. Take a good hard look at any No answers in these parts and try to introduce activities to fill in the gaps. (You can find lots of specific information about your marketing activities in this book.)

We divide the audit of marketing activities into multiple sections to reflect the reality that, in effective marketing programmes, you need to be active in each of the following areas:

- ✔ **Communications:** Sending clear, well-targeted messages through multiple channels and media.
- ✔ **Customer acquisition:** Actively reaching out to attract and retain good customers.

✔ **Customer service:** Interacting with customers to make sure that their experience is rewarding and to encourage them to become ambassadors for your business, product or service.

✔ **Information gathering:** Studying and tracking trends, listening to customer input and conducting other activities that help you find out about your customers and market.

✔ **Planning:** Organising and co-ordinating the activities to give them focus.

We're big believers in taking an activity-based approach to planning and managing your marketing. You can't just talk and write about marketing, you have to *do* specific things to get any desirable results. A marketing programme or plan really comes down to a set of actions that (we hope) has a positive influence on sales and profits. So the section of the audit where you evaluate your marketing activities strikes at the very heart of your marketing and can quickly tell you if your programme is coming up short.

Analysing your management and control

Control is sometimes hard to achieve in marketing. Some businesses don't really know what's going on in their marketing because so many marketing activities occur and customers are so widespread and difficult to track. For these reasons, many businesses waste time and money on their marketing and don't even realise it.

Writing everything down

One of the first things you should do to control your marketing is make a record of every action and expense. Keep good files and make careful lists.

This concept may sound obvious, but keeping track of your marketing can be difficult to do. For example, if you sell materials and publications to companies for use in their training programmes, you probably track any direct contact with clients and know who buys and uses what. But perhaps you also work with multiple distributors and publishers who may sell your publications to companies, sometimes without your knowledge. The situation can get even more complex: what if you sell publications to consultants who then sell training based on these publications to their company clients?

The result is you can't be sure who's using your products or which ones they've tried or haven't ever encountered. That lack of control becomes a problem when you want to send a letter promoting a specific product. You may send the letter to some companies that already use that product without your knowledge, which is a waste and makes you look disorganised.

Even worse, you don't have the names of all the companies that have used one of your products and so may be especially receptive to a promotional letter. You can work with all your firm's business partners to get them to trade their customer lists with you, but they won't all want to do so. Even controlling something as simple as your list of customers isn't as easy as it may first appear.

If you have a big enough budget, you may want to explore Customer Relationship Management (CRM) software. Marketers with smaller businesses or budgets may do better to build their own systems using any available tools. If you have under a hundred customers, a file cabinet with a folder for each customer works pretty well. Alternatively, you can use an Excel spreadsheet with a row for each customer and add notes in the columns for each update on what they ask about or buy. Some marketers use their accounting software as the core of their customer database because they're already capturing customer names, addresses and orders in it. Even if you don't have a fancy (and expensive) CRM system, you can and should track customer activity and compile notes about each customer.

Keeping the communication lines open

Another foundation of marketing control is what we think of as the human element, which encompasses how people are organised and the way in which they divide the work and communicate about it. Make sure that you clearly define roles and goals – this element is fundamental to good marketing management.

Make sure that you ask lots of questions and share lots of information to keep the communications flowing. We bet you haven't heard about all your customers' complaints or concerns – most marketing teams never do. We also bet that your business offers products that some of your customers don't yet know about; this issue is also a common communication problem in marketing. Management and control are all about making sure that your business has an efficient, effective connection to your potential customers.

Checking your creativity

The very idea of auditing your creativity may seem strange because auditing and creativity sound like opposites. But because creativity is an essential component of your marketing success, you do need to manage it, just like any other important business activity or asset.

How do you know if you're being creative? Consider the following:

- ✔ **Creativity means doing things differently and doing new things.** If your marketing seems routine, tame and overly familiar, it fails the basic creativity test: freshness. In this case, you really ought to try something new.

✔ **Creativity equals originality.** If you're not leading the way with a new idea, method or approach this year in your industry or market, you're not being very original. Yet you *are* a unique individual: your business is like no other, your products have many minor differences, your employees have unique cultural and geographical roots and so on. Tap into these differences to come up with original ideas and approaches. Try to make your marketing distinctive and special, not 'me too' and imitative. Why? Because the first person or business to try something new usually gets more money and success from it than any imitators.

Weaving creativity into your marketing gives your marketing activities more impact and helps your business grow. A pound spent on a dull, typical ad, mailing, brochure or website doesn't have much impact. In today's competitive market and unsure economy, businesses of all sizes need to figure out how to maximise every pound. However, if you have limited funds, you really do care how much impact your marketing has. A creative approach can increase your marketing's impact by 10 per cent or more. That's how powerful creativity can be, so please give this last section of the audit careful attention.

Using Audit Results to Focus Your Plan

When you look at your scores on all nine sections of the marketing audit, you can discern your *audit profile*, which is defined as the overall strengths and weaknesses from your audit. This profile is a useful planning tool. Use it to identify areas where you need to improve and areas where you have strengths you want to maintain and take advantage of. (If you haven't completed the marketing audit, see the section 'Auditing Your Marketing Activities' earlier in this chapter, and CD File 3-1.)

Professor Charles Schewe, of the University of Massachusetts Amherst, used a version of this marketing audit to help executives from electricity companies look at their marketing functions. They all faced the challenge that their markets were opening up to competition for the first time due to deregulation. This challenge meant that these utilities were no longer able to take their customer base for granted.

Of course, you probably haven't been able to take your customers for granted. Wouldn't having regulatory protection of your market area be nice? Ah, well, the days of regulated monopolies are ending and even utility companies have to find out how to recruit and retain customers.

The loss of regulatory protection of their customer base made the marketing audit a very powerful marketing tool for these companies. The marketing audit was a real eye-opener, to say the least: it revealed large areas of marketing in which the businesses simply weren't active. In some of these organisations, the audit led to an agenda that required several years to complete.

In your business, the results may be less radical than in the case of the electric companies, but we're sure that your marketing audit can lead to an agenda of some sort. Marketing audits always seem to reveal some needs and generate a few good ideas for positive action. Being fully customer-oriented is difficult; creating and integrating effective marketing actions in all areas of your business is very hard to accomplish, too. So a great next step is to review the findings – especially in areas of particular weakness or strength – and develop agenda items that help you to better attract and retain customers.

Immediately after completing your marketing audit, we recommend that you work up an action agenda based on your results. We would be amazed if you can't come up with at least five high-priority actions for your agenda as a result of the audit.

You can find a template on your CD (File 3-4) for developing your marketing agenda based on the marketing audit you performed. Print the template and fill it in to help turn your audit into action. Figure 3-1 shows you what a sample planning form looks like (although four more sample forms are on the CD, so you can develop a five-item agenda if you want).

Agenda item #1 is to: _____

Mini-plan for agenda item #1:

Who should spearhead this action? _____

By **when** should it be completed? _____/_____/_____

What special **resources** might be needed?

    Other people?

    _____
    _____
    _____
    _____

    Money? £ _____

    Special expertise? _____

    Special supplies/equipment? _____

What should this action **accomplish**?

    Key objective: _____

Figure 3-1: A sample planning form.

Formatting Your Marketing Plan

This section offers two alternative outlines for marketing plans. You can design a marketing plan in many different ways. No two plans are identical in their formats and structures because no two organisations are identical in their needs. Don't be afraid to adapt the planning outlines and templates to your own needs.

In the next section, 'Writing Your Marketing Plan the Easy Way', we show you how to use the planning template on the CD, so if you want to use our template you don't need to worry about the format; just skip to that section. However, if you're writing a plan from scratch, take a look at the two outlines that follow. One of them may fit your planning needs.

Here's a simple outline of a plan based on the Five Ps (which we describe in Chapter 2):

A Five Ps Marketing Plan

Situation Analysis (reporting on your customers, competitors, products and results from the past period)

Strategies and Actions (with Budgets and Timelines) for the Five Ps

Products

Placement

Pricing

Promotion

People

Budget Analysis

Responsibilities (who will do what)

Sometimes you may need a detailed situation analysis and a strategic examination of problems and opportunities. Here's an example of a plan outline used by a divisional manager at a large industrial chemicals company. The plan includes a good situation analysis, making it a strategic marketing plan. If you think you may need to change your strategy or basic approach, choose this outline:

A Sample Marketing Plan

Situation Analysis

Sales history

Market profile

Sales versus objective

Factors influencing sales

Profitability

Factors affecting profitability

Market Environment

Growth rate

Trends

Changes in customer attitude

Recent or anticipated competitor actions

Government activity

Problems and Opportunities

Problem areas

Opportunities

Marketing and Profitability Objectives

Sales

Market profile

Gross margin

Marketing Strategy

Marketing Programmes

Product Assumptions

After you choose an outline, of course, you have to start writing. This stage is when writer's block (and panic) may set in. A good way to simplify the writing challenge is to convert one question into many. The starting question you have is probably, 'What is my marketing plan for next year?' That's too big a question to answer in one sitting. Try breaking it down into a bunch of easy questions, such as, 'Would a newsletter be useful and interesting to our customers?' That question is very specific and one that you can probably answer on your own with a little thought.

If you decide that, yes, a newsletter may be appealing to your customers, you can think about a bunch of even more specific questions, such as 'How many people are on my mailing and email lists?' and 'Will I write the articles myself, or do I need to hire a writer or perhaps purchase the rights to reprint content?' By drilling down to specifics, you can turn a big, hard-to-answer question into a series of fairly easy detail-oriented questions. Each specific question and answer fits into one of the sections of your outline and fills it out into a useful document.

Writing Your Marketing Plan the Easy Way

What if you try to write your plan but end up with a lot of scribbled notes and no clear idea of how to complete it? Time for a template! This section walks you through the planning process using the planning template in File 3-5. The advantage of a template like this one is that your plan is already half-written – you just have to supply the details. The corresponding disadvantage, however, is that the outline and general approach are already decided for you, leaving you less scope for individualising the plan than if you write it yourself.

Luckily for you, the planning template in File 3-5 helps you produce a detailed, well-written plan. When you take a look at the template, you probably notice right away how detailed and lengthy the table of contents is. That's because the table of contents reflects the specificity of the questions that the template raises for you to think about. We divided the plan into lots of very specific small sections, so you never have to wing it and make up a lot of structure on your own. Instead, you always have specific small chunks of thinking and writing to do – which is much more manageable.

A marketing plan is really a collection of multiple smaller plans that work together. Each small plan is easier to write compared to a big plan, and so we want you to take this one building block at a time.

For example, if you look at the table of contents of the plan template in File 3-5, you see that the following subsection covers a plan for publishing a newsletter:

Harnessing the Power of Newsletters

>   Plans for Writing Our Newsletter
>
>   Plans for Designing Our Newsletter
>
>   Plans for Distributing Our Newsletter
>
>   Schedule and Budget for Our Newsletter
>
>   Expected Benefits

Obviously, this template is a plan for a newsletter, with places to describe how you're going to produce and distribute it, a place to summarise the costs and timing of the project, and an end-section to describe the benefits or returns from this newsletter plan (in terms of additional customer loyalty and orders, referrals from pass-along of the newsletter to new customers and so on; the template guides you on how to fill in each section). Filling in a paragraph or two under each of these headings and working up some estimates for costs and benefits isn't that difficult because a newsletter is a specific discrete thing to think about and plan.

At the end of the section on newsletters in File 3-5, you have bottom-line costs, the timing of those costs and also a sense of when you may get what kinds of returns from your investment in a newsletter. You can use these figures as a basis for entering some numbers in the summary row in your overall marketing budget for your plan (using the Excel spreadsheet template in File 3-6). And with the detail section of the plan to support that row of your budget, you can feel pretty good about the numbers you enter there. Build up your budget in File 3-6 in this way one line at a time as you do each smaller, easier-to-think-about mini-plan in each subsection of File 3-5. The big picture emerges from the details, and you'll be pleasantly surprised to find that the budget almost writes itself as you work through the plan. Similarly, the returns you predict from the newsletter can support a row in the Sales Projection Worksheet in File 3-7.

Using the marketing plan template

The best idea we had in a long while was to make the marketing plan template (File 3-5) rely on this book so that you can draw on each chapter as you write a corresponding section of your plan. In other words, this book becomes your master reference guide as you write your marketing plan.

A marketing plan template based on this book is helpful and practical. If you need to add more topics to the template, we suggest getting a copy of the companion book to this one, *Marketing For Dummies* (Wiley) – the most recent edition is also written by us – to provide you with the support you need to cover subjects beyond the ones that we cover here. (We mention some sections of *Marketing For Dummies* as optional reference aids in parts of the marketing plan template.) But if your plan is like most of the ones that we've worked on over the years, you're most likely to find more than enough information in this book and the template to get you through a planning process and produce a serviceable draft of your plan.

Combining the spreadsheets (Files 3-6 and 3-7) with the Word file of File 3-5 gives you a complete and very detailed marketing plan.

Gathering information before you start

Before you even start customising the template in File 3-5, we recommend taking a little time to assemble your marketing information. Make sure that you have records of last year's marketing activities, including expenses and all the sales records you can find. Also, if you have a little more time, use the audit and survey forms in the section 'Auditing Your Marketing Activities', earlier in this chapter, which provide good ideas and information that you can use as you work on your plan.

In addition, you may want to do a little extra research to gather more information about your market. For example, you may want to do one or more of the following:

- ✔ Ask salespeople or distributors about their views of quality, trends, competition and so on.

- ✔ Gather details of sales for the last year or more.

- ✔ Get breakdowns of sales by product, region or other categories.

- ✔ Get some general statistics on sales in your market or product category so that you can see what your market share is and if you're gaining or losing share.

- ✔ Collect any information on where sales came from; which sales and marketing practices worked best in the last year or two?

- ✔ Get prices on printing, ad purchases, design services or other costs you know you need to include in your budget.

- ✔ Quiz some customers about the quality of your service or product and get their ideas and suggestions on how to improve it.

- ✔ Plan some sales promotions and work out projected costs and returns. Special offers are a great way to get customer attention and stimulate new consumers to try your service or product.

- ✔ Collect cost and price information to use in budgets and projections. For example, what's the total cost for your business to deliver one unit of your product to a customer? What net price does the average customer pay after any discounts or special offers? And how do your prices and discounts compare to your competitors?

- ✔ Get information on any new products that you're going to introduce during the plan's period.

- ✔ Decide whether you want (and can afford) to hire a marketing consultant to coach you through the planning process. Or, if hiring a consultant is out of your reach, you can hire one to spend a day with you clarifying your strategy before you start writing. (Some ad agencies are also happy to help with general marketing planning, so you can ask local agencies for proposals, too.)

Researching this shopping list of questions may occupy you for several days or more. Simply gathering the information needed to do a good plan is a serious undertaking. Fortunately, all this upfront work helps make the writing part much easier.

Eventually, you have to roll up your sleeves and start writing. But don't just stare at a blank page or screen. (We're reminded of a quote from author Gene

Fowler: 'Writing is easy. All you do is sit staring at a blank sheet of paper until the drops of blood form on your forehead.') We want you to avoid writer's block, anxiety and the lack of structure that the blank-sheet-of-paper method provides! And we also want you to avoid the common mistake of making minor edits to last year's plan (if you have one). That method doesn't force you to rethink your marketing; it just creates something that fools you and others into believing that you've done real planning.

Instead, we want you to really write a plan because the writing process is also a thinking process, and coming up with good strategies and tactics takes a lot of thinking. But to make the writing process easier, we recommend following the template on the CD (File 3-5), because it includes detailed instructions for each section of your plan.

Saving time with the outline used in the planning template

File 3-5 contains a Word file written as if we were laying out a professional marketing plan, with a title page, table of contents, headings for each section and body copy. But instead of writing a specific plan for a client, we use the body copy to give you suggestions, examples and tips for how to fill in your own details. The outline of this planning template is as follows:

Introduction

Part 1: Programme Overview and Marketing Strategies

Overview of Last Year's Marketing Programme

Long-term Investments and Administrative and Overhead Costs

Audit Results and Agenda Items

Marketing Strategies

Part 2: Information and Skills Required for the Plan

Market Research

Creative Concepts and Plans

Guidelines for Written Marketing Communications

Testimonials and Customer Stories

Part 3: Advertising Management and Design

Planning and Budgeting Our Ad Campaign

Advertising Designs and Programmes

Part 4: Other Elements of Our Marketing Programme

> Branding through Business Cards, Letterhead and so on
>
> Brochures, Catalogues and Spec Sheets
>
> Pricing, Coupons and Other Promotions
>
> Harnessing the Power of Newsletters
>
> Media Coverage through Publicity
>
> Website Development and Promotion
>
> Trade Shows and Special Events

Part 5: Sales and Service Success

> Plans and Improvements for Our Sales Process
>
> Improving the Way We Close Our Sales
>
> Strategies for Dealing with Difficult Customers
>
> Sales Projections

Part 6: Marketing Budget

> Overview of the Marketing Budget
>
> Marketing Budget and Spreadsheet Printouts

The outline is detailed to give you a lot of structure, which is helpful when writing a plan. The most you have to create on your own is a paragraph or two per heading.

Also, you can incorporate many other forms on the CD (mostly Word and Excel files), described in other chapters of this book, directly into this planning template. Each time you use one of the other CD files, you're taking a shortcut to completing your plan. We want you to use all the resources in this book as fully as you can during your planning process so that it's as painless as possible! Our philosophy is that if you wanted to do things the hard way, you wouldn't have bought this book, and so we want to make your planning as easy as we can.

Developing Your Marketing Strategy

We don't need to guide you through every section of the planning template on File 3-5 because most of the sections have a chapter devoted to them elsewhere in this book. The section on your marketing strategies, however, doesn't have its own chapter, and so we discuss it here.

In the strategy section of your marketing plan, you describe the big-picture thinking behind your plan. The latter parts of your plan get into all the specifics – the whats, whens and hows. The strategy section is about the whys. Good thinking on the strategic level makes the rest of your plan much easier to write – and also much more profitable and effective!

We have to tell you before you write the strategy section of your marketing plan that strategic planning is difficult; perhaps it's the most difficult thing any marketer, manager or executive ever has to do. If you hire an expert consultant to do strategic planning with you, expect to spend many long meetings discussing strategy over a period of months. You probably don't have that kind of time today, however, and so we show you all the shortcuts we know.

We can help you craft a rough-and-ready set of marketing strategies in as little as a couple of hours, if you're willing to focus hard on the task for that long. If you have the time and funding to do a more formal planning process, by all means do, and use this section of your plan to summarise the results. But if you're in a hurry, don't skip the strategy section. Just follow our pointers and choose one strategy from our list, or perhaps (at the most) several strategies that seem to complement each other and fit your situation and opportunities well.

Basing your strategies on your core brilliance

Strategies have to be based on your product's genuine strengths: what we call *strategic assets*. The idea is simple and powerful: get in touch with your best strengths – the thing(s) you can contribute to your market and to the world – and make sure that you base your strategies and plans on them.

Think of your greatest strengths as the foundation of a lighthouse. Your strategies are the ground-level section of the structure. Later parts of your plan build higher, until your promotions at the top provide a beacon to draw customers into your anchorage. Your marketing plan has to be an integrated structure, based on a solid foundation of strategic assets. One person's version of a winning strategy is another's failure; the success of your strategy depends on whether you have the right foundation for it!

Deciding whether to adopt a new strategy or improve an old one

If you simply need to improve upon and continue using an already-successful strategy, say that clearly in this section of your plan and shape the plan to improve the efficiency of the marketing programme you used last year. If, however, you really need to shop for a new and better strategic approach, say so now and realise that you first need to figure out what your effective strategic plan is before you can expect to optimise any programme based on it. In other words, pick one of these basic orientations for your plan:

- ✔ **Efficiency-oriented:** Your plan needs to introduce a number of specific improvements on how you market your product but shouldn't alter your basic strategy from the preceding year.

- ✔ **Effectiveness-oriented:** Your plan needs to identify a major opportunity or customer problem and describe a strategy to respond to it.

Take a minute to think about the distinction between perfecting the implementation of last year's strategy and trying a new one. Which strategy you choose makes a big difference that affects everything else about your plan! If you use last year's strategy and just try to do it more efficiently, you can plan to do things on a fairly big scale.

For example, you can plan to do one big mailing a quarter (assuming that you do mailings – if not, imagine we're talking about advertising, trade show booths or whatever you do a lot of). But if you try some new strategy, don't plan to do a few big marketing activities because you may fail at one or more of them and blow your marketing budget in a hurry. Instead, plan to test a lot of smaller mailings and other kinds of marketing. Do a lot of marketing activities on a small scale and build in enough repetition to give yourself opportunities to build your expertise as you go.

Improving your current marketing strategy

When designing your plan's strategy, the first choice you have to make is whether you have a pretty good overall strategy right now or not. If it *is* good and should continue to work for the next few years, all you need to do in your plan is show how you plan to pursue that strategy efficiently. The main point of your plan is to do marketing like you did last year, but better. In that case, your strategy section can be short and sweet. Just describe the strategy and why you think it's going to continue to work and then say that the main contribution of your plan is to improve the efficiency of marketing by making certain improvements to last year's programme.

A marketing audit (see the earlier section 'Auditing Your Marketing Activities') or your independent research can guide you to specific areas where improvements are likely to pay off. Mention those general areas briefly in this section, but save the details for later in the plan.

Scrapping the old strategy and creating a new one

If you feel that a new strategic direction or approach is needed or you want to try one because you see good opportunities, your plan should be more effectiveness-oriented. You're going to define a new strategy that, if it works, brings you exciting new opportunities for sales, profits and overall business growth. So the critical issue for your plan and your next year's marketing programme is whether you can effectively achieve some new strategic vision and accomplish the new objectives that you set for that strategy. If you achieve even half of this new strategic vision, you'll probably be happy because doing something new isn't easy. Your plan should be about making your overall marketing approach more effective through a change of strategies.

Don't worry about sweating every detail of your new strategy. Just try to prove that it works without losing money while carrying it out. Next year, you can switch gears and design an efficiency-oriented plan that perfects this year's more experimental one.

If you're trying a new strategy and don't have proven marketing formulas, you can't write an efficiency-oriented plan. For example, if you don't do mailings to purchased lists right now, don't say that you're going to increase the response rate on mailings from 2.5 per cent to 5.5 per cent next year. Instead, plan on testing a variety of mailings, and allow for some of them to fail (a less than 1 per cent response rate) and hope to have one or two of them do pretty well (a 3 per cent plus response rate). But don't guess which ones are going to fail and which ones succeed.

Choosing your strategy

If you're sticking with your existing strategy, you still need to articulate it clearly in this section of your plan and explain why it's so good that it can power your marketing for another year. If you're pretty sure that you need a new strategy, use this section of the plan to say why and to elaborate on your decision. For example:

> 'Our strategy is a _____ strategy. Specifically, we are planning to
> _____.'

Can you easily fill in the blanks, or are you scratching your head?

Most people find completing those two simple sentences difficult, but we can make the task easier. In the following sections, we give you a master list of marketing strategies to choose from. You need to be using one (or possibly two or three, at the most) of these strategies in your marketing for the next year. Pick one strategy, and you're ready to fill in the blank in the first sentence.

The second sentence requires a bit more thinking on your part because it says how that strategy applies to your own situation and market. Our notes about each strategy (described in the following sections) offer clues on how to customise that strategy to your own plan.

By the way, we put the strategies in the order we want you to think about them; the easier ones are first. The farther you get into this list, the more difficult the implementation usually becomes. So all else being equal, we generally recommend using the easier ones.

Reminder strategy

The *reminder strategy* is a very simple communications-oriented strategy that reaches out to loyal regular customers to remind them to make a replacement purchase. If you have a solid base of loyal customers who ought to continue purchasing regularly, this strategy is for you.

You can implement this strategy fairly easily: just make sure that you give your customers periodic reminders and perhaps small incentives or rewards so that they don't forget your product and wander off to some competitor.

Acquiring a new customer costs ten times as much money as keeping an existing one.

Simplicity strategy

The *simplicity strategy* emphasises ease and convenience for customers. Can you simplify the purchase and use of your product or service to such an extent that simplicity alone can be a major selling point? If so, seriously consider this strategy, but be committed to keeping things simple – simpler than the competition. Otherwise, you don't have a durable advantage.

If you use the simplicity strategy, follow through with simplifying steps in all Five Ps (product, pricing, placement, promotions and people), not just in your promotional messages. Just saying that doing business is easier and simpler with your firm isn't much good – it really has to be!

Quality strategy

If you can figure out how to make a better-quality product or offer better service, by all means do so! The most durable and profitable strategy in marketing is to be better than the competition – in your customers' eyes, not just your own.

You can implement this *quality strategy* in many ways, such as by:

- Making fewer errors
- Having better designs
- Offering more reliable or rapid delivery

Pick one or two dimensions that your customers associate strongly with quality when they talk about your product category. Focus on these aspects and be prepared to redesign your business processes and your products to achieve noticeably better quality.

You may hear phrases in the world of marketing such as 'Total Quality Management' and 'Process Re-engineering'. These terms relate to ways that businesses can truly offer better-quality products and services without incurring high costs or raising prices above what customers can afford. You can fill whole books just looking at these topics – and people frequently do! – but these issues aren't worth covering here. Just note that if you're aware of and keen to pursue strategies such as these, you have to pursue them seriously in every aspect of your business. They have to go beyond marketing and filter through into the way the whole organisation operates.

Market share strategy

The *market share strategy* is a straightforward effort to get a bigger piece of the market than your competitors. Size often matters in competition, and so gaining on your competitors by using aggressive sales and marketing to get more customers or more sales pounds than they do in the next year can be a good strategy.

You can be fairly careful and conservative when you use this strategy when you don't need to gain a lot of market share quickly. In that case, you may think of this strategy as being based on the basic efficiency awareness that we describe in the section 'Deciding whether to adopt a new strategy or improve an old one', earlier in this chapter.

Other times, your goal is to make significant progress in capturing market share compared to competitors, even if you have to overspend on marketing and reduce your profit margin for a year or two. You can use this new strategic effort to achieve greater effectiveness by changing your position in the market. The prize is that, if you succeed in becoming one of the leaders in your market, you can hope for high profits in subsequent years as your payoff for investing in competitive growth now.

Positioning strategy

The *positioning strategy* is designed to create or maintain a specific image (or position) in the customer's and potential customer's minds. This strategy is psychological and all about how people think and feel. It uses words, stories and imagery to reach out to customers so that they form strong feelings or beliefs about your product. Often, this strategy looks at how customers perceive the competition because communicating your own unique position in the marketplace – and not a confusingly similar position – is best.

To design a positioning strategy, you really need to find out what people think and what they care about. You can use the exercises (and surveys) in Chapter 2 to get a handle on how customers see the product category in general and what they specifically like most about your product. You then build on these answers when deciding how to position your product in their minds.

In Chapter 2, we talk about the importance of being brilliant at what you do. In a positioning strategy, your goal is to communicate this brilliance in such a powerful way that you 'own' that claim to brilliance and are strongly associated with it in customers' minds. Clearly, this strategy is going to need a lot of brand-building and marketing communications in the implementation parts of your plan. (See Parts II and III for extensive how-to advice on branding and promotional communications.)

Product life cycle strategy

The *product life cycle strategy* adjusts your marketing to the growth stage of an overall product category. Any product category goes through a broad life cycle, from early introduction through growth, to a slower-growing maturity and, eventually, to declining sales and death.

Innovation drives this cycle: new products are invented and introduced, and then they catch on, eventually getting replaced by even newer products. As the cycle goes on, competition grows because the once-new product gradually becomes commonplace and easy for many competitors to make and sell.

The most fun period in this life cycle is the growth phase. During this phase, the market is beginning to embrace the new product and its sales take off. And during that phase, becoming a star by achieving high sales and profit growth is easiest.

You can use the life cycle strategy to refocus your efforts behind a rising star – a product or product line that you expect to experience fast growth in the next few years. Or you can use this strategy to adjust your expectations and refocus your efforts on competitive jockeying if you realise that your once-growing star is now fading and you don't have a replacement. Either way, knowing where you are in the life cycle of your product category is helpful, so that you can adjust your efforts and expectations accordingly – and seek a new product with growth potential if your main product is getting too old.

Market segmentation strategy

A *segment* of a market is simply a subgroup of customers with needs that make them special in some way. For example, if you sell breakfast cereals for adults rather than children, you're targeting (that's what marketers say) the adult cereal market. When you specialise in just one segment of a broader market, you can be more specific and helpful to your customers.

A *market segmentation strategy* often requires a broader geographical area – perhaps even national or international – because your segment of people or businesses with special needs may be relatively rare.

You may be using this strategy already, or you may decide to adopt it now as a way to compete more effectively in the market. Segmentation and specialisation can be a great way to make yourself more valuable to certain customers, which allows you to outsell more generalised competitors within the target group or segment of customers.

Market expansion strategy

If you're currently selling in a three-region area, a straightforward way to grow is to sell your product or services in two additional regions. This strategy expands the size of your market. But to use this *market expansion strategy,* you need to make sure that your new market area includes the right kinds of customers and that some new competitor isn't going to undercut your pricing or make entering the market in the new location difficult.

After assessing the new territory, decide on the main challenges of entering the market. Then base your marketing plan on what you must do to succeed in the new, bigger market you want to pursue.

Buzz strategy

The idea behind the *buzz strategy* is to create excitement about something new, hot, fashionable or trend-setting. Implementing the buzz strategy isn't as easy as it sounds – beware! However, sometimes a marketer has such a cool new idea that's so in sync with the times (and the current headlines) that it's a natural for buzz marketing.

If this strategy fits your product, put up cool or quirky YouTube videos, widgets and blogs, and post MySpace and Facebook pages. Plus, send press releases to let the media know you're a good example of a hot new trend. Also, consider doing some public speaking or product demos on college campuses, demonstrations at trade shows and fairs or whatever else you can think of to shamelessly pursue attention. (If you have a product you can give out, give it to up-and-coming celebrities who are also eager to create buzz.) The window doesn't stay open long, so hurry to make your mark before you're no longer the new thing.

If you aren't totally cool and hip and leading some new fashion or trend, a buzz strategy isn't for you. Lots of marketing pundits are excited about the idea of spreading the word through youth culture – but the concept is silly when your message is really just an advertisement in disguise. Kids aren't that easily fooled! You better actually *be* cool if you want anyone to view your YouTube video, befriend you on Facebook or download your widget.

Setting specific objectives for your strategies

A *strategic objective* states something you hope that your business will accomplish in the next year as a result of pursuing a strategy. If you're pursuing an expansion strategy, for example, you may set some goals for the number of new customers you want to acquire in each of the new territories.

If you're pursuing a positioning strategy, on the other hand, quantifying your success may be harder. You may have to do a survey at the end of the year to ask customers what they think and feel about your product. One objective may be to convince a significant percentage of customers that your product is better, faster and more sophisticated – or whatever the positioning goal is – than your competition. A second objective may be to increase your sales by a certain percentage as a result of communicating your special position in the market to prospective customers.

Set specific objectives that flow from your strategy and that also reflect your resources, such as the number of salespeople or the amount of money you have to spend. Good objectives require you to stretch a bit – but not too much. They should energise and give a purpose to the rest of your marketing plan. For example, if your strategy is to gain market share and try to become one of the top three in your market, a good energising objective may be to increase your sales at twice the speed of the underlying growth rate in your market (in other words, to grow twice as fast as the average competitor). Trying to grow much faster than that may not be possible.

You also use your strategic marketing objectives in your sales projections (use File 3-7 for that). One of your objectives must always be about sales, and this objective drives your sales projections. Pick a rough sales objective now, but expect to adjust it as you work on the tactical parts of your plan. Marketing activity is needed to generate sales. However, marketing activity costs money and takes time and effort, so you have to make sure that the sales objective seems realistic before you finalise it.

What are good marketing objectives? Whatever objectives you need to help you achieve your mission or growth goals. Your marketing objectives may be to:

- ✔ Attract attention and create a buzz
- ✔ Boost the performance of salespeople or distributors
- ✔ Change the way customers think of your offering (reposition)
- ✔ Cross-sell more products to existing customers
- ✔ Develop new channels of distribution (such as the Internet)
- ✔ Educate customers about a new technology or process

✔ Expand into new geographical markets

✔ Fend off a competitor's challenge

✔ Find new customers

✔ Generate more or better leads for the sales force

✔ Improve customer service

✔ Improve the distribution of existing products or services

✔ Increase the average order size

✔ Increase the perceived value of offerings to counter a trend toward price competition

✔ Introduce new products or services

✔ Recruit new distributors or retailers

✔ Reduce customer complaints

If you go through this list checking those objectives that apply to your situation, you probably come up with at least a few appropriate ones that you can use to guide your planning. If not, you can always make up some of your own. But make sure that you have clear objectives before you go into any planning process.

Running Goal-Oriented Marketing Experiments

Although creative experimentation is an important element of any marketing or planning effort, random experimentation is not. When you experiment, you need to have specific marketing goals and a rough idea of the kinds of marketing activities that may achieve those goals. Then you can focus your creative experimentation on finding out how to better achieve those marketing goals by refining your ideas until you have a unique approach that produces a winning marketing programme.

The formula you develop and continue refining through your marketing experiments is uniquely yours. No formula works for more than one organisation; each business needs to find its own marketing zone. Yet your formula can and should rely on certain transferable elements – the fundamentals that hold up in all marketing programmes. And the most easily transferable formulas have to do with marketing goals.

Specifically, you need to know that certain kinds of marketing initiatives tend to be appropriate for certain kinds of marketing goals and not for others.

You can use that information to help you define the basic structure of any marketing plan or programme – and narrow down those apparently random options – simply by picking one or a few marketing objectives. Then, focus on the marketing techniques that are most likely to help you achieve those objectives.

Planning Benchmarks for Marketing Communications

How much should you spend on marketing communications (*marcoms*) like advertising, the Internet, mailings, telemarketing or whatever you plan to use? Communicating with your market takes many forms in your plan and is probably a major part of it. If you want to truly achieve your strategic objectives, you need to have a plan that communicates well and often.

Avoiding random activity

Planning exercises can easily turn into random listings of possibilities. The poor planners run out of insights, information and time when they have to itemise the details of their marketing programmes. Their thinking often goes like this:

> 'What sorts of ads, mailings or other marketing communications should we use? Hmmm. Dunno. Maybe we should just list a bunch, so we make sure that some advertising and mailings are included in the budget.'

We guess that's a planning process, but not a very intelligent one! You can take many actions to promote your product or service. Often, people just try one thing after another, hoping to see sales increase without any real idea of what may work, why and how. We call this *random marketing*. It goes kind of like this:

> 'Hey, we need to do something to get more sales. Let's do some advertising.'

Or maybe:

> 'Our competitors are offering coupons. Should we do some coupons, too?'

And so on. What about trying some telemarketing? Or print advertising? Or even television or radio spots? Direct mail may be better. Hmmm. Lots of options. But which should you try? Is it entirely a matter of blind experimentation?

No. At least, it better not be, unless you have a lot of time and money to waste groping around in the marketing dark. Random marketing is like the old philosophical theory that if you put enough apes at enough typewriters for long enough, eventually they type a Shakespearean play by chance. With random marketing, you may produce a winning programme by chance. But you had better be very patient! The only difference between the old ape-at-the-typewriter theory and the typical approach to marketing is that nobody is silly enough to actually try the ape experiment, whereas the majority of businesses try random marketing. Then people wonder why their plans don't produce satisfactory results.

On the bottom of the spreadsheet in File 3-6, we include a row that calculates your total marketing communications spending by adding up any rows above it that involve spending on direct communications within your market. As you work on your plan, keep a close eye on this number and make sure that it's a big enough percentage of your projected sales to actually give you a good shot at achieving those sales projections.

What's a big enough percentage to spend on marketing communications? 'As much as you can afford' is one philosophy, but sometimes benchmarking against industry norms is best rather than just maximising marcoms. If your business is an average size in your industry, a spending level similar to the statistic from the industry closest to yours in Table 3-2 probably keeps you growing as fast as your competitors and the industry as a whole. To grow faster than your industry or to make up for being smaller than average, you probably need to allocate more money, perhaps even two to three times the average amount.

Table 3-2   Marcom Spending as a Percentage of Sales

Product or Service	*Spending (%)*
Services:	
Insurance	0.6
Advertising	2.8
Digital/pay TV	1.0
Nursing homes	3.4
Hospitals	3.0
Investment advice	6.8
Personal services	4.0
Services in general	2.5
Products:	
Ice cream	5.4
Furniture	5.0
Car parts/accessories	0.8
Greeting cards	3.3
Printed media (newspapers/magazines/ newsletters)	5.8
Food products	9.4
Toys	18
Computer equipment	2.5
Office supplies	4.2

Product or Service	Spending (%)
Building supplies	1.2
Retail stores:	
Watch stores	15.7
Department stores	4.3
Furniture stores	9.0
Clothing stores	3.2
Hotels/motels	3.9
Insurance agencies	1.6
Banks	3.8
Stockbrokers	2.0
Consumer electronics stores	3.8
Variety stores	2.0
Gift shops	4.5
Grocery stores	1.2
Restaurants/bars	4.4
Retailers in general	3.4

For more information . . .

In this chapter, we queue up a number of tools, techniques and benchmarks to help you with your marketing strategy and plan. Whether you just need to diagnose the situation or develop a full-blown plan, you should find plenty of guidelines in this chapter and its corresponding CD files. For more details on how to design and budget all the specifics of your plan, such as advertising campaigns, sales programmes and promotions, see the chapters that focus on each of these topics.

Often, a chapter in this book directly corresponds to a section on the market planning template and a section on the budget template, too. In addition, you can find complementary coverage of marketing plans in our other books in this series, *Marketing For Dummies* and *Digital Marketing for Dummies* (Wiley). We encourage you to seek additional resources as well. For example, William Cohen's *The Marketing Plan* (Wiley), although written for classroom use, has a number of good examples of marketing plans that we recommend as benchmarks. The 'Knowledge hub' at the Chartered Institute of Marketing's website (www.cim.co.uk) is also packed full of information to get you started. In our experience, the more support and information you have on hand when undertaking a planning process, the better.

By all means violate these norms if you like, but we do recommend thinking about how your business's marketing communications expenses compared to others in your industry. You should have a good reason in mind if you decide to be significantly different. For example, if you want to gain market share or grow your business's sales, you probably have to outspend the averages. But if your plan produces numbers that are dramatically different than the norms and you don't know why, you really ought to go back and look to make sure that a good reason exists for the differences.

Files on the CD

Check out the following items on the CD:

- ✔ **File 3-1:** Editable Marketing Audit, a Microsoft Word document
- ✔ **File 3-2:** Audit Score Form, a Microsoft Excel spreadsheet
- ✔ **File 3-3:** Marketing Agenda, a PDF format worksheet to use in a planning brainstorm session
- ✔ **File 3-4:** Marketing Plan Template, an editable Microsoft Word file
- ✔ **File 3-5:** Marketing Budget Worksheet, an editable Microsoft Excel template
- ✔ **File 3-6:** Sales Projection Worksheet, an editable Microsoft Excel template

Chapter 4

Cutting Costs and Boosting Impact

• •

In This Chapter

▶ Considering low-cost ways to boost sales

▶ Stimulating word-of-mouth referrals

▶ Using persuasive information and creativity to boost impact

▶ Narrowing your focus to increase effectiveness

• •

*I*n this chapter, we review a variety of ideas, tips and examples that help you to improve your marketing effectiveness and efficiency.

This chapter is especially useful for people who are in a hurry to find a way to increase sales and profits. Sometimes you don't need or want to do a full-blown audit and write a new plan (as we describe in Chapter 3) and instead just want to look critically and creatively at your business to see if you can do any quick fixes to help performance. Usually, you can!

Taking a Look at Low-Cost and No-Cost Marketing Ideas

In this section we look at various options that cost little or nothing to implement – some that you may not initially think about and some an ad agency may fail to mention to you.

You can quickly find the pounds adding up with most of the conventional forms of advertising. But you don't need to spend a lot of money on marketing.

Transit advertising

Generally you pay £70–350 to display your advertising poster on a bus or at a bus-stop shelter, depending on the size of the city.

Okay, it's not free, we agree – the cost's relatively low, depending on the size of the audience, the number of locations you require and the amount of time you want your ad to run. This commitment is fairly small on your part for a lot of exposure, and if your message connects with the public, you can expect a good return. (We recommend a direct response format, with a website and freephone number right there on the ad.)

An ad agency may direct you toward a local television ad, but that costs ten times as much to create and place as a small-scale outdoor ad placement. The good thing about marketing is that you always have alternatives that fit your budget.

Publicity

Spreading the word of your business throughout your home city or region for free can be difficult, but not impossible. If you can think of an interesting news story about your product, people or events, you can put your time and energy into contacting local media and trying to generate some editorial coverage rather than advertising (see Chapter 11 for more details on publicity).

You may not have a serious or *hard news* story to offer unless something bad happens (and honestly, we'd rather have no publicity than see a headline about a product failure or bad customer experience!), but being what's called *soft news* is fine. Local newspapers, radio stations and news weeklies need a lot of lighter filler stories with local or human interest. Here's where you come in. Let them know about a recent accomplishment or event or even offer your expert advice for businesses or consumers, depending on who you're trying to reach.

Publicity is free. We like free marketing.

The classic flier – tried, true and free

Flyers – single sheets designed to be put under windscreen wipers and through doors or stuck to public bulletin boards and other public spaces – are a great way to get the word out locally for almost no cost. You pay just a few pence to make a photocopy on colourful paper, and the turnaround at most copy shops is under an hour.

Although some locations regulate flyers and fine you if you violate the rules, you can still distribute them in plenty of ways and in many places. Also, some shops (such as coffee shops, supermarkets, grocery shops and convenience stores) have bulletin boards or other spots where you can post approved notices. If you want to reach a local audience, a flier may be worthwhile.

Look at what others are posting in your area and try to make your flyer look a little more appealing and easy to read. Most flyers cram far too much information onto the page. Select one or two simple, clean, easy-to-read fonts, and make sure that you design yours to be read in ten seconds or less, from a distance of a metre or more away. If you need to give a lot of information, refer to a website for follow-up or add a phone number for people to call.

The classic flyer works far better when you keep it simple. Copy your flyer in one colour and avoid complex designs.

Although you need to pay a minimal fee to print flyers, the great thing about them is that you pay nothing for the exposure. They're placed in public spaces for free. Displaying advertising for free is very hard to do, so be grateful for this rare opportunity and treat it with respect. Keep your messages appropriate – don't go using bad language or dodgy images where children may see them. Professional-looking flyers are best and always make sure that you're respectful when looking for places to post or distribute them. You are representing your organisation and business at all times and this encounter may be someone's first experience of your brand, so don't make it a disappointment by failing to be polite.

The information booklet or brochure

Many marketers forget about the value of technical or special knowledge. People don't want to be bothered with your sales pitch, but they love it when you offer to help them with their problem. And sometimes, the difference is just a matter of perception.

For example, imagine that you run a surf shop. Instead of churning out some ads boasting of the range of boards in stock, you create a publication (published inexpensively at the local copy shop) about caring for classic surfboards. Using an image of an old-fashioned board on the front, you can pack it full of historical information about the long boards that once dominated the sport, tips about the different types and which ones are most usable or collectible today, plus care tips, a directory of places to find and trade used boards, profiles of the best early surfers and their boards, and other interesting information.

Instead of plastering the shop's name, address, logo and product line all over the publication, relegate this information to the back cover. The product then feels like a useful booklet for people interested in surf boards without shoving anything down their throat. It is likely to get passed around enthusiasts and draw more people to the shop, which has positioned itself as the place where real experts go and the staff really care about classic boards and their owners.

The same strategy can work in many different businesses. Work out what's really important to your customers and position yourself as the expert in this area. If you're running a landscape gardening business, you may decide that your customers are concerned about the effects of pesticides and produce a leaflet all about organic lawns and how to care for them. Offer it to your current customers as a free gift and distribute it to the local nurseries and do-it-yourself stores for a small price. You can build trust with potential customers, who then come to you as an expert.

Better looking basics: Stationery, business cards and brochures

We can't believe how poorly most businesses dress themselves! They may have expensive ad campaigns or flashy websites, but if their mailings and business cards are poorly designed or cheaply printed, they're undermining their investment by not doing the basics well.

Take a hard look at your business card. Does it really present you and your business in the best possible way? Does it say 'Wow!' or does it just mumble? Please don't ignore the cornerstones of business communication. Make sure that you always make a powerfully positive impression. See Chapters 7 and 8 for some how-to advice to bump up the impact of these low-cost but high-value marketing tools.

Another hidden problem in most marketing programmes is a lack of consistency in image and presentation. If you don't present your brand name and related information in a consistent manner, both visually and verbally, you're not making the impact you ought to. Often, you can improve marketing response rates and boost sales just by reviewing the way you present your business in all existing formats, forums and media. Go for a consistent, impressive look and good things follow.

Spreading the message with electronic media

The profusion of various types of electronic media provides a number of different ways for you to get free or low-cost marketing.

Low-cost display ads in online communities

If you're looking to buy low-cost ads, social networks can be a great place to start. Begin, however, by considering which community is going to work best for your organisation's needs. For example, Facebook has a good spread of users across the age range, whereas MySpace has a lot of younger users. In the same way, people on Facebook tend to appear under their real names, whereas MySpace lets people build more fanciful profiles. Depending on who you're trying to target, you may want to advertise on one network more than another.

If you're a business offering services to other companies, think about ignoring MySpace and Facebook and sticking to a network like LinkedIn, which is solely for professional networking. Whatever your needs, an online community exists that can work for you!

Our advice to potential buyers of display ads on any of these pages is to visit the site, read their latest information about advertising options and buy the cheapest, easiest entry-level ad. Test a message. See what happens. If you don't get a good response, try adjusting the message. You can run a half-dozen inexpensive experimental ads and see if something clicks. If not, you haven't risked much of your budget. But if you find a formula that works, online communities are now so large that you can bump up the scale of your advertising easily and do some serious business on them.

Viral marketing on MySpace or Facebook

You don't have to buy advertising space to take advantage of the vast opportunities that cyberspace communities provide. With a little creativity you can reach a huge audience for very little cost.

A jewellery company with a range of products aimed at young children, Pugster, was looking for a free way to reach people. Although the company already had its own website, it was keen to find a way to promote its personality, tell people about special offers and differentiate itself from other jewellery brands.

Pugster already had a mascot in the form of Pinky, a pug dog that acts as the face of the company. So Pugster set Pinky up with his own page on social networking site MySpace (www.myspace.com), featuring blogs about jewellery, photos of products and downloadable Pinky wallpapers.

The company was careful to include lots of content on the site that wasn't just related to products on sale and people began 'befriending' Pinky. Because the face of the company was a cute dog rather than a more corporate image, people were happy to hear from Pinky. Now the company has more than 5,000 friends, who are engaged with the brand and open to its offers. The only cost is the time spent by Pugster employees replying to messages and updating the site.

You can use a similar strategy on Facebook, no matter what type of organisation you're marketing. You can set up a group for people interested in your products and ask people to become 'fans' or create a profile and get anyone interested to link to you.

The Cadbury Wispa bar, brought back from the brand graveyard after a successful consumer campaign on Facebook, now proudly sits on its own page with around 220,000 fans, all opening up their information to the company. Not just big businesses do this; schools and universities have set up profiles on Facebook to encourage donations and support from the people interested enough in them to befriend them on the site.

Getting things wrong in the social network space is all too easy. People don't mind a business making approaches to them if the services or products on offer are relevant or amusing. But don't just start spamming everyone with commercial impersonal messages.

And remember that though setting up MySpace and Facebook pages is free, you do need to maintain them if you're to have any success. This process can take up one of your most precious resources – time. You need to reply to messages from your new friends, post on their profile 'walls' and act as a real member of the virtual community that you're in. You can choose simply to post up some content, sit back and forget about it, but you aren't going to have much success that way.

Text messages – a personal viral marketing strategy?

You're a member of more online communities than you may think. We recently received some text messages from a beauty salon where we spent some money buying vouchers in the past, telling us about its latest offers and news. With offers of large discounts on various services, these messages were welcome information. Although text messages (otherwise known as SMS) are a very personal, informal medium, they're a good way to do viral marketing for the right message (something your friends and acquaintances don't mind hearing about). Check with your mobile telephone service provider to make sure that you have a plan with a cheap package rate for text messages; otherwise, they can be costly to send.

Of course, your phone can't by itself reach a very large audience – unless you can get people to pass the word along, or you can get lots of people to give you their mobile phone numbers. To make people keen to give you their numbers, you need to offer them something genuinely useful; for example, if you're a small clothes retailer, why not ask people to sign up to find out dates of sales before anyone else. But remember to make sure that you check out any data protection restrictions before asking people for their numbers. You don't want to be a spammer!

The information-heavy web page or blog

Websites are usually designed as if they're interactive sale catalogues. But the sites that have the biggest and most consistent traffic are usually ones that give away useful information and are less commercial in nature.

Baby products brand Pampers has a great website in this respect. The site is set out according to child age and filled with menu tips, advice for parents and blogs where people can debate issues. There is even a fun baby name finder. Product information about Pampers is available but kept low key – the site acts more as a portal for parents to meet, share tips and find out about child development than a pure sales tool. By creating this community for parents, the business positions itself as the expert in baby care, which it hopes makes parents – always anxious to give their kids the best care – seek out Pampers' products in stores.

Maybe you can do the same on your website. What special knowledge and information do you have that prospective customers may appreciate your sharing with them?

If you're an expert on something – anything – consider a blog. For example, once a week, the owner of a garden centre can post a new blog about some seasonal challenge for gardeners. In spring, the blog contains tips on which shrubs to prune now and which ones to leave alone until after they flower. In autumn, it covers bulb planting and how to put your lawn to bed for the winter.

Blogs are easy to create and post if you use a blog template and hosting service, such as the ones offered by WordPress (www.wordpress.org) or Blogger (www.blogger.com). You don't need to do HTML programming. You just need to have some interesting and/or useful things to say. If you're unfamiliar with this (completely free!) new medium, start reading other bloggers' work and get a feel for it before designing your own. If you want to know more about blog strategy you can also check out *Digital Marketing For Dummies* by Ben Carter and Greg Brooks (Wiley).

Pay-per-click advertising (keyword ads)

Pay-per-click advertising isn't free, but it's very economical and you can easily control your costs. You can turn it on or off depending on your budget and results. And you can keep fiddling with your selection of keywords, the price you bid for a click on a keyword and the phrase that pops up to promote your link.

You need a web page to link to, so if you don't already have one, you have to spend some money to create one. But web pages don't need to cost an arm and a leg (money is normally enough!). You can create your own simple one from an inexpensive template, so even that requirement isn't a major barrier to using pay-per-click advertising.

We give you more information about how to use this powerful and inexpensive medium in Chapter 6. You can also go to the relevant sections of the websites of Google (www.google.co.uk) or Yahoo (uk.yahoo.com), which explain how to use keyword advertising services. Pay-per-click advertising isn't rocket science, but it can help a marketing programme take off.

Widgets, gadgets and the like

You may hear excited marketing chatter about *widgets*. Widgets look like tiny square web pages that sit in their own window on another web page. Sometimes they're obviously commercial (for example, eBay has widgets that show specific eBay listings and their status). Often, widgets are informative, entertaining or fun; for instance, some of them are games.

If you search on the Internet, you can easily find a variety of businesses offering software you can use to build your own widgets, which may be a good idea if you're clever with your electronic fingers. If you come up with something that's really appealing, people may seek it out and put it on their home pages. Cool!

As they've become more popular, widgets have become yet another kind of paid web ad – more interactive and interesting than most, but sold as ad space by the same players you go to now for pay-per-click listings. Google, for example, promotes widgets under the name Gadget Ads.

Word-of-mouth or referral marketing

If your service is good enough, all you need is one customer. This customer is so impressed that she tells others to give you a try. And they tell others, who tell others. And soon you have more business than you need, without ever spending a penny on marketing.

Pay-per-click advertising heats up sales?

WarmFloors is an online retailer of under-floor central heating systems. Although the products are sourced from Scandinavia, WarmFloors is based in West Yorkshire. Founded in 2004, the founder and his partner were anxious to grow. But with no previous experience in the heating industry, the team was unclear on how to proceed and find customers for the new venture.

After a month or two of operations, WarmFloors turned to using Google's pay-per-click service AdWords. AdWords works by allowing businesses to bid on certain keywords to bring them up under sponsored links when people search using Google. By experimenting with paying for different keywords, WarmFloors was able to find customers searching for its very specific heating products who may have never come across the business otherwise. Within two years, WarmFloor had a turnover of £500,000 and now gains many customers from word-of-mouth recommendations rather than simply paid-for advertising methods.

Your quality needs to be notable and your people skills flawless, or else customers don't talk you up.

Business-to-business social network LinkedIn is an example of how word of mouth can help an idea to spread. Founder Reid Hoffman had the idea for LinkedIn when he realised that business today is done through building relationships.

Hoffman had been working on some ideas for one of his companies when he encountered some development issues. Having lunch with a friend, his pal recommends another friend who may be able to help. The friend-of-a-friend was able to offer some advice and Hoffman realised that without someone putting the two of them in touch, his problem would have remained unsolved.

LinkedIn doesn't market itself through expensive advertising campaigns but uses its own philosophy to promote itself. It simply tries to be the most useful resource for someone hoping to network, look for a job or promote themselves, and as a result people pass the information about the brand along to each other. By people linking on the service and telling their friends to get involved, it's grown to more than 33 million users around the world. Not bad for word-of-mouth marketing!

We hope that you can apply that story about the power of referrals to your own business. What can you do to make a more positive impression on each of your customers? How can you become their favourite vendor, service provider or shop? If you're better than 90 per cent of your competitors, word of mouth naturally lifts your sales and brings you new business. All you have to do is do your job well and make an effort to be friendly and likeable whenever you interact with customers.

If you're interested in any of the previously mentioned digital marketing techniques, read more in *Digital Marketing For Dummies* (Wiley).

Events, parties and charity fundraisers

New retail stores sometimes throw Grand Opening parties, which attract attention and draw in the curious. We like parties: they're events, and people go to events. All you need is some helium-filled balloons, beverages and finger foods on trays, and you can hold your own party. To pump it up, you can invite a local group of musicians to perform or tie into an art event. (If you let local artists display their travel or nature photos in your office or store, they show up for the party with friends and family members.)

Another good way to attract people and make your business visible is to offer space and support for a local charity to stage a fundraising or community event. Pick a charity that's compatible and of interest to your prospective customers, of course. Then let the enthusiasm draw a crowd.

Sponsoring a local sports or charitable event is another way to make your business visible in the community and to build goodwill. Mega-brands pursue these goals with multimillion-pound TV and print ad campaigns, but the smaller and/or local marketer probably builds a better image through events than through brand advertising. And the price is right – opportunities range from free to modest contributions or fees. And seeing your business name on children's sports uniforms or the list of hosts or sponsors of a local charity is a great feeling.

Whatever the event – fundraising party, sponsorship launch and so on – employ soft-selling to avoid things feeling too commercial. Get people in front of your name or to your place of business and allow them to meet you and your staff. Let them connect the dots later. We promise they'll remember you.

Ask for the business

A common marketing mistake is to fail to ask people to make a purchase. View every human interaction (whether in person, by phone, mail or email) as an opportunity to make a sale. We're amazed how these opportunities are often wasted. Are you asking for the sale whenever possible, and using proper sales techniques when you ask? If not, check Part V of this book which gives you ways to bump up your sales efforts.

Maybe this point is obvious, but a sales call is, at least in the short term, free. Yes, we agree that if you staff up with salespeople who receive a salary and/ or commission, the sales staff isn't free – but we're talking about you or other staff sometimes popping on your sales hat and getting out there to make a few calls.

That kind of marketing doesn't entail paying commissions to salespeople or sales reps, simply your remembering to ask for business on a regular basis. Our theory is that everyone in the business ought to do a little friendly soft selling. Making sales is the responsibility of everyone working for your business. If you can instil that value, you can generate a lot of business that's otherwise left unharvested.

We could go on for many more pages on the subject of low-cost ways to boost sales and maximise marketing impact. In fact, we have! File 4-1 is a printable tip sheet with a number of ideas you can check out. Maybe one of them works for your business. Have a look!

Harnessing the Power of Information

Information is usually free. Yet marketers rarely leverage this commodity of the information age to full effect. We can't believe how fluffy and insubstantial most marketing communications are. You only have to open any piece of promotional mail or visit any business's website to see what we mean. Do compelling, convincing, exciting hard facts jump out at you? No? Well, they should. Powerfully presented information has the power to make your marketing communications much more effective.

Here are some tips for pumping up your marketing communications with well-presented information:

- ✔ Pick your strongest fact or argument and emphasise it consistently.

- ✔ Prune your writing down so that you make your point clearly and simply.

- ✔ Strengthen your main point with three or more supporting facts or arguments.

- ✔ Use a *creative* approach to make your main point so that *people aren't bored* by it!

Most ads are mediocre in their performance. They do okay, but they're not stars. The same applies to sales letters, sales presentations, web pages and so on. Marketing is a lot like most other areas of human performance in that there is a dominant midrange of intermediate level performances, and not that many high-end examples. We bring up this point because of the cost impact it has.

To illustrate the opportunity, we're going to reach for the very first letter we find in front of us. Hmmm. It's an oversized white envelope bulk-mailed to us from our bank.

Now, what do our marketing eyes make of this mailing? Well, for starters, it isn't very attractive. The envelope seems to be made of the cheapest possible paper, and it's very plain and boring. No information appears on the front other than our address and the return address; the back is completely blank. Tearing it open, we find a folded set of pages that are labelled Account Statement and have technical information about our holdings.

This mailing is a wasted marketing opportunity! Plenty of space is available on the envelope, as well as within it, to print informative content about this bank's other services, how it can help us or what advice or tips it may have to make our financial lives better and more secure. And what would be the cost of adding information that may cement the relationship with customers and possibly cross-sell other services? Nothing. The mailing goes out every month anyway.

The next envelope in our in-tray is, we're amused to see, another statement from another bank where we do business. When we open it, we find that, in addition to our statement information, the bank includes a couple of sentences about various special accounts it offers and who's eligible for them, along with a customer relations number. That's better! A little information can go a long way in the world of marketing.

Here are some questions to help you assemble hard-hitting facts that can bump up the impact of any marketing or advertising you do:

- ✔ What technical specifications or qualities can you mention in order to make your offering look as good as possible compared to the competition?

- ✔ What qualifications or experiences does your business or team bring to its work that may impress potential buyers?

- ✔ What special degrees, memberships, awards or other honours have members of your team received?

- ✔ Who is already using your product or service? Get permission to name names or, better yet, ask for quotes or testimonials.

- ✔ What news coverage have you received that you can cite?

Facts and evidence, such as product specs, expert recommendations, media coverage or customer testimonials, have tremendous impact. They can increase the effectiveness of your marketing communications and thereby reduce the amount you have to spend on communicating. More effective equals lower cost; a powerful equation. Take a look at your marketing and sales and see where you can add more evidence and information.

Exercising Creativity: Ideas Are Free!

Creativity is the silver bullet of marketing programmes. It can slay overspending and bring new life to your sales and profits. Instead of searching for ways to cut costs or new media that are cheaper to use, go back to the drawing board and come up with some creative marketing concepts. If you get things right, it's like minting money in your basement – except it's completely legal.

One of the most successful ad campaigns for business magazine *The Economist* stepped away completely from the usual marketing methods used in that sector. Normally, adverts for publications attempt to ram home the publication's title as often as possible, but *The Economist* avoided this approach.

The marketing team at *The Economist* thought about what separated its readers in mentality from people reading other magazines. It decided on the important insight that *Economist* readers are part of a special club of brainy, informed types. As such, the team got creative and ran a series of ads based on the idea that if you understood the campaign, you were probably an *Economist* reader or the right type of person to be reading the magazine. The campaign played to people's vanity about their own intelligence and education; instead of following the usual rules of ads by making them easy to process, working out the advertiser acted as part of the campaign.

Some billboards featured classic Thunderbirds character Brains peeping into a poster with a red background – a colour associated strongly with *The Economist.* Others bore the text, 'Stop having to remind people who you are' on a logo-less red backdrop. In case these ads were too subtle, some of the campaign ads did reference the advertiser, such as a sign declaring: 'I never read *The Economist* . . . management trainee, 42.'

What all the ads had in common was creativity. Instead of telling people about what stories they may read in the current issue, the marketing concentrated on playing to people's desire to be part of an elite club. Now, although you may not have the budget to run a large-scale poster campaign, the idea is what counts. *The Economist* wasn't afraid to try a new approach, and you shouldn't be, either.

Don't despair, however, if you can't see a way to make a campaign like *The Economist*'s one work for you. Creativity doesn't have to be clever. In fact, headlines with clever puns are rarely as effective as the copywriter thinks they're going to be. (Usually, the joke turns out to be on the marketer.)

Creative concepts simply need to get the message across clearly and well. For example, a local insurance agency may have as its message that it doesn't just sell business insurance, it provides the benefit of 40 years of experience and expertise to its clients. Great! Service and support can make the difference. But how do you communicate this message creatively enough that it grabs consumers' attention and makes the point without your having to buy endless advertising and billboard space to repeat it?

Okay, get creative. How about a visual image to make the point? We're thinking about a spokesperson, someone who looks helpful, sage and business-like. This wise mentor-like insurance consultant is perhaps leaning over someone's shoulder, pointing something out to him as he examines a complex document. The grateful customer is smiling, nodding and saying, 'Thanks. I was wondering how to control our rising insurance costs! This looks perfect!' Perhaps a high-quality posed photograph of this scene can be used in ads and brochures?

That idea is called a *creative concept.* We're not boasting – we know it's not really all *that* creative. Not compared to an Andy Warhol canvas, for example. But it may be sufficiently creative to bring the message to life with words and imagery.

Thinking visually is often a good approach when you want to harness the power of creativity to make your advertising more effective. Studies generally show that print ads that are between ¼ and ¾ art (a drawing, diagram, map or photograph) have much more impact than ads that are mostly or all copy (words).

You can use creativity in all media, not just in print ads. Pump up your website the same way you would a print ad – except use streaming video instead of static art. (See Chapter 6 for more on visual appeals.) Also, make sure that your brochures, logo, business cards, billing statements and, in fact, all communications that reach customers or prospects are creative enough to draw the eye and attract attention.

 A dull speaker puts the audience to sleep, and dull marketing gets even less respect. Metaphors are a powerful creative tool for marketing. We give you more tools and techniques for creativity in Chapter 13, but even if you don't read that chapter right away, you can start to harness the power of creativity by using simple, powerful metaphors to bring your message home more effectively.

 The Australian winery Wolf Blass wanted to convey the sense that it's a bold leader in the industry. It decided to get this message across with a simple metaphor – the winery compared its brand to an eagle. The name 'WOLF BLASS' is always shown in gold capital letters with a gold line drawing of an eagle spreading its wings directly above. The message is also reinforced with words – the tag line that always appears next to their logo reads, 'Australian wine at its peak'. The link between the soaring bird and the idea of the brand soaring high is made in consumers' minds.

Can you compare your brand, product or service to a bird or animal? If so, this visual may be a good way to get your message across. For example, the camel epitomises sustainability because it can store and conserve water for its desert habitat. Perhaps a camel would be a good image to associate with a business that does energy audits and consults on green construction methods? See if you can come up with a good metaphor for your marketing message.

Narrowing Your Focus to Cut Costs and Maximise Impact

In Chapter 2, we introduce you to the concept of a marketing zone – the set of formulas that you develop for optimising your marketing and making it reasonably predictable and reliable. We also share the important insight that good marketing needs to have a tight focus and not be spread too thin. When you find your zone and get your marketing programme well tuned, you discover that you're focused in two ways: you know what your message is, and you know what your primary medium is for delivering it. This focus is the secret to economical marketing; it produces marketing programmes that generate a lot of leads and sales from relatively little effort.

Unfortunately, most marketing isn't well focused on either of these areas. Or is that a fortunate thing? Maybe so, because the result is that you can follow an obvious path toward better performance and lower marketing costs.

Directing your marketing message

What exactly is the benefit of your product or service? Why should people buy from you?

If your answer varies or is lengthy, confusing, unconvincing or uncertain, you need to focus your message more sharply. We have to be brutally honest with you: we don't think your message is clearly defined or communicated with sufficient consistency. We think your marketing communications lack focus. A lack of focus is a problem for 99 per cent of businesses, and that's why we imagine it's the same for you.

Take a look at any well-positioned consumer brand for inspiration on how to focus your message. Often they're good examples of highly focused marketing that hits the same powerful positioning message over and over.

And you don't have to be a multi-billion-pound consumer products giant like Unilever or Procter & Gamble to use this strategy. Think about independent smoothie company innocent. It is careful to use the idea that the brand is 'innocent' in every single aspect of its business. The fruit drinks contain no added sugar; the information on the bottles is written out simply and clearly in a childlike manner with transparency about all ingredients; and extra marketing material is also produced with the idea of being open in mind. The company also keeps a blog on its website, using much of the same friendly, approachable language to tell customers about new updates. For example, one recent post about launching two vegan vegetable pots for lunchtimes acknowledges that consumers demanded this product rather than the idea coming from the business. The brand looks modest and sensitive to its customers' opinions. The marketing message is 100 per cent pure, just like the products. No competing messages or confusion are allowed to cloud that message.

We probably don't need to tell you too much more about innocent because whether you buy the smoothies or not, you probably already know that anything the company produces is pure and 'innocent'. You know this by heart. But do your customers and prospects know *your* message by heart? Think about it. Do something about it.

To make sure that you're focusing your message precisely and basing it on a strong foundation of compelling evidence, open File 4-2 and take a look at the Message Pyramid, a simple way to illustrate your message strategy. We completed it for our example, innocent, so that you can see how you can use this tool to clarify and focus a marketing message. Give it a try!

Focusing your marketing programme

In Chapter 2, we introduce the concept of a well-focused marketing programme and use a pyramid diagram to illustrate it. The idea is simple but powerful: at least a quarter of your effort and spending should be concentrated on the single most effective marketing activity, or your programme is too scattered and unfocused to be effective. When you figure out what the right focus is, your marketing runs smoothly and profitably, and you enter what we call your marketing zone.

You need to focus your marketing programme on one primary method and several secondary methods because this approach is the most cost-effective and efficient way to market. Being noticed and getting heard is difficult. Lots of information is competing for consumer attention; what marketers call 'noise' exists in all the communications channels you're using to try to reach prospective customers. You have to focus your programme if you want to rise above the background noise.

For example, running a few 30-second radio ads a week probably doesn't produce any significant impact, because people don't really pay attention. You probably need to run a few dozen to get your message across, but you can't afford it if you're also spending money on billboards, a direct mailing, several new websites and an event at the same time you're trying to hit the market with radio ads.

If you lack tight focus, narrow your programme and concentrate more effort and resources in one lead marketing method. We have a hunch you'll see more bang for your marketing buck as soon as you identify the most productive marketing activities and focus your resources on them.

Don't get us wrong: you still need to have a lot of things going on at once in most marketing programmes. Your business cards and letterhead need to look sharp and use the same version of your logo and tag line as your latest catalogue or web page. Your packaging should be carefully designed to maximise appeal (if you sell a packaged good). Your list of customers needs a friendly mailing, telephone call or email at least once a month and so on.

You always have to juggle many activities and media, but you need to decide which are the most important – and be as tough as nails about defending their dominance.

Give your primary method between a third and a half of your attention and budget, or it doesn't have enough fertiliser to grow healthy sales and profits for you.

Files on the CD

Check out the following items on the CD-ROM:

- ✔ File 4-1: Tips for Boosting Sales
- ✔ File 4-2: The Message Pyramid

Part II
Advertising Management and Design

'You're not <u>quite</u> what I expected.'

In this part . . .

Do you ever advertise? If not, we can honestly say that you'd better think about starting because every business can benefit from well-designed, carefully placed advertising. If you do already use this powerful medium, then you no doubt know how expensive advertising can get and how hard designing an ad that really achieves its business objectives can be. Careful planning – which we show you how to do in Chapter 5 – is the answer to these problems. Ads can accomplish a lot of profitable objectives, but only if you clearly define them upfront and then design your campaign appropriately.

Ads absolutely *must* be well designed. They need to look good, read well, sound great, catch the eye, make a lasting impression and be the stuff of dinner conversation. In short, ads have to be powerful. In Chapter 6, we share ideas and techniques for building powerful ads that really make an impact on your customers and on your sales. Follow our advice and you won't ever run an ad that lacks power and punch.

Chapter 5

Planning and Budgeting Ad Campaigns

· ·

In This Chapter

▶ Calculating a practical average cost per ad

▶ Adjusting your budget based on gross profit

▶ Preparing a budget that achieves high ad frequency

▶ Designing business-to-business ad plans and budgets

· ·

*B*efore you start designing specific ads, you need to create an advertising plan. In this chapter, we help you plan how much you want to spend on advertising and how to spend it.

You can easily spend more money on your ads than you imagined in your wildest dreams – but please don't! In this chapter, we show you how to set some practical limits on your advertising campaign to make sure that you're laughing – not crying – all the way to the bank.

Selecting a Practical Approach to Ad Budgets

We feel like we need to start this chapter with a bold sign, flashing WARNING! in the middle of the road. If you're approaching advertising as a mid-sized or small consumer business or as a mid-sized business that sells to other businesses (business-to-business or B2B), you have to proceed with special caution. Why? Because all the expert advice and conventional wisdom about advertising is based on what works for giant consumer brands.

We don't know why all the advertising textbooks are based on what's best for Sony, McDonald's, Toyota, Coca-Cola and so on when most businesses need a very different approach, but that's how it is. In this chapter, we break with tradition and show those of you with small to mid-sized businesses how you need to approach advertising.

Your CD contains a White Paper we edited called *Budgeting for Advertising: A Practical Approach* (File 5-1), which explores the difference between a corporate ad campaign for a chain of restaurants and a local ad campaign for a single family-owned restaurant. The corporate approach has several attributes that don't apply to the local restaurant owner:

- ✔ Large scale (multiple stores throughout a region or a country), which makes frequent, expensive TV ads practical and effective for the corporate marketer.

- ✔ Deep pockets, which means that the corporate marketer can choose to invest in extra advertising without immediate sales payback.

- ✔ Focus on expansion, which gives the corporate marketer more reason to invest in pure brand-building without the need for immediate sales and profits to show for it.

When you operate at a relatively small scale and want to make profits every year, you can't just scale back the corporate advertising budget. Most businesses would need to spend their entire annual advertising budget to create just one high-quality 30-second TV ad and run it a handful of times. That ad would be useless because you need to run ads many times in order to make an impact. The most important rule for practical small-business advertising is *use cheap ads so that you can run them frequently without going broke!*

Setting your ad budget

Imagine that you're the owner of a local restaurant – a steak house, a seafood café, an upscale business lunch place or whatever would be most successful in your local market. To start with, you need to consider your advertising plan in the context of the overall budget. Is the business profitable? If so, some of that profit ought to be directed into advertising.

Advertising is a business expense, and so it comes out of pre-tax profits.

If you can afford to put 5 per cent of your gross sales into advertising *without posting a loss*, plan to do so. If not – if you have a profitability problem – stop worrying about advertising and start looking hard at your cost structure. Make necessary cuts first. Get the business at least to break even. If this means scaling back and reducing your payroll, moving to a smaller location with cheaper rent or otherwise changing your business plan, make these necessary changes first.

Advertising is powerful – but not powerful enough to dig you out of an unprofitable business model unless you have a lot of extra cash to invest and are *sure* that your business will be profitable if you increase the size of your customer base just a little more. Meeting these conditions isn't easy. Often, when people try to spend their way out of a loss, they find that they have to spend more on advertising than they had initially expected, and the losses get bigger and swamp them. Remember that you should be *spending gross profits* on advertising and making sure that the underlying business model is sustainable.

With that caution in mind, we now show you how to budget and plan an annual ad campaign, using a local restaurant business as our working example. Their goal? Growth of 10 per cent for their family-owned restaurant.

Table 5-1 shows the annual income statement for such a restaurant. It's a simplified budget, so please don't use it as a template for doing your business accounting. See *Business Accounting For Dummies* by Colin Barrow and John A. Tracy (Wiley) and speak to your accountant if you don't already have a budgeting process.

Table 5-1	Calculating a Percentage-of-Sales Ad Budget		
	Year 1	*Year 2*	*Year 3*
Sales	£1,366,770	£1,503,447	£1,653,792
Food costs at 35%	£492,037	£526,206	£578,827
Packaging at 5%	£68,339	£75,172	£82,690
Labour at 20%	£273,354	£300,689	£330,758
Overhead at 19%	£259,686	£285,655	£314,220
Total operating expenses	£1,079,748	£1,187,723	£1,306,495
Gross profit	£287,022	£315,724	£347,296
Advertising set at 5% of sales	£68,339	£75,172	£82,690

The two key lines in Table 5-1 for setting your ad budget are *sales* and *gross profit*. Total sales multiplied by 0.05 tells you what your 5 per cent target is going to be. Gross profits tells you if you can afford to spend 5 per cent of sales. In the case in Table 5-1, 5 per cent of sales is considerably less than gross profits, and so the ad budget is affordable and we recommend investing in advertising to help the business achieve next year's sales target of 10 per cent growth. (Remember to adjust the percentages to reflect your own expenses.)

If the 5 per cent goal isn't affordable (gross profits are too low to cover it), you may be forced to reduce your ad budget. Be a pragmatist and cut back – that's just how it goes. However, also make sure that you adjust your sales projections for the coming year, because less advertising means lower sales. And, of course, reducing your sales forecast reduces your gross margin (because some expenses are *fixed* – meaning that they don't vary with sales). Therefore, you also have to make some *cost cuts* in order to salvage your next year of business. Cut costs until you can project a healthier gross profit for next year. Don't try to advertise your way out of a flawed business plan – it takes more than advertising to succeed; it also takes firm financial management.

Planning your ad campaign

After you're confident that you can afford to put at least a few per cent of your sales into advertising, you're ready to think about how to spend that budget. Here's a simple, practical approach to planning your ad campaign:

1. **Decide how many ads you need to place over the course of the year and pick a goal for this variable.**

   For most businesses, the goal should be to run more than 100 ads per year. By number of ads, we're referring to frequency of exposure. You can accomplish the same frequency with one ad, run 100 times, as with five ads, run 20 times each. The best option depends on how effective the first ad is and whether you need to replace it. You can work out such details later in your process, but for now just focus on budgeting enough to run a high number of ads.

   If you're uncertain about how many ads you need to run, don't feel bad; this decision is tough; even the experts at big ad agencies have no hard and fast rules. However, keep in mind that major big-budget ad campaigns try to expose prospective customers to ads very frequently – perhaps many times a day. (Witness the frequent repetition of TV ads.) If you're a normal business – that is to say, not huge – you can't afford to do that. But what *can* you do? Can you at least expose people to your message once a week? How about two or three times a week? That may be an affordable goal. (After all, a single billboard can expose commuters to your message once every workday.)

   If high frequency proves not to be affordable for you, narrow your focus to a smaller target market, which allows you to run ads that cost less because they reach a smaller audience. You're better off reaching a small audience often than reaching a huge audience just a few times. It *does* take repetition to have an impact. And it takes repetition to make an impression. In fact, you really need to repeat your message frequently. Okay, you get the point!

2. **Divide your overall budget by your frequency goal.**

This result tells you what your average ad ought to cost if you're sticking to your calculations. If you buy ads the way big corporate advertisers do, you blow your budget on overpriced ads and can't afford to repeat your message frequently. That's why you need to do this simple equation before you shop for ads. In the example of a restaurant with an ad budget of about £68,000, a frequency goal of at least 150 ad placements would mean that the average ad cost should be around £450 (£68,000 ÷ 150).

3. **Armed with the knowledge from your analysis of what your total budget is and what your average ad cost ought to be, explore the options available to you in your local market.**

As you examine options, look for the media that reach your customers well. For example, if you have a local business, a newspaper that reaches the majority of homeowners in your city or town is a good place to advertise things homeowners buy, such as furniture, garden supplies or meals out (when people get sick of cooking-in). A national magazine on home remodelling isn't as good a match for you, because many of its readers are outside your market area.

Table 5-2 is an example of a spending plan based on a budget of £68,339 and an average ad cost of around £450, so that the business can run at least 150 separate ads over the course of the year. Actually, this plan will achieve considerably higher frequency – probably twice that much – because it includes some package buys. That's fine. There's no harm in exceeding your frequency goal – just make sure that you don't come in under it. In this example, we use ad prices for a typical small city, but pricing varies depending on the size of the population in your local area.

Contact your local media and ask for quotes or rate cards to get actual ad pricing. Most ads are sold by salespeople – real human beings who can talk to you on the phone, answer your questions and sometimes even negotiate a good deal if you ask nicely. So don't be shy; no price is set in stone. Spend a day or two calling and emailing to find out what the options are within your market area and price range.

Keep in mind that the rate per ad should come down proportionately with the frequency. Also contact media companies near to their publication date for insertion orders. Often, they're not at full capacity and are more willing to cut you a deal.

Table 5-2 Ad Plan and Budget for a Local Restaurant

Type of Advertisement	Cost*	Frequency	Total Cost
Daily local newspaper 3 column display ad (60,000 circulation)	£60	40	£2,400
Daily local newspaper 20 line ad at £13.50 linage charge (60,000 circulation)	£270	20	£5,400
Newspaper insert for 60,000 circulation (colour card at £40 per 1,000)	£2,400	10	£24,000
Internet radio ad package monthly	£1,600	5	£8,000
Google localised key term search advertising, monthly cap on costs of £300	£300	10	£3,000
Back of bus poster (at £140 per line, with 2 lines) monthly, per bus	£280	36	£10,080
Sponsorship of weekend crafts fair, with signage on site plus radio mentions	£5,500	1	£5,500
Single panel coupon in direct mailing to local households**	£600	11	£6,600
Total***		133	**£64,980**
Annual sales			£1,299,600
Ad budget as percentage of sales			5.0%

* Cost adjusted for any quantity discounts. ** Does not include cost of redeeming coupons, which depends on the nature of the offer. See Chapter 9. *** Total does not include package buy of radio spots, and so actual frequency will be higher.

A spreadsheet based on Table 5-2 is provided on your CD (File 5-2). None of the cells are locked, so you can edit it to fit your own ad plan. If you enter your annual sales in the correct cell, a formula calculates the percentage of sales your ad spending works out to, so you can keep adjusting your plan until you hit your percentage target.

Our budget for this family-owned restaurant is based on a mix of public advertising (bus posters and signs at an event), Friday and weekend newspaper display ads, experimental web-radio ads, Google key term ads, plus a newspaper special insert and coupon mailings approximately once a month (see Table 5-2). The local market will be fairly well saturated with advertising. The marketing zone pyramid (see Chapter 2) for this business is based on using newspaper advertising as the primary method, with two other types of ads (event sponsorship, bus posters) in secondary supporting roles, plus mailed coupons as the third supporting method. The Google keywords advertising and web radio ads are somewhat experimental, because we're imagining the restaurant is a traditional business. However, if either of them really makes an impact, we recommend giving them more of the budget next year and reducing the newspaper and bus advertising correspondingly.

Adjusting the ad budget for a B2B plan

If you're working on a business-to-business (B2B) marketing plan, you can use the same method and logic described in the preceding section, but need to favour professional venues for your advertising instead of consumer-orientated ads. You won't participate in a mailing of coupons to homes, but you'll probably want to pay to be listed in online business directories. Similarly, you should substitute advertising in business and trade publications for the newspaper advertising. And you'll probably spend less overall on advertising because you want to budget something for personal selling, trade shows and exhibitions, or other business-orientated marketing activities. However, the same basic rule applies: work up a budget that's pragmatic and sustainable because it's funded out of your gross profits and make sure that you buy inexpensive ads so that you can afford to run them frequently.

If personal selling is important to the business, B2B ad plans take second place behind the sales plans. Your sales force ought to be paid largely on commission (to reduce your risk), and commissions can range from 10 to 25 per cent, depending on the industry and business. The high commissions mean the cost of sales is much higher than with advertising – but usually price and quantity make up for the high cost of sales in a B2B plan.

If you're budgeting sales force commissions plus overheads (which encompass items such as sales collateral material and travel expenses), you're probably going to need to keep advertising to a more modest level – somewhere around 1 to 3 per cent of sales.

To get started, we suggest you work up an ad plan based on 2.5 per cent of gross sales and see what it looks like. Often, B2B marketers can get away with half as much advertising as consumer marketers, so you can start with this amount as your working assumption until you gain enough experience to know what your marketing zone formula actually is.

Tailoring Your Advertising Plan to a Specific Goal

The earlier sections show you how to modify the classic percentage-of-sales budgeting process, to keep it in line with your profits and make sure that you have realistic expectations about what types of ads you can afford. Other than these adjustments, the classic method is quite traditional, with many businesses using it with success.

In this section, we take a look at an alternative approach to advertising – known as goal-based advertising – which is a bit more sophisticated and may be worth the added trouble.

You use *goal-based advertising* (also called objective-based or objective-and-task-based advertising) to analyse the differences between ad options and decide which give you the best return on investment; you then design an appropriate ad plan and budget. This approach is common among large corporate advertisers, but you certainly can use it – and you may want to at least take a look at the approach before finalising your plans.

Goal-based advertising encourages you to take a step back and examine your motives and objectives for advertising. If you aren't sure why you're advertising or what you want to accomplish with it, do a careful analysis of your situation and market first. Then you can build a new advertising budget and plan based on your specific objectives using goal-based advertising.

You're not advertising for the right reasons if you're thinking things such as:

- ✔ 'We do some advertising just to keep ourselves visible, but I don't think it affects our sales.'
- ✔ 'We try to match our competitors' advertising because customers expect it.'
- ✔ 'We've always done advertising; I don't know if it really works, but we're afraid of what may happen if we stop.'

Take a look at Table 5-3, which lists examples of goals that advertising can help you accomplish and select one of these strategic objectives.

Table 5-3	Examples of Ad Goals and Indicators
Goal	*Indicator*
Boost sales	Sales rise when and where the ad runs.
Generate calls	The telephone rings off the hook in the week after the ad runs.
Generate by-mail responses	Responses come in by mail in large numbers the week after the ad first runs.
Introduce new product	Requests for and press coverage of the new product increase significantly right after the ad appears.
Switch customers from competing product	Sales go up next month as a result of switching.
Encourage word of mouth	Current and past customers begin to talk, stimulating sales to people who say they 'heard about you from someone they know'.
Increase your share of market	Your sales grow faster than the leading competitors' sales over the course of a year.
Recruit new distributors	You hear from multiple distributors who are interested in working with you.
Help build sales by building image or reputation	Sales grow gradually but definitely do grow, along with rapid improvements in image and enhanced reputation.
Attract more upscale buyers	You sell higher-priced products or find that you can raise your prices or no longer have to negotiate as many discounts.
Attract a different group of customers	Your sales to the new group increase over the course of a year.
Cross-sell new product to current customers	You sell more of the new product to your current customer base during the year than you did last year.
Get more shoppers to visit your store(s)	Monthly store traffic and sales figures increase.

After you have a clear goal or purpose for your advertising, identify appropriate indicators to track your success. Your sales figures are probably going to be an important measure, but profits may also be important, as well as more specific things, such as whether you succeed in raising your prices or increasing the average size of a sale. Think about what you want to accomplish and be prepared to measure it so that you can see whether you're making progress toward your goal.

The ultimate objective, of course, is to generate sales from your ads. For example, if you run an ad designed to get more people into your shop, the ultimate objective is to increase sales in that store. So you need to measure the ad by its impact on sales, as well as on more specific and short-term measures, such as the number of people visiting your shop.

Each statement in Table 5-3 includes an indicator of how you know if the ad's working, because we want you to be this specific when you define your own advertising objectives. That way, you can create or purchase advertising that has a very clear purpose in mind, and then you can watch its performance and see if it's doing what you said it ought to. One of the most fundamental rules of good management is that accountability is important – and advertising is certainly not above this accountability rule.

Every goal in Table 5-3 links to a specific outcome that you can track to see if you achieve the objective. If you see movement in the measure, the ad is working toward its objective. If you don't, the ad isn't working, and you need to improve it or scrap it in favour of a new design.

Budgeting based on goals

The concept of budgeting based on goals is simple: decide what you want to accomplish and then design an ad campaign that achieves your goals. Unfortunately, things don't work that way in reality, but it's a great theory. If you can apply this idea even partially, it can strengthen your advertising budget and plan.

Here's how to budget based on goals:

1. **Set your objective.**

   For example, you may choose the goal of expanding the customer base for a local restaurant by attracting a business lunch crowd to supplement your traditionally busy dinner seating.

2. **Clarify the gap between current and desired results.**

   For example, a restaurant owner may decide to create a three-fold increase in lunchtime business, while sustaining the current level of dinner business.

BROOKLANDS COLLEGE LIBRARY
WEYBRIDGE SURREY KT13 8TT

3. **Make a list of types of advertising that may be effective in achieving your goal.**

   For example, you may decide to hire someone to drop off menus and coupons at office buildings in your area in order to encourage local employees to eat lunch at your restaurant.

4. **Think about the scale of advertising needed to achieve your goal.**

   Is the gap between your current sales and your goal a large one? If so, you need to scale up your advertising in order to fill this gap. You'll probably need to bump up your sales by a factor of 25 to 50 per cent at a minimum.

5. **Set a target for your overall budget that is appropriate to (proportional with) the scale of your goals.**

   Don't set your sights high and your budget low, or you're bound to be disappointed.

After you've gone thoughtfully through these steps, you have a clearer idea of what may need to change in your approach to advertising. You also have some ideas for new and different types of ads and/or media to use, and a general sense of whether your historic levels of advertising are appropriate or whether you need to bump up your budget in order to accomplish an ambitious goal.

The strategic thinking involved in goal-based budgeting is especially helpful when you're trying to achieve something new and different with your advertising. However, coming up with a specific budget level through this goal-based approach isn't easy. We recommend starting with the more specific and practical percentage-of-sales method described in the section 'Selecting a Practical Approach to Ad Budgets' earlier in this chapter and then using a goal-based analysis to refine your budget and focus your approach to advertising.

Using an Advertising Objectives Worksheet

Although the goal-orientated approach is especially useful when you're designing individual ads, writing an effective ad is a lot easier when you have a clear goal or objective in mind. For example, if you work for a B2B supplier of industrial machinery and your goal is to boost sales of the business's newest product, you need to remember this goal when you design ads. An ad that tells the history of the business may be impressive and confidence-inspiring, but it doesn't address the goal of pushing the new product into the market. Instead, you need to plan some show-and-tell ads that convince prospects that this new product is superior. You may also want to think about a special offer, such as a one-month free trial. These ideas are focused on the goal, and so they make more sense than a general ad about your business.

To help you give your ads a purposeful focus, we include an Advertising Objectives Worksheet (File 5-3). Print multiple copies and use it for brainstorming as you think about what your ads should accomplish.

The worksheet in File 5-3 forces you to design your ad campaign one ad at a time. Each ad should stand on its own as a goal-orientated plan that makes both strategic and economic sense. Use the worksheet to estimate the costs and results of each ad. Plan to run the ad and others like it enough times to achieve your overall objective. The worksheet keeps you honest by forcing you to make a reasonable estimate of what each ad can accomplish. Its bottom line is the sum of the impact of each individual ad or flight of ads. Adjust the mix of ads in your worksheet until you're satisfied that you have a good selection of ads that achieves your goals efficiently (with a good return on your advertising investment).

The Advertising Objectives Worksheet is a helpful tool for analysing specific ads and for summing up their overall impact on your marketing programme. For the sake of analysis, an *ad* means a specific advertisement run in a specific medium a specific number of times. So, in a budget for a training materials business you may define ad No. 1 as '3 column ad on Conflict Assessment, three months in *Training* magazine'. And you may define ad No. 2 as 'Direct-mail script #22, to house list with new catalogue'. To keep track of these specifics, we write a clear description of each ad in the Description column of the spreadsheet.

When you use the Advertising Objectives Worksheet on your computer, you see (to the right of the Cost of Ad column) that the spreadsheet calculates the return on investment for each ad. If the result is 1, the ad breaks even, which means that its expected revenue-generating power is equal to its cost. If the result is above 1, you're making a profit on the ad. If you aren't sure which ads (combinations of a specific ad design and insertion in a medium of your choice) to use the most, look at this column and repeat the ads with the highest returns on investment.

If you aren't sure what to enter under the Reach (number of prospects) column in the worksheet, ask whoever sells space or time in the advertising media of interest to you. Almost all media selling ad space have statistics on whom they reach, and they almost always give away detailed profiles of audience or readership for free to anyone who's interested in advertising with them.

Note that the worksheet defines reach as the number of *prospects*, not just the number of warm bodies. Sometimes these numbers are the same; sometimes they aren't. For example, if you're promoting a product that mostly women buy, you want to enter the number of women (your prospects in this case) who read a magazine in the Reach column, not the total number of people in the magazine's readership.

Preparing a month-by-month ad plan

The Advertising Objectives Worksheet can be helpful as you work up a list of advertising plans for the year. After you've done your research on ad options and prices and have thought about what sorts of ads you need to run and how many of them you need, you should have a pretty good list. (It's never perfect – you'll no doubt revise it many times as you see what results you achieve during the year.) With this preparation, you can return to your over-all ad budget and prepare a more accurate and thoughtful version of it.

You then have two options. You can go back to the simple ad budget format in File 5-2 and revise it based on any insights your goal analysis gave you. Or if you want to create a more complex and detailed plan, you have the option of using the Advertising Budget Worksheets in File 5-4.

The Advertising Budget Worksheets in File 5-4 are two linked Excel spread-sheets. The first spreadsheet (see Tab 1) asks you to enter spending levels per month for all the different types of ads you plan to run. (Leave some of the rows blank – nobody should use all the options in this worksheet at the same time!) After you fill in the monthly worksheet, Tab 2 automatically produces a summary in the form of an annual budget. Handy, isn't it?

You may find as you use the worksheets in File 5-4 that your monthly plans produce an overly expensive annual budget. Keep an eye on the bottom line total for the year and make sure that it's reasonable. If you aren't sure what a reasonable overall ad budget may be, see the section 'Setting your ad budget' earlier in this chapter, and set a percentage-of-sales goal (roughly 5 per cent for consumer marketing, roughly 2.5 per cent for B2B marketing). Then review your goals and gaps and adjust accordingly. But don't forget that you have to fund the ad plan, so it needs to be less than gross profits. If not, worry about your costs and come back to your ad budget later.

Staying flexible throughout the year

Sometimes we speak to marketers who say something like, 'Okay, I've created a detailed ad plan and budget, but I'm still not sure that it's right. How can I be certain I've done it correctly?'

Our answer usually shocks them. The fact is, you *can't* be sure that your budget and plan are correct. There are no certainties in advertising. That means you need to stay flexible, keep an eye on performance and adjust your plan from time to time throughout the year.

Here are some ways you may want to adjust your plan:

- ✔ If sales are disappointingly low, consider cutting back on general brand-building ads while simultaneously increasing your sales promotions and direct response ads in the hope that they quickly boost sales.

- ✔ If one of the ads you run doesn't seem to be working, drop it from your budget and increase your spending on a more effective ad.

- ✔ If sales are higher than you expected and you're unable to increase your capacity fast enough, cut back on your advertising and channel some of that money into hiring more people, ordering more materials or whatever you need to do to meet demand.

These examples are adjustments that marketers can make at any point during the year.

Sometimes ad reps (the people who sell advertising space or time) try to lock you into big contracts by offering enticing discounts. But ask yourself whether the commitment is worth the additional discount. Remember you're trading flexibility for price. We favour flexibility, especially when we're trying a new ad campaign and aren't sure how well it's going to work. But don't forget that a few ads aren't enough in any medium or ad venue to make an impact. Mid-sized and small businesses are always at a disadvantage because they can't advertise at the high frequency of the marketing giants. Avoid spreading your ads too thin. Run at least a dozen ads in a row in the same place (for example, the same newspaper or website). As long as you think you're getting a response, keep advertising in the same place.

Files on the CD

Check out the following items on the CD-ROM:

- ✔ **File 5-1:** Budgeting for Advertising: A Practical Approach
- ✔ **File 5-2:** Annual Advertising Budget and Plan
- ✔ **File 5-3:** Advertising Objectives Worksheet
- ✔ **File 5-4:** Monthly and Annual Advertising Budget Templates

Chapter 6

Shortcuts to Great Ads

. . . .

In This Chapter

▶ Using do-it-yourself ad templates

▶ Taking a look at creative ad concepts and examples

▶ Knowing how far you can go with desktop design

▶ Placing ads by mail

▶ Surfing for web ad ideas and shortcuts

. . . .

Simple, inexpensive approaches to ad design are best for most marketing plans, because the goal is to keep your design and pre-press costs low. (As we discuss in Chapter 5, we recommend that you cap them at 5 per cent of your ad budget.) That way, most of your advertising budget is spent on actually getting those ads in front of potential buyers. If your ads aren't award-winners, that's okay. Just make sure that they're professional and simple enough that the message gets through loud and clear. And make them visually appealing because that's usually the secret to noticeable, memorable ads.

In this chapter, we help you conceive good ads and mock them up or (in some cases) design them fully, using nothing fancier than a basic computer running Microsoft Word. Word has a decent and simple-to-use drawing toolbar, plus a lot of basic templates, and it can produce output in the Acrobat Portable Document Format (PDF), which a growing number of printers and ad departments are happy to accept.

Following Do-It-Yourself Shortcuts

One of our favourite ways to think about a new ad we need to design is to leaf through a copy of the *Sunday Times Magazine*, studying the ads and pulling out examples of ad layouts that we think may fit our needs. (We like looking in the *Sunday Times Magazine* because its advertising space is expensive, so we usually find a lot of carefully designed ads that inspire us. However, if we're thinking about how to design a mailing, we prefer to go through the junk mail we receive for inspiration.)

Of course, you can't just cut someone else's brand name out of an ad and paste yours in. But you *can* get lots of starting ideas for different ways to communicate your message and achieve your advertising objective. (Make sure that you have a clear objective for your ad – something simple and persuasive to communicate.)

Trusting the tried-and-tested visual appeal ad

When you look at a large number of print ads in any well-read consumer or professional magazine, you begin to see some basic ad templates repeated over and over, each time with a fresh new combination of imagery and language. These ads use visual appeal to get the readers' attention.

Most commonly, many consumer magazines run one- or two-page full-colour ads featuring a striking or beautiful photograph with a simple headline that usually contains a play on words to help catch and hold attention (but you don't need to have a cute headline – serious is fine, too). The ad always includes the brand name and the tag line explaining the brand's basic brilliance and appeal.

If you don't already have a clear statement of what makes your product or service compelling to buyers, think about it and write a simple, compelling one-sentence description of why your brand is great.

At the bottom, the ad may have a sentence or two of explanatory *copy* (the written material). Figure 6-1 illustrates a basic layout sized for a full-page magazine ad.

The basic visual ad template in Figure 6-1 works for almost everything – including clothing, cars, cosmetics, travel destinations, business services and life insurance. Just vary the image and wording to fit your product. If the layout works for you, adapt it to a web ad, brochure, postcard or poster as well.

To make a visual appeal ad, start by seeking a photograph that's glue to the eye – and also make sure that you can somehow relate the image to the essence of your appeal. For example, if you sell computer maintenance services to businesses, you may choose the message, 'We keep you performing at your peak' and illustrate it with a beautiful photograph of a noble snow-covered mountain peak rising out of cloud-covered lowlands.

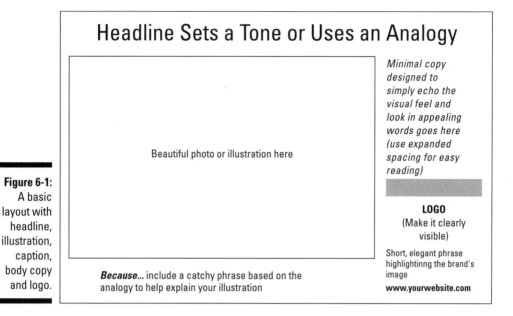

Figure 6-1:
A basic
layout with
headline,
illustration,
caption,
body copy
and logo.

But where are you going to find that stunning photo of a mountain peak? We thought you'd never ask! Go to stock photography websites and rifle through them to see if something strikes your fancy. Then use your headline to relate the image to your message. Here is a selection of websites where you can view and license photographs:

- ✔ **Corbis:** www.corbis.com
- ✔ **Fotolia:** www.fotolia.co.uk
- ✔ **Getty Images:** www.gettyimages.com
- ✔ **iStockphoto:** www.istock.com
- ✔ **Photolibrary:** www.photolibrary.com
- ✔ **Stockxchange:** www.sxc.hu

If you decide to use a stock photograph in your ad, contact the stock photography house directly to find out the cost for your intended usage. Charges typically range from as low as £100 to as high as £1,000, depending on what you have in mind. We usually budget £300 up-front for a photo, because that amount seems to be about the average for most pieces of work in the past.

Become a desktop publisher?

Increasingly, entrepreneurial marketers are designing their own print ads and submitting them in the PDF output option that all graphic design programs, and even Microsoft Word, support. (You may bump into the term PDF/X, which refers to certain standards for how you save the PDF file so as to make it more printer-friendly. If you're unsure of what the publication or printer requires, ask for instructions before you send the file.)

Consult the people at the publication in which you want to advertise (or the printer you want to hire to produce your brochure or catalogue) to find out the easiest and most inexpensive way to submit your ad designs. But don't let them talk you into buying an expensive new design programme you don't know how to use – just ask them if they can accept PDF files from whatever software programme you already know how to use.

Glossy monthly magazines may not accept a PDF file. Oops! For example, some magazines require you to submit your ad as a TIFF/IT-P1 (Tagged Image File Format/Image Technology) file because the company's digital printing processes work well with this format and errors

are kept to a minimum. However, you, as a desktop publisher, can't easily produce such a file. If asked for a specialised file format such as TIFF/IT, you need to find a provider of pre-press services. (You're not alone in this need; some ad agencies and graphic designers contract out for pre-press services, too.) Send your file in its normal format (for example, an Adobe Illustrator file when saved has a `.ai` extension; Photoshop files use `.psd`), and pre-press services or a friendly local graphic designer will, for a modest fee, convert it to the TIFF/IT format the magazine requires (and also allow you to proof and correct it).

Search the Internet for 'pre-press services' for quick access to hundreds of companies that provide such services. Note that you can also ask a pre-press service provider to help you with a PDF file so as to ensure the best possible colour reproduction and avoid errors with your type.

Many local and smaller publications (including some magazines and newspapers) offer design and pre-press services to the advertiser – sometimes for free! Just give them the design concept, with the images and language you want included.

Lots of good photographs appear on the Internet and in magazines and books. Use magazines such as *National Geographic* or do a Google search for images to look for the sort of image you want and then go to a stock photography company to find a high-resolution version for which you can purchase usage rights.

Don't try to use images you find online in your ad unless you track down the owner and get written permission. Purchased photographs from the stock photography suppliers aren't very expensive, but defending a copyright lawsuit is.

And don't forget the obvious: a good clear photograph or drawing of your product is sometimes the best art for an ad. If you have a product that's even slightly photogenic, maybe you can just use a photo of it and not bother with purchasing any other art.

To take a photo of your product yourself, use a high-end digital camera that can take images in high resolution – borrow one if you don't own one – and plenty of light. Professionals usually drape a white cloth under and behind the product, making sure that no obvious wrinkles appear, and then use two light sources, one from each side, a little to the front. Check for glare spots and move the lights or diffuse them through a screen of thin white cloth so that you don't have white-outs on your product.

If you're using a photograph of an industrial or business-oriented product, surround it with white space (a white background cloth for photography facilitates this) and then drop in arrows and text boxes to point out and describe three to six features that make the product useful and unique.

A clear, clean photo-based ad that emphasises information and specifications is often the best approach for business-to-business sales. If you do want to include a beautiful image of a tropical beach ('Let us show you how to work less and spend more time on vacation') or a mountain peak ('Here's how to make sure that your company reaches its peak performance zone'), keep the pretty picture and explanatory headline in the top third of the ad so that the product and its specifications can take up the bulk of the space.

Discovering some basic ad templates

The following sections offer you some basic designs that you can use as a starting point for your own ads. Each design is a fairly common type of ad that can work quite well when you drop in the appropriate words and images.

If you have some ideas about what you want your ad to achieve, try laying it out in one or more of these templates to get a decent rough cut of a design quickly and easily. All the following templates are on the CD as Word files that you can copy and edit.

Image ad template

File 6-1 has a basic Word template similar to the ad shown in Figure 6-1, for laying out an ad designed to communicate your brand's image to strengthen awareness and interest in your brand. If your objective is brand building, this format may work for you. Find a great image to help show others what you think makes your brand appealing or special (see the list of websites in the previous section for sources of photos) and then tie the image to the brand with clean, simple language in your headline and copy.

Many successful image ads use a central metaphor or simile tag line to connect the product to an unlikely object, place or event (a simile uses the words 'like' or 'as' in comparisons, for example 'as cold as ice' – if you equate something directly without using 'like' or 'as', it's called a metaphor). The compared item then becomes the central photograph or drawing in the ad. For example, imagine that you are a marketer of birthday or party supplies, and you want to say that your Instant Party Kit product is 'Like a Carnival in a Box'. With this simile in mind, you can visualise ad concepts. You may use an illustration showing a Brazilian carnival scene, visible through the cracked-open lid of a plain brown cardboard box. Figure 6-2 shows a simple line-art conception of this ad concept. It was created in a few minutes entirely in Word just to show you that you can do more designing than you may realise with this ubiquitous programme.

Figure 6-2:
An example of a small print ad that uses a simple simile with a visual to catch reader attention.

Each order of
Instant Party Supplies
is like a
CARNIVAL in a BOX!
www.instantpartysupplies.com

To come up with a good comparison for a metaphor or simile image ad, start by naming one or more qualities of your product that you want to communicate in the ad. Next, brainstorm other things that exemplify these qualities. An elephant represents a long memory, for example, and so a car mechanic service that maintains full service records in its database may want to use an image of an elephant sitting behind a service counter. The headline may be, 'We Remember', followed by copy saying something like, 'When did you last change your oil? What type of oil got the best mileage in your car? Do you still have any warranty benefits? What can you do when you lose your car keys while visiting Aunt Matilda up in Scotland? Whatever your problem, however foolish you think your question may be, don't hesitate . . . *Call us.* We remember!'

Okay, you get the idea. Now use these examples to come up with a comparison and an image for your own ad campaign.

After you visualise such an image, how do you bring it to life in your ad? You need to track down a suitable photo from a stock photography house (see the earlier section 'Trusting the tried-and-tested visual appeal ad' for a list) and negotiate usage of it. This photo may cost a couple of hundred pounds or more, so make sure that you like the photo and believe the ad will be valuable enough to justify the investment!

So, for the example of the Instant Party Kit in Figure 6-2, we create a clean line drawing of a three-dimensional box with the lid cracked open and combine this with a sliver of the chosen photo. How? You have several options:

✔ To do it yourself, use a drawing programme on your computer (such as Adobe Illustrator), or a photo-editing programme, such as Photoshop, if you're more familiar with one.

✔ Hire a graphic designer to create the visual for you if you don't know how. Local colleges are a great source of aspiring graphic and web designers who are willing to work at a reasonable price because they need to build up the experience for their CV.

✔ Get a newspaper, magazine or web ad seller to do the graphic design for you for free, as part of their support services for advertisers. It's always worth asking. People may be willing to go the extra mile to ensure that they get your business.

Informative ad template

File 6-2 is a template for an ad that emphasises information about the product. To analyse it, ask yourself: what are its important features or benefits, and how does it work? If you have a good story about your product, this ad design allows you to tell it clearly and well (see Figure 6-3).

You can lay out an informative ad in lots of ways. If you feel that the design in Figure 6-3 is a bit too technical, try the option in File 6-3, which floats a series of product or usage photos around a column of simple explanatory copy.

To design an effective informative ad, first make sure that you're clear on what's special and different about your product from your customer's point of view and then select three or more facts that communicate this benefit convincingly. For example, if your service is faster than your competitors, use facts like the following:

- ✓ Average response time for new service requests: 3.5 hours.
- ✓ Winner of multiple industry awards for the quality and speed of our service.
- ✓ Money-back guarantee if we take more than 24 hours to respond fully to your request.

These facts make the case in a compelling manner, and each supports the core claim to fame that the ad is trying to communicate.

Headline Goes Here
(Make it informative, about some appealing fact)

Small Headline
Overview of product or service here here here here here here.
More specific information here vfv dfsflkh sgsdg;j safdf jhk; dsgfdsl kfdsfmn.

Specifications:
- detail 1
- detail 2
- detail 3
- detail 4

(Let this text lead to the smaller headline and additional details in the right-hand column.)

Product photo or usage illustration (colour or black and white)

Descriptive caption

What Customers Are Saying

'testimonial'

'testimonial'

'testimonial'

Smaller Headline
about important technical details that differentiate this offering from others and make it better. Text text wara afdas.

Detail photo or diagram

BRAND NAME

Contact information here here here

Figure 6-3:
The informative ad template emphasises information that helps the reader see why your offering is special.

Don't let your facts wander off topic or you dilute the ad's impact rather than strengthen it. If the speed of your service is the most important thing for customers, don't start talking about how clean your toilets are and how many of your staff do community work. Stick to the core important facts.

Call-to-action ad template

Another option is to design your ad so that it asks the viewer to leap into action and request information or make a purchase right now. File 6-4 and Figure 6-4 show a basic call-to-action ad template that you can use to stimulate leads or sales by adapting it to your product.

Before you do, think hard about what incentives you can give the ad viewer to act immediately. Your objective is direct action, so you need to include some extra benefit or reason for them to act, beyond the basic elements of your product or service.

Main Headline (Short and Eye-Catching)

Secondary headline (explanatory, draws reader in)

Call to action in a short, clear opening paragraph saying exactly what you sell and why they should buy it right now.

Supporting information giving benefits, testimonials or other evidence to help close a sale or stimulate a visit to your website.

Additional benefits or special offers associated with this ad to encourage them to take action immediately. **Number to call.**

Illustrative photo or drawing, black and white or grey scale art

Small, short caption

Company Name Here

www.yourwebsite.com
Freephone number

Figure 6-4: A call-to-action ad asks the viewer to make a purchase right away.

You can ask the viewer to take action in a lot of ways, but these types of ads generally have several elements in common:

- ✔ A strong basic appeal with both emotional and intellectual reasons to choose the product or service.

- ✔ Added incentives to buy right now, such as a special time-sensitive discount or free add-on product or service included in the offer.

- ✔ Direct request or command to act; for example, to call a freephone number or go to a website and enter a special code to take advantage of an offer.

- ✔ Clear, frequent and varied options for contacting you and placing an order or requesting more information.

Try to include plenty of options in your ad because they tend to increase the response rate. File 6-5 is a template for a call-to-action ad that is, in essence, a mini catalogue, showing multiple products from which the viewer can select.

Creating Ad Concepts for Fun and Profit

The ad templates in the previous sections are layouts that show you how to create an ad in two dimensions using text and images. But every good ad has an important third dimension: the *conceptual dimension*. Your ad needs to engage readers on the conceptual level by grabbing their attention, stimulating their senses or engaging their creativity. It needs to make them think, feel, laugh or maybe even cry.

The conceptual dimension of advertising is what gives an ad its power. A clean layout and design help the concept jump off the printed page or web page and into the viewer's mind, but only when you have a conceptual design for the ad in the first place. We're going to take you beneath the surface of your ad to help you explore the conceptual dimension of your design.

Some ads start with a basic objective and graphic design, whereas others may start with the concept and then let the form follow naturally. Designing ads is a creative job, so don't feel you have to do it in any particular order.

So, how do you find a great ad concept that gives your ad design that extra zing needed to really make it work?

Well, ideally by being creative! Creativity is a good source for your conceptual designs: you think of something special that's easy and cheap to do, and you have a high-impact ad.

Of course, that's a tall creative order; otherwise, everyone would already be doing it. So we better give you some help. We have two cool ideas that aren't overused. They're adaptable general approaches that give your ad more stopping power and hold attention:

- ✔ In our first idea, we create ads that evoke a strong sense of mood by using words and/or an image associated with that mood.
- ✔ In our second idea, we create ads that communicate a mind-catching thought in the form of a wise quote.

In the following sections, we show you how to use these two shortcut design concepts. They're very flexible and adaptable. In fact, these concepts fit every business. You can easily adapt them to many different media (using the same design concept not only for a print ad, but also for a brochure, web page, catalogue, postcard or poster).

The mood ad

The premise of the *mood ad* design is that you can position your product or service in an appealing way by setting an emotional tone. You can accomplish the same goal in many ways – for example, a picture of a playful child conveys a happy, playful mood better than a thousand words.

To design a mood ad, ask yourself, 'how will our product or service make the customer feel?' Your answer reveals the emotional benefit you offer to people. Often, the feeling or mood that the ad conveys is an important part of making the sale.

Figure 6-5 contains an example of a mood ad for an insurance company (but please open File 6-6 to see it in colour). This ad combines an image of a gold pocket watch with the headline 'Loyalty' set in a classic-looking typeface (Rockwell) to convey a mood of quiet reflection about traditions, heritage and passing your values down to the next generation of your family. The goal of this ad is to capture the best mood for talking about life insurance – a topic that can be hard to broach without setting an appropriate mood first.

This ad for Coulter Insurance illustrates several points of good ad design. First, it takes an indirect approach to asking for business because more straightforward pitches may put people off. You don't want to read an ad saying: 'You're going to die and if it's anytime soon, your family will be ticked off at you if you haven't bought a good life insurance plan.' Also, the ad in Figure 6-5 not only sets a mood that makes talking about the subject of life insurance easier, but it also creates an analogy between the prospective customer and the valuable antique gold watch: 'Help them [referring to the prospective customer's family] learn the value of loyalty by setting a fine example yourself' is a subtle call to action that's made palatable by the fine example of the valuable watch in the illustration.

Figure 6-5:
This ad uses an heirloom pocket watch and the word 'loyalty' to convey a mood that helps to get people thinking about buying life insurance (see File 6-6 for a colour version).

Also notice how the copy in the Coulter Insurance ad has been overlapped with the grey of the photograph and laid over a series of soft vertical lines to create a strong vertical design element that draws the eye from the watch to the words. This pull of the eye is an example of what designers call *flow*. The goal is to create enough visual tension and interest that the viewer's eye enters and then travels around the ad in the order the designer has chosen.

In addition, the copy has been kept to a minimum, allowing the picture and headline to do most of the talking. Visual appeal is the key to success with almost all print and web ad designs.

Figure 6-6 also uses a photograph to convey a mood, combined with a headline (which, in this case, appears below the photo in place of the traditional small caption). The ad uses a simple, obvious description of how the customer is feeling: happy. But it adds a bit of intrigue with the idea of a 'happy secret'. The idea is that the viewer wonders what this happy secret may be. That secret isn't explained fully (it's good to challenge the imagination), but the ad implies that it can be found at Euphoria Day Spa.

Figure 6-6:
This print ad or brochure cover conveys the mood of someone whose spa visit has left them feeling beautiful, relaxed and self-confident.

This design can be the basis of a magazine ad (in which case, you probably want to add the business name and address, plus a small coupon or other call to action, at the bottom of it). Or it can be the front page of an elegant brochure or the front of a glossy card with services and rates listed on the reverse. If used for a brochure or card, you may want to use a header, such as 'Discover your own happy secrets', to carry over the theme on the next page and get the eye to flow into the listing of services. (By the way, this ad uses the typeface Humana Serif for the word 'happy' to make it pop joyfully from the block lettering of the Bank Gothic type behind it.)

Naming and illustrating a good mood, such as happy, loyal or relaxed, is a simple way to give your ad power. Try experimenting with a word such as 'reliable' (to describe a business service, for example) and looking up synonyms, such as 'dependable', 'careful' and 'trustworthy'. You can then add these words to your design if you want – for example, a local moving company may have a photograph of one of their trucks with all these words around it, like a picture frame. This concept uses a word or words to evoke a strong feeling and to associate it with your product or service.

Imagine that you run a business selling mobile phones to a health provider. Their phone calls are really important, and it's vital that they get through. So the most important point to emphasise to potential customers about your business plan is that your service plan offers better support than your competitors' plans. Your ads need to find a way to convey this advantage. The key word you use may be 'concern'; your business is concerned about each customer staying in touch with the important people in their lives. Figure 6-7 shows a basic layout concept for a service-plan brochure that uses words to convey the feeling that the business stands behind each customer and takes a personal interest in his or her success.

When you come to create a mood ad of your own, bear in mind that many possible feelings or meanings exist beyond the ones we illustrate here. And although we usually favour a strong visual image as the basis for ad design, as with all rules, there are exceptions. The brochure cover in Figure 6-7 makes do with creative use of text without a photo or other visual image. Can you design an ad or brochure that uses only text to set the mood or define the character of your product or service? This interesting design challenge may help you strengthen your understanding of your product's appeal – and perhaps even create something strong enough that you can use it in your next campaign! Here are some thoughts to get you started:

- List words in a long string to form unusual and powerful body copy or script.

- Ask a question and then let viewers answer it by ticking boxes next to words. (The copy may say something like: 'Is your ISP reliable? If so, surely you describe it as: careful, trustworthy, stable, available, helpful and supportive? What's that? You didn't tick all those boxes? Maybe you'd better send us an email. That is, presuming your current service lets you.')

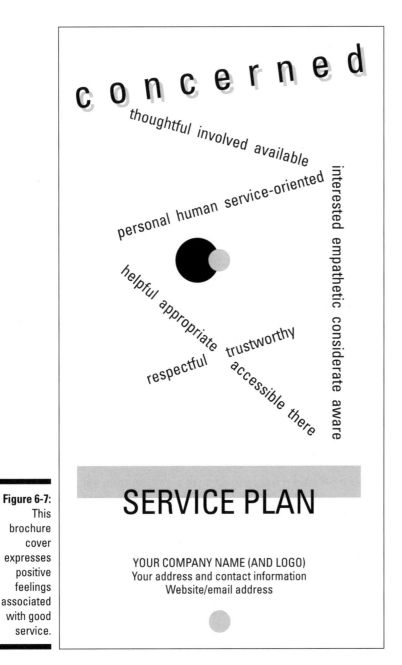

Figure 6-7:
This brochure cover expresses positive feelings associated with good service.

- Make a collage of words or a string of words (as in the design for a brochure cover in Figure 6-7).
- Create a simple crossword puzzle of the words that describe your product.

These design concepts all harness the power of the written word. Words are extraordinarily powerful: they can create a definite mood or feeling about your business or its product or service.

The wisdom ad

The wisdom ad is another simple-to-design, but potentially powerful, ad concept. The premise of the wisdom ad design (which you can use for any media from display ads to direct-mail campaigns, brochures, catalogues and sales materials) is that people like ads that give them the gift of wisdom. People value wisdom because it's in short supply.

So where can you find servings of wisdom to include in your ads? Our strategy is to go to the classics. People always like a great quote from a master writer or thinker, so a wise thought from literature can give your ad stopping power and increase its value to readers.

If you want to use a quotation, check that you're allowed to do so with the publisher. You can cite some older works of literature with no problems, but newer works may cause you some copyright issues if you don't check it out first.

Figure 6-8 shows an ad that uses a quote from the famous detective, Sherlock Holmes. The ad is executed in simple black and white for inexpensive back pages of magazines or for newspapers. This style of ad replaces the traditional headline with a thought-provoking quote. You can find thousands of quotes to choose from in any dictionary of quotations or online, just search for 'famous quotes'.)

The ad in Figure 6-8 uses a quote to draw reader attention. Many people like such quotes and may even cut out the ad just to help them remember the quote. A short message to the reader ties the quote into some positive attribute of the marketer's offering. The approach used in Figure 6-8 is a lot easier than writing a compelling headline or coming up with an original hook. All you have to do is find your hook in the form of an appealing quote and then tie that quote in to your products or services.

When you design an ad using a quote, pay attention to the little details that tighten the links from your offering to the quote. In Figure 6-8, an easy-to-recognise silhouette of Sherlock Holmes adds to the visual appeal, plus the reverse (white letters on dark field) phrase 'We agree!' in large type adds another eye-catcher to the design.

"It has long been an axiom of mine that the little things are most important."

- *Sherlock Holmes*

We agree!

That's why we:
- grgfdgytgf fgh hyuukghk jguihojhjlkf
- dfgfd ytty asdrhtj h jkiylghj kiry jkljlkvbnvaabt xvsdraab
- 655 fdyjh par fyutjf mjyfui

OUR COMPANY NAME. Getting the little things right, so you don't have to. Call or email for a free quote and audit today, or visit our website for more of those all-important details.

Contact info   contact info   **LOGO**

Figure 6-8:
Print ads relating the timeless quest for truth with the quest for better products.

To further refine the design, the copy has been set in an old-fashioned-looking type called Baskerville, choosing the semi-bold option for its stronger lettering. You have to be an expert on type fonts, as well as a Sherlock Holmes buff, to catch the subtle reference to the story about this Victorian-era detective called *The Hound of the Baskervilles*, but everyone recognises that the type matches the general style of the illustration and quote.

When working on a wisdom ad (or indeed any ad), try multiple designs and layouts until you come up with one that really seems to work.

Figure 6-9 shows another way to use a famous quote to draw attention and get people thinking about your offering. The ad uses a photo of a thoughtful young man whose eyes, you may notice, are looking downward towards the thought-provoking quote and the body copy about the online course offerings of the advertiser. The viewer tends to follow the gaze of the person in the photo to the headline, which makes their attention flow from the photo to the quote and then into the substance of the ad's body copy.

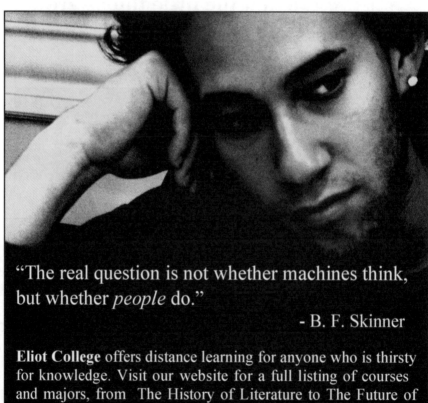

"The real question is not whether machines think, but whether *people* do."

- B. F. Skinner

Eliot College offers distance learning for anyone who is thirsty for knowledge. Visit our website for a full listing of courses and majors, from The History of Literature to The Future of Computing. At **Eliot College** we answer B.F. Skinner's question every day. Do you?   www.eliotcollegelearning.com

Figure 6-9:
This ad uses another famous quote to draw the reader in.

Using Visual Shortcuts to Make an Impact

In the preceding sections, we share concepts and designs that start with inspiration for advertising copy (or the written word), and then add an illustration to support the text. However, sometimes starting with a visual image works better (such as a photograph you really like), and you then find words to support it. An ad based primarily on visual appeal can transform an ordinary marketing message into an extraordinary one.

In the following sections, we look at strategies for using beautiful visuals to create powerful ads, catalogues, brochures, web pages or other marketing communications in a hurry or on a tight budget.

 If you want to make a big impact with a gorgeous photograph but need to work fast or have a small budget, you probably don't want to hire a professional photographer. Your best bet is to use stock photography, and you can find many vendors on the Internet, so don't be afraid to go shopping for a great image. (See 'Trusting the tried-and-tested visual appeal ad' earlier in this chapter for some web addresses.)

Think about the visual appeal of your ad this way. Every year, people buy expensive calendars featuring fine photography and hang them up where they look at one image for a full month. These same people are routinely exposed to many hundreds of ads each day but do their best to ignore and forget them. What's the difference between the calendar they pay for and treasure and the ads they ignore? One has beautiful photographs; one doesn't. So if you want people to treasure your marketing communications rather than ignore them, try giving people what they want – something beautiful.

 When we tell you to base your ad around a picture you really like, we mean one you like because it says something powerful about your organisation, product or service. Don't choose a picture that means absolutely nothing in relation to what you're advertising. For example, if you're a business consultant and you love a picture of a sprinter, that's great. If the message for your business is all about finding solutions at high speed, that makes perfect sense. But if you're a consultant specialising in careful, considered business development and just like the sprinter picture because it's an eye-catching image, best leave it well alone. You don't want your ads to be irrelevant. It's no good people saying 'Oh we love that sprinter picture . . . it's actually an ad for some business place,' without remembering your services.

Looking good with a beautiful landscape photo

We've collected a pretty large library of books on marketing and advertising over the years, and we went through the indexes of a bunch of them looking for the word 'beauty'. It's not there. Hmmm. What we think is that most people aren't designing their marketing materials (or even their products) to be beautiful. They're trying to make ads effective, clever, informative or persuasive, but not beautiful. So you can use a beauty-based appeal with the confidence that you don't have a lot of competition in using this shortcut to great advertising.

You don't have to stick to photographs alone to find beauty. You can offer customers beauty in plenty of other ways as well. A beautiful storefront, office space or even an especially elegant business card can create an aesthetic impact that pleases and impresses prospects and customers. Yet how many of the spaces where businesses receive or serve customers are actually made to be truly beautiful? A flowering plant or small garden, a gorgeous painting, photo or art poster, a fresh coat of paint and a little trim – all are small investments in adding beauty to the customer's world.

Here's an ad concept: why not select a really attractive photo of a beautiful natural landscape? The headline can say, 'Have a Beautiful Day!' In the bottom-right corner, you can put 'Brought to you by . . .' and add your logo or business name, plus a short one- or two-sentence update on what you're doing or any new upgrades or additions to your product line. Start this copy with 'Now offering . . .' or a similar phrase.

Keep the ad copy minimal and let the beautiful photo be your gift to customers and prospects. Also, don't clutter your photo with too many advertising messages. A beautiful ad achieves the objectives of burnishing your brand image and generating goodwill among customers and prospects, and both these objectives can help you close sales and retain customers later on.

Portraying an attractive person

People look at other people. Human are socially oriented; we can't help it. In particular, photos of people playing, laughing and having fun tend to attract viewers. Also, photos of children and babies are naturally attractive. And handsome or attractive people tend to draw and hold attention. (The ads in Figures 6-6 and 6-9 take advantage of the appeal of a photo of an interesting person.)

Don't make the mistake of thinking that a sexy, provocative-looking model will sell your product. Sexy images aren't very effective in advertising unless your product actually offers sex appeal. So go ahead and look for sexy photos if you're selling cosmetics or lingerie, but for most marketing needs, stick with photos that are interesting or attractive, but not overly sexy. Sex doesn't always sell if it's not relevant.

One way to use the natural appeal of people is to have a head-and-shoulders photo of an interesting or attractive person, using her as your spokesperson for your print ad. The spokesperson can say something in first person, like 'I'm glad I switched to (name of your business or brand)'. Placing that message in a bold headline, over an interesting, animated face, draws most viewers down to the copy to see why the person is happy she switched to your product.

Another classic concept is to have models using the product rather than just showing the product by itself.

People bring ads to life. Whenever possible, include photos of interesting people to draw the eye and engage the viewer.

Inserting a humorous cartoon

Humorous cartoons clipped out of newspapers or magazines cover many office bulletin boards and home fridges. People like a good cartoon. So another simple way to attract viewers to your print ad is to include a good cartoon.

This idea is easier than it sounds. Check out websites such as Cartoon Stock (cartoonstock.com), cartoonist Nigel Sutherland (www.nigelsutherland.com) or Moira Munro (www.moiramunro.com), or try the database of professional cartoonists of every type, style and price at The Professional Cartoonists Organisation at www.procartoonists.org. These sites should cue up thousands of humorous cartoons and give you the option of licensing them for professional use in an ad, newsletter, mailing, email, blog or web page. Have a look. You just need to think of some way to relate your product or service to a humorous cartoon, and you have yourself a great ad concept!

Giving Postcard Marketing a Try

The old-fashioned postcard is an interesting option for advertisers to consider. If you have or can buy a good mailing list of prospective customers, a colour postcard may be the cheapest and easiest way to get your ad message out.

If you don't have a list, you can buy one – search the key term 'mailing lists', and you'll be amazed at the number of businesses offering names and addresses for use in marketing!

Designing a postcard is a lot like designing a print ad, except that the photo is on one side (often along with a headline) and the body copy is on the other side. If you've already designed some good ads, you can easily adapt them to the postcard medium. And lots of templates and services can help make designing and mailing a postcard easy.

Figure 6-10 shows a simple postcard designed to be sent to homeowners to promote a heating and air-conditioning company's spring cleaning special offer. File 6-7 shows you this postcard in colour, and File 6-8 is a Word template for both the front and back of the postcard. The back is important because it contains the details of your offer – but notice how the copy is short and simple in the template. You should assume that the reader is going to give the text only a quick glance.

If you want to minimise design time, you can find plenty of postcard templates online. Type 'postcard marketing' or 'postcard templates' into your search engine and see what comes up. Firms such as Vistaprint (www.vistaprint.co.uk) offer one-stop shopping for postcard designs (including the art).

Some of the postcard marketing firms may offer mailing lists along with design, printing and mailing, so that they're truly one-stop shops. And because these businesses specialise in postcards, their designs may be better than average.

A good postcard needs to be visually appealing and bold and to have interesting and useful information – but not too much information. Keep it simple!

The standard postcard (which takes a postcard stamp in the United Kingdom) is A6 (105mm x 148mm), which isn't a lot of space for a marketing message. Yet it can economically communicate a single timely message and is more likely to be read than most mailings because the message is right there on the outside and the recipient doesn't have to open it. For these reasons, we recommend postcard mailings at least a few times a year for most businesses.

You can print postcards in small quantities, but you get a much better price if you have them printed by the thousands. A company such as Printed Postcard charges around £100 for 500 postcards but just £435 for 5,000. That's just the printing costs for a big box of them, though. Now you need to mail them.

Hand-addressing and stamping 5,000 cards takes a long time, so if you have anywhere near that many good names and addresses, consider contracting out for the mailing services, too.

Postcard stamps (for A6 postcards) in the United Kingdom are the same price as a normal letter stamp. At time of writing, this costs you 36p to send each postcard first class and 27p to send one second class. So expect to pay £1,800 to send 5,000 using first class mail, dropping to £1,350 if they go second class. However, if you pay for a mailing list plus mailing services, you can add up to a third more per card for the pricier ones. So a first class mailing can end up costing you (using 25 per cent extra for mailing list costs) £2,250, or £1,688 to go second class.

Figure 6-10:
This postcard design is best appreciated in full colour; see File 6-7.

Fresh paint, check!
Fresh lawn, check!
Fresh air? Hmm...

That means to reach 5,000 people costs just £2,250, which isn't bad. But are all those 5,000 genuinely good leads? The printing costs just a few hundred pounds, so why not get thousands printed, mail those few hundred for whom you have good leads and keep the rest to give out at a later date or to good leads when you do acquire them.

Using Web Pages as Ads

You don't necessarily have to confine your ads to the printed page. Think broadly about your options and don't be intimidated by the prospect of designing ads for viewing on a computer screen rather than a printed page.

Many businesses are springing up to offer simple ad templates for web advertising. Some of these companies are resellers of Google products, which leads us to ask, why not just go straight to Google? It now offers some very simple tools for the novice to use, so don't be afraid of trying your hand. Use an intermediary if you're really foxed, but Google offers something just as simple in most cases. A good place to start is www.google.com/adsense.

When using web ad design services beware – you may not be getting quite as much as you think you are when you open an account that promises free ad templates and great web advertising results. Make sure that you like the templates and support you're receiving and that the pricing isn't too much higher than Google's base prices.

You can get an almost instant website up and running in myriad ways, so you really need to think of websites as an easy way to post a highly interactive, content-rich advertisement. Marketers are eventually going to see websites as fluid, frequently changing, powerful advertisements. You may as well get ahead of the curve and start putting up websites to help communicate your advertising messages. You don't have to confine your Internet presence to one central static corporate site when web space is unlimited and lots of web traffic exists.

For example, if you're in the heating and air-conditioning business, you certainly need (and probably already have) a web page with a domain name based on your business name. This central corporate website is like a brochure describing your business – who you are, what you do, what your credentials are and what your happy customers say.

However, this corporate website should just be the spoke of your web marketing wheel. You should use pay-per-click advertising on Google to direct local searches to your website, plus the occasional paid ad or directory list-ing on high-traffic sites that reach your customer base.

And then you should consider specialised websites and/or blogs that relate to research topics of interest to your customers, such as:

> ✔ How to reduce energy costs and usage for existing home or office heating and AC systems (complete with a downloadable audit form bearing your business logo and contact information).
>
> ✔ How to prepare your AC and/or heating equipment for the off season.
>
> ✔ Spring cleaning for AC, including how to get ready for a summer of fresh, clean air (and why better quality air is also more economical to the homeowner).

These topics sound like good article topics for a magazine, don't they? That's the idea. You can create a web page or blog that is essentially an interesting, informative article for homeowners (Google and other vendors offer simple templates; check them out!). Homeowners have an interest in such topics, and they will search out your content and study it (assuming that you do your homework and give them informative, useful content, illustrated with photos from your own corporate sites to make it visually appealing, too).

Keep informative topic-oriented websites from looking overtly like corporate web pages or promotional pieces. Present your content like editorial con-tent, but of course give credit and a link to your business. Don't ever deceive consumers that a piece of information that exists for advertising purposes is pure editorial; this is certain to backfire. Instead, why not put 'Sponsored by BUSINESS NAME' and a web link and phone number for more information at both the top and bottom of each page.

Don't forget to look to other sources for content as well. Whether or not you write original copy, the key is to provide a source of useful information. Look to other vendors and businesses and credit them when you use their content. (Don't forget to ask permission first.)

If you want to create these editorial-style pages yourself, try out services including Typepad and Blogger.com. A growing number of easy-to-use web store templates can also get you up and running quickly. If you want to add in online payment options, check out PayPal (www.paypal.com) for other easy and inexpensive e-commerce options.

Files on the CD

Check out the following items on the CD-ROM:

- ✔ **File 6-1:** An image ad template
- ✔ **Files 6-2 and 6-3:** Informative ad templates
- ✔ **Files 6-4 and 6-5:** Call-to-action ad templates
- ✔ **File 6-6:** Insurance company ad
- ✔ **File 6-7:** Postcard design sample
- ✔ **File 6-8:** Postcard front and back templates

Part III
Power Marketing Alternatives to Advertising

'A great advertising gimmick, George, but who's going to see it up here on top of Everest?'

In this part . . .

*A*ds are powerful, but they aren't the only way to attract business. Other elements of your marketing communications are vital, too. In this part, we show you how to present your brand identity consistently in everything you do, starting with the basics of business cards, letterheads, emails and faxes. We also explore the important topic of presenting your brand on the web, and we guide you through the rewarding challenges of designing effective brochures, blogs and press releases.

Chapter 7

Branding with Business Cards, Letterheads and More

In This Chapter

▶ Clarifying your brand identity

▶ Designing your business name and logo

▶ Creating successful business cards, letterheads, envelopes and emails

▶ Strengthening your presence on websites and blogs

Making a professional impression when you're standing in front of someone in a suit, shaking their hand, is easy. But when you're presenting yourself at arm's length through marketing materials, you can all too easily come across as far, far less professional. Try to keep in mind that your business card, letter, brochure, catalogue or other materials represent you to potential customers. Most businesspeople tend to impose a lower standard on these materials than they would on themselves if they were there in person. But in truth, an even higher standard is necessary and appropriate. Why? Because you aren't present to make your case. And if you have sub-par materials, people assume that you don't take your business seriously enough to invest in a good image.

In this chapter, we show you how to examine how your brand looks, starting with the brand identity and then making sure that your business cards, stationery, labels, envelopes or boxes, faxes and emails all convey your identity clearly and well.

Establishing Brand Identity: Who You Are

Who are you? Your name and face are instantly recognisable to anyone who knows you. People who don't know you can easily begin to recognise you from your unique combination of name, face and voice. You have a clear identity as a human being – so clear that telling you apart from anyone else on the planet is fairly easy.

Well, maybe we're exaggerating. If your name is John Smith, you may not be too distinctive by name alone. But add your face to the name and now you're truly unique. We expect others to be unique and easy to identify. People become confused and even upset when someone doesn't look like a unique individual. No-one wants clones running around – they seem creepy. The same applies with businesses. You want to make sure that your product or service is so clearly identifiable and so well known that you never have identity problems in your marketplace.

To evaluate the strength of your *corporate identity* (logo, name and so on), consider the following questions:

- ✔ Does your letterhead look unique, and is it easy to identify at a distance, such as from across a room?
- ✔ What adjectives would someone use to describe your business if working only from a copy of your letterhead?
- ✔ Does your logo look more attractive and professional than your competitors' logos?
- ✔ Does everything you send through the mail, fax and email show your logo and identifying information in a clean, consistent and attractive manner?
- ✔ Do you include your corporate identity on all packaging and products in an appealing and consistent way?
- ✔ Do you (and all representatives of your business) carry attractive business cards in a proper case to give out whenever you have an appropriate opportunity?
- ✔ Do your emails include your corporate logo, name and contact information consistent with your letterhead and business cards?
- ✔ Is your corporate identity or brand personality (including your overall look and feel) consistent on the Internet as well as in printed material and signage?

These questions help you to identify immediate issues or opportunities in how you present your identity to the world. Marketing is in the eyes of the beholder, so you must make sure that everyone interacting with your firm or any of its products, services, publications, web pages, ads or other marketing materials sees your unique identity clearly and fully.

The best-looking logos, the most appealing names and the strongest presentations of identity are usually associated with winning businesses and brands. Like it or not, appearances matter. We always urge firms to make sure that they look like the business they want to be, not the business they were three years ago when they last ordered stationery. Updating your logo and materials doesn't cause any harm, and you often have much to gain. Don't be afraid to change the way you present your business or brands.

In the remaining sections of this chapter, we ask you to take a close look at some of the most important elements in the public presentation of your marketing identity.

Managing the Presentation of Your Brand Name

Whether you're selling your business or a specific product, your name and logo are vital.

Coca-Cola has a striking identity: the brand is easy to recognise anywhere, any time. The Coca-Cola Company writes its name in a distinct way that transforms the name into a logo design; and the firm always uses colour. Plus, the company puts its name everywhere in a clear, consistent manner so that consumers can't possibly forget it.

Nike uses another strategy. The company doesn't always write its name the same way, but it does always have the distinctive swoosh logo nearby. The swoosh brands every product the company designs and also appears on the company's letterhead, business cards and web pages, giving the firm one of the best-known brands in the world.

Are you as clear and consistent as Coke or Nike in the way you present your business name or brand identity? Hmmm. Maybe not. In this chapter, we help you work on that presentation.

Close your eyes for a moment and try to visualise the logo or name of your telephone company, bank and local taxi firm. How many of these logos and names pop right into your head, appearing clearly and easily in your mind? Not all of them, we bet. Depending on where you live, maybe only one or two logos or names are so well designed and consistently portrayed that you can actually visualise them instantly without a hint or other aid.

LloydsTSB has a particularly strong brand identity. The company is careful to always use the same strong blue and green in its signs and printed materials – not to mention the famous black horse – to help make it instantly recognisable.

Assessing your identity

Take some time to make sure that your marketing identity looks really good. A good marketing identity is one that:

✔ Makes a strong, positive impression on all who see it.

✔ Portrays you, your firm, service or brand as you aspire it to be. This way, as your business grows and achieves higher levels of success in the future, it grows into, not out of, your logo and look.

✔ Is highly memorable and easy to recognise, even from a great distance.

✔ Is consistently displayed wherever you have an opportunity to do so.

Give your business, product or service a clear, clean visual signature in order to pump up your identity. Always write the name of your business, product or service the same way. This approach means using the same typeface. Pick a font and style you like and stick with it. If you don't know how to design a great signature or logo, hire a graphic designer who can show you a portfolio of really impressive logo and identity work.

If you insist on a do-it-yourself logo in order to save money, here's the shortest and simplest set of instructions for creating your own:

1. **Finalise your name's appearance.**

   If your business name presentation varies, choose one version and stick with it from now on. For example, Vauxhall Landscape Services, sometimes known as South East London Landscape Services or Vauxhall Services, needs to choose one clear, simple version of its name, such as Vauxhall Landscapes.

2. **Use Word's library of fonts or the sample sheet at your local printer to choose a typeface you like for your name.**

   Avoid highly unusual, fanciful or hard-to-read types. If you aren't sure which you like best, print a sample sheet of several of your favourites and sleep on the decision overnight.

3. **Select a simple, clean small visual image or symbol if you want to add a visual element to your identity.**

   Sources include:

   • Your local print shop

   • Graphic designers

   • Online services such as iStockphoto (www.istockphoto.com)

   Or just use the first letters from your name to create a simple logo alongside a drawing you create yourself or source from a designer.

WARNING!

4. **Make sure that your name and image are unique.**

   Yes, you do need to avoid using a name and image that resembles another business logo. Check your region's phone directories, do a Google search and also check that your name and design aren't already trademarked. (In the UK, go to `www.ipo.gov.uk/types/tm/t-os/t-find.htm` to check for existing trademarks.) If somebody else is already using the same name and/or a similar design, revise yours to something that is unique.

5. **Pick a smaller, less bold version of your logo type, or a simpler, more common type (such as Helvetica or Times), to use for your address, phone number, web address and email.**

6. **Work up one idea into to several standard arrangements of your logo (name and graphic elements).**

   How are you going to lay out your name and graphic element on business stationery, business cards, magnetic signs for your vehicles and the banner of your website's home page? (See the upcoming sections 'Selling Your Business Cards' and 'Designing Your Letterhead and Envelopes'.) Also, do you want a colourful version of your identity for places to use where colour printing is easy?

   If you want to get more ambitious, you can try versions with several colours – but usually this experimentation gets overly complicated. Complex is bad when it comes to logos. Think about the power of the Coca-Cola identity. If Coca-Cola needs only red and white, you don't need to try all the colours of the rainbow for your business, do you?

If you're artistic yourself and willing to fool around for an hour or two in whatever computer drawing or design program you have access to, you can create a wonderful variety of identities in a hurry. Most such programs have libraries of line art; even Word has a rich variety of symbols in some of its fonts. Figure 7-1 is a simple logo design we made entirely using Word's text boxes and fonts.

Figure 7-1: A simple logo design using typefaces and symbols available in Word.

Business Name

Bringing the world to your doorstep

If we want to make the design in Figure 7-1 the official logo for our business, we either print all our cards and stationery on a good in-house laser printer or hire a designer to take our design concept and work it up a bit. Or maybe we just take it to a print shop and ask them to finalise it for us.

The technical editor for this book, who is a professional designer, explained to us why passing your logo concept on to an expert for finalisation is helpful. We're going to share her note with you because it shows how much is involved if you really want a high-end professional logo:

> *When I design a logo for someone, I am keeping in mind every intended use for that logo. Will they be putting it on a tradeshow banner, maybe embroidering a polo shirt? Designing a logo for these uses requires a professional that can supply several file formats, one of which had better be an .eps file that is scalable. The font should be converted to outlines so there is no room for error (such as a substituted font) when your logo is reprinted somewhere. It is understandable that someone may start with a homegrown logo, but they had better invest in doing it right for the future.*

'Selling' Your Business Cards

Your business card is often the first contact someone has with you or your business. Sometimes your business card is the only marketing communication that a prospect has, so you want to make sure that it follows the rules of good marketing communications by building both emotional and rational involvement. Therefore, your card needs to communicate the information that a prospect needs to figure out what products or services you have and how he can contact you easily. Also, make sure that it contains your web address.

Making a good overall impression

Imagine someone looking through a pile of cards that includes many competitors of yours. Why would a prospect choose yours? What about your card makes it call out to people? A strong logo and clean design are a good start.

Your card needs to make a powerful, positive personal impression. However, most cards don't. In fact, most are quite dull. Even the ones that are clean and professional generally emphasise information and ignore the need to make an impression.

To make a good overall impression, strive for a sophisticated, professional image with something different, such as a better-quality paper, a more beautiful logo, an unusual vertical layout, a useful fact or inspirational quote printed on the back, or an attractive use of colour to highlight your business identity. Above all, focus on a well-presented business name and logo.

Hold on! Just because you want to make a powerful, personal impression with your card, don't do anything crazy. You don't want to make a *negative* impression! An overly colourful, flashy card with a photograph plus gold, red and green coloured print is not the way to attract attention. Keep the design clean and professional.

Deciding on design details

When designing your business cards, remember that you want your card to make a good impression and to include enough information so that contacting you is easy. But at the same time, you don't want to overload it with so much information that the card is confusing.

File 7-1 illustrates four ways to lay out a standard business card, each of which is clean, simple and eye-catching. Even though business cards are small, you can design them in lots of creative ways. Your decision comes down to what you like and what best fits your business image.

Choosing flat or raised ink if using a printer

You can get business cards printed in flat ink or raised ink. *Flat-ink printing* is the standard printing. In *raised-ink printing*, the printer uses an ink, dusts it with a plastic powder and heats it in an oven that melts and expands the powder, giving the type a raised look and feel. Almost all printers offer both types of printing for business cards, and the choice you make is largely one of taste.

Here's our favourite, if you want serious elegance: ask your printer to help you find a specialist who can make a *die* (metal stamp) of your logo and have it *embossed* (so that it sticks up a little bit) on your card, along with flat-ink printing of the business name, tag line and your name and contact information. Embossing takes longer to make and is considerably more expensive, but it really stands out.

Setting your margins for the printer

You need to design only one master version of your business card, and the printer takes the process from there. Most printers are happy to accept a PDF file produced by Word or any of the desktop graphic design programs.

Whatever you use, make sure that you keep the print from being too close to the margin. Printers like to have space from the edge of the design to the edge of the paper. The amount of required space varies from printer to printer. To be safe, check how much should be left around the edge, because paper can sometimes shift from side to side when going through the press; this amount of space ensures that the cutter doesn't clip off any text that's too close to the edge of the card.

Pondering paper stock

The printer is likely to have a raft of different paper for you to choose from for your business cards.

Of course you have to pick paper that matches your budget, but don't forget the importance of making a good first impression: paper is not an area to skimp on.

When you've made your selection, ensure that you use matching (lighter but similar looking) paper for your stationery and envelopes so that people see them as part of a clearly defined professional presentation and image. Some papers differ in weight but match in colour and finish, so you can easily match your cards with the lighter paper of your letterhead.

Some printers offer package discounts on letterhead, envelopes and cards when you order them together, so getting them all printed at the same time is often cost-effective.

Here are some additional sources of online information and templates for designing your own business cards:

- ✔ **VistaPrint** (www.vistaprint.co.uk) offers colourful card designs to which you simply add your text. The prices are low because the company uses digital laser printing. This option is a good way to get starter cards when you don't yet have the time or skill to develop your own logo and look.

- ✔ **Microsoft Office Online** (http://office.microsoft.com/en-gb/templates/CT101043091033.aspx) gives you access to a huge variety of designs that you can quickly download and adapt to your needs in Word.

- ✔ **Logiprint** (http://www.logiprint.co.uk/en/business_card_template_uk.html) allows you to create your own business cards online and then order them direct from the site for delivery by post.

- ✔ **Hewlett-Packard** (HP) (www.hp.com/sbso/productivity/office/buscards.html) offers a page of good quality card templates maintained by Hewlett-Packard (which makes many of the printers used for desktop publishing of marketing materials). All you have to do is double-click the card you like and the file downloads to your desktop. You can then open and edit it in Word and print. These templates are easy to use and allow you much more design control than the template pages maintained by printers.

Sourcing great business card templates from the Internet

You can design your own business cards using Word, which offers a number of free templates, or other software packages such as InDesign. We've included a Word document on the CD in File 7-2 which has some pre-designed cards that you can adapt and print out at home. If you have trouble opening this file, go to www. avery.co.uk, click Templates and Software, and then Templates and either Blank Templates or Pre-Designed Templates, depending on your needs. When you've chosen the right template you need to supply your name and some basic info to be allowed to download the template. Having done so, you can add your own information to the free template.

To create a PDF of your formatted template, click the print button in Word or choose Print⇨ PDF in the Print Dialog Box and then Save as PDF. If this process doesn't work, search 'save as PDF' in your Word Help. The Word program has a lot of variations, but this function is somewhere in your version – don't worry!

File 7-3 shows a card design we created using one of the HP templates from the Hewlett-Packard website. We like the vertical format and the stripe on the side, although we ended up adjusting the size and location of text boxes and replacing the stripe provided with one we constructed ourselves, because the original contained an odd irregularity. Sometimes you have to fiddle with templates to get a card that satisfies you, but starting with a template is still worthwhile because it can reduce design time significantly.

Notice that the card design on File 7-3 doesn't have a margin all around it. Instead, the green stripe is supposed to *bleed*, as printers say – in other words, it goes to the edge of the card and so must be printed slightly over the trim line. Bleeding is a simple technique to use and many templates allow you to do this. If you're printing yourself, run one sheet to check your alignment and then adjust your template until you get the desired ink or toner coverage.

Figure 7-2 shows the two business card designs we created using free Word and HP templates. They're rendered in black and white here, but of course, you can do colour versions of them if you want to.

We go into quite a bit of detail about the mechanics of designing and printing business cards, because the skills and knowledge that you accumulate are transferable to producing other essential materials, such as stationery and brochures.

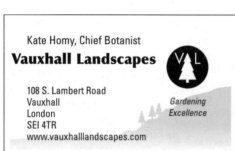

Figure 7-2:
Cards
designed
with free
Word and
HP
templates
for desktop
printing.

Designing Your Letterhead and Envelopes

As with business cards, a letterhead and envelopes may be the first encounter someone has with your business, and first impressions are obviously important. But even if customers have done business with you for some time, the look and feel of your stationery has a subtle but powerful impact on their attitude towards you. Good letterheads can help retain a customer or stimulate a referral. So, as with business cards, a letterhead is a surprisingly important marketing investment. Make sure that you have a clean design that impresses customers favourably.

As with your business cards (see the preceding section), you can order these items from a printing house or you can do them yourself. Word has envelope and letterhead templates (see the Tools menu), but you can easily create your own template in Word, too, because all you need to do is use text boxes.

Here's how to create a text box in Word:

1. **Choose View⇨Toolbars⇨Drawing to display the Drawing toolbar (if it's not already shown).**

2. **Position your cursor on a blank section of your page and click and drag to create a box size you're happy with.** To expand or change the size of the text box, click the box and move your cursor over one of the small squares embedded in the frame of the text box. When the cursor changes form and is directly over one of these boxes, click and drag the frame of the text box and then let go when you're happy with the size.

3. **Add multiple text boxes if you need to break Word's rules of formatting.** For example, you can move words closer to each other or overlap them.

Traditionally, the letterhead was printed in black ink, and the business name and address were centred at the top. You don't need to respect this tradition; anything that looks good and fits your image well is fair game.

Colour is fine, too. And unless you do business on a fairly large scale, you can desktop-publish your stationery (a colour laser printer is our preference for durability), which means that having colourful stationery doesn't cost you expensive printing bills. You can also use Word templates to make up labels in any size you need, with matching identity and colour scheme.

Leave room for the letter, invoice number or fax number on the stationery you design and confine the design to the left third of the envelope (because the remaining area needs to be reserved for stamp and address).

File 7-4 is a PDF file showing a creative, colourful letterhead design based on the logo from Figure 7-1. File 7-5 is a Word version of the same design, in which you can edit the text and adjust the colour scheme as you desire, in case you like the basic design concept and want to use it as a template for your own letterhead.

Keeping Visual Control in Faxes and Emails

Many businesses use a decent letterhead and yet send faxes using a generic cover sheet with designs. (Please avoid the templates in Word!) Other businesses create inconsistent and unprofessional-looking faxes.

You don't need to compromise in this way. You can simply use your letterhead for faxes, centring the header FAX MEMO at the top of the page, with the date centred in smaller type below it. Then use the standard memo format of left-justified for the 'To:', 'From:' and 'Re:' lines, including both the name of the recipient and their fax number. At the bottom, beneath your signature, provide your own fax number if the contact address on your letterhead doesn't include it. You can also say in a note at the bottom, '3 more pages to come' or whatever, to make sure that the recipient receives all the pages you send.

Nowadays, email is favoured over fax, so you need to give more thought to how your emails look. For starters, we recommend using your business domain name for emails, too, so that every email address reinforces the business identity. This change is easy to do because host servers generally offer email options. Check with your web host for details, or if it's not helpful, switch to someone else.

Next, consider creating a standard identity and appearance for emails. However, to keep it simple (and avoid your emails being filtered into Junk folders), this look shouldn't include art elements such as a logo or specific type style and colour. In other words, your basic email identity needs to be boring. Sorry, but the text that emails are made of isn't intended for use in graphic design. If you want to make it pretty, you have to resort to the methods used for designing websites – and we're not going to go into HTML coding and other oddities of making emails pretty, because emails with HTML coding and fancy designs get filtered so often these days.

We suggest that you just create a standard set of text lines for your business identity and contact information, plus a short marketing phrase describing what you do or what makes you great, and paste this signature into the bottom of every email you send. (You can also include a link to your website, but it too may trigger filtering in the more finicky systems.)

To bump up your emails beyond this basic format, consider getting a product such as Email Templates (www.emailtemplates.com), an add-on for your Microsoft Outlook programs that gives you lots of capabilities for sending personalised email marketing messages to your contact list, including some HTML template options.

Simple text emails tend to avoid spam filters more efficiently than fancier ones.

Conveying Your Image through Design, Paper and Print

Your image in your business card, letterhead, brochures, faxes and emails (plus signs, trade show banners and any other marketing materials) needs to reflect who you are and what you do.

If you're a stockbroker or a business consultant, you may want to have an established conservative look for your design, ink and paper selections. Communicating a sense of stability and longevity can be important in these fields. Therefore, ask yourself what types of typeface, ink colour and paper leave this impression? Perhaps Times Roman lettering, centred in a traditional style at the head of the paper, printed in conservative black ink on an old-fashioned creamy paper made with cotton fibre and a subtle watermark. Such paper is more expensive than lighter, more modern papers but is consistent with a conservative, solid sophisticated image.

Make sure that you order blank sheets of your chosen paper as well to use for second pages, because a regular piece of white paper doesn't match.

Here are some tips for choosing an appropriate style based on your profession:

- **Law firm:** Stick with a conservative top-centred layout for stationery using Times New Roman or Century typefaces. Avoid colour and design-oriented logos. Just present the partners' names in a traditional, trustworthy font.

- **Insurance:** Insurance agents need to be almost as conservative in their logo designs as lawyers. However, adding a list of the types of insurance you provide is helpful, because many people are uncertain about who sells what in the insurance industry. Also, if you've been in business for a long time, add 'Since 1975', or whatever the date your business set up as this helps position you as trustworthy and professional.

- **Massage therapy:** Balance the idea of being trustworthy with that of being helpful and healing. A rounded block-letter type of font meets these two goals. (Ask your printer to show you what Euphemia UCAS Bold and Helvetica Neue look like – or Google them to see them online.) Consider a logo featuring a pair of hands palms-down, as if in the midst of a massage. Avoid strong or bold colours (which may imply a heavy-handed approach), and instead plump for a subtle use of soft pastels. Include credentials on business cards to increase the sense of professionalism and trustworthiness.

- **Building:** We rarely see a business card that looks adult or professional in the building business. Avoid the temptation to use large type, a strange mix of bright colours and a simplistic icon of a house or other building. And please, no icons of hammers! All of these give the impression of a very basic business, rather than a more sophisticated operation. Since builders have a reputation for being unreliable, try to develop a more serious image that doesn't bring to mind all the usual clichés about builders not turning up or overcharging. Try to break with tradition by using 11 point Times New Roman, Arial or any simple, traditional font. Instead of a simplistic piece of clip art for a logo, have a sophisticated logo designed for you; or just use your business name as the logo (in 16 point type – not any larger, please).

Notice that we don't recommend a wild and crazy design for *any* of these professions. Whatever you do, stick to a clean, professional look. Even if you're non-traditional in person, be fairly traditional on paper. Otherwise, you scare people off before they get a chance to know you.

You need to project a clear, strong personality each and every time you present your business. Capture and convey your brand personality on your letterhead, envelopes, faxes and business cards. Even if you don't work with an expensive designer, take the time to explore many options and make a thoughtful selection of paper, ink, typeface and logo (if you use one). Extra care and a little extra investment here go a lot further than most people realise to help make sales and marketing successful.

Here's an idea you can act on easily, with or without a designer's help. Go to a larger print shop and select a distinctive paper for your business – something that you feel has a unique, appropriate and appealing look and feel to it. Then order letterhead, business cards, envelopes and even labels all on this distinctive paper. This subtle design element can boost the image and appeal of a business.

Maintaining Your Identity on the Internet

We want to compliment Royal Mail on being a good example of how to present a corporate identity on a website. If you go to www.royalmail.com, you see a beautiful version of the Royal Mail crown logo displayed prominently in the upper-left corner. The logo seems to stand proud surrounded by white space and positively shines out at the audience. Click any of the many tabs to navigate through pages for different countries and services, or go to the corporate page, and this nice version of the Royal Mail logo is always there to greet you. That's how websites should handle logos and identities, but most sites don't do it nearly that well. Does yours?

Whether you confine your logo to the top-left corner or use a full-width banner at the head of every page, the goal is the same: anyone navigating your site ought to have their recollection of your identity constantly reinforced. Web pages allow for excellent graphics with high resolution, strong colours and good backlighting on the viewer's computer screen, so use them to present your logo attractively. Make sure that your web pages help to build the strength of your firm's marketing identity.

Many websites try to squeeze too much information or too many tabs at the top of the page and end up overcrowding the business identity. Make sure that you leave 2–5 centimetres in all directions around your name and logo. Also, set the logo against a contrasting background so that the background colour doesn't wash it out.

A blog is a website maintained by an individual who posts frequent text entries of commentary and news and may also post digital photographs, music or streaming video. Entries are commonly displayed in reverse-chronological order, with the latest at the top.

Blogs focus on a topic of interest to a group of readers, who are expected to revisit often in order to see the latest posting. Most blogs are personal activities, but you can write a blog to forward your professional interests and promote yourself and your business. For example, Tom Glocer, the CEO of Thomson Reuters, currently keeps a blog in which he talks about his work at Thomson Reuters, as well as wider issues such as technology, information publishing and globalisation (see http://tomglocer.com/).

Blogs are a simple, quick and usually free way to put your content on the Internet, and increasingly small businesses (as well as large ones) are turning to blogs for web marketing. In fact, some small business owners and entrepreneurs are using blog-hosting sites to create their main web presence – the blog takes the place of a more traditional (and complex) web page.

We recommend using portal host sites for blog creation, such as www.blogger.com or www.typepad.com/, which make getting a blog up and running startlingly easy. For example, the blog at http://coppersblog.blogspot.com/ currently has a handsome blog created on Blogger that looks a lot like a corporate website, but was much easier to create and is simple to update with new information (and it's an interesting insight into the world of British policing, too).

You're always going to need a business card and stationery, but increasingly email, websites and blogs are great ways to interact with prospective customers and build awareness of your brand identity. These new media are additions to the old, rather than replacements, which means more opportunities for marketers to make a splash.

Files on the CD

Check out the CD-ROM for the following materials:

- ✔ **File 7-1:** Four standard business card designs
- ✔ **File 7-2:** Business card sheet for printing
- ✔ **File 7-3:** Colourful business card made from a free HP template
- ✔ **File 7-4:** Sample letterhead design with strong visual appeal
- ✔ **File 7-5:** Editable Word version of sample letterhead design

Chapter 8

Creating Eye-Catching Brochures, Catalogues and Spec Sheets

In This Chapter

▶ Deciding which marketing materials you need

▶ Designing brochures that make a strong impression

▶ Knowing when to use digital brochures

▶ Creating catalogues, booklets and books

▶ Making spec sheets

*I*f you sell something expensive or complex, you need a detailed brochure or glossy catalogue and perhaps additional information in a binder or pocket folder, on a CD or DVD, and if possible, an informative website. If your offering is fairly simple but you want to make sure that prospects are impressed, excited or trusting enough to buy from you, you need a smaller brochure that emphasises design and visual appeal over information. And no matter what your business, a collection of press clippings, an informative or interesting booklet, a great promotional video or other supplementary marketing materials can be helpful too.

In this chapter, we help you to work on brochures, spec sheets, catalogues and booklets, all of which are essential parts of a good marketing programme. We also touch on modern CD, DVD and web versions of the introductory brochure, which are, in our opinion, the most exciting new direction in brochures. Finally, we encourage you to get creative in your design and approach. Hundreds of millions of brochures are in print right now. Most end up in the recycling bin. This chapter shows you how to make yours stand out!

Considering Your Needs

Brochures, spec sheets, catalogues and flyers are really just variations on the same theme. In all these marketing materials, you include essential information about your offerings, plus additional information and images to attract and hold interest. And you make sure that you present your brand identity correctly and memorably (see Chapter 7 for more on your business identity). This section provides a decision-making guide to help you select the format you need.

Simple one-page spec sheets or flyers

If you need only one page of information and plan to place it beneath a letter or in a pocket folder, you can just design a one-page spec sheet (for technical information) or flyer (which contains more interesting information and/or images than a spec sheet). Think about how you can use photographs, product specifications or charts to make it visually appealing. Also add a call to purchase, saying how or why to buy.

Multi-page brochures

If you have more information and need multiple pages, or if you expect to fold the material for mailing or displaying in a rack, create a brochure layout and design. Another consideration to keep in mind is that brochures – when done well – can look more sophisticated and professional than single sheets. The folding and/or binding shows that you took care to create it, and invite the reader to open the brochure up and see what's inside.

File 8-1 contains an example of a conventional template for a three-panel brochure design. This brochure has two sides so that when it's folded, each of the six panels, front and back, is used. Replace the text with your own (the template is filled with nonsense text right now).

Microsoft Word includes templates for a variety of brochures. Each version of Word hides these templates somewhere different, and we're not going to give you specific instructions for finding them. Instead, we suggest you type **brochure** into Word Help and let your program tell you where to find the templates.

The more visual your brochure is, the better. If you can't think of any good photographs and a cartoon (see Chapter 6 for artwork sources) doesn't work, consider using colourful rectangles or triangles, which are easy to draw using the Word Art toolbar. (See the many options under Shapes, the pop-up menu that's symbolised by a circle, square and triangle in the Word toolbar.)

Figure 8-1 is an illustration of the outside three panels of a standard brochure made to be printed on A4 paper. It uses only the standard options and menus in Word to draw this illustration, just to show you how easily you can make strong, eye-catching designs. For display in this book (which is printed in black ink), the brochure uses shades of grey, but we would choose appealing colours if we were designing an actual brochure for desktop or print-shop production. (If you make up your own brochure, take care to line up folds and leave room between them for a margin around every illustration and block of text.)

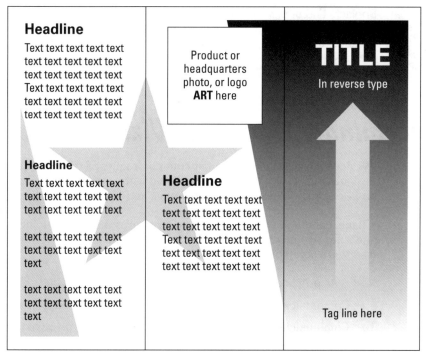

Figure 8-1:
Simple visual elements can pump up a brochure's visual appeal.

Catalogues and booklets

When you want to include a lot of information, such as descriptions of multiple products, a brochure may get a bit overstuffed. In these cases, you probably need to make a catalogue or booklet instead.

When multi-page publications focus on portraying and selling an assortment of products, they're usually called *catalogues*. So if you have an assortment of products, you probably need a catalogue. But don't overlook the less common, though more expensive, option of a *booklet* or book. For example, if you run a boatyard, you can compile a booklet on how to maintain your boat, geared to boat owners.

What's the difference between a catalogue and a booklet in terms of producing them? Not much. Both booklets and catalogues contain multiple pages that are bound together by centre-folding and stapling or by the spiral binding or glued (unsewn) *perfect binding* methods. (Perfect binding is how paperback books are made. See the sections 'Captivating Catalogues' and 'Marketing with Booklets and Books' later in this chapter for more on these products.)

Booklets and books can work wonders in generating interest in what you do and in positioning you as an expert in your field. (If you're daunted by the prospect of writing a booklet, hire a writer to help you.) Try looking at the Freelance section at www.journalism.co.uk, which contains a long list of freelance writers available and their specialities by sector.

Becoming a Brochure Wizard

'We need a brochure' is the most common request a marketing consultant or designer hears from clients. Seems like clients always need a new brochure, and we think we know why: the old ones aren't working.

Clients can't find what they want in brochures that aren't doing their job, and sales people can't make many sales if the brochure they send to clients isn't up to scratch. A good brochure:

✔ Gets prospects excited about doing business with you.

✔ Communicates enough information to support a purchase decision.

✔ Communicates enough feeling to create a strong, positive impression or image.

✔ Serves as a simple mini-catalogue that describes your various products or services.

✔ Supports *all* your marketing activities by serving as a handout for salespeople, a great mail piece for enticing prospects, a useful update for existing customers, a giveaway at events or trade shows, the perfect accompaniment to a formal proposal or press kit and so on.

Whenever you present yourself to the public, you can use your brochure to break the ice. Because brochures can be such effective icebreakers and salesmakers, you may want to create a line of brochures – one for each purpose, service or product, plus a general one that presents your business well. Single-purpose brochures are more effective and easier to design well, so we usually recommend creating a separate brochure for each major need or purpose.

Brochure design considerations

We recommend keeping a file folder somewhere in your office labelled something like 'Brochures I Like'. Whenever you see an appealing brochure, toss it in that folder. That way, when you have to think about designing your next brochure, you can empty the file folder and look at lots of appealing approaches. One of them may inspire you.

Function and purpose

Just like an ad, a brochure should have a clear message and audience. Who are you designing the brochure for? What do you want to tell them? What do you want to do? If you think these questions through before you start, your final brochure is more effective and focused than most.

Major design elements

Think about the major design elements of a brochure. Most brochures present a narrow front panel first. This panel needs to have a simple, clear, large headline, along with enough visual and/or written information to make it clear who should read the brochure and what it contains.

You can use the front panel like a book or magazine cover, with a title at the top, plus art and a few short lines advertising the contents. Or you can include some of the content on the front cover – but if you do, make sure that you leave some room for a large (25 point or bigger) title and a large version of your logo or other visual element.

 If you plan to use the brochure for mailings, make sure that you design it to meet postal requirements. Avoid oversized brochures, which cost considerably more to mail. A standard three-panel brochure printed on A4 paper makes a good mailer. The middle outside panel should be set up like a business envelope, with your name and address in the upper-left corner. If you want examples, Word has a number of brochure templates that meet this requirement. (Find the ones in your version of Word by typing **brochure** in the Help dialogue box.)

Infinite materials at your fingertips

Brochures are unusual in the variety of options they present. Unlike a flyer, you're working not just on one piece of paper, but also on as many as you want to include. And you have options about how you fold the paper.

In addition, you have more options for materials than you do for ads or letters. Brochures can be printed on regular or coated paper, but you can also get creative and use heavier card-like papers or even foil paper, embossed covers, clear or opaque covers and so on.

In fact, if you don't mind assembling brochures by hand, you can even include unusual materials, such as cloth. (For instance, how about a silk sheet between the cover and the first page?) Nothing's stopping you from using a leather or wood cover, although we don't recommend using exotic materials unless they tie into your image or relate to your product line, and you have the time and money to execute them properly (for example, a hard-wood floor installer should certainly consider a varnished wood cover).

Brochures give your marketing imagination plenty of scope!

Sizes and shapes

We suggest looking first at simple, inexpensive standard design options before going crazy; they're more economical because they use standard paper sizes. And you can vary these paper sizes by folding them in different ways, so that you still have plenty of room for creativity.

The easiest option is to use standard A4 paper, which you can work with hori-zontally (known as *landscape* format) or vertically (known as *portrait*). With a little imagination, you get five excellent brochure layouts out of this standard paper size: horizontal half-fold, accordion-fold, tri-fold, and the vertical half-fold and fold over.

You can also use these different design options with different sizes of paper, in order to generate different impacts. Each of these five fold variations makes a unique page size and therefore supports different approaches to page layout and design. In designing your brochure, think like a painter who first decides which size canvas to work on.

Sometimes you want your brochure to have an unusual shape or size to help it grab attention or make a statement. In this case, the added expense of a non-standard paper size makes sense. For example, a car dealership may print an oversized, heavy glossy-coated stock brochure cut in the shape of a car. The cover may show the owner, key salespeople and key service people as if they're riding inside the car, viewed through its windows. Such a bro-chure costs more than an ordinary one, but may be worth the expense if the brochure is highly appealing and memorable.

If you intend to mail your brochure, make sure that it meets postal regulations and fits in a standard-size envelope. Otherwise you have to find unusual enve-lope sizes and pay extra postage. Start with a search at the printer for unusual envelope sizes; that way, you don't get stuck with a great design that you can't match with an appropriate envelope. You can also check out the Royal Mail website to work out what your envelope size and mailing weight means to your postage costs (www.royalmail.com).

Paper characteristics

Paper is usually packaged in bulks of 500 sheets called a *ream* and comes in different weights: choosing a heavier (thicker) paper may give a look of quality. Heavier papers also reduce the chance of seeing text on one side of the paper through the other, again giving a more expensive look.

Lighter weight paper, such as stationery paper, is sometimes called *offset paper* and heavier card stock, such as the paper used for business cards, is called *cover stock*. You can use either type for a brochure.

Try folding and handling different types and weights of paper before you decide what to use. But remember that if you intend to do mass mailings of your brochure, the heavier papers may cost more for postage. Weigh and price the postage on several options before you make your final decision.

Also consider the finish or texture of the paper you use. Paper with a texture or grain feels nice but may not be advisable if your brochure has photos because the texture of the paper breaks up the ink for the photo, making it look coarse or muddy. If you're reproducing a lot of photos, stick to paper with a smooth surface to keep them sharp and clear.

Layout tips

Local printers usually use one of several computer programs for page layout: Adobe InDesign, Adobe PageMaker or Quark Xpress. Your printer has at least one of these programs. In some cases, these programs can read layouts that are constructed in other programs, but check with your printer beforehand to find out what the shop can handle.

Increasingly, professional printers can work from Word files, which is helpful for occasional designers who don't want to buy and master a new program. Newer versions of Word incorporate a basic Adobe Acrobat output capability that allows you to convert your Word file to Acrobat's format (Portable Document Format, or PDF) – which printers are also increasingly willing to use.

The printing industry as a whole is more accommodating to Word users than it used to be, and you may be able to design a serviceable brochure or flyer in the basic word-processing program that your computer already has, and then have a local printer produce it directly from a CD or email attachment. This option is definitely progress for budget-conscious marketers!

When laying out the text and artwork for your brochure, keep in mind that printers need a *margin* – the blank space that's needed on the edges of a document so that the printing press can grab the paper and pull it through the press. Check with your printer for specific needs. The margin area needs to be totally free from text or images. (If you want the ink to *bleed* – run to the edge – the printer needs to print on larger paper and cut it down after printing.)

Next, think about how you want your text and artwork laid out on the paper. You won't find any absolute rules for how many illustrations or pictures you can use in any one brochure, but you can follow these general guidelines:

- ✔ **Shoot for a balance between text and artwork or photos.** Too much text can be boring, and a well-placed photo or illustration can break it up nicely. Use at least one visual element on every other page or panel.

- ✔ **Place an image and/or an opening statement or paragraph on the front panel of your brochure, to catch your readers' attention.** This front panel needs to draw readers to the brochure and make them want to check out the information inside. You have to catch many people's attention with this important panel, so consider how people are likely to receive the brochure. If it's in a display rack, will the rack hide most of the cover? Maybe, therefore, you want to design it to compensate for the rack.

- ✔ **Consider using a strong photograph both for your cover design and as a visual theme for the entire layout.** File 8-2 is a brochure template you can use, with the cover featuring a striking photograph that's repeated in variations inside. Figure 8-2 shows a grey-scale version of this brochure's cover, with the strong photograph featured in its design.

- ✔ **You may hear your printer refer to *serif* and *sans serif* typefaces.** Serif typefaces have little feet-like appendages on their ends, whereas sans serif typefaces don't have those feet. (This paragraph is in a serif typeface.) Think about a combination of serif and sans serif type in your document. For example, use a sans serif type for your headings and serif for the body copy.

- ✔ **You measure type in point size.** For example, ten-point type is a small point size:

    The quick brown fox jumps over the lazy dog.

    A large point size is 24 point:

    # The quick brown . . .

- ✔ **Make sure that the body type is readable; the size should be no less than 10 to 12 point.** Consider your audience. If the people reading this brochure are elderly, use a bigger type size, such as 14 to 18 point.

Also avoid large areas of *reverse type* (where the type is white or a light colour on a dark background) because it's much harder to read.

✔ **Try to stick with one or two families of fonts within a brochure.** Too many font styles can look sloppy and confusing. Each family has many styles (for example, **Bold**, *Italic* and <u>Underline</u> in the Times New Roman family), so you have plenty to work with. And don't forget that you can change the size to add variety. For example, you can use all the following variations in size in a single brochure – the largest for major headers and other sizes for minor headers, the body copy and the fine-print details.

Helvetica 10 point

Helvetica 12 point

Helvetica 14 point

Helvetica 16 point

Helvetica 24 point

✔ **Mix up straight paragraphs with other ways of laying out text, such as checklists, tables and columns.** The changes of pace you create keep the text appealing.

Figure 8-2: This brochure cover features a strong photographic element to draw the eye.

Headline type

Headline type is made for just that: headlines. It's usually bigger, sometimes bolder and often more ornate than the regular text.

Headline type isn't meant for the body of the article – it would be too hard to read. Its purpose is to grab readers' attention and draw them into the article below.

Headline type is usually used on brochure covers and paragraph headings.

Body type

Body type is used for the main body of the text. Because it needs to be simple and easy to read, bold is usually (but not exclusively) restricted to serif fonts, which are easier on the eyes, especially at smaller type sizes.

Times New Roman is the classic body copy and the most readable of all the fonts. Garamond is an elegant alternative. Helvetica and Arial (both sans serif fonts) are more clean and modern, and they're attractive, too.

Type alignment

The way type lines up on the page supports an image or conveys a feeling. For a formal, conservative look, use *justified type* (where both the left and right sides of the type align at the margin). A *ragged right margin* (text not lined up on the right; used in this book) gives a less formal look. You can also centre text, and sometimes you can justify the text on only the right side, as when it floats in open space with a photo or box to the right of it. Figure 8-3 shows you what each of these options looks like and how printers and designers refer to each option.

The quick brown fox jumped over the lazy dog. The quick brown fox jumped over the lazy dog.The quick brown fox jumped over the lazy dog. The quick brown fox jumped over the lazy dog.The quick brown fox jumped over the lazy dog. The quick brown fox jumped over the lazy dog.The quick brown fox jumped over the lazy dog. The quick brown fox jumped over the	The quick brown fox jumped over the lazy dog. The quick brown fox jumped over the lazy dog.The quick brown fox jumped over the lazy dog. The quick brown fox jumped over the lazy dog.The quick brown fox jumped over the lazy dog. The quick brown fox jumped over the lazy dog.The quick brown fox jumped over the lazy dog. The quick brown fox jumped over the	The quick brown fox jumped over the lazy dog. The quick brown fox jumped over the lazy dog.The quick brown fox jumped over the lazy dog. The quick brown fox jumped over the lazy dog.The quick brown fox jumped over the lazy dog. The quick brown fox jumped over the lazy dog.The quick brown fox jumped over the lazy dog. The quick brown fox jumped over the	The quick brown fox jumped over the lazy dog. The quick brown fox jumped over the lazy dog.The quick brown fox jumped over the lazy dog. The quick brown fox jumped over the lazy dog.The quick brown fox jumped over the lazy dog. The quick brown fox jumped over the lazy dog.The quick brown fox jumped over the lazy dog. The quick brown fox jumped over the
JUSTIFIED LEFT (Ragged Right)	**JUSTIFIED RIGHT (Ragged Left)**	**CENTRED**	**JUSTIFIED**

Figure 8-3: Your options for aligning type on the page.

Text wrapping

With *text wrapping*, the lines of text end right where they bump into artwork. Word offers a variety of text-wrapping options in its Formatting area. (If you don't know where that is in your version of Word, type the term **text wrap** in your Word Help and follow the instructions.)

You can choose to have the art bump the text so that the text wraps around or beside the art, or you can make the art float independently. (The same basic options exist in any design program.)

Printing or do it yourself?

One of the first things you have to decide when creating a brochure is how to produce it. Traditionally, this decision means whether you have it photo-copied or printed, but today the main choice is between professional print-ing or making it yourself on your own ink-jet or laser printer (usually called *desktop publishing*). Some factors to consider when deciding how to produce a brochure include:

- ✔ If you have large runs of 1,000 pieces or more, having them profession-ally printed is better than using your desktop system.

- ✔ If you have small runs (under 1,000 pieces), professional printing usually isn't cost-effective, because the price per unit goes up as quantity goes down. Digital print or desktop-publish instead.

- ✔ If you have a lot of photos in your marketing piece, professional printing tends to produce better quality. However, newer desktop printers can fill this need quite well at quantities between one and 100.

- ✔ If you want your brochure to last a long time, professional printing is far more durable than desktop printing because the ink sinks down into the paper, locking it in and making it impossible to remove. However, a good colour laser printer gives desktop printed brochures almost as much durability as professionally printed brochures.

- ✔ If you want to minimise costs for small numbers (under 100), why not just design the brochure in Word and print it on brochure paper on your ink-jet or laser printer? Printing yourself gives you the ability to adapt the design to your immediate needs.

Colour

Adding colour to your brochure grabs the viewer's attention and makes the brochure more appealing to the eye, but for professionally printed brochures, each added colour can require an additional print run and thus adds cost. You can add colour in different ways, such as by using:

✔ **Pantone Matching System (PMS) colours:** Printers use a universal ink colour system called the Pantone Matching System. This system allows printers to match ink by referring to swatches that show the colour along with the exact mixture of inks needed to obtain that colour. So if you want to add colour to a professionally printed brochure, you need to ask a printer to let you see a set of PMS colour samples so that you can select from it.

✔ **Four-colour process:** In this process, printers achieve full colour by separating the image into four basic colours: cyan, magenta, yellow and black (CYMK). Printers shoot film of the image in each of these colours and break the colours down into tiny dots (or increasingly, they ask for four digital files from you to substitute for the old-fashioned films). These dots, when arranged next to each other, create the full colour effect, and you can see the arrangement of dots only with the aid of a magnifying glass, or loupe. The effect of the four-colour process is excellent – it can reproduce fine art or photography quite accurately. But four-colour printing is expensive because of the extra film work or digital separations involved, as well as the need for four print runs through the press.

✔ **Alternatives to four-colour process printing:** Some alternatives allow you to have a variety of colours but still keep costs down. When using PMS colours, you can ask to screen the colour(s) at different percentages. For example, your brochure may have only two ink colours, such as black and blue. Using the blue screened back to 80 per cent, 60 per cent and 20 per cent gives the impression that you're using four different blues when you're actually using blue at 100 per cent, 80 per cent, 60 per cent and 20 per cent. Using this method, the printer can do all the blues on one run through the press. And although the shades of blue plus the black give the feeling of five colours, the brochure needs only two print runs – one for black and one for blue.

✔ **Ink-jet and colour laser printing:** For very small runs, you can use any decent desktop printer. For example, many ink-jet printers can produce a good quality colour brochure using brochure paper. You have to print and fold them yourself, so you don't want to make more than 10 or 20 at one sitting, or you'll go mad! But for small runs, the desktop option is great.

When laying out a brochure for any of these printing options, avoid large fields of solid colour because they add to the cost of a printed piece, and some electronic printers have a hard time keeping the ink consistent throughout the field of colour. In some cases, you can screen large solid colours to give them more consistency (for example, use blue at 85 per cent instead of 100 per cent – it still looks like dark blue but prints more consistently and with less trouble).

Watch out for any printed areas that reach (or bleed) all the way to the edge of the paper. To print to the edge of your sheet of paper, the printer has to print a larger sheet and cut it down – and that adds up to extra costs for you.

Artwork

Illustrating a brochure adds visual appeal and, if the illustrations are appropriate, makes it more persuasive. 'Seeing is believing', as the saying goes! But as with type design, you need some basic technical knowledge before you're ready to select artwork for your brochure. The catch is that how you want to produce the final output partially determines how you choose and prepare your graphics in the first place.

When you design a brochure or other printed product, keep in mind that the artwork needs to be in a file that has reasonably high resolution: 300 dpi (dots per inch) is the standard for most printing jobs. Pictures for the Internet need to be low resolution: 72 dpi is standard for web images.

When we say that the rule is 300 dpi for your printed photos and 72 dpi for web photos, we're assuming that you *aren't changing the size of the picture* to any significant degree when you print it. If you do, the resolution doesn't automatically adjust with the size. The amount of data in the image file is the same, no matter what size you make the picture in your printed product. Therefore, you can get in trouble if you give your printer a JPEG file of a photograph that's saved at 300 dpi, and then ask for it to be blown up to twice its current size. Now the resolution is cut in half and the quality is poorer. Oops. When you shrink an image, you run the opposite risk – you may make it higher resolution and therefore it may look out of place against other images on the same page with a lower resolution.

Graphic designers resize images and adjust their dpi in order to fit the design and medium (resizing is easy in programs such as InDesign and Photoshop). We don't cover these technicalities here; instead, we suggest that you ask your printer (or web designer) if your photograph is the right size and resolution, and if it isn't, ask her to help you adjust it.

Your printer or designer may ask you whether you're going to provide a bit-mapped image or a vector image. Most photographs are bitmapped. Logos created by graphic designers are usually vectored. Here's a brief overview of the two options so that you know what your printer is talking about when the question comes up:

  ✔ **Bitmapped images (or raster images):** When you *bitmap* an image, you digitise and store the image, using small squares (pixels) arranged on a grid to represent the image. Bitmapped images are fine, as long as the image stays at the same size or smaller. If you blow it up, though, the small squares grow larger, making them noticeable and giving the image a poor appearance. File 8-3 compares a bitmapped image with a vector image to show how they look when enlarged beyond their original size.

✔ **Vector images:** Designers use *vector images* to get around the problems of blowing up bitmapped images by using mathematical equations to represent the lines and curves in artwork. The art stays clean and clear at any level of enlargement because the computer program literally redraws it to the new scale. Most logos are vector images because they're reproduced in many different sizes for different uses.

The examples of bitmapped and vector art, shown in File 8-3, are both examples of line art. *Line art* consists of any black and white image with no grey areas or screens. These images can be anything from line drawings to black and white logos.

You can also print forms of art other than line art – in other words, art that has greys or shades of colour in it. (Photographs are a good example.) But – wouldn't you know it? – doing so adds more technical issues. Avoid using anything drawn in pencil, such as drawings or sketches, because these images are difficult to reproduce. If you have to use a pencil drawing, the printer may suggest making a *halftone print* of the image to save the grey areas from *burning out* (disappearing). (A halftone print is a high-quality option using screens; your printer will know all about it.) Follow this advice and don't grumble about the minor added expense.

Photography

Traditional printers usually like to work from black and white photos that you supply (assuming that you want one- or two-colour output). Colour photos, especially *low-contrast photos* (photos that don't have a lot of difference between dark and light areas), tend to muddy up when you reproduce them in black ink. But sometimes you have to use colour photos because that's all you have or because your source is colour photos from other marketing materials, such as your website or a PowerPoint sales presentation.

Do your best to find and use high-contrast photos (with lots of difference between the dark and light areas). High-contrast photos have more definition and reproduce better.

If you or a photographer are planning to take pictures of your products, facilities or people, make sure that you use a high-contrast film (one designed to produce sharp, clear images). In general, slower films give higher contrast and sharper images. When shooting with a digital camera, you can set the shutter speed to anything you like. However, the principle remains the same: you need plenty of light!

Clip art and stock photography

You can use copyright-free images, such as clip art and photos, when budget constraints eliminate the possibility of hiring professional illustrators or photographers. These images are copyright free, so you don't have to pay royalties or get special permissions to reproduce them. They're usually available on disk or CD, and you typically pay a modest fee to the publisher.

You may find some stock photography websites that are running promotions in which they offer some images for free as a way to attract new customers – if so, grab some art while you can!

Crop and fold marks

Crop and fold marks tell printers where they need to cut or fold a marketing piece. You need to mark these instructions on your original piece with a *hairline* – the smallest weight printed line possible – to ensure accuracy.

The following list briefly explains the standard terms and symbols that you need to know to communicate with your printer or binder:

- **Crop marks:** *Crop marks* are guides that show the printer where to cut a page. If you need to print your brochure on larger paper and then cut it down (as when the ink bleeds all the way to the edge of your page or when you specify a non-standard size), the printer uses the crop marks to cut in exactly the right place.

- **Fold marks:** *Fold marks* tell the printer where to fold the paper. But make sure that she understands which *way* to fold the page!

- **Score marks:** *Score marks* indicate where the printer should *score*, or lightly cut, the paper. When using heavy paper, you sometimes need to score before you fold in order to get a clean, crisp fold. In that case, you need to mark the fold line as a score line, too.

- **Perforating marks:** You use *perforating marks* when a brochure includes a coupon or postcard that you want people to tear out. Perforating marks show the printer where to make the *perforations* – a series of short cuts in the paper.

In addition to providing marks to show where you want folds, scores and the like, you should also make a mock-up of your brochure. It doesn't have to be fancy, just cut and tape it together. The point of a mock-up is to show the printer how the finished product should look. The mock-up helps the printer to interpret your marks and instructions and avoid confusion.

Making Digital Brochures

Including a CD-ROM or DVD along with the printed materials in mailings and client proposals can be a good move. A CD-ROM can contain lengthy documents in PDF or Word formats, as well as extensive photographs, PowerPoint slide presentations and even video. Or, if you have high-quality video about a product or service, you can use a DVD to distribute a video brochure (basically as an infomercial on a disc).

You need to weigh up whether the circumstances justify using the more extensive capabilities of a CD-ROM or DVD, instead of (or in addition to) a traditional brochure. We recommend using a CD-ROM or DVD in either of the following situations:

- ✔ If your business story is complex and detailed, and prospective customers need and want to do extensive background research before buying.
- ✔ If you want to make a good impression by using a new medium in a creative way.

If you have trouble visualising how to set up a CD-ROM brochure, think about the design as a web page. Why? Because you (or any competent web design firm) can create web-page style designs, just like any you see on the web; the only difference is that you launch them off the CD-ROM. In fact, you should also put the digital brochure on your website and include the link in the cover letter for the CD-ROM and on the label of it, because some of your customers or prospects may prefer to view it that way instead of having to load a CD-ROM.

We don't have space to cover the how-tos in detail, but if you don't have the budget to hire someone who knows how, other useful references can help you, such as *Digital Video For Dummies, 4th edition,* by Keith Underdahl, published by Wiley.

Captivating Catalogues

If you think of a catalogue as an elaborate brochure, you'll be pleased to discover that you already know a great deal about how to design and print catalogues if you read the earlier section 'Becoming a Brochure Wizard'. That's because everything we write about brochures applies to catalogues as well. In fact, many simple catalogues are indistinguishable from brochures in their basic design, use of paper and layout. The only difference is that a catalogue focuses on describing a product or service line, which is what makes them catalogues instead of brochures – brochures are the equivalent of looking through a shop window to get an idea of what products are on offer. A catalogue offers the same experience, but gives more detail including specifics such as sizes, colours, quantities and prices.

Design considerations

We go into considerable detail about the design of brochures in the earlier section 'Layout tips', because we believe many marketers can and should roll up their sleeves and get involved in designing their own brochures. By getting involved, you don't feel intimidated by the project and can feel free to create and replace brochures whenever you have a need to.

The same is true for simple catalogues prepared in the same style as brochures. You can design one-sheet catalogues with one or more folds and have them printed at the local print shop or photocopied quite easily. But if you want to get into more elaborate multi-page catalogues, you may do better to work with a specialist.

Consider hiring a designer who specialises in catalogues. Creating a catalogue involves more than just the mechanics of design and layout, although these alone can become quite complex when you have many pages. The biggest challenge, however, is to sell your product effectively in the pages of a catalogue. How you present each purchase option (in copy and art), what you choose to feature on the outside and inside covers (where you get the most impact), whether you include an index and what sort of look and feel you go for are all quite sophisticated and difficult decisions, so we recommend spending the extra money for an expert's input.

Printing a multi-page four-colour catalogue can be costly, and mailing it adds up, too. You may as well invest enough in the design to give yourself good odds of getting a profitable return on that investment.

For a less expensive alternative, print a handsome brochure that highlights your best-selling products and directs the reader to your website. Design your website as if it's a high-quality catalogue, with large or pop-up photos of your products, detailed supporting information and an e-commerce store, as well as easy-access email and telephone contact options for enquiries.

For a very low-cost approach to do-it-yourself online catalogues, take a look at eBay (`www.ebay.co.uk`), which supports vendors with templates and makes showcasing your products, accepting orders or running auctions easy. Many vendors use an eBay store as their primary catalogue and website, and run occasional auctions at low starting bids as a way to promote their store to eBay users.

Benchmark catalogues for your reference

You can easily find good examples of multi-page full-colour catalogues by examining your mail. Clothing retailers usually have well-made catalogues that can serve as your benchmarks. Also look at glossy, sophisticated magazines in newsagents for interesting approaches to graphic design that you may want to earmark for a catalogue. We recommend keeping a folder of catalogues that appeal to you, so that you can review their designs next time you need ideas.

Notice especially how good catalogues:

✔ Use their front covers to feature special products or offers or to create appealing moods.

✔ Organise their contents in intuitive ways so that readers can quickly find sections of interest.

✔ Vary the page layouts so that each page doesn't look like the last and avoids monotony.

✔ Give readers plenty of ways to reach the business with questions or orders, including telephone and fax numbers (and perhaps a website) on each page, as well as a clear, flexible order form.

✔ Contain clear, accurate, sufficient information about products to support purchase decisions. (They answer all the customers' questions well.)

✔ Are positive in their emotional appeals, using smiling people, enthusiastic language, bright, warm colours, or all three to create an 'up' mood in readers.

Good catalogues break up space into smaller blocks by using a column or grid pattern to display multiple products on most of the pages. If you can tighten up the space used for each product without damaging the selling power of your coverage, you can generate more revenue per page. And because design, printing and mailing costs vary with the number of pages, hardworking pages make for a more successful catalogue.

Notice that many of the most visually appealing and readable catalogues aren't too cluttered. They have that magic ingredient of great designs – white space. *White space* is the open space that you can see on the page without text or images. Amateur designers (that's most marketers, by the way) tend to cram too much onto a page, which makes focusing on any one item difficult. Open up your design with a little more white space than people usually use, and your catalogue becomes more readable and attractive.

Less is more

Here's an example of the power of white space. A business that sells office supplies wants to liquidate a lot of inventory by publishing a special sale catalogue. At first, the business's catalogue uses a cover design featuring a photo of a warehouse stacked high and thick with all sorts of products, making the outlet like a maze. Across the photo, in big type, runs the title 'Everything Must Go!' The design is overpowering, and it hurts the eye to look at this cover.

The business reconsiders. It publishes a catalogue with a cover that is mostly white. This design shows an almost entirely empty, clean white warehouse interior, cavernous in its emptiness except for one lone box far off in the corner with a man in a dark business suit standing looking down at it. Across the top of this design runs the headline, 'Everything Will Go'. This new design is visually appealing and entices curious shoppers into the interior of the catalogue to find out more.

Estimating How Many Copies to Circulate

The number of catalogues or brochures to mail varies enormously. Whereas a regional business-to-business marketer may be content to send a catalogue to only a few thousand names, a national business-to-business catalogue usually needs to go to at least 10,000 names, and sometimes four or five times that number. Consumer-oriented catalogues on specialty topics (like model railways) may go to a small number of names, but consumer ones usually need to go to hundreds of thousands of people to be really successful.

Set your circulation target based on the following factors:

- **The size of the potential market:** Try to reach at least half your potential market through your mailing. But if your catalogue or brochure is new, test it on smaller samples first to make sure that it's profitable.

- **The amount of your inventory or capacity:** Try not to send out so many catalogues or brochures that you risk being unable to fill your orders. Otherwise, customers become upset and don't respond the next time.

- **The size of your in-house list of past purchasers:** You can, and should, try to supplement your in-house list. But don't let new names that you purchase dominate your mailing; getting a good response from them is just too hard. Build your list gradually until you have a substantial (for your market) in-house list instead of trying to supplement 1,000 past purchasers with 100,000 names from purchased lists.

✔ **The size of your budget:** In the real world, the fact that millions of people buy gardening supplies is irrelevant if you only have £3,000 to spend on launching a new catalogue of specialty garden tools. Spend cautiously so that you can afford to recover and try another mailing, even if the first one is an abject failure. The path to success is paved with failures, so make sure that you can afford to survive a few low-response-rate mailings. Eventually, you'll discover a mailing design and strategy that really pays off for you – but only if you can afford to stay in the game long enough for luck to strike!

Spectacular Spec Sheets

'Just the facts, ma'am.' Too often marketers forget to communicate enough information or to communicate it clearly enough so that people can make informed purchase decisions. Marketing communications are often maddeningly vague to serious buyers, who want to know exactly what you do, how your equipment performs, what the specifications are, what the terms are and so on. What, exactly, are the facts?

Enter the specification, or spec, sheet. A *spec sheet* is a simple, clear one-page technical description of a product (or, rarely, a service). It contains all facts – or mostly facts; it may also have a testimonial or two and a nice photo or illustration. It often uses a tabular layout to provide consumers with detailed information that they need to make a purchase decision. Spec sheets serve this purpose well, providing the hard-core informational backup to support more imaginative or persuasive marketing materials. We believe that everyone ought to prepare spec sheets for each product or service they sell. Not all prospects want one, but those who do really appreciate it.

Include a spec sheet in the sales collateral for a product if technical specifications are important to buyers or prospective buyers. For example, use spec sheets for video monitors, fire extinguishers, food processors, outboard motors, golf clubs, toasters or remote-control toy cars, because buyers of these products may well want or need to know something about the product's specifications.

Formatting your spec sheet

Spec sheets are usually A4 pieces of paper with printing on only one side. Include your business's name, logo and contact information on the top or bottom of the sheet. Title it 'Specifications for <product name/code>' at the top (or just beneath your business identification). Date it because specifications often change, and you may issue updated sheets in the future.

Use your business letterhead for a simple, quick spec sheet. You can use Word's table option and your office printer to create a simple but professional spec sheet on your letterhead.

Set up the spec sheet in two columns, with the left column listing a category of specifications (size, weight, voltage and so on) and the right column giving a specific measurement for each category. Use numbered footnotes to define any ambiguous or obscure terms or units. Avoid lengthy descriptions, and don't try to sell the product. Spec sheets give specifications; they don't promote. Hopefully, the product or service is good, and the specifications do the selling for you!

Here's a simple template for spec sheets:

Specifications for <product>
Date/date/date

Category	Data
Category	Data
Category	Data
Category	Data
Category	Data
Category	Data

Business Name
Address
Phone/Fax
Email/Web page

Ensuring that your spec sheet is up to scratch

Spec sheets should be *clear*, *readable* (don't use type smaller than 11 point, please!), *accurate* and *sufficient*. Verify all the data you include on the spec sheet and include everything needed to describe the product.

To ensure that your specifications are sufficient, look at spec sheets of competing products. Also *ask customers or prospects what information they need.* If you're using units that aren't universal, provide conversions (for example, give the dimensions of a product in both inches and centimetres). And verify all specifications with product designers and producers. Ask them whether they're *sure* of the specifications. You don't want to be wrong. (If you're in one of those industries where regulations or legal liability are issues, also have a qualified lawyer review your spec sheet before printing it.)

If you employ a graphic designer or advertising agency to typeset your spec sheet, leave time to check its accuracy thoroughly after the design is finalised but before it's printed. The design process can introduce errors into spec sheets. Also, designers may want to jazz up your spec sheet. Discourage this urge. Keep spec sheets clean and simple and save the creativity for other marketing materials.

Marketing with Booklets and Books

Consultants have long used the power of a book to promote their firm and its services. As their job is to work for clients, they have no tangible products of their own to point to. Creating a book allows them to set out their philosophy, their methods of working and to create a difference between themselves and their competitors in potential clients' minds. In fact, any business whose expertise is important to its customers, including doctors, lawyers, architects, accountants and so on, may benefit from having its own book or booklet.

A book can be a powerful demonstration of your expertise, allowing prospective customers to get to know you well enough to decide whether they want to work with you. Of course, the risk is that they decide you don't know what you're talking about, so be sure to approach books with caution. If you aren't a writer yourself, you can find ghostwriters that specialise in creating books for business clients – try checking out www.journalism.co.uk and looking under the Freelance menu to find specialist writers for different business sectors. If you have a PR company that you already work with, ask them for help too.

One heating and air-conditioning company published a short but nicely done booklet called *How to Increase the Comfort of Your Building* to promote its services. The booklet addresses upgrades and improvements to both residential and commercial structures, with short chapters explaining how and why to install different types of systems. The booklet has attractive pictures and diagrams (provided by the suppliers whose equipment this company installs), plus mini case studies of successful projects. The three top people in the company wrote the booklet, and their photos and biographies appear on the back cover. Whenever company employees interact with new or potential customers, they include this booklet as a handout, and it makes a strong, positive impression that helps land the company many good jobs.

If you keep your booklet short and sweet (64 pages or under, centre stapled) and provide much of the content yourself, you don't need to pay a lot for ghostwriting. Writing your own material can save you quite a bit of money because the better ghostwriters charge anywhere from a few thousand pounds to a hundred thousand, depending on the project! When the time comes to produce the book or booklet, you can do it in-house using Word – if you're very brave – but we recommend working with a local print shop.

Files on the CD

Check out the following items on the CD-ROM:

- ✔ **File 8-1:** Product Offerings brochure template in Word
- ✔ **File 8-2:** Brochure template with photographic design elements
- ✔ **File 8-3:** Illustration of bitmapped versus vector line art options

Chapter 9

Planning Coupons and Other Sales Promotions

*M*any marketing experts use the term *sales promotion* to describe the use of coupons, discounts, premium items (special gifts) and other incentives to boost sales. Coupons are probably the best known and most widely used sales promotions, but you can use plenty of other ways to give prospects an incentive to make a purchase. In this chapter, we look at a variety of options, explore some of the best ways (and worst ways) to use them and include an analytical approach that helps you figure out whether a specific incentive is going to prove profitable or not.

Calculating the Importance of Profit

Making a sale is easy if you don't care about profits. Cut the price enough, and almost anything sells. Witness the junk people buy at car boot sales and flea markets. But you're in business, so you don't want sales when they don't make you money. And sales promotions don't always make money.

Take a look at the new car business. New cars are very expensive and as such, you need to have lots of disposable cash, or a strong incentive, to buy one. Car retailers try a number of different techniques in order to generate a sale through their marketing.

Here's an example of some of the offers that you're likely to see when reading car marketing material:

- ✔ '0% finance available'
- ✔ 'Great deals on trade-ins'
- ✔ 'Buy now, pay later'
- ✔ 'Hire Purchase available'

The showroom is aware that people view cars as expensive and therefore require a number of reasons – above and beyond the emotional connection they've made to a particular brand – in order to complete a purchase. Closing the deal can become particularly difficult for the car dealer in tough economic times.

When trying to sell older cars, even these incentives aren't enough on their own, so car dealers are forced to offer price incentives: you often see '20% off all models only this week' or in the case of second-hand car dealers 'best price for cash' marketing messages.

These offers shift stock, but are they a wise strategy? That depends on how consumers react to them:

- ✔ If customers get into the habit of waiting for offers such as these to be made, the car retailers lose the ability to sell any of their older vehicles at the full price. Heavy discounts are great for the consumer, but they may damage long-term sales strategies.
- ✔ If these communications aren't too frequent, however, any customer that buys an older car at a reduced price recommends the dealer to his friends and has a positive memory of the experience. This outcome also means that sales of the newer makes aren't detrimentally impacted.

In reality, both reactions are common in any sales promotion. Some consumers only shop based on price and never buy at the ticket price. However, when using sales promotions such as the above, as well as attracting the bargain hunters, you may also remind some customers that they like your products or introduce yourself to them for the first time, building a purchase history with you that carries over into non-sale items. And that's a great return from a sales promotion.

Discovering How Promotions Affect Sales

A sales promotion can basically have one or more of the following five effects on the market:

✔ **It takes your competitors' customers.** The promotion encourages the consumer to purchase a new brand or do business with a new vendor.

✔ **It attracts brand-new customers.** The promotion may draw in new users who've never bought products like yours.

✔ **It stimulates repeat purchases.** The consumer is more likely to keep buying the product or doing business with the vendor because of the promotion.

✔ **It stimulates bigger purchases.** The consumer buys sooner and/or in larger quantities as a result of the promotion. (Be careful, though; sometimes a corresponding decline in purchases occurs later on!)

✔ **It gives away profits to people who would have bought anyway.** This result is the risk you run. What if all you do is cut prices to customers who would have bought at a higher price? Sometimes customers load up during a promotion and then don't buy later at their normal rate.

The first four scenarios are positive. They help generate more sales and grow your customer base. That's a good result for coupons or other sales promotions, and it's the reason marketers call these things *sales promotions*. Multiple paths can lead to those increased sales and sometimes the increases are long term rather than short term. If you don't see a clear link from your coupon or discount programme to increased sales, forget it. You're wasting your time and your business's money.

Planning Coupon Programmes

Boy, have I got a deal for you!

These classic words (or offers to the same effect) are the bread and butter of many marketing initiatives. Offering a discount gives people a reason to buy. It attracts their attention and converts vague intentions into immediate actions. However, discounts also cost you money and that's not so good.

How much will a discount cost your business? Will the increased sales more than offset the cost? If you don't know, you better find out. You need to do some careful thinking and forecasting before you offer any discounts or distribute any coupons.

If you print and distribute coupons, any number of things may happen:

✔ Prospects may ignore them.

✔ Some prospects may redeem the coupons and become loyal, profitable customers.

✔ Everyone may ignore the coupons except those people who constantly shop for deals – and these people don't become regular customers unless you *always* offer them a deal.

✔ Some stores may *misredeem* the coupons (apply the coupon to the wrong product – we say more about misredemption in the later section 'Filling in the blanks'), in which case you end up paying the coupons' face value but not winning new sales.

✔ Existing customers may use the coupons to buy just as much as they would have without the coupons, in which case you've just given away profits.

✔ New sales may flood in, making you very happy – until you realise that the costs of the coupon programme are high enough that you've lost money in the process of winning that new business.

In other words, you can't really be sure what's going to happen, and a number of bad results may occur. Good things may result, too, but those aren't a certainty.

Enter *coupon profitability analysis*. If you do a careful analysis of several possible scenarios upfront and crunch the numbers on each scenario, you have a much better idea of the likely outcomes. Often, when people do a formal analysis, they're horrified at the results. They find that their initial ideas and assumptions have fatal flaws, and they realise that they were about to throw away some or all of their profit margin in exchange for very little new business. So we highly recommend doing a careful profitability analysis, which we describe in the next two sections.

Also, remember to experiment and gather data from your experiences. Finding those formulas that put you in your marketing zone (see Chapter 2) takes time and experience.

If you did some coupon programmes in the past, running the numbers on them is a great idea to see how they worked out. Were they really profitable or not? The answer isn't obvious unless you do a proper analysis. And when you do, you can discover a great deal from these past efforts that can help you design more effective and profitable coupon programmes in the future.

Creative experimentation – and taking lessons from your experiments – is at the heart of all great marketing!

Basics of coupon profitability analysis

To perform a coupon profitability analysis, follow these steps:

1. **Identify all the fixed and variable costs of the coupon programme.**

   Fixed costs are costs, such as design expenses, that don't change with the quantity of coupons. *Variable costs* are costs that increase with the number of coupons printed and distributed.

2. **Figure out how much product you think you can sell directly to consumers because of the coupon redemption.**

3. **Figure out how much money you make by selling that product.**

4. **Subtract all those expenses from the profits you've earned to see if the coupon programme is profitable or not.**

As you can see, the basic idea is to estimate all your costs, redemption rates and other important statistics, and then add an analysis of the impact on your sales and profits.

This four-step method is perhaps not quite as simple as it seems, so take a look at an example for 1,000 coupons with a face value of £10 each. This example appears in Figure 9-1 and as a PDF in File 9-1. A £10 coupon is quite valuable, so the redemption rate should be high – in this example, it's estimated at 8 per cent (which means that eight coupons out of every hundred distributed are redeemed). When all costs are worked in, the net impact is estimated to be a gain of about £2,431 in net profits. This coupon programme ought to more than pay for itself – and if it attracts some new customers who then come back and buy again, it will have a good long-term impact, too.

To perform your profitability analysis, follow the step-by-step instructions we provide in the next section.

Coupon profitability analysis step by step

Please use the interactive spreadsheet in File 9-2 to work through your coupon profitability analysis. To use this Excel form, make a working copy (so you don't accidentally mess up the master file's formulas) and then fill in the boxed cells with numbers representing your plans for a coupon programme. The spreadsheet calculates everything else to figure out your costs and profits.

Coupon Profitability Analysis

WORKED EXAMPLE FOR YOUR REFERENCE

Number of Coupons	1000
Face Value of Coupons	£10.00

Fixed Costs:
(Costs required to create and manage the promotion)

Design and consultation fees (if any)	£500.00
Setup costs for producing coupons	£250.00
Other fixed costs (describe)	£50.00
Total Fixed Costs	**£800.00**

Incremental Costs:
(Costs varying with number of coupons)   *Incremental costs running total....*

Production costs per thousand coupons	£10.00	£10.00
Distribution costs per thousand coupons	£50.00	£50.00
Legitimate redemption rate	8.0%	£800.00
Misredemption rate	1.0%	£100.00
Processing costs per coupon redeemed	£0.10	£9.00
Other variable costs per coupon (describe)	0	£0.00
Total variable costs		**£969.00**

Total Costs: **£1,769.00**

Incremental Profit Contribution:
(Number of incremental sales x profit margin on product)

Number of sales directly from redemptions	80
% of sales that would have occurred anyway	25.00%
Number of incremental sales from redemptions	**60**
Profit contribution per sale	£70.00

Total incremental profits resulting from coupon programme   **£4,200.00**

Bottom-line Impact of Coupon (Net Profit)

Net Profit (Incremental profits minus coupon costs)   **£2,431.00**

Figure 9-1:
Analysing
a coupon
programme
using the
spreadsheet
in File 9-2.

The general categories of costs are:

✔ **Fixed costs:** These costs are the costs of designing your coupon, printer's set-up costs and so on. Be sure to include all fixed costs that are necessary to create the coupon and programme.

✔ **Variable costs:** These costs vary with the number of coupons. Note that many such costs are conventionally measured on a cost per 1,000 coupons rather than on a cost per individual coupon. When you get quotes from printers and businesses that handle coupon redemptions, these quotes are likely to be in costs per 1,000 coupons. (If not, please convert.)

Filling in the blanks

The following paragraphs go through the coupon profitability analysis line by line and show you how to enter appropriate variables, so you can see how a coupon programme may work. You have to fill in 13 cells in order to complete an analysis of a future scenario or past programme. Are you ready? Good. Here we go.

Number of coupons: _____

How many coupons do you plan to distribute? If you're planning on giving them out through a shop or other public site, you may not be able to guess accurately how many coupons people are going to pick up. So just take your best guess, print a specific number and then test several levels of distribution: say (a) the entire print run, (b) ²/₃ of it and (c) ¹/₃ of it. If the programme seems like it may be profitable at all these levels, trying it is probably a good idea. Often, however, businesses distribute an offer to a mailing list of a known number or to the subscribers of a publication. In these cases, you can use basic circulation or list data to determine how many coupons you're going to distribute.

Face value of coupons: £_____

What are you planning to offer the users of the coupon? Typically a coupon gives a discount on the purchase of a single product, so that's how we set up this spreadsheet. Enter a pound sterling value representing the amount for which the coupon is good. For example, if you plan to offer a £20 discount off the next purchase of a carton of your special industrial cleaning fluid, enter £20 in this cell.

Ah, but how much of a discount do you need to offer to get a good response? We were afraid you'd ask that! A good but vague rule is to offer just enough to get someone's attention. If you offer too much, well, you're just giving the product away. If you offer too little, nobody pays attention.

Regular coupon marketers run lots of experiments until they find some formulas that tell them what discount to use. If you don't have any idea of what to offer, you need to run some experiments yourself. Start with a nice safe number. Safe means from a bottom-line perspective, which means a number that's considerably less than your profit.

For example, say you make a cool new cat toy that you sell at wholesale to pet stores for £1.75, which they mark up to a retail price of £2.49. When you examine your costs, you find that it costs you approximately £1.20 to make and deliver each unit, and so your profit is £0.55 on each cat toy you sell. Now, offering a £0.55 discount would be a costly experiment, wouldn't it? But you can readily afford a £0.25 discount. On the other hand, is that discount enough to get anyone's attention? Maybe not. The redemption rate may be pretty low. So perhaps a £0.35 coupon is better. This discount still leaves a little profit to cover (we hope) the costs of the coupon programme, but offers enough of a discount that it may get a reasonable response rate from cat owners. You may want to start there and see what happens.

Design and consultation fees: £_____

If you hire a graphic designer, marketing consultant or ad agency to design your coupon, you're going to have to pay him. Enter the cost here.

Set-up costs for producing coupons: £_____

If you're having a printer produce your coupons, you'll have some set-up costs. Enter those costs here. If you're buying ad space in a newspaper or other publication for your coupons, you probably don't have to pay set-up costs, so just enter a zero.

Other fixed costs: £_____

If you expect to incur any other upfront or fixed costs, be sure to add them in here. Forgotten costs come back to bite!

Production costs per 1,000 coupons: £_____

If you're having a printer produce the coupons, he can give you this number (along with the set-up costs, earlier in this list). Ask him what the costs are at several different volume levels because a sliding scale based on quantity may apply. If you're inserting your coupons into a publication, just enter zero here. The next line item is the one for you!

Distribution costs per 1,000 coupons: £_____

What will the newspaper, trade magazine or coupon booklet publisher charge you for inserting your coupon in its publication? What will stores charge you for placing your coupons at the point of purchase? What will some hot website charge you to put your discount offer in a banner ad? If you're using someone else's service to distribute your coupon offer to prospective customers, enter that service's cost per 1,000 coupons here.

Legitimate redemption rate (percentage of coupons properly redeemed): ____%

What percentage of your coupons are people actually going to use towards the purchase of your product? It may be 100 per cent, but we doubt it. Usually, only a small percentage of coupons are actually redeemed. Often, for under-a-pound discounts on consumer non-durables, just a few per cent of coupons are redeemed. For larger discounts and/or higher-cost items, the rates may be higher, even over 10 per cent. But again, there's no substitute for experience, so if you've done similar coupon programmes in the past, use them as your basis for estimating. If not, well, recognise that you're running an experiment and don't do anything on such a large scale that you regret the results later!

Misredemption rate (percentage of coupons redeemed wrongly/for the wrong products): ___%

Programmes rarely work exactly as you hope. Sometimes the shop assistants or order fulfilment staff apply the coupon to the wrong product. Sometimes somebody finds some way to scam you. If things can go wrong, they will. So build a little error into your projections and make sure that it doesn't kill you.

The problem with misredemptions, obviously, is that you end up paying the face value of coupons but not getting a product sale in return. So the misredemptions come directly off the bottom line. Fortunately, misredemption rates are generally quite low.

Processing costs per coupon redeemed: £_____

If you're using a totally computerised system in which the coupon is scanned or the discount is applied to a customer code number, you don't really have any appreciable processing costs. Your system (or some shops' systems) just processes the things automatically. But most coupons actually end up being handled by someone somewhere, and that handling costs you money, whether you use a redemption service or hire someone to do it. If you plan to have someone do it by hand, estimate how many he can do per hour and work out what it costs per coupon. Enter your estimated processing cost per coupon in this blank.

Other variable costs per coupon: £_____

If other incremental costs exist that we didn't think to include, due to the specific nature of your business, put them here. If not, just enter a zero on this line.

Percentage of these sales that would have occurred anyway: ___%

The spreadsheet calculates the number of sales from coupon redemptions, based on the number of coupons and the legitimate redemption rate you entered. If, for example, you plan to distribute 100 coupons and you anticipate a 5 per cent redemption rate, the spreadsheet calculates that you will sell five units as a result of the coupon programme.

Now, many people just chalk up all five of those units as resulting from the coupons. In other words, they give the coupon full credit for all those sales in which customers redeemed a coupon. But is that fair? Maybe not. What if some regular customers would have bought anyway, but at full price rather than at the discount rate? Then your coupon isn't really bringing you their business.

So in this blank, you can account for those regular users who would have purchased anyway. You do so by estimating what percentage of all redemptions they comprise. Make it a high percentage if you think that the distribution method that you're using will reach lots of regular loyal customers. Make it a low percentage if you think that the distribution method will reach mostly new prospects – such as users of your competitors' products. Make it a zero if you're introducing a new product that doesn't have any regular users.

Profit contribution per sale: $_____

How much do you actually make in profits from each product that you sell? Calculate this number based only on the direct costs of making and selling one unit of the product. That number is the profit contribution per sale, and hopefully it's a positive contribution!

And the bottom line is . . .

When you've filled in all those blanks, you get the answer. In fact, you get a number of answers. The spreadsheet tells you what your fixed costs, variable costs and total costs should be, assuming that your estimates are correct. The spreadsheet also figures out how many new sales you should get as a result of coupon redemptions. Finally, and most important, the programme calculates the total *incremental profit* – that is, the amount of money that your coupon programme makes or loses.

Testing multiple scenarios

Because this spreadsheet has built-in formulas, you can (and should) test many different variables in order to get a feel for the range of possible outcomes. For example, we highly recommend that you test several different redemption rates. Build low-, medium- and high-redemption-rate scenarios. Make sure that the coupon programme appears profitable at all likely redemption rate levels before you run it, because you can never project redemption rates with complete accuracy.

Discovering from experience

When the coupon programme is complete and you have the actual redemption numbers, compare each variable with your upfront forecast for it. Take lessons from your mistakes – yes, you will make mistakes. You can't forecast any coupon programme with complete accuracy. In fact, unless you run very similar programmes routinely, forecasting any programme with even rough accuracy is hard to do! So the name of the game is to discover all you can from your experiences.

Here are some really useful questions to use in debriefing yourself and preparing to design even better coupon programmes the next time around:

- Did you do enough coupons to reach your market?
- Did your method of distribution get enough coupons to your target market?
- Did you offer enough of an incentive to attract new business (indicated by sufficiently high redemption rates)?
- Did you offer more of a discount than you needed to in order to attract new business (indicated by far higher redemption rates than expected)?
- Were your fixed costs higher than you expected – and, if so, how can you cut them next time?
- Were your variable costs higher than you expected – and, if so, how can you cut them next time?
- Were too many coupons misredeemed – and, if so, how can you reduce errors and/or cheating in the future?
- Did processing each coupon cost more than you expected – and, if so, how can you reduce this handling cost next time?

When you look at these specific questions, you're working on the key variables that drive the profitability of coupon programmes. Finding out more about each of these variables and how to control them gives you more control over the bottom-line profitability of your programme. Like anything you do in marketing, experience helps you refine your formula.

Asking yourself: Ah, but did it work?

You need to ask yourself one more question after distributing a coupon or other sales promotion, a question that has little to do with the profitability of the coupon programme: 'Did the coupon achieve my broader marketing objectives?' In other words, did your coupon do one or more of the following:

- Attract new customers, some of whom will become regular buyers
- Help ward off competition
- Boost sales for the period
- Introduce customers to a new or improved product or service
- Support or enhance other advertising or sales initiatives
- Help cushion a price increase
- Help cross-sell another product to existing customers
- Help motivate the sales force by giving them a new sales incentive or tool
- Make your distributors, retailers or other intermediaries happy and more willing to push your product or service
- Help you gain access to greater distribution
- Help you migrate customers to direct or web-based purchasing
- Increase repeat-purchase rates
- Maintain or increase your market share
- Attract frequent switchers – those customers who are always looking for a deal
- Attract a specific attractive segment (or group) of customers with an offer designed for and distributed to them
- Make a profit

As this lengthy list demonstrates, many reasons exist for distributing coupons or offering special deals. Sometimes marketers are willing to run a coupon programme at or below break-even costs in order to accomplish their marketing objectives.

The most important objective may not be to make a profit, but rather to give your salespeople an incentive or tool for boosting distribution. In this case, you may be happy to lose money on the coupon as long as you get greater distribution, because you figure that the aim is so valuable that it's worth investing in. But even so, make sure that you know how much you're going to lose and keep the programme under control.

Some Alternative Approaches to Sales Promotions

Plenty of alternatives exist for your sales promotions, when you want to offer some incentive to prospects but don't want the scheme to be price-based and cost you directly on your profit margin. As with so much of marketing, only your imagination limits the options in this area.

Collect examples of clever sales promotions from other marketers – especially marketers who aren't in your industry and don't compete with you. When you look around at all the ideas people try in the world of marketing, you can often find something that adapts well to your business and industry.

The following sections describe some alternatives that usually build sales or loyalty without costing you as much of your profit margin.

Offering free food

Face it: people love to eat, at least if the food is good, the location is pleasant and the company is tolerable. So put some marketing imagination into ways of using free food as an incentive. We only recommend taking this approach, however, when doing so makes sense for your business.

At Christmas 2008, we witnessed employees of the now-defunct Zavvi music store handing out free curries to try and encourage sales, but as no direct link exists between curry and CDs, we doubt the offer did them much good – which may seem obvious, as they're now out of business. Try making the food you offer relevant to your product offering; so if you're a travel agent having a special promotion on holidays to Mexico, why not offer people free Mexican food to get them in the mood? If you're a bookshop and have a special push on cookery books, why not offer free cookery lessons with a chef?

Giving gifts

Maybe you can try making better use of gifts, also known as premium items. Many businesses do. If you're launching a direct marketing sales promotion, how about using 'lumpy envelopes' with interesting, even funny, gifts inside them. The contents can be simple and useful or simple and zany – it's up to you. If your envelopes are three-dimensional, people open them, and almost 100 per cent of them get read – which is way above average for direct mail. Sometimes spending a little more on the packaging of your offer to make it interesting and memorable pays off well.

Offering rewards for repeat business

We highly recommend looking at loyalty rewards programmes. Many businesses are exploring this concept. A loyalty programme can be something as simple as the coffee card that collects stamps each time you fill up until you earn a free coffee, or something as complex as an airline's frequent-flier club, with all its rules and benefits and tie-ins to other businesses' sales promotions.

Or maybe you can find a unique formula of your own. Have a look at the different incentives offered by the most successful loyalty schemes in the UK: Tesco Clubcard, Nectar and the Boots Advantage Card. You can find out a lot about what makes up a good loyalty scheme by checking out the leading players in the market, even if you don't have their marketing muscle.

Files on the CD

Check out the following files on the CD-ROM:

- ✔ **File 9-1:** Coupon profitability analysis example
- ✔ **File 9-2:** Excel spreadsheet for doing your own coupon profitability analysis

Chapter 10

Spreading the Word
with Newsletters

*N*ewsletters are a great vehicle to deliver information about your field in general, or to bring people up to date about your business, product or organisation. Depending on the content, you can publish them monthly, quarterly or yearly. (We like the idea of sending out a newsletter for the holiday season, even if you don't do one any other time of year.)

Like brochures (which we discuss in Chapter 8), and letterheads, envelopes and business cards (covered in Chapter 7), newsletters reflect your business's personality and need to be consistent with the look and feel that you reflect in your other publications.

In this chapter, not only do we share enough technical information to help you create great newsletters, but also we do our best to convince you to treat newsletters as a very powerful and important marketing medium.

Grasping Why You Need a Newsletter

We really like newsletters as a marketing medium, and if you don't currently have a newsletter, we strongly suggest that you consider creating one. (If you do have one, see whether you can make it even better.)

Here are just a few reasons why you need a newsletter. Newsletters are:

- ✔ Relatively cheap to produce (but that's just the beginning of why we like them).
- ✔ Great engagement devices that get people involved and interested.
- ✔ One of the best ways to express your business identity and values.
- ✔ Remarkably flexible – you can use them to convey information, promote your own offerings, share customer testimonials, provide interesting or amusing content, share a funny cartoon and so on.
- ✔ Relationship builders that help retain good customers, as well as attract good prospects.

Best of all, most of your competitors don't know how powerful a well-done newsletter can be. So you have a chance to outflank them on this one!

You have both knowledge and news that may be of interest to customers and prospective customers. Use a newsletter to make sure that they find out what you have to share with them. Think of newsletters as a great way to spread the word about your business, products or services, and people.

Also, keep in mind that *publicity* – editorial coverage about your business in the media – is usually very effective at raising awareness of what you do and building a positive reputation. When you write and distribute a newsletter, you're in essence creating your own editorial content. Therefore, the publicity is in your control, and a newsletter is a good way to strengthen your publicity programme.

You can also use a newsletter to make connections with people. Let the newsletter share some of your personal (or your business's) warmth and enthusiasm, along with the facts. You may hear people talk about *relationship marketing* – a buzzword that generally means building a more genuine, meaningful, lasting business relationship with your customer. In our minds, a newsletter fits in wonderfully with this strategy. A newsletter gives you many opportunities to explain yourself and present the readers with useful information, entertainment and other gifts on the printed page or via email, CD-ROM or website.

When you first think about publishing a newsletter, don't fall into the easy trap of committing to something that's too ambitious. You don't need to publish every month: once a quarter or irregularly (meaning only a few times a year or less) can be effective and easier to accomplish. Start out with a comfortable schedule, maybe quarterly or bi-monthly, and work up to a monthly publication when you have the resources and content to do so. Give yourself enough time to write a good newsletter – and also to continue doing your other marketing tasks.

Be careful in planning the frequency of your newsletter and never commit to more than you can produce.

Examining the Elements of a Newsletter

The following sections describe the most important parts of a newsletter. Electronic newsletters don't always have these elements, but in our view they should, because these elements help attract and hold reader attention.

Masthead and nameplate

The *masthead* is the area that appears at the top of the newsletter. The most important element of the masthead is the *nameplate*, which is a full-width display of the newsletter's name, issue number and date. Sometimes the masthead is made up only of the nameplate, but in more complex designs, a business logo, *teasers* (small boxes of text describing articles inside) or even a teaser photo may be added to the masthead.

The design of the masthead should remain consistent throughout all your newsletters, changing only the date and volume/issue numbers. Consistency in the masthead brings identification to the publication. If you change the masthead, people don't recognise your newsletter each time they receive it.

Mastheads usually contain a nameplate with the following:

- ✔ The name of the newsletter – usually done in a headline typeface – that reflects the nature of its contents.

- ✔ The name of the person or organisation that publishes the newsletter.

- ✔ The date of issue, as well as issue and volume numbers (if you're committed to making the newsletter regular; otherwise, this information can be omitted).

In addition, give some thought to the headlines and any teasers that advertise your articles. They should be designed to integrate into the look of your nameplate but also to attract enough attention to entice the reader into each specific piece. Your nameplate is usually the boldest design element, with the main article headline taking second place to it, followed by other headlines and illustrations.

Readers can look at only one thing at a time, so as you write and design a newsletter, have a plan for the order in which you want readers to look at each element. The masthead is the boldest element, so it is seen first. Make it pop out through bold design elements: large size, big type and contrasting or bold graphics.

The masthead area of your newsletter is important because it announces your intentions and sets a tone for the entire newsletter. Pick a title that draws attention and defines or brands the newsletter effectively and yet keep it short enough that it can be set in large bold type in the nameplate. Figure 10-1 shows an example of a striking nameplate and effective newsletter name.

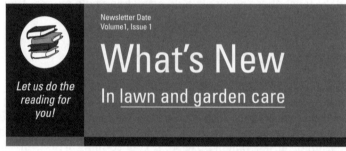

Figure 10-1:
A strong
nameplate
design
draws
reader
attention.

Lead Story Headline

Browse the web and professional publications for article ideas. Always find three or more sources, and digest the story in your own words.

Modules

Newsletters, like newspapers, web pages and blogs, are usually laid out using *modular design*. Modular design divides the available space into rectangular modules, creating a grid into which the masthead elements, the articles and the illustrations must fit.

Thinking about your newsletter's modules helps you to organise your newsletter visually. The rule is simple: as long as you keep each section in its own rectangle, you can combine a wide range of elements. A vertical rectangle may include a headline, columns of body copy and an illustration with caption, for example.

File 10-1 provides a visual illustration of how modular design works.

Articles

The most important article in each issue is called the *lead story*. Give your lead story the most visible headline and more space than any other story – between a third and two-thirds of the space on the front page.

The lead story needs to be extremely useful to the reader or extremely interesting. For example, a useful lead story tells readers how to do something – solve a problem or accomplish a goal, and an interesting lead story shares news or gossip about people and events that are especially engaging to your readers. Similarly, your other articles should also be useful how-to tips or interesting news.

When you decide what articles to include in your newsletter, make sure that you cover a variety of topics. You want to have something of interest to everyone. And make them good journalism, not just disguised sales pitches.

Keeping it short and sweet

Make sure that your articles contain solid nuggets of useable information, such as when and where events take place, what happened (news is always of interest), what will happen (forecasts are always of interest) and how to perform tasks successfully (how-to tips and lists are great).

Also, make sure that you tell stories. Tell who did what, when and why they did it, how they did it and what happened. Insert a photo of the person the story is about, if possible. People read the news for stories and the same is true with newsletters. Include case histories, interviews with people who are telling their stories or simple news stories describing an event or happening.

Write short, to-the-point articles, by which we mean 100 to 300 words. That is very short, as you discover when you start writing. Choose Word Count in your Microsoft Word program to count words and cut text if you're over your word limit. Don't worry too much about making them perfect; short articles don't have to be brilliantly written because they allow the reader to get the key information quickly, so just bang out three to ten short articles and call it a wrap!

You can create articles that are digests of interesting tips, facts or examples you glean from other sources – but if you rely on sources, be sure to give them credit. For example, you can say, 'According to a recent Gallup survey, 55 per cent of . . .' or 'A Feb. 2009 article in *Industrial Engineering* magazine included these three tips for safer workplaces . . .' Also, try to assemble three or more sources, even for the shortest of articles, so that you're truly adding your expert value, not just revising someone else's article.

If you're a poor writer or not confident about your skills, you can hire a writer to do the newsletter for you. Most writers, however, don't know enough about your business to write a really smart, useful newsletter. Therefore, consider writing poorly written but functional articles yourself and then hire someone to edit them. Or work with a writer or publicist who knows your industry.

Our feeling is that you need to manage the writing aggressively to keep it interesting and useful. Otherwise, the newsletter just becomes another throwaway; if you're too scared to do anything that isn't bland and dull, you shouldn't do a newsletter at all.

Grabbing and holding the readers' attention

Design is as important as writing in making an appealing newsletter and building a following for it. Lay out articles in such a way that they capture the readers' attention and invite them to read on. Break them up with new paragraphs at least once every five or seven column centimetres (two to three inches). Interrupt long flows of text with headers, tables, bullets or an illustration. Add a *sidebar* (a very short piece or how-to tip that relates to the main article) to increase the appeal for readers.

Try to use interesting sentences, especially at the beginning of each paragraph or section. If the first sentence grabs readers, you probably keep their attention for the rest of the paragraph.

The best way to ensure that each paragraph and major section of a newsletter article has an engaging and attention-grabbing introductory sentence is to go back and write (or rewrite) them *after* you've written the article. Take a half hour or more just to craft good lead sentences that queue up the content of the paragraph or section. Sentences that stimulate the imagination by asking an interesting question or challenging a common assumption are also good.

Imagine that you're editing an article for a business newsletter that contains the following paragraph:

> *The Divisional Quality Improvement Team leaders got together last week for a leadership training event that included classroom study, a self-assessment of their leadership styles and two hours of 'experiential training' on a high ropes course. The training was sponsored by Corporate Headquarters and lasted for six hours. It took place at Sleepy Hollow Retreat Centre in Brighton, East Sussex.*

The preceding paragraph is an example of the kind of writing that consigns most corporate newsletters to the recycle bin. If you have time, get some quotes from people about how scary the high ropes course was and how it really taught them what true teamwork is all about. Maybe someone overcame a fear of falling about which you can include a personal story. Content can always be improved when you put on your storyteller's hat. But even if you don't have time to perfect this article, you can do a great deal by simply adding good introductory sentences. For example, you may amend that boring article as follows:

> *What lengths – and especially heights – will our volunteer team leaders go to in order to improve their own performance? The Divisional Quality Improvement Team leaders got together last week for a leadership training event that included classroom study, a self-assessment of their leadership styles and two hours of training on a high ropes course. The training. . . (and so on).*

By adding a catchy opener, you greatly increase the rate of readership for that article. If you can work a few quotes in from participants or witnesses, you make it even more interesting. Add a photo and you have a really engaging story!

Headers (like this one)

Headers (also called headlines) should be set in a larger and bolder type than the body of the article. Don't make a header too wordy, but ensure that it contains enough description to invite the viewer to read on. Check out a well-designed newspaper to see how it uses headlines to draw readers in. *The Guardian* is a good example of a broadsheet model, and *The Sun* is a good example of a tabloid.

You can use special headline typefaces for your headers or use bold type from the same typeface family used in the body of the article. Figure 10-2 illustrates some of the headline typeface styles. Your printer is sure to have numerous options, and you probably have some good ones to choose from in your Word library of typefaces (also known as *fonts*), too.

Arial Black

Charcoal CY

COPPERPLATE GOTHIC BOLD

Delta Jaeger Bold

Helvetica Neue Black Condensed

Impact

Optima ExtraBlack

Times New Roman Bold

Figure 10-2: Headline typeface styles.

This book uses a bold italic version of the Georgia typeface for headers. Bold versions of fonts often work well for headers, so keep that option in mind. The last example in Figure 10-2 is a bold version of the body copy font you're reading right now, Times New Roman.

You don't want to use too many type styles in a single publication. As a rule, we recommend sticking to one type style for most or all your text. But headers are the exception. You can try a contrasting style for the headers because it sometimes adds an appealing contrast to the design. You may also want to use a separate font for figure captions. (This book uses Times New Roman for body copy, Georgia bold italic for headers and Arial for captions, for example.) Sometimes it looks good to set sidebars in a separate style, too.

Figure 10-3 shows a header added to a paragraph. Note the impact of contrasting styles and sizes of font.

Use plenty of headers. When in doubt, break up an article with more subheads. People have short attention spans, especially if the writing isn't the greatest in the world. So give them many smaller chunks to read, each wrapped up nicely in a good header.

Team leaders on the ropes

What lengths – and especially heights – will our volunteer team leaders go to in order to improve their own performance? The Divisional Quality Improvement Team leaders got together last week for a leadership training event which included classroom study, a self-assessment of their leadership styles, and two hours of experimental training on a high ropes course. . . .

Figure 10-3: Header and body copy.

Type

Type comes in different sizes (known as *points*). The body of an article should use a clean, conservative typeface set large enough so that you can read it easily – usually of size 10, 11 or 12 points. (If readers are middle-aged or older, 12 point is your minimum.) A serif font style is more readable than a sans serif style.

Serif fonts have the little decorations at the ends of the lines of font, as you can see in the serif font in which this text is written. Times New Roman (this book's type-font) and Palatino are popular and attractive serif fonts. *Sans serif fonts* have clean edges. Save these fonts for headers unless you want a clean, modern look for your text. Helvetica is the most popular sans serif font. Figure 10-4 illustrates the difference between serif and sans serif letters.

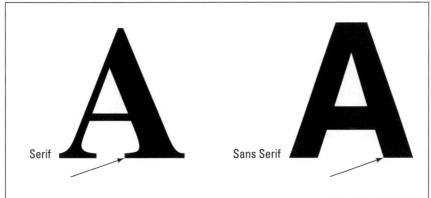

Figure 10-4:
Serif and
sans serif
letters.

Serif

Sans Serif

If the type is too hard to read, you lose your readers' attention.

If you're designing in Word, avoid using Times. The Times font is designed for viewing on-screen, not for printing and it's often the default font. Switch to Times New Roman, which is optimised for the printed page rather than the screen. (This paragraph is set in Times New Roman 10 point; it reads well, doesn't it?)

Never select a font because it has a cool name. Stone is a neat-sounding font, but we don't recommend it for most uses. Apple Chancery looks and sounds interesting and pre-teens like to use it for school papers, but avoid it for business uses because it's hard to read. Also, avoid all fonts designed to look like handwriting, comic book scripts or old typewriters, unless you have a really, really good reason to use them. You have hundreds of fonts to choose from, but most of them are inferior to the classics we mention earlier in this section.

Columns

Use columns whenever you have a large amount of type. The eye may waver and jump from line to line when it has to follow lines of type that go across a full page. If you break up the same article into two or three columns, the line is shorter, so the eye focuses for a shorter amount of time and doesn't get sidetracked.

Leading and kerning

Leading (pronounced *leding*, to save you any embarrassment!) refers to the space between the lines of type. Layout programs have an automatic setting for adjusting the leading, but you can also change it manually.

Adjusting the leading manually comes in handy when you're trying to get just one more line to fit in a particular article. By adjusting the leading to a smaller size, you can scrunch up the lines and allow that extra line to fit in. Type size and leading are usually written in this form: 10/12. The type size appears before the slash and the leading size appears after it (so 10/12 indicates 10 point type is typeset on 12 point leading, hence 2 points separate each line of type).

Kerning, also known as *character spacing*, refers to the space between characters (letters). Like leading, layout programs adjust the kerning between letters automatically, but you can manually override this command, too. Sometimes you need to tighten the kerning in order to fit an article into the available space.

Figure 10-5 shows you the type of spacing that leading and kerning control.

Try to be fairly consistent with leading and type size throughout the publication because irregular type and leading sizes look out of place.

Figure 10-5: Leading and kerning control the spacing of your type.	Leading → The quick brown fox jumps over the lazy dog. Then the lazy black cat crawled under the fence. The quick / Kerning

After you write and lay out your newsletter, check for *widows* and *orphans* (stray words or short lines at the end of a paragraph that end up on their own at the beginning of a line). Also, watch out for sections of words (when they're hyphenated) that are broken awkwardly or misleadingly. For example, if the word 'therapist' is hyphenated at the end of a line into 'the-rapist', you can correct this manually.

You want to make sure that the reader's eye can flow naturally and easily from line to line. Redesign as necessary to eliminate any rough spots where the reader may get hung up or confused.

These rules of good layout apply to all marketing copy, including printed and web ads.

Flow and readability

Make sure that your newsletter flows. If you have to continue articles on another page, don't make finding the continuation difficult for readers. If possible, keep articles together to make reading less frustrating. (And remember to keep articles short – under 300 words. If they're short, you don't need to break up many of them.)

Size

You can publish newsletters on virtually any size of paper. The main determining factor is the amount of content you have (think smaller if you have a limited budget!). Newsletters can range from both sides of an A4 sheet to an A3 sheet that's printed on both sides and folded in half. Or you can add more sheets and staple at the fold to make longer newsletters.

Photos and artwork

As with brochures, you can use photos and artwork to make a newsletter article more interesting and to create an appropriate mood or feeling. *Text wrap* – when text wraps around a box containing artwork instead of stopping above the box and continuing below it – can also be an effective strategy in a newsletter.

For technical information about how to handle artwork, what your options are in photocopying and printing, what screens are, how to handle colour and so on, turn to Chapter 8. We cover these details in our discussion of how to design and produce brochures, and you can directly apply this knowledge to newsletter design and production, too.

If you're desktop publishing a newsletter yourself in small quantities (see the next section), the main consideration for art is your printer. Do you have a good quality colour printer? If so, you can make quite crisp full-colour pages with high-quality photos and other graphics. Just drop photographs into your master document (which you can design in Word). Make sure that your photos are high enough resolution, at least 300 dpi (dots per inch), to print clearly. If you aren't sure about an image, try printing it. If the quality looks fine, it is fine. The proof's in the pudding, as they say!

Doing It Yourself: Templates for Desktop Publishing

As with brochures (see Chapter 8), you have a wide range of options for newsletters, from hiring experts and offset printing (expensive but easy and good for high quantities), to doing everything yourself. Most businesses realise, however, that communicating often with their customers and prospects is important, even when they don't have a big marketing budget, which is where the do-it-yourself desktop approach comes into its own.

So, how can you write, design and produce your own newsletter without spending any money? Good question! We're glad you asked.

The first thing we want to say is, why make the process complicated? Start with a one-page newsletter. Yes, just one page. If you find after a few issues that you're getting the hang of it and want to write more than that, expand to the back page. After another couple issues, maybe you can switch to printing on tabloid paper and folding it down the middle so that you have four pages. But start with one page if you've never written or produced a newsletter before.

Also, why commit to monthly production? Many newsletters are monthly, but that schedule means you have to start writing the next issue at the same time you're printing and mailing the current one. If you have a business to run, creating newsletters takes too much of your time. We recommend starting quarterly. A seasonal theme is easy and gives you a break between issues.

Figure 10-6 shows the top third of a simple but eye-catching one-page seasonal newsletter template. You can access the template in File 10-2, which is a Word document set up for three brief articles. This newsletter uses blue, green and yellow and looks quite summery. All you need to do is drop your text, business name and address into the template and print!

Notice how this newsletter uses two columns, one of them wider than the other and how the nameplate sits above the wider column. This innovation breaks the rule of making the nameplate go all the way across the front page, but rules can be broken in design – only, however, after you think about the exception and make sure that your unusual design really works.

What if it's not summer? Then you have to shop for a seasonally appropriate graphic and shift the colour palate to something better suited for your first season of printing: orange leaves and brown headlines for autumn, a green fir tree for winter or pink or purple tulips for spring. You may be surprised at how a good seasonal design or photograph attracts reader interest.

Date can be put here

SUMMER
newsletter

Your Business Name

Short, pithy tag line can be added right here!

Lead Story Headline

Lead story body copy. Lead story body copy. Lead story body copy. Lead story body copy. Lead story body copy. Lead story body copy. Lead etc.

Figure 10-6:
The banner of a simple seasonal newsletter template (see File 10-2).

Short Article Headline

Short article body copy. Short article body copy. Short article body copy.

Plan to print your simple one-page seasonal newsletter on a colour ink-jet or laser printer; if you want to make more copies than your printer can handle, shop around for a copy shop or print shop with a digital laser printer.

The trick with contracting out for digital colour printing at low quantities (fewer than 500 copies) is to shop for price. Many copy shops charge around 50p a page for good quality colour copies or prints, and that won't do. You ought to be able to get the price down to a third or quarter of that. If you can't, consider buying a colour laser printer with rapid *through-put* (which means it was designed for quantity printing) and make your own. You cover the cost of the new printer in the first issue or two, compared with having a copy shop print a several-hundred-copy run at 50p a page.

If you want to get more ambitious and desktop publish a four-page newsletter, see the editable Word template in File 10-3.

The front page of the What's New newsletter template in File 10-3 is set up for two columns of body copy, which gives sufficient visual interest when combined with the bold masthead design. However, the second and third pages are set up in three columns, which makes for an interesting change when you open the newsletter. Generic photos currently fill these interior pages, which you can replace with something appropriate to your articles.

We recommend that you read the text in the template in File 10-3 because we have inserted a variety of tips and suggestions for how to write a good newsletter. Of course, you replace our writing with your own in the version you create for your customers, but we thought it would be fun and helpful for us to provide some additional advice within the template.

Before you produce (print) your four-page newsletter from the template in File 10-3, please proofread your writing carefully! Amazingly, loads of errors and typos get past your eye the first few times. Read your newsletter over repeatedly and get someone else to proofread it too.

After all the typos and corrections are taken care of, you're ready to check formatting one more time. Is everything lined up neatly and in place? Are any of the articles too big for their text boxes? If they are, the endings disappear, so you need to click and drag the bottom edge of the text box to expand it, or better yet, cut some of the words out of your article.

When you're sure that everything is just right, you have three basic options for desktop printing. You can print the sheets one at a time, just the way the template cues them up, and then staple them. Or to save paper and make the newsletter look more professional, you can print two-sided. In some versions of Word and some printer interfaces, you can automatically print two-sided. The simple way, however, is to just print the odd-numbered pages first and then turn them over and feed them through your printer a second time, printing only the even-numbered pages.

If you want to produce a longer newsletter, simply add more pages that are copied exactly from pages two or three of the template in File 10-3. These pages are the interior ones, so they should be consistent in style. Consider asking experts to write columns for you or look for interesting recent articles and blogs on the web and ask the authors for (written) permission to reproduce their work in your newsletter. Give them credit, and they may be tickled to be included.

Measuring Your Success

You know that your newsletter is a good one if you get positive feedback from readers and requests for copies or subscriptions.

You can ensure this outcome by employing good design plus good writing. To be more specific, the design should be visually interesting with plenty of features to avoid long boring-looking columns of text. Colour also helps. Short articles with good how-to tips, interesting facts and exciting stories also help your newsletter achieve popular appeal.

BROOKLANDS COLLEGE LIBRARY
WEYBRIDGE. SURREY KT13 8TT

If you have an article that seems to lack excitement, look for a short paragraph that can stand on its own as a sidebar (for example, an interesting fact from a survey). Create a small box with its own headline and put the paragraph there. Also look for illustrations that complement the article.

Even though most marketing-oriented newsletters are sent out for free, you can and should build a mailing or emailing list for your newsletter. Communicate with your list occasionally to check that recipients are enjoying their complimentary copies of the newsletter and ask them whether they'd like to request any special topics or have any stories for you to include. (Interviews with customers are a great way to built interest!) Also ask them whether they want you to send the newsletter to any of their colleagues.

Positive feedback from current readers and a growing mailing list are both good signs of a successful newsletter.

Saving a Tree: Electronic Newsletters

We live in a computerised world, meaning that interesting variations to traditional printed products are extremely popular. In this section, we discuss a few of the most common variations.

Emailing a Portable Document Format (PDF) attachment

Many organisations have switched their newsletters from print mailings to email documents, which isn't a bad method if your target readers check their emails routinely and like to receive news this way.

To use this method, write and design the newsletter as if it is for one or more A4 printed pages. Then convert it to a PDF file and attach it to an email addressed to your subscription list. The email subject line simply needs to announce the newest issue of the newsletter so that recipients know it isn't spam and don't delete the attachment before opening and reading it.

By designing the newsletter for a standard sheet of paper, you allow recipients to print it themselves if they want (and many people do if the content is good because having a hard copy for easy reference is useful).

Emailing an HTML page

Another option is to design a simple half-page-size newsletter in HTML as if it is for a web page. Then insert it directly into an email so that it appears on-screen for the recipient. With this method, you get the content in front of your recipients without having to depend on their opening an attachment.

Some people don't like receiving big visual emails – they think you're hijacking their computers – so you have to decide whether or not your audience objects to this approach. Also, many email systems automatically screen out emails with HTML embedded in them, so if you use this method, consider offering it as a downloadable PDF as a backup option.

Sending hybrid emails

Hybrid emails basically display what looks like a banner ad from a web page or, even more simply, a one-line link. When the reader clicks the link, their web browser opens, and they're taken directly to a web page.

Of course, in this way you can deliver your newsletter content on a web page, which opens up the options for design. For example, in addition to conventional articles, you can include high-quality colour photos, animation and even streaming video. You may have difficulty making a text-oriented description of a routine event interesting, but imagine how much more appealing your coverage can be if you show a video of the event on your website with a short caption underneath.

A very simple way to make your newsletter available online is to post a notice about the latest issue on your website with a one-click option for downloading the PDF version of the newsletter. And you can archive past issues and have them available for download, too.

Trying blogs rather than newsletters

Quick now, what's the difference between a newsletter and a blog? Um, hold on, let's see . . . Well, the blog has opinions and editorial content you gather and write in your own words, and the newsletter – oops, so does the newsletter. Well, how about this for a difference: the newsletter is updated periodically, but the blog . . . now, wait, so is the blog. Okay, we give up. What *is* the difference?

Well, actually, we're not sure. In practice, blogs are often more editorial and personal than newsletters, but you can use a blog as your electronic newsletter if you want to simplify (and cut the costs of) your design and production.

Why not do a really modern newsletter that uses a blogging template instead of bothering with traditional printed paper at all? And to publicise it, you can send emails (or hybrid emails as described in the preceding section) with the link each time you do an update – or you can allow your customers to sign up to receive RSS updates. RSS is short for Really Simple Syndication and is an online service that notifies you each time a blog is updated. Search for 'RSS Readers' online for more information or check out *Digital Marketing For Dummies* by Greg Brooks, Ben Carter, Frank Catalano and Bud Smith (Wiley) for more information.

A great thing about blogs is that you can keep adding the new content above the old because endless room exists on the Internet. So a new reader can have access to all your past writing, not just your current news.

Do a Google search for the latest offerings in blog services or check out the following links for places where you can create and publish a blog rather than a newsletter:

- ✔ **TypePad** (www.typepad.com) is our first suggestion because it's easy and offers clean, business-like design templates.

- ✔ **Blogger** (www.blogger.com) is a very simple-to-use system that shouldn't cause too many problems for first-time bloggers.

- ✔ **Wordpress** (www.wordpress.com) is a very easy-to-use system, but be warned that it doesn't accept – in its free form – adverts, so if you hope to monetise your blog, this may not be the best option for you. Or choose to pay for your service and bump up its capabilities.

Mailing a CD

Although not as exciting as blogging, burning a newsletter to a CD-ROM and sending it by mail is another practical and easy option. This tool makes sense when you have a lot of complex content that may be too expensive for a printed newsletter and you have old-fashioned mailing addresses for your customers rather than email addresses.

Don't waste money sending a CD-ROM to people who don't recognise your name. They need to trust you before they dare put a CD-ROM into their computer, for fear of computer viruses.

The CD-ROM can contain your newsletter, in printable form (as a PDF or Word file) or in colour designed for on-screen display. Your CD-ROM can also contain supporting information and materials – almost anything that you can imagine – because a CD-ROM has so much more capacity than a printed newsletter.

Use the CD-ROM to provide more and better photos to illustrate the newsletter. Or put the latest copy of your full catalogue and price sheet on the CD-ROM in folders that readers can open when they need this information.

A Few Thoughts on Logos

We touch on the subject of logos and how to design them in Chapter 7, where we talk about branding. We thought we'd add to that advice here, in the context of newsletters, because designers and writers are often asked to create a dynamic, exciting-looking newsletter for a client whose logo is dull and boring. Oops. Fundamental problem. What can be done?

In our opinion, the newsletter is a good place to experiment with bumping up your visual branding. You can give the newsletter itself an exciting logo and name and you can also consider displaying an exciting new version of your business's brand name in the masthead. We prefer the latter option because the most important marketing goal is to bring fame and fortune to your business, not to your newsletter.

If you try your own hand at masthead designs, you may discover that finding symbols and shapes and combining them into dynamic logo designs is easier than it seems at first. If so, why stop there? Maybe you should revisit your corporate logo or product logo, too. If it's dull, see what you can do.

The simplest way to create a visually appealing branded look for the nameplate of your newsletter is to turn the name itself into your design. Set the name in an interesting font, for example. Or – and this is a trick we've seen used several times with success – make the first letter of the newsletter's name much larger and turn it into a design element.

Although a good graphic designer can certainly do much that the desktop publisher can't do, don't despair if you haven't got a budget for design! All you need is a little ingenuity to create an exciting, well-branded newsletter that draws customers to you and builds your reputation.

Files on the CD

Check out the following items on the CD-ROM:

- ✔ **File 10-1:** A newsletter marked to show how modular design is used
- ✔ **File 10-2:** Seasonal newsletter Word template
- ✔ **File 10-3:** What's New four-page Word newsletter template

Chapter 11

Taking Advantage of Publicity

*T*his chapter is probably the one that small or medium-sized businesses are tempted to skip over, because creating newsworthy stories about your business may seem out of your reach. Don't feel discouraged! Publicity is a very real part of your marketing plan, and it's one that *is achievable* for you. Besides, understanding what publicity can do for your business can save you some serious money in advertising costs.

Understanding and Using Publicity

Publicity tells the story of a business, executive or employee within the organisation. A good publicity campaign results in a positive public image and attracts new customers and makes you a more desirable employer.

Publicity is a special, powerful tool, but it doesn't have to be complicated to do. When you understand what it can (and can't) do, you can add publicity to your marketing toolbox. A little publicity goes a long way toward boosting brand awareness and generating sales leads.

Imagine that you own a medium-sized tool manufacturing business that caters to the car repair market in North London. Growing your business has two components:

✔ Producing the best quality products available (satisfied customers keep coming back and refer other customers).

✔ Getting name recognition to attract a whole new customer base.

Suppose that you place a story in the business section of the largest newspaper (by circulation size) in the region. (We discuss how to place a story in the section 'Pitching Your Release to the Media', later in this chapter.) The story is about the fact that your business just received the most sophisticated machine in the world to produce the kind of tools that garages need.

The first result of this positive publicity is that new customers call you to find out more about what you can do for them. In addition, your existing customers gain more confidence in your products because the newspaper article validates the fact that your business is progressive. Another positive result is that potential employees and current employees become aware of your cutting-edge capabilities and consider you a good firm to work for, and employees naturally want to work for the best.

So, with one carefully placed article, you've increased your firm's name recognition, reinforced that your business is the best and highlighted the fact that you're a great place to work because of your cutting-edge technology. Not a bad result.

Another valuable way you can use this article is to post it on your website and send a copy of the article (with a cover letter and a product information sheet) to new and potential clients. (Note that you need permission from the publication to make copies of the article – but permission is routinely granted to you if the article is about you.) You may even do something as simple as placing a reprint of the article in the envelopes that hold your employees' payslips or your customers' invoices.

In short, editorial coverage creates a publicity-marketing umbrella with which other forms of marketing can't compete. Just think about it: are you more likely to hear two businesspeople saying, 'Hey, did you see North London Tooling's new direct-mail piece?' or 'Hey, did you see that article in *The Islington Gazette* about North London Tooling getting that new machine?'

Publicity versus advertising

We find that people often don't understand the difference between publicity and advertising. Think about the issue this way: advertising is what you pay for, such as posters, brochures, newsletters, billboards, direct mail and advertisements. You write a cheque to produce them and place them in front of an audience. Advertising involves *paid placement of marketing messages*, which is not the case with publicity.

Story ideas

Your publicity programme is a powerful image builder. If you aren't sure what story to tell the world, here are some ideas you can use:

✔ How you have cutting-edge technology

✔ How you have a quality product or service

✔ How your business gives back to the community

✔ How you're helping to conserve energy and recycle

✔ How many awards your business has won

✔ How your business is growing – renovating, relocating and updating

✔ How you're offering summer work experience to help secondary school students

✔ How your management kept the business healthy through difficult economic cycles

✔ How your business has started a new advertising campaign

You don't pay for an interview on a radio or TV programme or for the space a newspaper or magazine uses to write about your business. If a local business programme interviews you or a TV station comes to your business and video-tapes a special event for the evening news, it doesn't send you a bill.

Publicity falls into the editorial side of any media company's business, not the advertising side. Therefore, not only is publicity free for your business, but also it's inherently more interesting and credible than space or time that you pay for.

Publicity is *not* the same as advertising.

Publicity versus public relations

Publicity is not the same as public relations; in fact publicity is a tool that falls under the public relations umbrella.

Public relations, as a function, generally includes all sorts of other stuff, such as how you relate to your community – which may or may not generate profitable publicity for you. We focus on getting you publicity, because that's what you need to promote your business.

Publicity is obtaining free editorial coverage based on factual, interesting, breakthrough and newsworthy information about your business, product or service.

Now, the question is, how do you get that publicity?

When to hire a pro

Many businesses hire a professional public relations company to help them obtain publicity. Often, hiring a good public relations company is a much better investment of your marketing pounds than advertising, but keep in mind that you need to pay several thousand pounds a month for a major publicity campaign. Hiring the professionals is useful, if, for example, you need to target a particular type of trade media where you don't have any contacts or experience. Or if you don't have much time to send out press releases and follow them up, it might be better to call in the professionals than carry out a badly executed job yourself. If that doesn't seem necessary or affordable right now, consider doing a simpler campaign yourself. This chapter covers the essentials of do-it-yourself publicity.

Be newsworthy

To generate publicity, you have to find something about your story that lends itself to generating news coverage. Here are some criteria to determine if your business's story is newsworthy:

- ✔ **Show of progress:** One way to determine whether your business is a good candidate for publicity is to determine if the information you can share about your business, product or service shows progress. Progress is always newsworthy because it's new, and so counts as news.

- ✔ **Local angle:** The closer a story is to people's homes or business, the more important it is to them. In many cases today, so much generic global information is available through the Internet and syndicated wire services such as the Associated Press that the real gem to a reporter, especially a local paper reporter, is a real person at a real business telling a real story with a real local angle.

  To give you the best chance of making it into a newspaper (or in a magazine or on the radio or on TV), you need to do your homework before you approach the media. Specifically, you need to prepare some thoughts and information, and you need to package your contributions to the media in one or more of the forms that they're used to working with. (The later sections 'Developing a Media Kit' and 'The Press Release That Gets You Publicity' look at the forms in which the media like their information and how you should prepare your stories.)

- ✔ **Unusual:** Your business's story is different – not the same old story recycled over and over again.

- ✔ **Timely:** Of course, you want your story to make sense considering the business conditions or the time of year.

By the way, *timely* means that your business is doing something before anyone else. If you're the third firm to send a press release about new ideas for holiday gifts, the media is a lot less likely to pick up your story than if you're the first one.

✔ **Necessary and important:** Your business provides a needed service or is doing something significant for the local or regional area that's *important right now*.

Getting your story out there

The way to generate publicity is to let journalists know about anything that you can point to as having news value because it represents significant progress, has a local angle, is unusual, is timely and/or is important right now.

Sounds easy, doesn't it? I know what you're thinking:

✔ My business is doing lots of great things that are newsworthy.

✔ But no one from the media calls the business to ask about it. Why not?

✔ How is the media going to know what's important to me and my customers about my business, product or service?

Well, nobody in the media is going to cover your business unless they know what's newsworthy about it. Media professionals don't read minds, you know. So you simply have to tell them – but don't send them every single detail of your business operations. Remember to filter what's newsworthy before sending out thousands of press releases. Local journalists won't thank you if you clog up their inbox with lots of untargeted and uninteresting 'news'.

Telling journalists about your business

The idea of you calling a business reporter at the largest paper in your region and telling him about a new product or service you offer, a sales record your business achieved or the expansion your business is making within the area isn't so far-fetched.

And yet most – really almost all – businesspeople never pick up the phone and call a journalist or editor to share their information. When have you ever initiated such a call? What, *never?* Those editors must be getting the idea that you don't like them. They may think that you don't *want* news coverage.

All media professionals need information, and most of them need and want some help gathering that information. The days of the reporter with a notepad, trench coat and hat seeking out a great story are (almost) gone for good. Reporters still have *beats* (specific subject areas), but their beats are probably the largest companies in the area, or an entire market sector.

No business reporter today can do his job effectively without the help of others to keep him informed. And under the 'others' category are professional publicists who work at public relations firms, seasoned public relations professionals who work internally at companies and *you*.

By becoming a liaison with the media, you can help your business accomplish one or more of the following aims:

- ✔ Inform people about how to choose, buy and use your product or service.

- ✔ Persuade consumers to buy your product or service.

- ✔ Counteract misconceptions about your product or service.

- ✔ Get customers in your store or on your website.

- ✔ Get information to the public on issues your organisation is concerned about.

- ✔ Bring people to an event or a series of events.

- ✔ Recruit highly qualified employees.

- ✔ Attract investors.

Because reporters need help gathering information that isn't readily available – such as a breaking story about your business – the chances of your business getting coverage for what it's doing are pretty good; but only if you package the news and deliver it to the journalist in the right way.

Finding good stories is always a problem for journalists. And their problem is your opportunity.

Take a look at File 11-1, which is a press release announcing the launch of a voting period in a global advertising awards ceremony. (We show you how to write a good press release in the section 'The Press Release That Gets You Publicity', later in this chapter.)

This release tells a simple yet compelling story: The Festival of Media Awards is designed to celebrate the very best in media work and the contribution made by great thinking in media and advertising. The award's creators, C Squared, decided to create a People's Award that allowed the media industry to vote for the work that they felt was the best that year. This press release was intended as a call to arms for voters to go online and pick their winner. The release was timed just before the voting site went live, and the resulting coverage from journalists in trade publications was used to drive a lot of traffic and voters to the site.

Developing a Media Kit

Before you write and send your first press release, you have to do some homework. You need to create a media kit to support your press releases. (Some newspaper people and many publicists still call this a press kit.)

If you want to create a physical media kit to accompany a physical press release (as opposed to an emailed one), read on. A *media kit* usually consists of a folder (with two inside pockets) that includes one or several news releases about your business, photographs that relate to the information in the releases, a background sheet with an overview of interesting facts about your firm (such as its history or milestones), bios and photos of your management team and any other information that compiles a complete overview of your business as it stands today.

The media kit serves as the basis of your publicity programme because journalists can always refer to it at a moment's notice for factual information about your business.

The primary purpose of a media kit is to help news people report your story as thoroughly as possible. It saves the reporter's time and shows that you and your business are competent and serious about providing accurate, up-to-date information.

Assembling your kit

To start assembling your physical media kit, purchase some shiny folders from an office-supply store. These folders are available in many colours and sizes. Make sure that the folders are big enough to hold all the information you want to offer. You can insert all your information inside the folder and interchange the information as needed. Some businesses even print stickers for the cover (with their name and address on the sticker) because doing so is a low-cost alternative to printing directly onto a folder.

But why be cheap? First impressions are the most important, right? You can instead choose to have your local print shop create some bespoke folders, including your business name, logo and address and contact details.

If you anticipate moving your office, you may want to print a smaller quantity or leave off your address and phone number and focus on putting your name and logo or a picture on the cover.

You can find many additional uses for this printed media kit folder. When you're not using it for publicity, it makes a great folder to give customers. You can use it to interchange price sheets and information easily. You can also use it as your employee handbook to hold information that employees need. You may even find yourself bringing one to the bank when you visit your loan officer or passing them out at the pressroom at a trade show. Consider the many uses a media kit folder can serve and design it flexibly. (For example, don't print 'media kit' on it!)

Considering using your web page as a media kit

Many businesses choose to provide the information in a media kit to the press via their website. Go online to a big company website such as Google and click the About Us tab that's usually found at the bottom of any home-page. From there you can quickly find a link called Press or Media Kit that takes you to pages showing you the kind of information that these businesses feel is useful to help journalists write about them.

You can easily do the same, putting your media kit information under a tab called Press or Media along with an archive of your press releases. Journalists are often happy to visit your site to pull off the background information that they need.

Increasingly, electronic (email) distribution of press releases is replacing hard copy mailing, because doing so saves time and money in getting your message out, and is more convenient for the journalist and eco-friendly. So a win all round! However, if you want to make an impact with a journalist, maybe by adding a novelty item in with your information, doing so is a lot easier with a hard copy media kit than in the Subject line of an email!

Creating the hook

Now for some bad news. Did you know that most media kits never get more than a passing glance from journalists? In general, media kits don't generate publicity. Not on their own.

You need to find the essence of your story, known as the *hook* – that is, the part of your story that journalists and editors notice after it's sent to them in a good press release. The hook is what's really exciting about your executives, staff, products, services, earnings, special event or milestone. Without a hook, your media kit is just a foundation for generating publicity, and is not news.

Good versus bad press releases

A good press release is professionally typed and printed on original letterhead. If you're using an email version, the same rules apply: ensure that it's properly set out and gives off a professional air – this isn't an email to your mum! A press release includes the name of the contact person, phone number and email address, date and the words *For Immediate Release*. It also:

- ✔ Has a great headline

- ✔ Is double-spaced

- ✔ Is clearly interesting

A bad press release – one that ends up in the rubbish (both virtually or in the real world) – is:

- ✔ Too long

- ✔ Missing a much-needed visual, such as a photograph, which helps tell the story

- ✔ Not newsworthy

- ✔ Too soft or self-promotional (this isn't a sales pitch)

- ✔ Poorly written with obvious mistakes

- ✔ Lacking valuable information that makes the story more interesting

- ✔ Lacking in attention to details

- ✔ Late or untimely

The hook is the newsworthy aspect of your current press release, and it forms the basis of, and helps you to create, your press release.

The Press Release That Gets You Publicity

The best way to decide what your newsworthy story should be is to ask yourself what's new at your business. So, ask yourself now:

- ✔ Have you launched a new product?

- ✔ Did you add new employees?

- ✔ Did you have outstanding earnings for this quarter?

- ✔ Are you expanding in the region?

- ✔ Are you soon merging with a new business?

- ✔ Is it your anniversary?

- ✔ Do some of your employees run in marathons or volunteer for a local charity?

- ✔ Does your business support a youth football team or league?

Whatever your story is, whether you received a new contract with a major client or just received an award, you want to put it on paper (or an email) in the form of a press release.

Because space and time equal money, keep your press release brief and newsworthy. How? Imagine that you're writing a short article for the front page of your local paper.

Getting a reporter to take notice

Try putting yourself in the reporter's seat for a moment. A reporter receives possibly hundreds of press releases each week, often scanning only a few paragraphs of each release and making quick judgements. Your release has to rise to the top of this weighty pile of communications. And the pile is far bigger at larger newspapers, where you may be most eager to get coverage.

Make your press release as professional as possible so that it sticks out in the memory of a reporter. Make it stand out! Here are some of the tricks. Your press release needs to:

- Consist of news that's really news, not just promotional material. (*Newsworthy* means something that represents significant progress, has a local angle, is unusual, is timely and/or is important right now.)

- Contain the name, address, phone number and website of your business. Also, give the name, phone number and email address of the person to contact (probably you) for further information.

- Be short. Yes, short! (No more than one page of A4 is a good guide.)

- Be word-processed and printed on your business's letterhead on a laser printer. If you're sending an email make sure that you take the same care and attention and save the release as a PDF or a Word document, so that when opened it displays the same attention to detail as a physical release.

- Be spell-checked and read over by several different people for accuracy.

We're serious about checking your release for accuracy and professional appearance. In many cases, you're sending it to editors and writers, and they know when a press release is well written and professionally laid out and printed. Have several people at different levels in your business read over your press release. You'll be surprised at what different people may see. The third reader often finds a mistake that the first two missed or adds some insight that nobody else thought of.

You won't believe the amount of badly written, misspelt, untidy and confused press releases that we receive on a daily basis. Bad presentation and errors really do affect how the reader of the press release views your business; if you can't get the press release right, why should they believe that you can run your business to a high standard?

Making sure that your release is news ready

A good press release reads like a news story, which is exactly the point. A good release sounds as if it's ready to be inserted in a paper. Here's how to write one that meets this important criterion:

1. **A good release starts with a *headline*.** A short title at the top tells the media what your hook is. 'Local business agrees to support youth football leagues for five years.' 'Tooling business adds cutting-edge equipment.' 'Authors explain the secrets of generating publicity.' Whatever your hook, start right off with it so that readers get it right away.

2. **A good release has a *lead paragraph* that covers the who, what, when, where and why of the interesting subject that you're sharing with the media.** Then, subsequent paragraphs clearly and cleanly elaborate upon that story with details and interesting tidbits.

   Who, what, when, where and why is the journalist's mantra. Let it be yours when you write a release; otherwise, a story isn't fit for print (or air) until the journalist answers those questions. In a way, you can think of that opening paragraph as providing the *bait* for your hook. And that bait is the who, what, when, where and why that provides a journalist with all the essentials needed to turn a hook into a story.

3. **A good release needs to follow through on the promise of the header and lead paragraph with a few more paragraphs of *supporting text and images*.** Make sure that this supporting text is truly relevant and to the point, not boringly repetitive. Provide some interesting or important background information. Throw in a quote or two from a business representative, if you like. Give some evidence to support your contention that you've actually done something important or unusual or timely. And if at all appropriate, provide a photo or other visual to illustrate the story.

Pitching Your Release to the Media

When you have your press release and media kit ready, you need to make a *media pitch*. In other words, you have to sell your story.

Make your first media pitch by choosing one reporter and trying the process out. Select the main paper in your region and pick the reporter who covers the subject area most affiliated with what your business does.

For example, if your business is an art gallery and is opening a new exhibit, you obviously contact the art editor at your local paper. If your business just bought a huge piece of land to develop over the next two years, find the reporter who covers housing and development.

You may also call the section of the paper that best relates to your business and ask who writes about your specific topic. You can usually find someone who's happy to point you to the correct contact.

Here's a list of some typical speciality areas found at a large daily newspaper:

Art	Film
Books	Fashion
Music	Business
Property	Science
Education	Society
Sports	Entertainment News and Reviews
Events Calendar	Television and Radio
Technology	Theatre
Food	Travel
Women's Page	Home and Garden

Lots of options, aren't there?

Before you approach the most appropriate person, confirm the reporter's name, business address and phone number via phone. You have to be sure that you know who you want to talk to and how to contact him.

Including a cover letter

To pitch your press release, you need to put together a short, clear cover letter that tells the reporter why you think he should write about your business. It can go something like this example:

Dear Doug Smith,

I enjoy your feature article every week as you overview housing and development in North London. I particularly enjoyed your article dated 1 June, 2009, regarding the proposed new library and housing project in Islington. I think your readers will enjoy hearing about the land my business is purchasing for development and our plans. The attached press release specifically outlines our plans.

I have also enclosed a media kit, which gives you background information on our business and a visual rendering of the proposed project. Digital versions of these illustrations can be emailed to you, or they can be obtained in the pressroom on our website. I will follow up with you shortly.

Best Regards,

John Builder

Now you're actually ready to make the contact. Put your cover letter, press release and kit into an envelope (don't fold them!) and send them via first-class mail.

You can use the above example of a cover letter as a template for the cover of your emailed press release. Simply use it in the body copy of your email, but instead of talking about emailing the illustrations to the journalist, simply add these, along with the media kit, to the bottom of the email along with the press release – the journalist then has everything to write your story!

Ensure that you don't create a very large file by adding so many attachments, because it may not go through to the journalist. If size is a concern, highlight the fact that more information is available on your website in the Media Kit section, or let the journalist know that you can email this information if required.

Remembering to follow up!

You absolutely must make a follow-up call. If you want to be successful with publicity, never send anything that you don't follow up with. Four or five days after you send your package, make a follow-up call and talk to the media person about your potential story. You may get voice mail, or you may actually get a live person on the phone. In case you do talk with the reporter on the phone, be sure to have the media kit and press release right in front of you so that you can quickly discuss key points.

If you get voice mail, which is most common, make sure that you've practised a solid voice mail message that goes something like this one:

'Hi, Doug. This is John Builder. You may not recognise my name, but I'm the Director of Marketing at North London Construction Services. I read your articles all the time in the Islington Gazette and sent you a press release that I think is something you can use and is something that your readers will be interested in. As you know, my business has just purchased a tract of land, and the package I sent to you reveals our plans for the land. You can reach me at 0207 123 4567. I look forward to talking to you soon.'

We can't emphasise enough the importance of calling a reporter. Don't be shy and think you shouldn't call because you'll be bothering the person. If you don't bother reporters just a little bit, they probably don't notice you or your story.

Making the follow-up call is far easier when you have something in mind that's worth saying – and that you know the reporter is going to want to hear.

A clever strategy is to offer some significant detail that wasn't covered in your press release (either on purpose or because it wasn't confirmed yet). Then you can feel good about calling because you have another piece of valuable information to share with the reporter. For example, you can amend the earlier call script to include this additional sentence: 'We've just got approval last night from the local planning committee for our plans, so I thought you'd like to know that we begin building next week.' Now the story is timely, and you probably get a prompt response.

The time at which you get the best response from a journalist varies depending on their deadlines, which are different depending on whether the publication is daily, weekly or monthly. Take the time to find out when the journalist's copy deadline is and even ask when calling is best. This way you're more likely to call at a time when the reporter can talk, and also ensure that you're calling in time to get your story coverage. When you know this information, you can make a short reminder call about your release the day before the deadline in case a reporter is desperately looking for one more story to fill the next issue.

Dealing with rejection

When you pitch a story, you're selling your hook to journalists. (See the 'Creating the hook' section earlier in this chapter.) It may not seem like real selling because you aren't asking for money, but it's still sales in that you need to select a target, make an approach, find a way to present your information and ask the person to do something that's beneficial for you.

And sometimes people do. But often, the media ignores you and declines to cover your story, in which case, you need to deal with rejection, just as you do in personal selling. (See Chapter 18 for helpful advice.)

Remember that rejection means nothing to journalists and should also mean nothing to you. Maybe they just don't need your story right now. Or they just don't think the hook is very sharp. Or they don't think the story is very relevant to their area or focus. But because you presented yourself professionally and politely, they're still happy – in fact, more than happy – to see your next release or hear your next voice mail follow-up on a mailing. So rejection doesn't preclude later coverage.

A journalist who rejected you in the past is more likely to cover your business than someone who has never heard of you. Even though a journalist declines to cover a specific story, he or she generally makes a mental note of the source and puts you in a physical, or at least a mental, 'possible sources' file. Your well-prepared, professional letter, press release and media kit earn you the right to be a source of news in the future.

So don't let rejection worry you. You're still closer to coverage than you were before you made the contact.

Creating Your Mailing Lists

Start by targeting one reporter at the largest paper in your area. Pick someone who has written stories like yours in the past and develop a relationship. This person can probably do more for your business's exposure than all your marketing efforts combined. Then build relationships with additional reporters, until you have a good in-house list.

As you build your list you may find that breaking it down into multiple categories, or even into separate lists, is useful. You'll have occasions when you want to make a mailing to a specific type of medium – large local dailies, smaller daily papers, weekly newspapers, trade magazines, local television or radio. Begin by keeping them in separate lists so that you can easily extract them for a particular use. Also, if your geographic areas become larger, you can easily expand these more specific lists.

You may need only one or two lists of a very limited nature to begin, but planning for future lists at this time as well pays off. You get a good understanding of what your growth potential is, and you establish a workable pattern for your lists: how you keep them, the type of information you collect – that sort of thing. As you prepare more and more lists, you can shuffle and combine them for temporary or immediate goals, eliminating the need to build a new list each time you send out a mailing.

The lists you may eventually be building can include:

- ✔ Business hometown media.
- ✔ Branch offices' hometown media.
- ✔ Wire services that have a bureau where your business is based.
- ✔ Daily newspapers (A list: big papers).
- ✔ Daily newspapers (B list: smaller papers).
- ✔ Weekly newspapers (C list).
- ✔ Television and radio stations (with business shows that may cover your business).
- ✔ Trade, professional and technical journals and blogs.
- ✔ Consumer publications (usually national; look for a reporter who covers your subject and thinks you're unique).

Finding the names for your list

Deciding what sorts of lists you want to compile is one thing, but actually creating those lists is quite another. Where are you going to find the names of the appropriate editors, writers and other journalists?

One suggestion is to go to a local newspaper stand in your city and buy all the publications that someone who uses your products or services would read. (You probably read many of them anyway.) You can find out who's writing about your subject and start a print database that way.

All magazines and newspapers print what in the industry is known as a *flannel panel* – essentially a list of the names and contact details of reporters and the beats that they cover. This list is often found on the inside cover of the magazine or in pages close to the editor's leader article.

If you make business-to-business sales, you also want to compile a list of contacts at trade and industry publications. You can always find at least a few publications read by purchasers in any industry. Put those publications on your list. If you aren't sure what your customers read and what professional associations they belong to, ask them!

For radio and television programmes that may offer opportunities for exposure, you can simply go through a TV guide published by your local paper. If you see that the local ITV station in your area offers a business-focused programme every Sunday morning, you know that the producer of that programme needs to appear on your media list.

What? You were thinking Jeremy Paxman, Jonathan Ross, Peter Snow and the front page of the FT? Your business may produce products or services that warrant exposure nationally, but for discovering the process of publicity, we recommend focusing locally to start with. You can use the experience you gain and the techniques you master on a local basis for regional and national publicity. Going to the local media first to gain experience and confidence is far easier. And, in truth, most publicity is local and regional. Over the long run, this media is where most businesses get the ongoing exposure they need.

Opting to buy a list

Another option is simply to order a list from one of the media list-management companies in the country, such as Gorkana (`www.gorkana.com`) or Media UK (`www.mediauk.com`). These companies hold databases of key contacts across TV, radio, newspaper, magazine and any other media you can think of. They are a great repository of media contact information, and if you don't have the time or resources to generate your own media list, you should definitely buy from these companies.

Don't over-send to your lists. Make each and every contact with the media count, just as you want every contact with your customers to count.

Going Online: Web Publicity Tools

Nothing beats studying your market (whether a local area, region or industry) and digging up good editorial contacts for personalised calling and mailing. However, taking advantage of the power of the Internet to supplement these traditional activities is also helpful. Two key strategies are to send your press release to an email list and to post your press release on web newswires, where editors often check for story ideas.

Sending releases to your email list

You may want to use two kinds of email lists. The first is the personal list of editors and writers who have given you their emails and recognise your name when you email them. This list comes from your research and contacts and builds gradually over time. By the time you've done your tenth press release, your prospecting and follow-up calls should have generated enough personal contacts to provide a decent email list.

Use your email list judiciously by writing personal emails only – don't blast generic-sounding emails to your personal media contacts, or they won't want to accept your next email or phone call.

The second kind of email list is an impersonal list of editors and writers that you don't know – yet. However, if you send a short, interesting release to them, a few of them may take an interest in your story and email or call to find out more. This approach is a good way to expand your reach and pick up new contacts for your core media list.

If you're using one of the media list brokers we highlighted earlier in this chapter (in the section 'Opting to buy a list'), they supply email contacts as well as telephone and postal contact information. You can also find commercial sources for email lists, and you can hire a firm to do a bulk emailing to editors.

Lots of media list vendors offer thousands of email addresses for a very cheap price, but they don't sort and check their names very well. Pick a vendor who specialises in business names by title or job and won't send your press release to a generic email list.

Also, keep your email press release short and simple and ask the recipients whether they're interested in future releases and, if so, to reply to you. This way, editors and writers with an interest in your business news can add their names to your in-house list, and you don't bother the rest again.

Using web press release services

For a modest fee, a variety of companies can blast your press release to thousands of journalists. If you have news that may be of broad interest, a press release service is worth a try. At the time of writing, tens of thousands of individual journalists (85,000 globally according to the website) use the PR Newswire service, so you definitely put your news in front of a lot of media people when you use these channels. This service does come at a cost, however, which varies depending on how you use it. Check out (www.prnewswire.co.uk) for prices and more information.

However, keep in mind that most journalists aren't going to be covering stories such as yours; finding an interested journalist is something of a needle-in-the-haystack problem, so getting wide exposure for your press release is important, but not the be all and end all.

Talking it to the street

We hesitate to mention it, but another great way exists to get out there and generate some great visibility for yourself and your business without buying ads or even creating a media kit and press release. That is simply to be a public speaker at events that attract people who may become customers or may lead you to customers. When you speak at a local business club or group or a conference, you're taking your content directly to interested people rather than relying on the media to distribute it for you.

Many organisations seek out speakers including local chambers of commerce, continuing education programmes and large corporations. Don't be afraid to ask to put on a seminar. Be the first to suggest and produce a seminar to pave the way to additional opportunities. Don't forget to record your presentations. You can place video and audio files on your website or integrate them into your email newsletter to secure future speaker engagements. And often, when you know you have a speaking event on the calendar, you can use it as a source of publicity by creating a press release and notifying an appropriate media list that you're making a presentation. Tell them what you plan to speak about, why it's a new or important approach and who the sponsor and audience are. Send out your press release a couple of weeks ahead of the event, but not too far ahead; otherwise, the media forget about it by the time it occurs.

Also, keep your release brief and newsworthy, emphasising information that perfect strangers may take an interest in. Go to PR Newswire (www.prnewswire.co.uk) or a similar service to read current news releases from other marketers. Which of them are most compelling to you? Use those releases as models when you write your own.

Another good way to use PR Newswire and similar services for planning your release is to type in a key term related to your story and read whatever releases pop up. You can then differentiate your story from these stories and make sure that you add a new twist or some fresh news so that your release stands out.

Files on the CD

Check out the following file on the CD-ROM:

   ✔ **File 11-1:** A well-done press release

Part IV
Honing Your Marketing Skills

'In your marketing plan, you said you wouldn't spend unnecessarily. I thought that only applied to your business!'

In this part . . .

Sales and marketing always benefit from the dramatic boost that creativity can give your appeal, so in this part you'll find lots of tips and techniques for harnessing the power of creative marketing. Writing is also essential to almost everything in marketing, from the lowly sales letter to the modern website, so we include a hands-on chapter on how you can make those marketing words and phrases ring out and draw in customers.

Because we're big believers in understanding and empathising with your customers, we start this part with a chapter on what we think of as real-world research: practical, affordable ways to find out what's happening in your industry and ways to stay ahead of the trends. If you want to be a leader in your market, you always need to be sniffing the wind!

Chapter 12

The Customer Research Workshop

*T*he concept behind market research is simple: knowledge about people's needs, preferences and habits can be useful to you as you seek ways to boost sales. Although professional market researchers tend to use highly complex sampling and statistical analysis methods to look for subtle refinements to their advertising and marketing plans, these techniques are worse than useless for the average marketer. Fortunately, simple insights that help grow your sales *are* of value, and this chapter helps you seek and find them.

In this chapter, we cover the best ways to conduct customer research: interviews, customer service audits and experimentation. We also point you to files on the CD that help you with these methods.

Talking to Your Customers

Before you turn to consultants and experts to solve your business challenges, speak to your customers first. Simply ask them a few questions about what they like or don't like about your service and products. Doing so can help you a lot more than the most high-flying – and highly paid – consultant can. This approach is true no matter what market sector you work in and whatever the size of your business.

If you're doing marketing for an ongoing business, asking for customer feedback is your single most powerful technique for planning or improving your marketing activities. Somewhere in customers' heads or hearts is the answer to every question, including how to grow your business tenfold in the next three years. You just have to get that information out of them in order to profit from it.

We go through the example of Premier Inns in some detail (in the sidebar 'Hotel marketing') to show you how asking simple but powerful questions about market trends and consumer behaviour patterns can help you find your marketing zone more easily (Chapter 2 is all about your marketing zone). But if you're not in the hotel business, don't worry. Whatever your business, you can gain some insights that help you to increase sales, reduce customer turnover, raise prices and increase profits.

So how does the type of information that Premier Inn obtained help you to market your business? Well, if you work in the leisure industry – anything from running a B&B to being the manager of a top international chain hotel – customer satisfaction concerns you, and the process undertaken by Premier Inn shows clearly that satisfaction is directly related to both repeat bookings (more business) and also to recommendation (more business again – a friend or family member recommending your business is even more powerful than the best paid advert).

Whatever your business area – the leisure sector, an engineering business or even a high street retailer – you can apply this process to your firm. Asking your customers about every aspect of their experience with your business is valuable information for you as a marketer and helps you to conduct better marketing campaigns.

For example, if you know that your customers value service over price, you can focus your marketing messages on that aspect of your business, instead of getting involved in price wars with competitors.

If you're a small business, you don't need to engage the services of a massive international research company. You know your customers well enough to ask them a few questions yourself!

Why not try getting in one expert who can give your sales staff a training day to help them better understand how to conduct surveys and get useful information out of your customers? They can be provided with a written guide with step-by-step instructions and questions to ask. Role-playing can be used to train them how to ask the questions.

If you don't have the staff to do customer interviews, advertise at a local college or go to a temp agency to find people to carry out the work. Just make sure that you train them and then conduct a mock interview with them to see how well they perform. If they aren't professional and pleasant throughout the mock interview, send them back and hire someone more competent. You can even use work experience people if you really want to keep costs down!

Hotel marketing

The hotel industry is one of the most competitive business sectors in the UK. The loyalty of consumers to certain hotel brands is increasingly important, because prices have become more competitive due to the online comparison engines of companies such as Expedia and eBookers, which offer consumers a view of all the prices on offer at a glance. The Premier Inn chain employed market research to help them compete in this tough market.

Premier Inn previously measured customer satisfaction via a brand-level postal survey, but the company needed to obtain monthly feedback at an individual site level. Therefore, it hired market research company ORC International to help discover more about its customers.

ORC replaced the previous postal questionnaire with an online survey, providing a cost-effective and practical method, particularly given the high proportion of bookings made online.

Although understanding the overall customer experience in booking and staying at a hotel is crucial, in order to improve business performance and profitability companies need to identify the main elements that drive customers' satisfaction and their likelihood to recommend. *Key driver analysis* – finding out what element of a stay in a Premier Inn was most likely to influence a customer to rebook or recommend the hotel to others – was therefore conducted to establish which elements of a stay at the Premier Inn were most likely to impact on the overall ratings, helping the company to determine future priorities.

The research captured opinions from over 350,000 respondents. By the end of 2007, over 1 million guests had been sent an email inviting them to complete the survey (emails were sent the day after their stay to ensure that their views were captured soon after their visit).

Since the survey programme started in March 2006 and subsequent improvements were made to parts of the Premier Inn service, the proportion of guests saying that they 'definitely would' recommend Premier Inn to others increased by 5 per cent. The proportion giving an overall satisfaction score of 'Excellent' rose by 6 per cent, with 84 per cent of respondents giving a positive score. All the *key performance measures* – a set of standard goals that the chain set itself to measure the impact of changes it made, informed by the customer feedback – indicated a rising number of loyal customers who were likely to return and recommend Premier Inn to others. Significant improvements were seen in virtually all the measures, but in particular the staff, breakfast and appearance of the rooms.

If you're going to use your sales staff to do the questioning, the main thing to focus on is that market research is not sales: instead, it's a conversation with the customer that helps you hone your marketing and sales process. It isn't a sales pitch!

All you have to do is ask

Whenever you have questions, concerns or a desire to boost performance, the first action you need to take is to talk to your customers. Customers usually know how to talk, after all, and getting them talking about your product or service isn't too hard. Often, they're flattered that you value their opinions.

Just remember when you're doing research, no matter what your customers say, don't argue with them. Got that? We don't care if their views are based on incorrect information or a false interpretation. You're doing research, not debating. For customer interviews to work, you need to avoid defensive reactions. Act like a dispassionate third-party who just wants to clarify exactly what the customer thinks. Then study their reactions later and decide what to say in your next ad campaign, brochure, blog or sales pitch.

Try calling a few customers and asking them whether they're willing to participate in an informational interview to help you with your research into how to improve your product and/or service. You may be pleasantly surprised at how many of them are willing, and even eager, to provide their input after they see that you're sincerely open to constructive criticism. Most customers feel like their opinions aren't wanted, and they're thrilled to find someone who cares.

Keep in mind that your customers probably don't know what they know, so the research process isn't as easy as just asking them what to do. You need a system, a method and the willingness to sift through a lot of junk information for a few pearls of wisdom or a single startling insight. But doing customer research is definitely worth the effort.

To ensure that you, your salespeople or your temps/work experience employees conduct successful customer interviews, try using the Customer Debriefing Form on the CD (File 12-1), which you can adapt to your specific needs and print multiple copies for use in interviews. Try it. We guarantee you'll discover at least one new and useful thing about your own business when you ask customers to open up and give you honest feedback.

Auditing Your Customer Service

Whether you market a service or a product, every marketer needs to take a close look at the quality of their service. For example, a business that makes and sells products wholesale, for others to sell retail, may seem to be strictly a product-based business. However, as soon as you start asking buyers at stores about their suppliers, you discover that they care a lot about service. When they need to reorder, can they easily reach someone? If a defect exists, can they get help, a refund or a replacement in a hurry? Service matters, even if you think you're in a product-oriented business.

How good is *your* service? A good way to find out is to ask customers for an overall rating of it. Surveys like the 7 x 7 survey in Figure 12-1 (and on your CD as File 12-2) give you an idea of whether customers think that your firm is good, fair or poor to do business with.

Customer Satisfaction Survey

Please answer these questions while thinking about your customer service from

Dave Lane Home Improvement

Scale: 1 = Strongly Disagree   to   7 = Strongly Agree

1 2 3 4 5 6 7 I am highly satisfied with all aspects of customer service.

1 2 3 4 5 6 7 I definitely will make more purchases from this business in the future.

1 2 3 4 5 6 7 I commonly recommend this business to my friends.

1 2 3 4 5 6 7 This business is highly responsive to customer needs.

1 2 3 4 5 6 7 This business's service is faster than typical of the industry.

1 2 3 4 5 6 7 This business's employees are helpful and cooperative.

1 2 3 4 5 6 7 This business is good at solving my problems.

Thank you for your input!

Figure 12-1: An example of an effective customer satisfaction survey.

Surveys like the template in File 12-1 allow you to take the temperature of customer service quickly and easily. If the answers aren't near the top of the scale, you know your patient is ill!

But then what? What if customers don't like you as much as you'd like them to? How do you know what to actually *do* about it? File 12-2 includes suggestions for interpreting your score on the customer satisfaction survey by examining each of the seven questions. If you collect a few dozen or more surveys and then average the scores for each question, you have enough information to compare the scores on each question. A difference of two or more is probably significant. Look at your lowest scoring question and focus on correcting your marketing and service based on the following suggestions:

- ✔ Question 1 is a general customer service question. If your score is 3 or less on question 1, look for the reasons in low scores on any of the other more specific questions.

- ✔ Question 2 measures a customer's future purchase intentions. If your score is low, focus on delivering a quality experience and product, and follow-up after the sale to make sure that users are happy with their purchase.

- ✔ Question 3 measures customer willingness to make referrals. If low, focus on boosting positive word of mouth by raising overall quality and, in particular, by making sure that you notice any problems or critical incidents and resolve each one positively.

- ✔ Question 4 measures your responsiveness to customers. If low, make sure that you recognise and react to customer requests, complaints or problems quickly and visibly. Also train service employees to demonstrate more empathy (sympathetic listening skills).

- ✔ Question 5 measures service speed. If low, work on handling customer orders and needs more quickly and reliably.

- ✔ Question 6 measures your overall helpfulness to customers. If low, work on providing supportive services characterised by being accessible and available to customers and eager to meet their specific needs.

- ✔ Question 7 measures how well you resolve customer problems. If low, make sure that you have appropriate processes for identifying and resolving complaints or customer concerns, including ways of compensating customers for service interruptions.

The customer satisfaction survey asks questions about six specific components of customer happiness. Any one of them can sabotage your customer relationships and cause customers to complain and, eventually, to leave you. The survey helps you identify what specific problem is bothering your customers. We can't tell you what to fix – only your customers can. Your customers have specific expectations about you that you need to explore and understand.

Review the sample survey on your CD (File 12-3) and consider printing and handing out copies to a few dozen customers. You may need to offer them an incentive to complete it, such as a special gift or a discount on their next order, but the cost is often worthwhile to find out what problems they see in your service.

UPS, like other delivery companies, traditionally assumed that speedy delivery was the key to success. Competitors competed on speed, and customers always said they valued speed and were upset when packages came late. So UPS understandably focused on speed. Their drivers raced in and out of offices and up and down driveways trying to beat the clock.

Then UPS talked to some customers who said they thought the drivers were in too much of a hurry to be friendly or helpful. Customers said they wanted drivers to stop long enough to answer questions and give advice. This response revealed an entirely different dimension of customer service that the company had ignored in its quest for speed.

When the company bigwigs realised that the drivers' friendliness and helpfulness were important to customers, they changed the company's approach. The company gave new instructions to its drivers and gave them permission and training to provide more in-the-field customer relations and advice. Customers were much happier when the drivers took time to talk with them, and customer loyalty increased.

Performing a customer service review

Probably 25 per cent or more of your customers aren't too happy with your product or service. And you won't know most of their concerns unless you look for them because less than 5 per cent of unhappy customers complain. The other 95 per cent are like the sunken part of an iceberg: they're a serious hazard to navigation, but nobody can see them – except maybe other customers. People are about five times more likely to tell others about bad experiences than about good ones. So those hidden grumblers are spreading the bad word without your knowledge. Time to find out what's troubling them.

How are you going to get to the bottom of hidden, complex customer attitudes toward your service? An audit is the best approach. A *customer service audit* uses a survey to explore the specifics of what customers want and how well they think you deliver what they want.

Here's a five-step process for performing your audit:

1. **Identify specific attributes of customer service, such as speed, friendliness, convenience, availability or quick response times on complaints.**

   In other words, break down customer service into as many components as possible so that you can get specific in managing them.

2. **Ask customers how important each specific attribute of service really is.**

Some aspects of service are more important than others. And when you know what your customers value most, you know where to put your efforts so that you can do the most good.

3. **Ask customers how well your service performs on each of those specific attributes.**

Do they think your business is doing well or not?

4. **Think about the responses.**

Specifically, look for gaps between customer priorities and your product/business's performance. If you're performing less than wonderfully on your customers' top-priority service attributes, you'd better work on those areas right now. If you're doing wonderfully on issues that they rank as low priority, you can slack off a bit in those areas, which can give you room to improve on their higher priorities. So think about what changes you can make to better match your service performance to your customers' service priorities.

5. **Make changes.**

Often, surveys and analyses like this one end with a nice report or to-do list. To make your audit pay off, you actually have to *make some changes* in how you deliver your customer service. So create an action plan and then remind yourself to check on your execution next week, next month and so on until you see real, lasting improvements in high-priority service specifics.

Using the audit template

Figuring out what to ask customers is the hardest part of doing a good customer service audit. This task seems easy, but don't be deceived. If you just ask customers about the obvious issues, you may miss something important! So take plenty of time to brainstorm a long list of specific aspects of customer service. Then ask a few customers whether you've covered everything and add any ideas that they suggest.

The start of every great customer service audit is a thorough, detailed list of what good customer service comprises. When you have yours ready, place it where everyone who interacts with customers can see it routinely! Also, put it in your next marketing plan along with action steps on how to improve on all the items on the list.

Here are some candidates for good customer service, taken from a variety of businesses and industries, to get you started:

✔ Answering the phone quickly

✔ Apologising for delays

✔ Being available when needed

✔ Being consistent and predictable

✔ Being creative at problem solving

✔ Being reliable

✔ Billing accurately

✔ Friendliness of personnel

✔ Getting a job done right the first time

✔ Helping to solve problems

✔ Honouring frequent-user offers fairly without tricky small print

✔ Informing customers quickly and fully about problems

✔ Keeping things neat and clean

✔ Making up for mistakes or delays with offers of real value

✔ Matching competitors' capabilities

✔ Matching competitors' prices

✔ Not arguing over who's responsible

✔ Not pestering with irritating sales pitches

✔ Not stuffing bills with junk-mail advertisements

✔ Not using rude letters to collect bills

✔ Not using rude phone calls to collect bills

✔ Performing only the necessary work

✔ Performing only the requested work

✔ Politeness of personnel

✔ Product/service ready when promised

✔ Product/service made convenient for customer

✔ Prompt warranty work

✔ Providing frequent-user benefits

✔ Providing loan equipment when your customer's is being repaired

✔ Providing useful information

✔ Reminding customers when their products need maintenance

✔ Reminding customers when they need supplies

✔ Responding fairly to complaints

✔ Responding quickly to complaints

You can copy this list, employ the similar one on File 12-3 or make up your own. Then ask a few customers to look at your list and tell you if it describes the issues they care about. Encourage reviewers to point out any issues that may be missing; using their feedback is a good way to get the most complete list possible.

After you have a good long list, you can prepare a survey and systematically ask as many customers as possible to respond to it. A basic survey should look like Table 12-1, whether you plan to fill it in yourself or have your customers do it.

Table 12-1	Customer Service Survey	
Customer Service Element	*How Important Is It?*	*How Do We Do on It?*
Politeness of personnel	__not important	__poor
	__slightly important	__fair
	__important	__good
	__very important	__excellent
Getting job done right the first time	__not important	__poor
	__slightly important	__fair
	__important	__good
	__very important	__excellent
Apologising for delays	__not important	__poor
	__slightly important	__fair
	__important	__good
	__very important	__excellent
Prompt warranty work	__not important	__poor
	__slightly important	__fair
	__important	__good
	__very important	__excellent

Customer Service Element	How Important Is It?	How Do We Do on It?
Not arguing over who's responsible	__not important	__poor
	__slightly important	__fair
	__important	__good
	__very important	__excellent
Things ready when promised	__not important	__poor
	__slightly important	__fair
	__important	__good
	__very important	__excellent

Surveying successfully

The key to performing the survey successfully is to ask a lot of customers the questions and use an efficient method that allows you to talk to your customers as easily and quickly as possible.

If customers are willing to fill in a written survey and return it, let them do so. (Your response rate improves if you offer a gift, such as a coupon, pen set or something relevant to your business, as a reward.)

Sometimes, though, customers don't pay much attention to written requests, in which case, you need to ask them in person, by email or over the phone to answer some questions for you.

Face-to-face interviews in which you explain that you're auditing your customer service and then ask customers to rate each statement while you fill in the form get reasonably high participation rates. (If you're too busy to do face-to-face interviews, consider recruiting students or temps.) Telephone requests in which you ask the same questions have somewhat lower response rates than face-to-face interviews. Email requests (if personal) get moderate response rates. Mail requests get the lowest response rates.

If you aren't sure which method works best or whether a particular method of administering the survey may be biased in some way, try two or three different methods. Collecting a good number of responses is key. And be polite, always explaining who you (really) are and why you need the information (to improve your business's service), and always get permission to ask them some questions. Then at least you don't make any enemies, even if they decline to participate.

What constitutes a lot of responses depends on your requirements. How many do you really need? Statistically, survey research firms often want to get several hundred or more responses, but then they want to do fancy statistics in which they chop up the responses into little subsets by cross-referencing one response against another, so they need big starting numbers. You probably don't. A dozen responses tell you something useful. Two or three dozen responses give you more certainty that the results accurately represent your customers. Don't be obsessive about getting responses; just get as many as you can in a few weeks of effort, at most.

Analysing the results

When analysing the results of a customer service audit, look for discrepancies between the first and second ratings: the first rating is the importance to the customer and the second rating is how good your business is. Here are a few key points to remember:

- ✔ If your business is doing well on an important service attribute, you can leave well enough alone.

- ✔ If your business is doing poorly on an important service attribute, you need to improve your performance on it right away.

- ✔ If your business is doing well on an unimportant attribute, consider putting less effort and resources into it so that you can emphasise a more important attribute instead.

Often, you find that you're putting lots of energy into something that isn't too important to your customers and not putting enough energy into something else that really matters to them. For example, in the case we describe in the preceding section, UPS had been focusing only on speed, not on helpfulness and friendliness. Table 12-2 shows some sample results of these ratings.

Table 12-2	Sample Results and Display Format	
Customer Service Element	*Average Importance*	*Average Performance*
Politeness	3	4
Right the first time	4	2
Apologising for delays	3	4
Prompt warranty work	2	4
Not arguing	4	3
Average Scores	3.2	3.4

This table illustrates the common problem of over-performing on some elements of customer service and under-performing on others. Note that we give each rating a number from one to four using the following conversions.

1 = not important	1 = poor
2 = slightly important	2 = fair
3 = important	3 = good
4 = very important	4 = excellent

That way, comparing the results on each item is easier. If your performance rating is equal to or above the importance rating, well, you don't have any trouble on that element. But if your performance rating number is below the importance rating, this result suggests that you need to make the item a higher priority.

Using numbers also permits you to average each customer response and compare your overall performance rating with an overall importance rating for all the elements you tested.

This mathematical exercise is helpful, but don't let it blind you to item-by-item problems and opportunities to improve. In the example in Table 12-2, you can see that averages can be deceptive. Performance averages higher than importance. Does this high-performance rating mean everything's fine? Not at all! The higher average performance rating suggests that the firm is putting too much effort into some items: it's over-performing in areas where performance isn't very important to customers.

If you get a high average performance rating combined with over-performance on the most important service elements, you're in a position to celebrate. But as long as you see under-performance on any important elements, you know you have an opportunity to improve your service.

Using Experimentation as a Research Technique

You don't always have to do a survey or ask customers for input in order to do good research. Sometimes all you have to do is carefully track what you do and what happens.

This approach is the scientific method applied to marketing. For example, a business that sends catalogues to people on their mailing lists is always testing different designs and methods. Is putting the colour-printed catalogue in a brown paper mailing sleeve or letting the colour cover show better? We don't know, but if you send some catalogues one way and some the other and then compare the response rates, you'll find out in a hurry.

The first step in using a scientific approach is to identify your marketing variables. *Marketing variables* are any aspects of your product, service or marketing communication that you can control and change and that may affect results. Variables for a mailing include the size of the envelope, whether it contains a customised (personal) cover letter and whether it has a special time-sensitive discount offer.

After you determine your marketing variables, start varying them and tracking the results to see what works best.

We don't know exactly what your marketing variables are or what combination and approach is going to boost your sales most effectively, but we do know that you can find out, if you take a scientific approach and are willing to experiment. Every business has its own successful, but unique, set of marketing formulas. You're responsible for doing the research and experimentation necessary to find your own formulas. If you always take an inquisitive approach, you'll find and polish your own winning formulas.

Files on the CD

Check out the following items on the CD-ROM:

- ✔ **File 12-1:** Customer Debriefing Form (template)
- ✔ **File 12-2:** 7 x 7 Customer Satisfaction Survey
- ✔ **File 12-3:** Customer Service Audit (template)

Chapter 13

The Creativity Workshop

● ●

In This Chapter

▶ Understanding how creativity affects the Five Ps of marketing

▶ Being practical and yet creative at the same time

▶ Getting your creative juices flowing to come up with profitable marketing ideas

▶ Leading a creative project or team effectively

● ●

*Y*ou can't succeed without the new, no matter how much you're in the marketing zone. And producing the new is where creativity comes in. Whether it's just a new, fresh set of direct mail, advertisements or blogs to keep attention high, or a major rethinking of your product line or distribution and pricing methods, you certainly need to be doing something new. Every good marketer's mantra needs to be: 'What's next?'

In this chapter, we clue you in on just how important creativity is to marketing success, and we show you how to spur your creativity when you're stumped for more ideas. We also give you advice on how to manage a creative team or project. Although managing something creative may not be your core strength, you can still find out about and practise it. And you won't be on your own – creative teams can be drawn from anywhere in the organisation, from distribution to graphic design. Your job as the marketer is to become an expert in managing their ideas and the creative process.

Creativity's Impact on the Five Ps

A good way to think about your marketing activities is to create a chart in which the left-hand column is labelled Old and the right-hand column is labelled New. In the Old column, list every element of marketing that you're doing at the moment. Hopefully, a number of things you do work well enough so that you don't have to change them right now. In fact, if you're in your marketing zone (which we describe in Chapter 2), quite a few things should be working well and don't need to be thrown out. Highlight the good items in the Old column – and cross out the ones that are outdated, so you can shift resources to something new and better.

Now you need to list some things in the New column of your table, and that's where creativity enters the picture. When you want to benefit from creative thinking, framing the project using the Five Ps can be helpful (flip to Chapter 2 for all about the Five Ps). This approach gives your efforts some structure. Try creating subheadings for the Five Ps – product, price, placement, promotion and people – down the side of the sheet and across the Old and New columns. In the next five sections, we discuss creativity for each of the Five Ps.

We tell you lots of stories about creativity in the following sections because getting inspiration from others is often the easiest way to get your own creative juices flowing. Collecting your own examples of creativity is also a good idea.

Product innovations

Products often come to life as a result of creativity. To see the power of creativity, all you have to do is think about the products that you use every day. Look around you right now and ask yourself how many of these products existed ten years ago. Where was the iPod? Even the Blackberry phone was just a pager ten years ago. Spotting dozens of new ideas with just a quick glance around is easy to do.

New products and clever variations on old products are the bread and butter of marketing. Some are made possible by new technical breakthroughs, but many product innovations have nothing to do with technology. Sometimes the innovations are fresh combinations or forms of traditional products and services. For example, leasing used to be available only for big companies that ran fleets of trucks or cars. Then someone had the bright idea to offer leases to car buyers, and he created a new kind of product – a car lease.

The example of leasing cars involves an innovation in how to price a product – in fact, it uses a new form of pricing to change the product. Therefore, this innovation creates a hybrid model because it affects two of the Five Ps in combination. Creativity often defies categories, and that's okay. Where do you think that terrible management-speak phrase comes from: people were 'thinking way out of the box' when they invented products such as the iPod, Blackberry, Post-it notes or even the online auction site eBay.

Perhaps you don't manufacture any products yourself but run a business that resells products made by other people. If so, the way to be creative about products is to 'shop out of the box'. Find a new, exciting supplier who's making something unusual. Be the first to introduce a new product line.

Pricing innovations

Price-oriented creativity is at the heart of thousands of discounts, coupons and other special offers. We recently attended a fundraising rally at a local school. Instead of offering us the usual raffle tickets to win a prize at the end of the evening, everyone was handing out the details of a website called Yellow Moon. This gift website offers discounts to shoppers, and when they buy, a certain amount of cashback goes to the school. Although people may hand over small amounts of donations on the day of the rally, by simply buying gifts (which they would have bought anyway) at Yellow Moon, the school can keep benefiting for months or even years afterwards.

Sometimes you can make creative changes in when or how people pay rather than in how much they pay. For example, think of the model operated by low-cost airlines. Before the likes of Easyjet and Ryanair appeared in the UK, the price of a seat on a plane was generally fixed. Trains had long run various advance prices rewarding early bookers, but flights tended to have a single cost. Whether you were buying a seat two weeks before the flight or on the day, it was the same fee for the service.

But then the low-cost airlines developed a charging method that meant those people booking early got cheaper prices whereas those booking on the day paid more. Some airlines even varied the price depending on popularity; if some flights were filling up slowly, fares were lower but those going fast were more expensive. Now many different industries use the same model, and most people accept that if they book in advance, they're likely to get a better deal.

Here's an example of a price promotion from the National Maritime Museum in Cornwall that may inspire you. Museums can't live on ticket sales alone; they depend on people buying more expensive annual memberships. So the National Maritime Museum has a marketing programme that offers visitors taking out an annual membership during their visit a refund on the ticket they bought for that day. Usually, some people take this offer up, keen to get a free visit alongside the membership, and the museum wins new supporters this way. Can you use a similar strategy to upgrade customers to more expensive or long-term purchases? We recommend spending a half hour brainstorming at least 20 ideas for how to achieve this goal in your business. Then take the best one and see what happens when you implement it.

Placement innovations

Placement is where and when you present your product or service to customers. For example, if you're a food or drink brand, most people can easily find you sitting on the supermarket shelf. If you're a shampoo, it stands to reason that you might be available in a chemist. But if you want to surprise potential customers or appeal to them in a more exciting and alluring way, you may need to innovate with your placement. Appearing somewhere unexpected or original can make a big impression with prospects and convince them to try your product or service.

Many of us have at one time or another stayed in an upmarket hotel and wanted to take home the gorgeous sheets, toiletries or art that we experience during our stay. Hotel groups have caught on to this desire, and many now have physical and online catalogues from which their guests can order the same luxuries to take back home.

For example, if you love the woven stripe sheets at the Hilton, you can log onto the website www.hiltontohome.com and pick up a set for your own bed. Or if you've stayed at the Radisson hotel chain, you may have your eye on its toiletries, which you can buy from www.radissonguestboutique.com.

This type of merchandising is a little touch that makes people feel as if they can buy into the luxury lifestyle but at almost no cost to the hotel, which buys these items in bulk anyway. You don't expect to find hotels in the catalogue business, but the idea seems to work.

Placement innovation can work even if you're not a big brand. If you're an artist in the UK, for example, you've probably already built your own website, so interested buyers who know your name can see your work. You may even have a physical gallery showing your work. But if you're only doing this part-time or you don't have a lot of time to carry out larger promotions, a community art site is a good bet. Community sites enable you to post up your work so that interested people who're searching for art can find the images they like, even without being aware of the artist. The site essentially markets your work with very little effort on your behalf.

To see community sites in action, go to www.apob.co.uk and visit the community art galleries featuring more than 2,000 artworks.

If you're a relatively small-scale marketer, look for ways to take advantage of group websites. They're the shopping centres of the Internet, bringing you into contact with many more prospective customers than you can afford to attract all by yourself.

What's the future of distribution in your business? Can you think of some ways to take costs out or reach more customers more conveniently? Creative placement is often behind the best business plans and the biggest profits.

Promotion innovations

What you name a product and what you say about it can make or break your business plan. Promotional creativity is the most important and attention-getting form of creativity in business. Turn on any TV, and every time a show breaks for commercials, you can see dozens of examples of efforts to make promotions creative. You may not have the budget to do creative television advertising, but you can apply the same kind of creative thinking to whatever you can afford to do.

For example, take the simple brochure, something almost every marketer uses. Does your brochure cover stand out and catch the eye? If not, apply your creative thinking to the challenge of making it more notable. A strong new photograph, a catchy headline or an interesting shape or size can set your brochure apart. (See Chapter 8 for details on how to design a good brochure.)

What about your ads, business cards and signs? Are they creative? Hmmm. Signs are an interesting challenge because if they get too creative, they can put people off and be hard to read. Your brand image needs to constrain your creativity. Tie the creative concept to the business so that the look and match is a good one. For example, a tax accountant shouldn't use a bright orange hot air balloon full of clowns as his new logo. Something more cautious and conservative is better – how about a firm-jawed sea captain, his hand steady on the wheel of his ship?

Also, look for creative ways to get your message in front of people. Take, for example, an agency in London that's renting forehead space for logos (so now you see a company logo on people's foreheads as they walk around town). A bit crazy? Yes, but many good ideas seem that way, at least at first. Or how about the strategy of renting spaces for a new car model in front of the finest restaurants in order to get it in front of prospective drivers? Maybe these ideas don't work for you, but see whether they inspire you to try something new that *does* fit your business. For example, if you've never tried them, consider having some nice fridge magnets made up as giveaways. People use them, and it's nice to have your business name and contact information in people's kitchens.

Or how about T-shirts? If your customers wear them, try giving away an appealing design that has a subtle, attractive brand image or marketing message on it. People wear your marketing message if you make it attractive enough. If you aren't sure how to make a T-shirt design that's appealing and fashionable, ask your daughter or any teenage girl who cares about fashion. You won't be alone in adopting this strategy; many large companies use panels of teenagers to help them find out what's hot and what's not. (See *Marketing For Dummies, 2nd Edition* by Greg Brooks, Ruth Mortimer, Craig Smith and Alexander Hiam (Wiley) for lots of ideas and information about creative ways to use signs, banners, flags, T-shirts and other silk-screened products, such as bags.)

People innovations

Here's a wild and crazy idea: how about taking turns answering the phone live and not allowing it to go to a computerised answering system? In this age of computerised phone systems, having real live knowledgeable, friendly people answering customer calls is a radical idea. So few businesses offer this service today that it may give you a real competitive advantage.

Another way to innovate is to think of times and places where you can meet customers and prospects in person. Can you attend an event or conference that would expose you personally to good prospects? Can you have some kind of party that draws in customers and prospects?

Also give some thought to finding new people to help you sell. Personal selling can be very effective, but finding the right sort of salesperson is tricky. Someone who's been in your customers' shoes is probably better than someone who's a professional salesperson but doesn't know your industry inside and out. Being able to identify with and talk shop to prospective customers is probably the key to good salesmanship. In most cases, doing so works better than high-pressure sales techniques.

When, where and how you have people interact with customers is a very important part of your marketing. You can do it innovatively and well, or you can do it poorly. The difference between a bad server and a good one determines whether or not you go back to the restaurant a second time. At Pret a Manger food stores in the UK, the staff are encouraged to be friendly. Sometimes they even offer regular customers a free coffee or drink if they're loyal to the brand. It doesn't happen all the time or cost the firm a fortune, but it spreads a little bit of goodwill that keeps people buying there.

People can be your most important and valuable asset – but only if you can find ways to connect them meaningfully with your customers. Spend time thinking about how you and others can make more and better human contact with existing and future customers. Throw a party. Go to a convention. Make a sales call in person. Ask a happy customer for a referral. Put your staff in fresh new uniforms. Many creative ways exist to harness the power of people in your marketing.

Being Creative but Also Practical

In business, we find that creativity needs to be a cyclical activity, not a continuous one. After you come up with and introduce a creative idea, you often need to repeat and perfect it, milking it for profits before doing the next creative thing. In marketing, perfecting an idea may mean testing several new creative magazine ads, discovering that one of them seems to *pull* (generate leads or sales) especially well, and then repeating the ad for the rest of the year or until consumers finally grow tired of it and stop responding well.

Being creative takes effort and money. A new idea for an ad or brochure requires someone to design and print it, which involves time, effort and usually money. So focusing your creativity where it can do the most good is important. Creativity helps you find your marketing zone. Then, when you prove the concept works, keep doing it with only minor variations for as long as it continues to be successful.

Harnessing your creativity for profit

The pure artistic approach to creativity is just to be as creative as you can for the pure joy of it. In marketing, you usually have some practical objectives – although creativity should also be fun, because you can't come up with winning creative ideas unless you're in a good mood and are relaxed enough to free your imagination. A good way to keep creativity fun but also profitable is to decide what your creative goals are, and then be creative within the discipline of your business goals.

For example, you may think that the time's come to do some brainstorming for ideas, but don't ever run a completely unstructured session; always start with a clear strategic goal, such as:

- Thinking of ways to freshen up an aging product
- Coming up with attention-getting ideas for a new promotional event
- Improving the business's website or printed brochures
- Designing a fun and effective new trade show booth
- Thinking of a better new logo and tag line to use on the business's letterhead and in advertising

Each of these topics can provide the focus and purpose to a wild and crazy brainstorming session. Setting a goal for the session is a good idea, such as 100 new ideas for modernising or renewing a product. Focusing on quantity rather than quality is more important for creative idea sessions. If you're only aiming for one really good idea, people self-censor their ideas and aren't as freely creative. But if you say that the goal is 100 ideas – any ideas, no matter how stupid or crazy – you probably get 200. And ideas tend to build on each other, so as the group generates more and more, the quality begins to take care of itself, and you usually get at least a handful of really promising ideas out of the crop of hundreds.

Refusing to get carried away

Our editors asked me to put this topic in. Editors often have to rein us creative writers in and keep us focused and disciplined. You may have to play editor with creative ideas in your marketing, too. An editor seeks the best and cuts the rest. Use this strategy with your creativity.

Sometimes a wonderfully entertaining, creative ad comes on TV, and everyone talks about it. But here's the interesting thing: half the time, people remember the ad vividly but aren't sure what product or business the ad is for. That creativity isn't useful because it doesn't connect the impression the ad makes with what the ad is selling.

To make sure that you aren't getting carried away, stop for a moment and ask yourself whether the creative ad, brochure, web page, event or whatever is in danger of becoming its own product instead of selling yours. Try to avoid the trap of creativity for its own sake. Entertaining or amazing an audience without making any sales is expensive. You aren't doing creativity just for the fun of it in marketing!

Generating Creative Concepts

We use the term *marketing imagination* throughout this book, and this concept is probably the most important factor in marketing success or failure. Your ability to imagine new approaches is vital to your success as a marketer. The salesperson who invents an opener or comes up with a strategy for generating leads is the one who sells the most products. The small business that seeks new ways to promote its products or services makes a bigger impact at lower cost. And the advertiser who creates an imaginative message captures consumer attention and makes more sales.

In contrast, any marketer who fails to be creative or who tries to just use last year's formula or borrow directly from others is destined for failure. Marketing demands more creativity than any other business activity. So it seems only fair for us to help you be more creative in your approach to marketing. In this section, we give you techniques to help you engage your creative imagination and come up with breakthrough sales and marketing ideas.

Revelling in the irreverent

Seek out and enjoy unconventional or downright crazy approaches. Any examples of how people can flaunt the rules of convention are inspirational. Even if they have nothing to do with marketing, irreverent attitudes can inspire your marketing imagination. For example, today's wild teenage fashions end up in tomorrow's high-end clothing lines because most of these designers' new ideas are inspired by teenagers who are trying to break conventions, not make them.

When we're having difficulty suggesting new creative ideas in our work, we like to watch the 1990 film *Crazy People*, starring Dudley Moore and Daryl Hannah. This comedy is about an advertising copywriter who goes over the edge and gets sent to a psychiatric hospital, where he and his fellow patients create such crazy and wonderful ads that his agency ends up begging them for more. The story is silly, and it makes us laugh. But more importantly, it shows that creativity comes from thinking freely and not sticking to the rules, which is a pretty big inspiration.

We recommend any comedy, whether it has something to do with business or not. Humour is based on unusual viewpoints, and it helps you loosen up and find your own creative perspectives.

We also recommend keeping an eye out for crackpots and others who do things strangely on the fringes of your industry. For every successful business, a dozen marginal ones operate outside the normal rules and rarely amount to anything. But sometimes these businesses have the weirdest ideas, and when you combine those weird ideas with a sound understanding of how the industry works, they may just lead to breakthrough insights. So don't forget to pay attention to the crazy people in your own industry. Sometimes they're better at inspiring your marketing imagination than more successful, but conventional, role models.

Forcing yourself to develop alternatives

The quest for new and better alternatives is the essence of creativity. The marketing imagination is never content – it's always seeking new approaches.

We once interviewed a man who developed advertising for a massive consumer goods company. He told us that to create a successful deodorant advertising campaign, he and his ad agency had sat down in one session and come up with more than 100 ideas. His company hoped that it would come up with one good advertising campaign as the result of the session, which it could use over multiple years.

Was generating this many ideas tricky? Yes, but doing so was worthwhile. One idea above all the others got everyone talking at the session, and at first, the company executive wanted to go with this idea. But the agency took away the top ten favourite ideas and worked them up a little into some mock ads. The result was that seven didn't really work very well. The message was too complex, got lost or just didn't appeal.

Ultimately, just one idea stood out as the one that made sense to everyone when the agency tried showing the campaign in different channels, including the Internet, print, direct mail and TV versions. But this idea wasn't the one that the company executive had liked earlier on in the process. If he'd stuck with just that one idea, he'd have lost the chance to find out what really worked further down the line. Having alternatives is always important.

Ensuring that you don't overplan

Most experts tell you to write a careful plan. Marketing plans and business plans in general can help you anticipate the future and make sure that you're ready for it. But they can also destroy creativity. Plans hurt creativity in two main ways:

- ✔ **If you have to write everything down upfront, you don't have the opportunity to come up with creative approaches later.** The weight of the planning exercise deadens creativity. To decide all the year's marketing activities in just one week of planning is pretty hard. And it's certainly not fun. People who have to do that task aren't going to spend much time being creative. They're going to approach marketing in a mechanical way, looking up costs and writing them down one after the other until they fulfil their obligations.

- ✔ **If you have to follow a detailed plan, that plan does the thinking for you, and you miss the opportunity to discover, experiment and invent as you go.** Rigid plans and micro-planning that structure every decision and action are the enemies of creativity. They keep people from reacting and creating.

To make planning creative, leave room in your plan for improvisation. Of course, you face budget limits, and you need to follow broad strategies that you expect to work. But also leave room for modifying the plan. We like to revisit our plans every month or two, and, if we get a better idea, we simply rewrite our plan around it. Your plan is only paper. Throw it out if it's getting in your way and write a new one!

However, make sure that your plans aren't too detailed. For example, specifying that you're budgeting so much for publicity, most of which should focus on generating press about your business activities, is one thing. That example is fine because it leaves you plenty of room to invent clever ways of getting publicity. But planning exactly how you're going to spend that publicity budget is quite another thing. For example, if you specify one press release a month to the in-house press list of 250 names, you've just guaranteed that nothing imaginative is going to happen all year. Don't overplan!

Identifying your personal barriers and enablers

A *creativity barrier* is anything that gets in the way of your creativity. And plenty of things can do just that. Being more aware of those barriers helps you discover how to avoid them or minimise their impacts. Here are some of the most common barriers:

- ✔ **Pressure to conform:** Thinking and behaving differently from others is taboo in many organisations and industries. This approach means that people are more conservative than they need to be.

- ✔ **Perfectionism:** If you worry too much about how well you perform, you may be afraid to try anything really new. Sometimes we remind ourselves that when it comes to creative innovations, 'If it's worth doing, it's worth doing poorly!'

- ✔ **Overconfidence:** Assuming that you're doing the right thing without stopping to question yourself is all too easy. Overconfidence keeps you from examining your assumptions or developing and considering alternatives.

When you know that a creativity barrier affects you, you can guard against it. Awareness is the key.

Creativity enablers are factors that help you be more creative. They work in the opposite direction of barriers, helping you overcome barriers and leading you to creative insights. Here are some of the more common enablers:

✔ **Open-mindedness:** An open, accepting approach to other ideas and methods is a great enabler. If you're open-minded, you often receive inspiration from others that you may otherwise miss.

✔ **Role models:** Creative innovators are great enablers. Try to find and spend time with such people. They can get your creative motor running in no time!

✔ **Persistence:** Perhaps the most powerful enabler of all, persistence keeps you trying even when your initial efforts at creativity fail. Often, the only major difference between highly creative people and those people who aren't creative is that the creative people don't give up as quickly. Do you?

Incubating ideas

Incubation is just what the term suggests. You sit on a problem or idea, keeping it warm, until it hatches a solution. But first, you have to lay that egg. In other words, start by focusing hard and furiously on your subject of concern. Research it thoroughly and bang your head against it over and over all week long. Wear yourself out. Then relax. Time to sit on the egg that you just laid. Take a little time off. Or work on something else. Just stop to have a quick look at the problem or to turn it over in your mind every now and then.

After you let your problem or idea incubate for a while, you may begin to hear from it. It starts to call your attention back to it as new ideas and approaches come to mind. Then, and only then, is your idea ready to hatch. When you revisit the issue and give it your undivided attention again, you may find that you have more and better ideas than you had before.

Because incubation works so well, try scheduling your marketing development efforts to permit incubation. For example, rather than planning to spend three consecutive days writing a new brochure, why not schedule two days to study it and begin work on it, take three days off the project for incubation, and then one final day to complete your work? The result will be more imaginative and better because of the incubation period, and yet you haven't spent any more of your work time on the project.

Breaking problems down

When we get stumped on a project, we use a strategy called breakdown brainstorming, and we've used it to good effect on many difficult tasks. The idea behind *breakdown brainstorming* is to put some creative effort into thinking about the task itself instead of moving directly to formulating solutions.

For example, say that you're working on a web page, and you want to do something creative and special. But what? You're stuck. So break down the task into as many subproblems or subtasks as you can imagine. Your list may include issues such as 'attract people to our site', 'make our site more entertaining', 'create an opening page for the site that really wows people' and 'find a game people can play on our site'. Now you've broken the broad problem of designing a good website into many smaller problems, some of which may fire your imagination more easily than the broader definition of the problem.

Competing with each other

You're more likely to come up with a creative breakthrough when you have two or more individuals or groups working on the same creative task at the same time. So why not create a contest for yourself and a few other associates or friends? Pick a good reward – sometimes a joke reward is best. Give each person or group the same amount of time and the same starting information. Then compete to see who comes up with the best ideas!

Recording more of your own ideas

You often have ideas that you discard or forget. If you get in the habit of recording more of your ideas, you may find that some of them are more valuable than you thought. Also, your marketing imagination becomes more active when it gets attention. By simply making notes or recordings of your ideas, you stimulate their production and soon generate many more.

We record ideas in several ways. We keep notebooks in which we write down any good ideas that come to mind as and when they emerge. We can then flip back through the pages if we're trying to find a new idea and pick one for more exploration. We also keep files of interesting articles or clippings (as well as bookmarks on our web browsers) to spark off thoughts when we need them.

Come up with your own system for recording ideas. Whatever works best for you is the right one, so try several. Or you can enlist others in your quest for ideas. You may want to provide everyone in your business with an idea journal and reward the best ideas with an award every month or quarter.

Looking hard at your assumptions

Many smaller businesses assume that TV advertising is too expensive for them. That's a silly assumption. You can buy local television advertising very cheaply in most markets, and you can even find relatively inexpensive national cable ad slots. We're not saying that all businesses ought to advertise on TV, but some certainly can and don't realise it because of their assumptions. In a recession, many media owners are cutting the price of their advertising space, even the big TV channels, so with some negotiation perhaps you can afford it after all.

All marketers make assumptions and, in general, most of their assumptions are questionable. For example, assuming that your business isn't newsworthy is a common assumption, so your business never explores the potential of publicity (turn to Chapter 11 for all about publicity). And many people assume that they can't manage word-of-mouth marketing, so they do nothing to try to build referrals. Watch out for such assumptions! They keep you from considering many creative alternatives.

You can create breaking news by sponsoring a benefit concert for a charity. You can encourage positive word-of-mouth referrals by offering a prize to the customer who brings you the most new customers. You can . . . hang on; it's your turn to come up with an idea now!

Talking to ten successful people

We recently ran into a friend who's an artist. She complained that she needed to reach a broader market with her work but didn't know how to go about it. We suggested she look at her own ideas and experience to find out how best to market herself. The answers to your problems are often closer than you think.

We suggested that she chat to ten artist friends and discover how they were marketing their work. Each artist probably has a slightly different approach. By listening to each of their stories, she can start seeing more possibilities. One person using a community Internet site may spark off an idea. Or another artist getting local firms to hang art in receptions may also suggest a new path. After compiling these ideas, she can work out which of these techniques may work, separately or together or in a new version for her own work.

Asking ten people how they do their sales and marketing is a wonderful discipline. Put on your journalist's hat, take along a pad and pencil, and collect information about how other people practise marketing. You're sure to come across something new and different that gives you a good idea for your own business.

Managing Creative Projects and Teams

When you have a group of people trying to be creative together, all sorts of complications arise. The first issue to watch out for is overly critical feedback. If one person tells another that an idea is stupid or won't work, the other person is going to hesitate to present more ideas. So try to instil an open-minded, positive attitude in your group of creative marketers. Praise creativity, even if it isn't practical. The more you recognise and reward creative behaviour, the more creative ideas you're going to have to choose from.

Also, recognise that different people are creative in different ways – and some people are more creative than others. The classic creative personality is very inquisitive, open-minded, and artistic but not very organised or focused. Do you have someone in your office or on your marketing team who has great ideas and lots of imagination, is interested in all sorts of odd topics, but can't keep his or her desk clean? If so, this person is a great one to put in charge of looking for new product ideas or coming up with better headlines for new ads.

But don't ask this person to make sure that you meet all the deadlines for submitting ads to magazines on time. Obviously, for this part of the creative process, someone with a more organised personality and a clear focus is a better choice.

If you can, build creative teams out of people with contrasting personalities so that the team has all the complementary strengths needed to take a project from idea stage to execution. In marketing, you have to turn creative ideas into practical projects and complete them on time and within budget. This task requires a challenging balance of different kinds of personalities, skills and roles. Some people can do all these things themselves, but most can't. Working with at least two or three other people whose creative profiles are different from your own is wise. Doing so makes passing the baton and filling all the roles needed to bring great ideas to practical fruition easier.

We include a great tool for managing creative groups or building creative marketing teams in File 13-1 on the CD: *Creative Roles Analysis*. Print as many copies as you need for each member of your staff or team so that they can take the assessment and discuss who's best suited to play which roles on creative marketing projects. If you want to dig deep into the topic and discover more about your own and the rest of your team's creativity, make sure that each member completes it. (We also include instructions for interpreting and using the results on File 13-1.)

Files on the CD

Check out this file on the CD-ROM:

▮ ✔ **File 13-1:** Creative Roles Analysis

Chapter 14

Writing Well for Marketing and Sales

Sometimes marketing seems as if it's all about writing. We can't recall an ad in any medium that doesn't contain some writing, and writing dominates many ads. Similarly, coupons, contests, memberships and other special promotions need clear writing to communicate their benefits and rules to customers. Even sales materials rely on writing. Many people do sales approaches or follow-up proposals to businesses in writing rather than verbally. So you can see why writing is an essential core skill for all marketers.

But how do you go about the process of conceiving and writing great ads, direct-mail letters, brochures, websites, signs or other marketing communications? Every good marketing communication starts with ideas that make it persuasive and effective. Marketing is all about getting across your offer in a compelling manner that gets attention and helps shape opinions and actions.

We ask a lot of our marketing communications, whether they're ads, mailers, web pages, catalogues, brochures or other forms of communication with our customers and prospects. So you need to do quite a bit of thinking in order to come up with ideas that really work. In this chapter, we share some techniques that can help you differentiate your communications from the pack.

Avoiding Power Words and Phrases

If you search for help with marketing and sales writing on the Internet, you're inundated by expert advice and products that have one common theme – write using stock phrases and words that are guaranteed to sell. Often called *power words* or *power phrases*, these overused, exaggerated words are supposed to make your communications effective. More often than not, however, they have the opposite effect – they make you sound like a huckster or con artist with nothing substantive to say.

Self-styled experts tell you that you should use power words and power phrases that 'guarantee success', 'boost sales dramatically' and so on. The trouble is that consumers aren't actually idiots, so marketers can't afford to be. If your writing is full of stock catch-phrases, it looks like it was cut and pasted from old ads or sales letters. Don't make the mistake of trying to punch up your writing by filling it with exaggerated claims and generic power phrases.

Table 14-1 lists examples of words and phrases that you'll probably be told to use. Please don't! You can use these sorts of words and phrases if you want to sound like a million other salespeople, or you can craft a simple, clear communication that says what it means and means what it says. You don't have to sound like a marketer to make a sale. In fact, not sounding like a stereotyped sales copywriter is much better.

Say that we want to write copy for a website describing an Internet-based business service. We can fill up the screen with trite power phrases, such as 'Unbelievable! You have to try this to believe it! A remarkable breakthrough that will save you untold time and trouble! Enjoy the ultimate in complete business support on the Internet by taking advantage of this unique limited-time offer, for preferred customers only. Act now and . . .' But what are we really selling? What are its genuine benefits? Nobody really knows. All that we make clear with this kind of writing is that we don't have a fresh phrase or thought in our heads.

Table 14-1	Power Words and Phrases to Avoid
Overused Power Words	*Overused Power Phrases*
Daring	What you should know
Blockbuster	Proven steps to . . .
Revolutionary	Act now!
Astounding	Unlock the hidden . . .
Dazzling	The shocking truth about . . .

Overused Power Words	Overused Power Phrases
Mammoth	Limited edition
Powerful	For preferred customers only
Remarkable	Enjoy the ultimate . . .
Electrifying	A breakthrough!
Vital	Once in a lifetime opportunity
Incredible	Let me show you how to . . .

Now here's a straightforward approach to describing the business service that the preceding copy failed to sell effectively: 'You can upload your financial, accounting, sales and marketing information easily, no matter what business software programs you use. As soon as you log onto our site, you start getting integrated reports, error flags, expert suggestions and other services to help you run your business better in less time and with less effort and expense.' This copy works because it describes the user's experience and benefits and nothing else: it's clear, concise and sounds honest.

Marketing communication is like any other communications in that less is more. Try to make your marketing copy as clear and simple as possible. If any power words, phrases or other stock elements of traditional marketing-speak slip into your writing, cut them. Never say 'trust us' or 'trust me': that's what con artists say. If you have to tell the prospect to trust you, you or your offer must appear untrustworthy. Fix the underlying problem instead. Deals shouldn't sound too good to be true or be packaged in superlatives and over-excited prose. Keep your writing calm, professional, concise and factual. Let the facts do the convincing. If your offer or claim is unconvincing, dig up facts or testimonials to make it believable (check out the 'Obtaining and Using Customer Testimonials' section later in this chapter and Chapter 15).

When writing for a website, follow the rule of sticking to the core benefits, just as if you're writing for print. However, keep the copy much shorter. Most of your paragraphs on a website should be one or two sentences only, which means that avoiding clichés is even more important. If you need to give more detail, provide links to supporting pages or PDF documents. Also, before you start writing for a web page, make a list of a half-dozen key terms that help interested buyers find your page on search engines. Then make sure that you work these key terms in naturally as you write.

Writing Persuasively

As a marketer, you need to create effective writing for ads, sales letters, websites, press releases, catalogues and many other applications. Whether you do most of this writing yourself or use others to help draft it, you need to make sure that the writing is *good*: clear, interesting, professional (no obvious errors, please!) and – most important – persuasive.

To write or not to write yourself

Are you a good writer? Sorry for the personal question, but you need to be honest about your writing talent. In ad agencies, specialists called *copywriters* do the writing – and they're excellent writers. But most people aren't. If you enjoy writing and are at least moderately good at drafting and editing clear, interesting copy, by all means write your own marketing materials, sales letters and ads. If not, read on.

We're writers and so are used to avoiding the mistakes or pitfalls of bad copy. But we know lots of great marketers and businesspeople who don't write well and probably never will.

So, what can you do if writing isn't one of your strengths? Here are a few ideas:

- ✔ **Take advantage of templates.** Published books of business letters can provide a good starting point, allowing you to customise and refine a letter rather than having to start one from scratch. If you suffer from writer's block, a starting draft – even a poor one – may break the logjam and get you writing.

- ✔ **Make friends with writers.** Some people love writing and editing and enjoy the challenge of improving your copy. These eager volunteers can exercise their talents when they volunteer to help you write. Return the favour by doing something you're good at, and they aren't; then everybody's happy.

- ✔ **Hire a writer.** Most writers are underpaid, so you can probably afford one. But don't assume that all writers can produce good marketing copy. A novelist writes 300-page stories, not short direct-response ads. Look at writers' portfolios and select the person whose portfolio includes the kind of writing that you need. Also, check samples of their writing. If the style doesn't fit your taste, keep shopping.

- ✔ **Hire an ad agency.** This strategy is the expensive approach, but sometimes turning the work over to the pros is a good idea. However, still insist on checking the portfolio of the copywriter assigned to your work and refuse to sign a contract until you have a writer who obviously can do just what you need.

Dusting off your writing skills

Think back to your English classes at school, when you explored the many ways of making a point through writing. Perhaps you had an assignment where you needed to show how a character in a story feels when something bad happens to her. Well, you have two basic options. You can just describe her feelings:

'She was hollow. Empty inside. She felt cheated and alone. In fact, she'd never been so down in her life.'

Or you can create an imaginary scene that portrays her feelings:

'She slumped against the railing of the bridge, tears streaking her cheeks, tempted by the cold waters far below.'

Both approaches communicate your point that the character is having a really bad day, but they do it in very different ways.

Which way is best? The approach you take depends on what you're trying to accomplish, the context and the reader. It depends, in part, on your taste and style as well. A single best way to make a point doesn't exist, but when you recognise and experiment with alternative approaches, you're more likely to find a good solution in any situation.

✔ **Copy good writing . . . sort of.** Sometimes we keep copies of great articles or adverts to use as inspiration. However, we don't copy the writing directly; we use it only as a general model to inspire our own creative work. Copyright laws apply to any marketing materials or ads that you collect. Remember in school how teachers taught you how to use source materials to write a paper but warned you not to plagiarise? Same rule applies here, except now you can go to court rather than the head's office. So be careful when using other marketers' work for inspiration.

These strategies are for marketers who find writing painfully difficult. If you don't mind sharpening your pencil and crafting a careful paragraph or two, the rest of this chapter can help you make your marketing copy more effective. Oh, and even if you don't do the writing yourself, as a marketer your job is to make sure that it's engaging and persuasive, so maybe you'd better read this chapter anyway! Someone has to manage the writing project and approve the final copy and that someone should be you.

Engaging and persuading your audience

Basically, you can engage and persuade people in one of two ways:

✔ By appealing to them with a compelling, logical argument.

✔ By appealing to them with an engaging story.

Or you can use a combination of these strategies. But the point is, these two strategies are always options when you're communicating. And thinking about which option to use is a wonderful source of inspiration whenever you need to create strong marketing communications.

In this section, we show you how to write incredibly effective *copy* (the words or story behind any ad or other marketing communication) that you can use for a print ad, a direct-mail piece, a brochure or catalogue, a web page, a broadcast fax, a radio or TV commercial, or whatever. The basic strategy applies to anything, even to a personal sales presentation. And the strategy's based on using these two very different ways of making a point when you communicate.

Straight facts or a little drama

Thinking about whether you want to make a factual argument in your ad or dramatise your point with some sort of story is always helpful.

Every marketing communication has a factual and a fictional version awaiting discovery. So which approach should you use? Or should you try something that's a combination of the two forms – part fact and part fiction? Simply posing this question opens up many possibilities to you as you develop your ad or other marketing communication. This section shows you the difference between factual and fictional versions of a marketing communication.

Imagine that you're designing a letter that you want to send to prospects of a training firm to introduce a new training programme that instructs employees in how to handle customer complaints effectively. We call this programme Handling Angry Customers, or H.A.C., for short. And we assume that the programme is great and companies that use it to train their employees have happier, more loyal customers and make lots more money as a result. How do you convince managers and training directors that H.A.C. is a good service? What should the introductory letter say to catch their attention and get them interested in the training? You have a couple of options.

Just the facts, ma'am

First, we suggest that you rough out a factual letter. A *factual letter* makes a logical argument, such as the following:

> *Dear Manager,*
>
> *Everyone knows that it costs ten times as much to win a new customer as it does to do business with an existing customer. Yet companies routinely lose their good customers because of errors or slip-ups that anger those good customers and open the door for defection. What can you do to keep your customers from leaving you? What can you do to make sure that they buy*

more next year instead of less? What, in short, is the secret of high customer loyalty?

People. It comes down to people in 99.9 per cent of the cases, according to our extensive research. We studied the companies with the most loyal customers in a dozen different industries, and, in every case, these winning companies have more sensitive, better trained employees. Employees who know what to do when customers are upset or angry. Employees who know how to convert each problem into an opportunity to build loyalty instead of losing business.

That's why we designed Handling Angry Customers (H.A.C.), the radical new customer-service training programme that has a measurable impact on your customer retention rates – or you get your money back.

That argument is pretty powerful. It makes the case for the H.A.C. service quite forcefully. And most people who want to describe a new service for business-to-business sales probably choose a factual approach based on argument, just like this copy employs.

A flair for the dramatic

But remember what your schoolteacher told you about all the different ways of making your point? You should also be able to present the H.A.C. training programme in a completely different manner using the tools of the dramatist and telling a story (or stories) rather than arguing the facts. For example, you can draft some copy for that direct-mail piece that goes like this:

Dear Manager,

I want to share a story that I think you'll find interesting.

Rick, the purchasing manager for SysTech, was a man of action. He hated to waste even a minute of his company's precious time. Yet today, he was doing something uncharacteristic. He was doing nothing. He had been doing nothing for four and a half minutes already, and it was obviously wearing on him.

Rick was on hold. On hold with your company, to be specific. He was on hold because he had called to complain about a minor problem with the last order and been put on hold by one of your employees who didn't know how to handle the call.

In contrast, your employee was quite busy. She was busy asking anyone she could find what to do. She had no idea how to solve Rick's problem. But she sensed the urgency in his voice, and she, too, was well aware of the ticking of the clock. Finally, after searching fruitlessly for the appropriate paperwork and getting a wide variety of unhelpful advice from her associates, your employee came back on the line. Five minutes and sixteen seconds had passed since she'd put Rick on hold. You don't want to know what Rick said in reply when her first words to him were, 'I'm sorry, sir, but I can't find any record of that order. Are you sure you really sent it in?'

Accidents happen, as the old saying goes. But whether you recover from them gracefully or lose a customer for life depends on how you handle those accidents. If that employee had only received Handling Angry Customers (H.A.C.) training, she would have known not to put poor Rick on hold even for one minute. That violates the Adding-Insult-to-Injury principle, which says that you must handle all unhappy customers with a high degree of consideration and support. And never, ever, put them on hold or question their word when they are upset!

But Rick doesn't care any more. He's already busy placing his order with one of your competitors. A competitor who has recently trained all its employees in the H.A.C. programme and is not likely to lose a customer over a minor problem. You may as well throw Rick's business card away. You're not likely to do business with SysTech again!

This example uses a dramatic approach to make a point, creating a plausible scenario that catches readers' attention and draws them forward. It makes readers wonder whether such dramas are playing out right now somewhere in their own business. And if so, well, they are certainly likely to question their staff's ability to handle angry customers and wonder if a little training may not be a wise investment . . .

If you switch on your TV, you're bound to see a number of examples of both factual and fictional styles of advertising within a short period of time. Some TV spots make rational arguments, presenting facts and attempting to make you believe their product claims. Others present dramas, tell stories and try to affect your attitudes toward their products by making their stories compelling.

Considering which option is better

Which works better, an argument-based factual communication or a dramatic fictional one? Well, no hard and fast rule applies. Sometimes one approach works better, and sometimes the other one does.

If your business wants to send a letter to training managers and executives to introduce the new H.A.C. training programme, you need to consider both options and develop and test ads using different styles. One letter will work to the extent that its arguments are persuasive and the other because its dramatic scenario is compelling – but you don't know until you try both.

With both approaches in hand, we can test two very different types of letters. We can simply divide the mailing list in half, send out the two different letters and wait to see which one more training managers respond to. The odds are that one letter or the other pulls significantly better. If you don't write both versions, you never have the chance to find out which approach is best in this specific situation.

Always think 'test' when you're working on a marketing communication. You can run one ad one week and another ad the next. You can mail or email multiple letters by randomly dividing your list into sections. You can try different brochures on different customers or prospects. You can always find a way to experiment and compare multiple options. And when you do, you discover far more than most of your competitors ever will, because most people aren't thoughtful enough to design even the simplest of experiments.

Hybrid ads: Have your cake and eat it, too

Here's another way you can take advantage of the fact that ads can take a factual or dramatic approach. Why not incorporate both approaches into one ad? Using this strategy, you can create a hybrid that works better than either form on its own. At least it's worth a try. Test these three versions of any sales-oriented communication letters:

- ✔ A straight, rational, persuasive argument based on facts.
- ✔ A dramatic ad that's based almost entirely on a story or scenario.
- ✔ A combination of fact-based argument and a brief story to dramatise your point.

After you create a factual and a dramatic version, developing the hybrid of the two is no big deal. Then you have three versions of your sales communication to test, and experimenting with them is easy because you can measure the response rates.

We prefer communications that combine argument and storytelling. We find that the hybrid approach often makes the most effective ad or direct-mail letter. You can even use this approach on the Internet.

For example, you can include storytelling on a web page or in an electronic newsletter. Whenever you have the opportunity to engage the reader long enough to communicate any details, a combination of argument and storytelling can work wonders. You can use a picture that tells a story in a print ad, combined with written arguments. You can combine personal testimonials from happy customers with a factual description of the benefits of your product in a brochure (see Chapter 15 for how to get customer quotes). You have no limits when you're incorporating elements of both argument and narrative into a single marketing piece.

You can even incorporate both styles in personal selling by weaving some case histories or testimonials into a sales presentation. We're amazed at how rarely salespeople use the extremely powerful tool of storytelling.

Over the years, we've noticed that the most successful salespeople tend to weave three or four stories into each sales presentation. They often use stories about other customers to illustrate a point. Similarly, some of the most effective sales collateral – brochures, catalogue sheets, audiovisuals and other materials that the presentation refers to – are full of stories. They may include actual case histories, customer testimonials or generic stories written to illustrate how the product or service works.

Never underestimate the power of storytelling when you weave it into sales presentations!

A work of art: Fact and fiction combined

When you create hybrid ad copy using both arguments and storytelling, you tap into both the rational and emotional sides of your customers with relative ease.

To show you what we mean, we created a hybrid of the two approaches we showed you in the earlier section 'Straight facts or a little drama' for the H.A.C. training programme. We lead with the story version for the simple reason that people often react initially on an emotional basis and then engage their rational minds. So an opening appeal to emotion is a great initial attention-getter. And a strong finish based on rational facts and arguments is a great way to cement those initial emotional responses by adding rational conviction. When we combine the two approaches into one (tightening them up a bit to avoid making the hybrid too lengthy), we get the following direct-mail or brochure copy:

> *Dear Manager,*
>
> *Rick, the purchasing manager for SysTech, hates to waste even a minute of his busy day. But he's actually been doing nothing at all for four and a half minutes now.*
>
> [Show picture of a man in shirt sleeves and a tie, phone to ear, looking at his watch in exasperation.]
>
> *Rick is on hold with your company. He was put on hold when he called to complain about a problem with his last order.*
>
> [Show picture of frazzled employee, phone in one hand, making a palms-up gesture as if to say, 'I have no idea how to handle this.']
>
> *If this were a real-life situation, you can imagine that your employee would be busy trying to solve Rick's problem. Five minutes and sixteen seconds have passed since she put Rick on hold, and you don't want to know what Rick says in reply when her first words to him are, 'I'm sorry, sir, but I can't find any record of your order. Are you sure you really sent it in?'*

A major source of hidden losses

Every manager knows that it costs ten times as much to win a new customer as it does to do business with an existing customer. Yet companies routinely lose good customers like Rick over slip-ups that anger those good customers.

Did you know?

According to our research, the vast majority of employees fail to pick up on signs that customers are unhappy or respond appropriately to them.

What can you do to keep your customers from leaving you?

People

It comes down to people in 99.9 per cent of the cases. Our studies show the companies with the most loyal customers have more sensitive, better-trained employees. Employees who know how to convert each problem into an opportunity to build loyalty instead of losing business.

That's why we designed Handling Angry Customers (H.A.C.), the radical new customer-service training that has a measurable impact on your customer retention rates – or you get your money back!

'My employees are performing 100 per cent better since their H.A.C. training, and I'm getting a lot of compliments from my customers. They really notice the difference.'

– Charlotte McGwire, President, Global Food Supply plc

You can take the first no-obligation step toward higher customer loyalty today by calling us or returning the enclosed postcard to get your Course Overview booklet and video today. And if you respond before the end of the month, you qualify for our introductory 15 per cent discount. Take a decisive step towards educating your employees by contacting us to preview or schedule the Handling Angry Customers training today.

Sincerely,

Millicent Marketer

Head of Training Programmes

Combining an opening story with hard-hitting fact-based arguments and ending with a simple call to action generates a nice response rate, because it pushes two powerful buttons. It appeals to emotion and logic, which means that it stands a good chance of creating immediate involvement with readers who have reason to worry about how well their employees handle customer problems and complaints.

Getting attention means having full reader involvement – both emotionally and rationally (see the later section 'Designing for Stopping Power' for more on grabbing attention). This hybrid letter grasps attention and turns it into action by combining an emotional appeal (based on a story) with a rational appeal (based on factual argument).

Other ways to spice up your copy

We made some other improvements to develop the hybrid example:

- ✔ **Call-to-action paragraph.** We finish with a final paragraph containing a *call to action* – details of what the reader can do next, along with some incentive to do it now.

- ✔ **Headings.** We drop in a few headers to break up the text, which makes it more readable. The headers entice the eye, drawing the reader into each section. They also reinforce the points by hitting the reader over the head with them.

- ✔ **Text boxes.** We add a text box that readers can read independently of the main copy.

The text box reinforces the copy and gives readers with short attention-spans something to jump to. Specifically, it quotes a customer who had a good experience with the product. Such testimonials are often very powerful and tend to be under-used in marketing communications.

- ✔ **Visuals.** We come up with some concepts for visuals (appropriate if the medium permits). A couple of simple black and white photos may work well in a two-page letter; and if this was copy for a brochure, we can opt for nicer full-colour photos (budget permitting).

Developing a hybrid letter like this one to a high level takes quite a bit of care, but the effort is worthwhile when you get increased responses.

What makes hybrid ads so effective?

We demonstrate in the preceding section an obvious bias for hybrid ads, letters, sales presentations and other communications that combine the best of fact-based argument with the best of narrative. This strategy is our favourite because it has two things going for it:

- ✔ **Creating a hybrid letter is usually the third step in a creative process.** Generally, people tend to create ads or ad concepts in the order we list them in the previous section – that is, first, they create the rational argument based on facts; second, they create the dramatic persuasion based on storytelling; and third, they develop the hybrid that includes some of both tactics. You have an advantage using the form that you created previously, because by doing so you spend more time and invest more effort in your ad. You really had to work hard to develop two completely different approaches and then find a good way to combine them. So the hybrid form represents more creative energy and a higher level of involvement on the marketer's part. And, in general, when you put more of yourself into an ad, you get more out of it.

- ✔ **Creating hybrid ads uses the fact that humans have both a rational and an emotional side.** In fact, many scientists believe that arguments literally appeal to a different side of the brain than stories do. By combining appeals to both our rational and emotional sides, hybrid ads tend to cast the broadest net. And when both the rational and emotional appeals work well, these ads build the highest involvement on the parts of their readers, listeners or viewers.

Getting Serious about Testing Your Copy

In the preceding section, we show you how to combine a rational appeal with a story to make a direct-mail piece that has high impact. Good strategy, but does it work? Of course, you never really know how any marketing communication is going to work until you try it. But you have no reason to market blindly. You can use a lot of easy ways to test what you've written and see how it performs. In this section, we show you a few of the best tests.

Checking your writing against screening criteria

One way you can test your copy is to check your writing against the statements we provide in the following two sections. Develop your screening criteria from these statements and then evaluate your writing against them. Ask others to evaluate your copy in the same manner, too. For ads that are purely fact-oriented and rational, or purely emotional and story-oriented, you can use just the six statements that apply to their specific form. Or, go ahead and evaluate each communication using all the statements, because you can't always be sure that you know the ad's real appeal.

Evaluating rational arguments and fact-based appeals

Ideally, your copy needs to be convincing and persuasive and not lead to counter-arguments. Your copy should also be believable and honest – don't over-claim.

Use the following statements as your criteria when evaluating writing with a rational appeal:

- ✔ I find this writing very convincing.
- ✔ I agree with the main points completely.
- ✔ I can't think of any reasons to avoid this product/service while reading/ listening to/viewing the copy.
- ✔ I don't feel like arguing with the writer/speaker.
- ✔ The writing makes sense to me.
- ✔ This ad is important.

Your goal is to create an ad that people don't feel like arguing with. Ads that generate the fewest counter-arguments are the most persuasive.

Evaluating emotional appeals and stories or case histories

An ad's emotional appeal, story or case history needs to be engaging and interesting. It should engage feelings to a significant degree and be realistic and believable.

Use these factors as your criteria when evaluating writing that uses emotional appeals:

- ✔ I find the writing compelling.
- ✔ The writing holds my attention.
- ✔ I feel that the copy describes a situation that may easily apply to me/my business.
- ✔ I like the ad.
- ✔ The ad is definitely true to life.
- ✔ I relate easily to the feelings of the people in this ad.

Evaluating hybrid ads

Hybrid ads involve both rational arguments and emotional stories, so you need to evaluate them using both sets of criteria (in other words, all 12 statements described in the preceding two sections).

Figure 14-1 shows a form you can use to evaluate marketing communications based on the need for both rational and emotional appeals. You can also find this form on the CD (File 14-1).

On the form, notice that we alternate the items measuring the effectiveness of your argument with the ones measuring the effectiveness of your story. The story-oriented items have odd numbers, starting with item number one. The argument-oriented items have even numbers, starting with item number two. So an ad that's effective as a story scores high on the odd-numbered items. And a great hybrid letter, such as the one we show you in the earlier section 'A work of art: Fact and fiction combined' scores fairly high on all items and receives a high overall score.

You can use the form in File 14-1 to check your own work and refine your drafts as you work on customer letters or any other marketing communications. Or you can take your research to a higher level by soliciting customer input.

Evaluation Form 1 (Argument/Story Effectiveness)

Please circle the number that best represents your feelings toward the marketing communication you have been asked to evaluate. Thank you for your help.

Scale: 1 = not at all to 5 = definitely

Item A

#1.	1 2 3 4 5	I found it compelling.
#2.	1 2 3 4 5	I found it very convincing.
#3.	1 2 3 4 5	It held my attention.
#4.	1 2 3 4 5	I agreed with the main points completely.
#5.	1 2 3 4 5	I felt that it described a situation that could easily apply to me/my business.
#6.	1 2 3 4 5	I could think of no reasons to avoid this product/service.
#7.	1 2 3 4 5	I liked the ad/marketing communication.
#8.	1 2 3 4 5	I did not feel like arguing with the writer/speaker.
#9.	1 2 3 4 5	It was definitely true to life.
#10.	1 2 3 4 5	It made good sense to me.
#11.	1 2 3 4 5	I could relate easily to the feelings in it.
#12.	1 2 3 4 5	It is important.

Figure 14-1: Evaluation Form 1 (Argument/ Story Effective- ness).

Getting other people's opinions

You can use the statements in Figure 14-1 to evaluate a marketing communication before you even try it out in the media or mail it. If you show your ad to a half-dozen or more people who are similar to your customers (or are your customers), you can find out what they think of it and, often, you can find ways to improve the ad before you spend money and take the risk of using it.

We recommend talking to some of your friends in the industry and to some of your most friendly customers, as well as to some people you don't know quite so well, to sign them up for ad-evaluation duty. You can point out that the procedure is quick and painless, and they must simply look at drafts of marketing communications and then fill in a quick one-page-or-less questionnaire by circling some numbers. So their duty is easy, and they get to have a peek into your marketing operations and may get some good ideas of their own. Or you can sweeten the pot by offering participants a discount to make their participation more worthwhile.

Having a panel of even a few people who you can run your communications past before you finalise them is a really wonderful thing. In addition to asking your panel to respond to some specific questions, such as the ones we give you in Figure 14-1, you should also spend a few minutes debriefing them in person or by phone to find out what they really think about your marketing piece. Try asking them to identify several things they like and dislike about the piece as an easy way to get them talking.

And while you're having people read and evaluate your marketing communication, you can also ask them to make sure that it's simple, error-free and clear (some of the common problems that we always find ourselves correcting when we do communications audits).

If you really don't have the time to put together an informal audience panel to test your ad, at least test it yourself and get others within your organisation to test it. Any evaluation is better than none!

Creating options and picking a winner

Another way to use research is to develop and evaluate three or more communication pieces. We know that designing three ads, letters, brochures or whatever is more work, but if you mock up three different designs and then compare them using evaluation questions (like the ones we gave you in the earlier section 'Checking your writing against screening criteria'), you're more likely to end up picking a winner. Many ad agencies develop at least three different ads, and sometimes as many as a dozen. Then everyone argues over which approach is best.

If deciding which approach is the best is difficult, you may have the luxury of multiple good options. But in our experience, one option often rises to the top, and it's rarely the first concept you develop. So creating more options and testing them before you make a decision really does pay off!

Evaluating for High Involvement

Does your marketing communication get *high involvement* from your audience? In other words, do your readers notice it and become interested in it or do they just pass it by, flick over it or scroll past it without paying much mind?

Because most people ignore most marketing communications, involvement is an important first step toward winning customers. You need to win their attention and interest, and you need to get them involved in your effort to communicate.

In this section, don't worry about the content of your material or whether you convince people. Instead, focus on how you build high involvement (often requiring both rational and emotional responses), which is often essential when you're designing an ad for a crowded place (such as a magazine full of ads), where your biggest challenge is just winning some attention. A TV spot, a magazine or newspaper ad, a banner ad for the Internet, (yet another) mailing or an outdoor poster must grab attention and build involvement in a hurry, or else customers pass it right by.

So how do you create high involvement for an ad? Here's a hypothetical example:

> A picture of a laughing baby probably creates emotional involvement, especially in parents of young children.

> A table showing that babies whose parents feed them organic baby food have fewer health problems later in life than those whose parents feed them conventional baby food demands rational involvement.

> Combine the picture of a laughing baby with the data from our imagined study showing that organic baby food is healthier and you have the potential to capture full involvement, because the ad appeals to both the rational and emotional sides of the parents you want to reach.

A number of large ad agencies actually measure rational and emotional involvement with questionnaires as a way of evaluating ads. Then they plot the results on a graph like the one shown in Figure 14-2 (which is also in File 14-2 on the CD). Ads that plot high and to the right win the most involvement on both dimensions. And these ads tend to be more effective, all else being equal, especially in situations where catching your target audience's attention is hard to do.

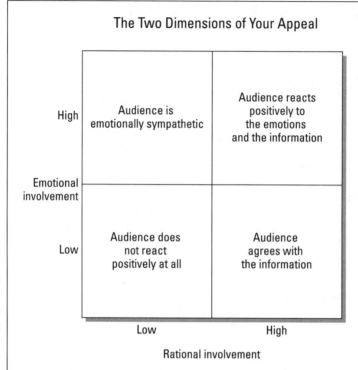

The Two Dimensions of Your Appeal

	High	Audience is emotionally sympathetic	Audience reacts positively to the emotions and the information
Emotional involvement			
	Low	Audience does not react positively at all	Audience agrees with the information
		Low	High

Rational involvement

Figure 14-2: The two dimensions of your appeal.

ON THE CD

So here's another way to evaluate your own marketing communications or to have a panel or group of people representing your audience evaluate them: simply ask people to rate each marketing communication by filling in Evaluation Form 2 (Emotional/Rational Involvement), shown in Figure 14-3. This form is available on your CD, in case you want to print some copies (File 14-3).

If you're testing multiple ads or other marketing communications, simply ask your panel to evaluate each one using the scale in File 14-3, which has room to evaluate up to ten options at a time, lettered from Item A to Item J. Label each ad or other communication clearly with one of these letters to make sure that you can accurately decode the data you collect.

Even if you have only one or two communications to evaluate, consider including others that you collect from the marketplace – especially ones that you think are effective because of their track records. Looking at the range of responses that customers give to a variety of options is always interesting, and doing so gives you insight into how to interpret their responses. For example, if people rate your new brochure design at 3.9 on average, and the average for competitors' brochures is only 3.1, you probably have a winner, even though your absolute score isn't at the top of the 1 through 5 range.

To maximise involvement, look for designs that score reasonably high on both the odd- and even-numbered items in Figure 14-3 and in File 14-3. But if you designed your communication to have either a highly emotional or a highly rational appeal, don't expect to score high overall. Instead, look for top marks on the items that measure the dimension of involvement that you're aiming for (odd-numbered items measure rational appeal and even numbers emotional appeal).

Evaluation Form 2 (Emotional/Rational Involvement)

Please circle the number that best represents your feelings toward the marketing communication you have been asked to evaluate. Thank you for your help.

Scale: 1 = not at all to 5 = definitely

Item A

#1.	1 2 3 4 5	I found myself caught up emotionally in it.
#2.	1 2 3 4 5	I was interested in the information it contained.
#3.	1 2 3 4 5	I got a definite sense of the feelings it is trying to communicate.
#4.	1 2 3 4 5	I could follow the logic of the argument easily.
#5.	1 2 3 4 5	It has a definite emotional appeal.
#6.	1 2 3 4 5	I thought it was well researched.
#7.	1 2 3 4 5	It captures my own feelings quite well.
#8.	1 2 3 4 5	It is a good source of useful ideas.

Figure 14-3: Evaluation Form 2 (Emotional/ Rational Involvement).

Interpreting Your Ad Research to Select or Refine a Design

In this section, we examine the data from three different ad designs, each one a draft of a possible direct-response ad designed to run in the Sunday magazines of various newspapers. We're just going to describe these ads, not show them, because we want to focus on how you interpret research about people's reactions to them:

✔ The first design uses an eye-catching photo and a brief story as its focus.

✔ The second design presents several little-known facts and builds an argument for the product based on them.

✔ The third design is a hybrid of the first two, combining a smaller photo and brief quote from a customer with a short discussion of relevant facts.

Here's how a panel of 15 prospective customers evaluated each ad on the customer involvement scales (see the preceding section for more details on this scale) and also on the emotional/rational appeal scales (see the earlier section 'Checking your writing against screening criteria' on story-based versus argument-based appeals).

We simplified the results by coding them as L = low, M = medium and H = high.

Ads	Average Scores			
	Appeal		Involvement	
	Story	Argument	Emotional	Rational
1. Photo/story	H	L	H	L
2. Facts/argument	L	M	L	M
3. Hybrid of 1 & 2	M	M	M	M

You can see that the panel's reactions to the ads are nicely summarised in this type of table. At a glance, you get a feel for the strengths and weaknesses of each of the options. The first one had high appeal as a story and also achieved high emotional involvement. It bombed on the other scales, though, reflecting its lack of hard information. The second ad got medium scores for the appeal of its argument and its ability to involve people rationally, but it bombed on the other scales because it lacked emotional impact. And the third ad, the hybrid ad, received medium scores across the board.

So which ad is better? A conservative marketer would probably pick the third ad because it seems to have something for everyone. We usually favour hybrids with a combination of stories and arguments and the ability to create both rational and emotional involvement. Our choice based on this data, however, is definitely the first ad. We like to see exceptionally high scores on anything, even if they require a sacrifice on other dimensions. Grabbing attention with an ad is hard, so one that packs an emotional punch is obviously a good choice.

If you're still worried about ad number one's low scores on the argument and rational involvement scales, feel free to fiddle with it and do some more testing. Perhaps you can make it just a bit bigger and work a line or two of copy in at the bottom with some compelling facts. Even an asterisk with a footnote citing some facts or statistics may raise those low scores to the medium range without diluting the ad's emotional impact and bringing down its other scores.

So you can work with ad number one and try to formulate a better hybrid ad, but we wouldn't mess with it too much. An emotionally powerful ad is a rare commodity, and you may mess it up if you add too much. A good rule for marketing communications is that less is often more.

Designing for Stopping Power

Another important consideration for any marketing communication is how well it screams for attention. Not all marketing communications need to shout out to their audience, but many benefit from the ability to grab attention. *Stopping power* is the ability of a marketing communication to attract immediate notice and command attention.

Ask yourself some questions. What does your logo look like? Do people stop and give it a long look because they find it interesting? Do they want to open an envelope because the logo on the outside is striking and catches their eye? Well, maybe not – most logos lack stopping power.

We were impressed by a new logo that Xerox Corporation unveiled in 2008 because it had strong stopping power. According to the company's press release in January 2008, the logo 'is a lowercase treatment of the Xerox name – in a vibrant red – alongside a sphere-shaped symbol sketched with lines that link to form an illustrative X.' The press release included a JPEG of the logo design, which we put in File 14-4 for your reference.

What gives this logo stopping power? The vibrant red certainly helps, but Xerox's new logo is strong even in black and white. It uses chunky strong letters and an appealing three-dimensional-looking circle with an X on it that really does draw the eye.

This chapter is, of course, on copywriting, so how can we translate the concept of stopping power to writing? You can, and should, showcase your copy visually, with appealing layouts, bold headlines and subheads, and so on. And a strong illustration also helps. But you also need some words that leap up and grab attention, so as to stop people from whatever else they're doing and make them start reading.

A strong caption, headline, first line or last-line special offer may be where you put your stopping power. Make sure that it's in at least one of those places. The need for words that jump up and stop people in their tracks is behind the use of the clever and catchy headlines you see in magazine ads. For example, instead of saying, 'Home remodelling services that meet your needs', which isn't exciting enough to make you want to read an ad or brochure, you can have a headline that reads, 'Home is where the heart can afford to live well'.

What does that headline mean? Good point. We have to make up something in the first paragraph that ties the phrase into our ad for home remodelling services. But we like the headline: it's catchy and makes you wonder what comes next. So if we're writing a print ad, brochure or web homepage for a construction business that specialises in home remodelling, we can start with this headline and weave some copy to go along with it. For example, the first paragraph can say:

Home is where the heart can afford to live well

Too often, people live in their dream homes only when they are sleeping. Our hundreds of happy clients can tell you that they live that dream every day in homes that reflect their special tastes and desires. With free consultation by our architects and hundreds of design concepts in our virtual reality remodelling software, you can fall in love with your new home before we drive a single nail. And no hidden costs apply – we show you exactly how you can make your dream affordable.

After this eye-catching headline and interest-building first paragraph, we would simply provide clear, factual information about the business and its services. The main copy of this ad needs to support the exciting opening claim with solid foundations. Then, depending on what you're using the copy for, you can add some kind of call to action at the end, such as, 'Call or email today for a free home-redesign kit or to schedule a no-obligation, free visit from one of our redesign professionals.'

Does sexy sell?

Many marketers assume that a sure way to give any marketing communication stopping power is to put something sexy into it. If you show some attractive people in suggestive positions or even just put the word 'sex' in the headline, people take a quick look to see what's going on. But generally sex has nothing much to do with what you're communicating, so that sort of stopping power doesn't work well. People just move on again after they realise you've tried to trick them into paying attention.

So, putting a sexy photo on the outside of a direct-mail envelope probably doesn't increase the response rate, and it may irritate some of your prospects. Stopping power isn't really that simple at all.

Stopping power's great virtue is that it gets you in. And when you're in, when you've captured the genuine attention of a prospect, the rest of your design can go to work.

To really generate stopping power, you need to give any marketing communication six different qualities. Here are some qualities an ad can use in order to generate serious stopping power:

- ✔ Audience participation
- ✔ Beauty
- ✔ Curiosity
- ✔ Drama
- ✔ Emotion
- ✔ Surprise

You may surprise readers by talking about your product in an unconventional way. When we write a headline about home remodelling services that says 'Home is where the heart can afford to live well', we make people curious and even a bit surprised by this unusual phrasing. The words encourage them to want to read more, stimulating participation on their part as they try to figure out what the headline means. This headline has stopping power.

Do your marketing communications have stopping power? Maybe, but probably not. Most communications don't. In fact, if you think about this concept, most communications having high stopping power is impossible. Stopping power requires qualities that make the communication stand out from the crowd and not everything can stand out. So an ad with stopping power is always going to be rare.

Beauty also has stopping power – a lot of stopping power. When a product design is beautiful (for example, a new car), the thing to do is just show the product in the ads. Its beauty makes people stop and look. If you don't have an inherently beautiful product or if you have a service that people can't easily see or you can't easily photograph, consider finding a beautiful image to represent your product (see Chapter 6 for all about choosing images for adverts).

Measuring stopping power

As in the previous sections, where we use evaluation forms to rate communications on their appeal and involvement, you can use a simple evaluation form to measure a communication's stopping power. What you can measure, you can manage, so when you start evaluating your communications with the stopping power form, you may find yourself working more stopping power into your marketing. You can give more stopping power to any marketing communication. And stopping power always helps to get attention and gives your communication the opportunity to do its job.

Following up after getting attention

Having a catchy headline or other device to stop people and make them pay attention for long enough to start reading is great. However, the writing itself must be appealing to start with, or the powerful headline doesn't help much. Your writing needs to be clear and strong. To achieve clarity and strength, rewrite and edit with these two related goals in mind.

Yes, that's what we said: *rewrite and edit!* As authors, we always remember what one of our mentors said years ago: the art of good writing is rewriting. This fact can be taken as bad or good news. Are you an optimist? Then think of the good news: you just need to draft a few paragraphs quickly and you're well on your way! Rewrite them rigorously a few times, and you probably have some pretty good writing. (If you're a pessimist, you may feel discouraged by the thought that you're going to have to spend hours reworking a single page – but hey, that's the secret to good writing! Just budget enough time and make a really big pot of coffee.)

As you write and rewrite with the goals of clear and strong language in mind, ask yourself this question: 'What's most important to my reader?' For example, if you're selling home remodelling services, you may answer that question by deciding that they care about good work, completed on budget and within schedule. If your ad is full of words that don't emphasise these most important qualities of your service, rewrite until the important points burst off the page and into the reader's mind.

Applying Great Writing to Your Website

Open any of your own web pages and take a hard, objective look at them. Are they visually appealing, drawing your eye in so that you want to read what's on screen? If not, add a unifying design element, such as a central photo or a bold headline. Or, reduce the clutter and make it clean and easy for readers to approach.

Next, read the first text that catches your eye. Is the text clear? Interesting? Brief? Does it make you want to read more? Probably not. Most of the writing on the Internet is just terrible. Really awful. Unclear, too complicated and full of errors of usage and grammar. We've never seen a website we didn't want to edit. Here's a quick checklist of things to work on if you want to try to improve the clarity and appeal of your website's text:

- ✔ **Can you reduce the number of words?** On the Internet, shorter is usually better. You can tighten your text by eliminating unnecessary words and by choosing words that express your meaning more succinctly.

- ✔ **Can you make everything crystal clear?** Understanding all the writing on the average website is amazingly difficult. That's because business insiders (like you) who write the text have a hard time imagining how ignorant people like us can be when visiting the site for the first time. For example, we just went to the Xerox website. Nice logo but what on earth is the iGen3? This product is apparently gaining a new 'press matching system', which is being boasted about on the website's front page, but we have no clue what this term means. Next time you look at your own website, imagine how it may read to people like us who have fresh eyes and little or no knowledge of your business.

- ✔ **Can you make the key point clear?** Every web page, like any form of writing, needs to have a clear point. The headline and topic sentence should express one clear, simple claim to fame. What is it? We rarely can tell because web pages tend to be divided into lots of little sections and zones, each one competing for attention with all the others. Make sure that you have an overarching message. Your home page ought to devote at least one-third of its area to conveying a key message about what makes your business or service special and brilliant. And you need to mention this message in different variations as reminders on most of the other pages on your website, too. *Focus* is the key ingredient in great web writing!

- ✔ **Can you reduce errors?** Oh, sure, your site doesn't have any typos, inaccuracies, non-functional links or other errors . . . and now do us a favour, and just check it carefully one more time anyway. Thanks!

Don't take time and space to try to wow your viewer with elaborate high-tech bells and whistles. Stopping power is unimportant on websites because viewers don't wander by on the street and suddenly spot your ad. They choose to click through to your web address, so you already have their interest. Keep the writing clear, clean and focused, so as not to lose their interest.

Avoid these common pitfalls and your web writing is as tight, appealing and effective as the rest of your marketing communications. And remember to make sure that you have factual arguments that persuade logically and/or interesting stories that appeal emotionally in everything you write for marketing. Stories can work well on web pages, just as they can work well in sales materials, direct-mail letters or personal sales presentations. If you can obtain permission, include a quote or testimonial from a happy customer with one or more of these case histories. A good story always creates high involvement and makes your point persuasively.

A Final Check: Auditing Your Marketing Communications

Auditing your communications regularly is vital to make sure that they are at their most effective. When you do this audit, you're likely to find you need to:

- ✔ **Make the writing briefer.** If you can shorten the number and complexity of words, you make the communication easier and quicker for customers and prospects to read. These changes mean that more people read and understand your message. And that's a very good thing!

- ✔ **Correct errors.** You may think accuracy isn't an issue, but we're often surprised at the number of errors that we find in marketing communications. Trust us, somewhere in your printed materials or on your website or in an ad, your products or services are misrepresented. Wrong names, inaccurate technical details, incorrect addresses or product codes, and old prices may be creating confusion and losing the business sales.

- ✔ **Identify omissions.** In every business marketing materials, many places exist where the information is insufficient for customers or prospects to take the next step toward purchase. Sometimes all you need to do is add something as simple as a contact address or phone number; other times, you need to provide instructions for how to select the right product or option. But the most common of all is that you have to explain what the business is and does.

  For example, we have a nice golf umbrella sent to us by a business that had recently rebranded. The umbrella was designed to bring attention to the new name. But unfortunately, because most people don't know the name, they have no idea what the business does or what those words mean. Many probably simply believe the name is a brand of umbrella. The giveaway promotional item is a nice idea, but it would work better with a website address or some sort of logo or contact information so anyone interested can find out more.

✔ **Achieve consistency.** Each individual marketing message is part of your overall message, and you need to view each one that way. A worthwhile exercise is to find the major and minor inconsistencies in how you communicate and then come up with ideas for how to standardise across the board. When you communicate a consistent message, each individual communication helps create and maintain a strong, professional image in the marketplace instead of creating a weak, inconsistent or confusing one.

✔ **Improve persuasiveness.** We're amazed at how boring most marketing communications are. We like seeing writing jump off the page or the computer screen and seize readers by their eyeballs. Think carefully about what it would take for you to part with your money when reading an ad; why should your customers be any different?

We share these common corrections to marketing communications with you so that you can try to fix the problems yourself. Perform your own audit of every piece of written (or scripted) marketing communications your organisation does, looking for ways to make each item the best it can be.

Create an Ad on (Legal) Steroids

The headline can work magic, especially when combined with a good visual. We illustrate this point by designing our own ad that captures the idea that headlines and images can combine to have considerable marketing power.

The easiest and best way to write a strong headline is to start with an analogy or metaphor that captures the core concept. In this case, the concept is that a good headline can tie into the photo and be powerful. Imagine that we're working up an ad for our own firm's design services and we want to explain that we write powerful ads with strong headlines. Here's a way to express that idea with an analogy: 'A headline with a good photograph is like a traditional picture and caption on steroids'.

This statement isn't the headline. Not yet. It takes several stages to create a strong headline. Next step: we ask ourselves whether we like it. Are we on to something? If we say yes, we continue to work on it by simplifying and clarifying it. For example, we may decide that the statement is clearer and better this way: 'Should *Your* Ad Be on Steroids?'

Good! We've got a strong headline concept that seems to capture the point we want to make in an exciting and intriguing way. But how to illustrate it? Hmmm. How about a photo of a cricket player swinging a bat that has our headline written *on* it? Right there on the face of the bat: 'Should *Your* Ad Be on Steroids?' Beneath the ad, we can have a paragraph of copy such as:

> *Why not? It's perfectly legal in the great sport of marketing. The more power you can give your ad, the better! And when the power comes from words – plain, simple old-fashioned words – nobody gets hurt. But you may hit a six.*

Our ad can go on to describe the powerful copywriting and creative services of our marketing business. You can use the same technique in any consumer or business-to-business ad, including for *your* firm.

The bra firm Wonderbra ran a series of outdoor ads with the cheeky headline 'Hello Boys' above a lingerie-clad woman.

Now, a normal caption for that photograph may say something obvious and ordinary, such as 'A great bra to make you look your best'. However, that doesn't make for an exciting ad because it's too obvious and ordinary to catch the eye or hold the imagination. Hence the need to bump up the power of the writing with an analogy or idea that puts that caption on steroids.

After all, the term 'Hello boys' not only puts out an amusing call to women who want to look attractive in their underwear to attract men (plus men who may buy the brand for their wives or girlfriends) but it also refers to 'boys', the slang term for a woman's chest. Although some people may feel that the ad's a bit sexist, it certainly grabs attention! This ad manages to capture a big idea in a simple headline, and it's an excellent example of good headline writing.

Your challenge as a copywriter is to push through the early ideas and drafts of your ad and refuse to stop until you have a concept that supports a powerful headline. A headline that pumps the power of steroids into your ad. Most ads don't have this kind of power. And most ads don't get high readership and response. Hmmm. Wonder why? Maybe somebody decided to play a defensive stroke instead of swinging for the boundary (that's enough of the cricket metaphors).

When you design or commission your next print ad, web ad, poster, billboard or brochure, take the extra time to pump up an ordinary photo caption and make it into a caption on steroids. All great headlines are just that – captions on steroids.

Obtaining and Using Customer Testimonials

You can increase the persuasiveness of your marketing writing by adding a quote from a happy customer. For example, a restaurant ad that says, 'Our food is the best in the city' is less persuasive than an ad for the same restaurant that quotes a food critic who says the same thing. If you've received good publicity, check with the publication (or other media) to make sure that it doesn't mind you quoting the story and then include a short, accurate excerpt in your own marketing materials.

What if the media hasn't published glowing reviews that you can quote? You can still obtain testimonials, which are positive quotes from customers or other credible sources. However, you have to ask for them and then edit them into something short and clear enough to put quotes around and add to your brochure, sales letter, website or other marketing communication. (In the case of radio, TV and streaming video for the Internet, you also have to record the testimonial.) And most important, you have to obtain written permission from the source (or, if the source is under age, a parent) to use the testimonial in your marketing.

Chapter 15 contains lots more info on using all sorts of quotes and testimonials.

Files on the CD

Check out the following files on the CD-ROM:

- ✔ **File 14-1:** Evaluation Form 1
- ✔ **File 14-2:** Two Dimensions of Your Appeal
- ✔ **File 14-3:** Evaluation Form 2
- ✔ **File 14-4:** Press release about new Xerox logo

Chapter 15

Using Testimonials and Customer Stories

*J*ust imagine if a dozen of the best-known and most admired people in your industry wrote you personal testimonials saying how special your product or service is. Or if the top people from the best companies in your market gave you permission to print their endorsements in your business literature and ads. And what about having excellent customer quotes, lauding your business (or product) and saying how superior it is to all the competition?

Almost nothing beats the power of personal references, testimonials or quotes. When a credible, objective party says 'buy', your prospects are going to listen. Ads, sales sheets, brochures, letters and web pages are all more effective when they include a quote or case history.

Using Testimonials Effectively: A Real-Life Example

Some marketers have used customer quotes and testimonials for years, especially in direct-response print ads, brochures and letters. But most marketers ignore this powerful technique.

One business that uses quotes and examples from its past customers is the bookselling website AllYearBooks (www.allyearbooks.co.uk), a specialist business selling yearbooks to those schools, universities or individuals who want to compile a memory book.

These days, numerous businesses are willing to print books, and with so many easy desktop publishing programs, schools and universities no longer need a special yearbook company. They can probably have a pretty good attempt at making the yearbook up themselves and then have it printed in fairly large numbers.

So AllYearBooks needs to offer something that shows it can go a little bit over and above what schools or universities can handle themselves. Aside from lots of product information about what the service offers, customer quotes make up an important section of the website.

The business noted that many people may feel uncomfortable using online sites to create yearbooks without some feedback from other institutions that have gone through the same process. As a result, AllYearBooks has a great long list of testimonials on its site, from staff, pupils and individuals at many of the UK's most prestigious schools and universities, including Jesus College, Oxford and Bourne Grammar School. The idea is that potential customers check out what the website has to offer and then see who else has used it, deciding 'Oh well, if it was good enough for them . . .'

Borrowing a Page from Books

The book business uses testimonials frequently. Some authors plan their cover quotes before they even write their books. Publicists rush advance copies or bound galleys of books to key reviewers early in the book-production process in the hope of snagging a quote from a favourable review in a well-known newspaper or magazine. Authors network madly to line up the addresses of experts and celebrities and then shower them with letters and samples of their writing in the hope of getting cover quotes from the rich and famous. When you see several impressive quotes on the outside of a book, you know that the author or his publicist devoted dozens of hours to securing those well-chosen words.

When Harvey Mackay was writing his first book, *Swim with the Sharks Without Being Eaten Alive,* he launched a major campaign to line up celebrity endorsements. If you ask enough people, some of them are bound to say yes just because the exposure is good for their image, too. Well, Mackay asked lots of people for quotes, many of them well-known celebrities. And more than 40 gave their testimonials for promoting what went on to become a runaway bestseller. The reading public had the distinct impression that Mackay was already a celebrity himself, even though in truth, he had really been networking with most of those respected, successful endorsers and didn't know them personally.

Understanding Why Quotes Work

But why go to all the trouble to secure a few brief quotes? Because a good quote sells.

Basically, the idea is to let someone the prospect *believes* do the selling instead of you. You're the marketer. Nobody is going to take you seriously when you say that your product or service is superior. If you don't believe us, here are some statistics to prove it. According to e-business information supplier NetExtract, 71 per cent of UK online shoppers seek out reviews before buying. Satisfaction for those who recalled customer reviews on the retailers' sites is also 10 per cent higher than those who said no reviews were offered, claims the Online Retail Satisfaction Index. If you aren't using customers to recommend your service on your website, you're missing out on a chance to put across a flattering review of your products or services.

To make the quote powerful, you need to get some quote or story from a source that the prospect is going to believe, and you need to make that quote or story available to a prospective buyer at or near the point of purchase. (The *point of purchase* is the time and place where the prospect makes a decision that affects your sales.)

When people are at the point of purchase, the timing is right: they're interested in what you have to sell, and they're ready to consider your offer seriously. At this moment, they want to believe in your product or service. If they find your claims credible, they'll probably buy your product or service. But prospective customers are naturally suspicious, and this is the time when testimonials and other evidence of product quality and believability are the most powerful. For instance, testimonials can reach out to someone who's just picked up a book and is considering purchasing it but isn't quite sure whether the book will really meet his expectations.

Using Quotes in Catalogues

In the preceding section, we say that testimonials work well at the point of purchase when someone is considering buying a product off the shelf. But many other possible points of purchase also exist. Sometimes people make their purchase decisions while in front of a salesperson; sometimes they decide when they're in front of their computer looking at a web page; and sometimes they decide when they're reading a direct-mail piece, such as a sales letter or catalogue. All these instances are points of purchase, so using testimonials or customer stories in them can be effective as well.

Catalogue shoppers often need supporting evidence when they're examining the claims about a product in a catalogue. To them, a product may sound good, but is the catalogue overstating the product's virtues? How can the shopper be sure? Again, a testimonial from an expert or a quote or example from a satisfied customer at this point of purchase can lift sales by helping the involved shopper believe the marketing claims.

When you're selling expensive products or services to businesses, providing enough evidence to make your claims believable is especially important.

Seeking Customer Testimonials

In truth, the use of testimonials and customer stories is a relatively rare marketing strategy. If they are so effective in lifting sales at the prospect's point of purchase, why don't marketers use them more often?

We think part of the reason most marketers don't use testimonials is because they're not aware of the power of this technique. Marketing or advertising courses at business schools don't teach this technique and marketing textbooks also don't cover this topic. Plus, this strategy isn't a common practice among marketers and managers. And because using testimonials is an uncommon strategy, most people are unclear about how to use them. They aren't even sure who to ask for a quote or how to ask them. In this section, we show you how to obtain good, useful customer testimonials.

Whom to ask for testimonials

The first thing stopping many people from lining up testimonials is that they aren't sure whom to ask for quotes. So that's the first thing to clear up. Basically, *you can ask anyone who has a legitimate, authoritative opinion* about your product, service or business. If someone obviously should have an opinion, you can certainly ask for it. Here are some of the more common prospects to consider when seeking a testimonial, case history or other useable contribution:

✔ Your customers.

✔ Friends in management positions in businesses or in other positions of recognised authority, such as accountants, doctors or politicians.

✔ Experts in your industry or technology, such as well-known authors, professors or journalists.

✔ People who run a consulting, real-estate or insurance firm; they're always looking for exposure, and the public often sees them as experts.

✔ People who you can get to sample or review your offerings (such as in a test market, in-store sampling or introductory promotional offer).

✔ People who are sufficiently well known and routinely get such requests and have an established system for handling them.

✔ Editors of newsletters, magazines or e-newsletters about your industry.

You have or can make plenty of opportunities to talk to people in most of these categories. So asking them for their opinion on a specific question concerning your business can be perfectly natural. Take advantage of these opportunities to pop the question and see what raw testimonials you can harvest just by enquiring.

Some people may not be within your circle of regular contacts. Don't despair. If they're well known, they're probably used to such requests. They may have a publicist, secretary or assistant who handles requests for testimonials or other public appearances routinely. Just call or ask around until you find out what the proper approach is, and then send a professional written request.

With celebrity endorsers, you may want to suggest some simple phrases or quotes that they can consider using if they don't have the desire to write their own from scratch. Also, be sure to describe the sort of use you intend to put their quote to, with specific references to how neatly and professionally you're going to present it and how many people you expect to see and read (or hear) it. That way, the big fish can decide more easily whether this is a good exposure opportunity for him.

Whenever you ask for a testimonial, enclose a short, simple release form for the person to sign, which says something like 'I freely give [place your business name here] permission to use the following quote from me in its marketing communications and to cite me by name as the source of this quote.' Check with a lawyer for more specific advice about how to craft the best release statement.

When you approach a well-known individual for a quote, your odds of success are a lot lower than when you approach your own customers or other people you already know. Also, the turnaround is going to be considerably slower. But don't worry. If you keep trying, you'll probably line up one or two as a minimum. And even if you don't, customer quotes are often more believable and more compelling than celebrity endorsements anyway.

Don't be too pushy when asking people for quotes. Some people just don't feel comfortable lending their names. Often lower-level employees in a business don't have the authority to lend their names and titles to others without clearance from their bosses, which isn't that easy to secure. Other people are simply not into the idea of participating in your project and don't have any interest in seeing their names in your marketing materials. That's fine. Don't bug these people or businesses. For every one of these people, there's another person who loves your product or service and enjoys taking part in anything that gives him exposure. Just keep looking until you find people who are happy to contribute. They're out there waiting to be found, and so few people ask for their contributions that they're probably happy to help if you ask.

Stay far away from people who raise the question of payment. Anyone who says, 'Sure, I'm willing to give you a quote. How much are you offering?' isn't thinking about the opportunity as a simple favour that may come round to help them some day in the future. They're trying to milk the situation. People who think that way are likely to come up with other ways to bother you for money in the future.

And besides, you don't really get an objective testimonial if you pay for it, and it certainly doesn't mean as much as one given because someone genuinely likes your product or service. And if it ever becomes public that you paid for this recommendation, your potential customers will think you're an untrustworthy business – if you're as good as you say, why pay for a quote?

So when you bump into someone who wants to profit from your request for their feedback and assistance, just thank them kindly and back out as gracefully and quickly as you can.

What to request in a testimonial

The next stumbling block that stops many people from getting testimonials is that they don't know what to ask for. Basically, *you can ask people for any information or opinions that wouldn't embarrass them in public.*

Your request for a testimonial should be specific because this makes your request easier to answer and less easy to object to.

Here are some examples of specific requests:

✔ What the person's opinion is of your product or service.

✔ A description of how the person used your product or service and what happened as a result.

✔ What the person's view is of where the industry, product category, technology, economy or whatever is going.

✔ Information about which of your products or services the person uses.

✔ How often the person uses your product or service or how much of it he uses.

✔ Why the person uses your product or service.

✔ What the person thinks the best things about your product or service are.

✔ Who the person would recommend your product or service to.

✔ What the person would recommend your product or service for.

And the less well you know someone, the more specific your request needs to be. When you ask close friends for a reference, they generally say, 'Sure, just tell me what you want me to say.' But people you know more casually are not likely to be as easy to work with. To them, a general request for a favour like that may seem inappropriate or difficult. So be more specific as you work outward from your immediate circle of friends and associates.

Ensuring a helpful response

Being specific in your questions is important if you want to receive a helpful answer. Think about the difference between asking someone for one of these specifics versus just asking them for a recommendation or testimonial. Imagine you know us vaguely as the owners of a business from which your business buys some computer repair services. You don't normally think about us or our services unless you have a problem with your computers. But today, you've just received an email from us asking for a personal quote from you recommending our service to other businesses.

What do you do with this request? Perhaps a flat refusal, but you don't actually want to be rude. So, probably nothing at all. You may dash off a hearty recommendation and send it back by email, but that scenario's not very likely because the request is so broad and poorly defined. What should the recommendation say? How long should it be? How should you write it? If you just ask someone for a vague recommendation, you're asking him to do something that's difficult and poorly defined – and something that doesn't offer him any obvious major benefit to justify the difficulty of the task.

Now try a more specific request using one of the suggestions from the list in the preceding section. Imagine now that we emailed not a generic request for a recommendation, but something like:

> *Dear Ms. Franklin,*
>
> *As one of your regular suppliers for several years, we are writing to ask if you can tell us what sort of businesses you think our computer repair services are especially well suited for.*
>
> *Would you recommend them for large businesses? Small? High-tech? General?*
>
> *Do you think the businesses need to have a lot of technical expertise to take full advantage of our services or not?*
>
> *Your opinion would be especially helpful right now as we are preparing our marketing plan and designing our marketing materials. Just a quick sentence or two is all we really need, because we are sure you are busy.*
>
> *Thanks so much for your input!*
>
> *Sincerely,*
>
> *Simon Smith and Dave Curry, Owners, ABC Computer Services*

This email script asks for one simple, clear thing: who the customer would recommend your services to. That's a very easy question to answer for any reasonably happy customer. You're likely to get a positive response, such as the following:

> *Dear Simon and Dave,*
>
> *Got your note. Happy to help but in a hurry. Basically, I'd say ABC's services would be useful for any business within this geographic area, as long as they have computers that need maintenance. I think your service is great! By the way, can you remind Joanne that she is supposed to get us a bid on a new graphics workstation? Thanks.*
>
> *Anne Franklin*

Congratulations! You just landed a testimonial in the raw. It may not look like much right now, but with a little work it can become a powerful marketing tool.

If you want to use this script as a template for your own efforts, you can find it on the CD (File 15-1).

Processing the testimonial

When people give you a quote, you usually get their unedited writing. To process this raw testimonial, you need to isolate and refine the language. Here's an example of a sentence from a customer that needs some editing:

'Basically, I'd say ABC's services would be useful for any business within this geographic area, as long as they have computers that need maintenance. I think your service is great!'

This recommendation is a start, but it isn't quite as short or punchy as it needs to be. Tightening up the text a bit by cutting superfluous words (such as *'basically'*) and by substituting briefer words or phrases for lengthy or poorly chosen ones is perfectly reasonable. Just don't make the recommendation say anything that it didn't originally. For instance, you can't add 'I love this business' if that thought isn't there to start with. But you can massage the text into the following form without violating the spirit of the original quote:

'ABC's services are great! They're useful to any business in the area with computers that need maintenance.'

We moved up the bit with stopping power and changed 'would be' to 'are', because present tense is always stronger for testimonials. And now that we isolated and cleaned up that offhand sentence from the middle of your customer's busy email, the quote is beginning to show some real promise as a marketing communication.

Seeking permission to use the testimonial

Your testimonial isn't finished until you *have permission* to attach its author's name to it. So you need to email the source again, this time asking for permission to quote the earlier email. You may do so using a script such as:

Dear Anne,

Thanks so much for your email. We're attaching that bid Joanne promised you. It took her longer than she expected, but the good news is she found some alternatives that offer the same performance at a lower cost. One of our bigger suppliers is discounting several high-end models to get rid of back inventory, and we can pass the savings along to you.

Your answer to my question was very helpful. Thanks for participating. It helps us refine our strategies, and we're also considering including a few quotes from customers in our next brochure or other marketing communications. With a little editing to shorten it, the answer you gave reads, 'ABC's services are great! They're useful to any business in the area with computers that need maintenance.' If you have any objection with our referencing this quote or would like to review specific uses of it, please let us know. Otherwise, we will include it in our upcoming brochure, alongside some other quotes. Thanks again for your help.

Best,

Simon and Dave

We scripted this reply carefully to keep it low key. We don't want to put images in the customer's mind of her name and quote being plastered all over late-night television or on a huge billboard beside the motorway. We want to keep the reply professional and cool in tone so that she just glances at it and thinks, 'Wonder why they want that? Not much of a quote really. But it is what I said after all, and what harm can there be in it?'

Note that you have two options in how you solicit quotes. The first option is to ask a specific question in order to generate a quote (as Simon and Dave did in the preceding example), and then – if you like the quote – seek permission to use it in your marketing. A second approach is to ask upfront for permission to use a quote, and then ask specific questions to generate one. If you're sure that the person will co-operate, try the latter. If you aren't so sure what response you're going to get, try the former. Then you don't have to deal with the embarrassing situation of having to decline using a quote because it isn't as positive as you'd hoped!

Assuming that you solicited a quote first – one that you like – you have more than one way to ask for permission to use it. You can assume permission and just write to confirm, as we illustrated in the preceding example, or you can assume that you don't have permission and ask for it.

The following example represents the latter approach (it's also on File 15-2). This script takes a slightly different tack in other ways, too, emphasising the positive responses from customers, which tends to make people feel good about being part of the event.

> *Dear Jane,*
>
> *Thank you for your response to my questions. I appreciate your help and am frankly amazed by the many positive responses my request generated from our customers. Although we certainly intend to continue improving our services over time, it is gratifying to know that so many customers currently have positive things to say about our business.*
>
> *I'd like to include your quote in our future marketing materials and would appreciate it greatly if you'd confirm that this is acceptable in a return letter, fax or email. And, in addition, if you'd like us to include some background information about your business or products, send that along as well.*
>
> *Once again, thanks for your assistance. Your participation in this outreach project is greatly appreciated, as is your continued business. Do let me know if we can do anything more for you.*
>
> *Sincerely,*
>
> *Matt*

If you don't mind being just a little bit pushy, you can end your communication to a prospective recommender by telling him to contact you if he objects to you using the quote, the way we did in our sample email reply to Anne Franklin. Then, if you don't hear back, you can reasonably presume that you have the person's permission to use it.

But if you think that customers may object to that approach, end the email with a request that they respond one more time to confirm their permission to let you use their quotes. Then you have to wait for their replies, and some percentage of them don't ever get back, forcing you to give up or to go begging with a reminder email or phone call. But some customers *will* return a confirmation. After all, the quote is in their own words, and they already sent it to you, so saying that you have permission to quote them isn't a big step.

Either way, if you ask enough customers to start with (say, at least ten), in the long run you end up with sufficient authority to include quotes from some of your customers in future marketing communications. If you line up even three or four quotes with this technique, you're in a position to harness the power of testimonials in your marketing.

What if some people get cold feet but you liked their initial quotes? Even if some people balk at permitting you to use their names, you can still find good uses for those quotes. After all, they're legitimate quotes, and you have (we hope you have!) hard copies of the source emails, letters or written notes on the phone conversations in your files. You can use the quotes, attributing them to a general description of the person and/or business. 'President, financial institution' or 'Bank Executive' may do fine if the local bank's president ducks your requests and never confirms that you can attribute the quote directly to him. A quote is a quote, and it can add value to marketing communications even if you have to attribute it to an anonymous 'Regular Customer'.

Don't ever attach someone's name to a quote unless that person has explicitly allowed you to do so.

Putting those testimonials to use

The final step is using the quotes effectively in your marketing efforts. Put them together on a single sheet of paper so you can get a good feel for how they read and can decide what order you want to see them in.

Include as much information as possible regarding the person endorsing your product or service. Many marketers are afraid to ask permission to include all someone's details, and so they list Greg B., rather than a full name. This type of acknowledgement, however, simply gives the perception that the recommendation may be fake.

Avoiding legal traps

Many countries regulate advertising, so you always have to be careful to make honest, well-supported claims in any marketing communications. This point is certainly true for testimonials. The Office of Fair Trading in the UK recently launched two spoof websites to highlight the problem of false customer testimonials, particularly in the health and weight loss areas. The websites are for Fatfoe pads (www.consumerdirect.gov.uk/fatfoe), which pretends to suck out fat as people sleep, and Glucobate (www.consumerdirect.gov.uk/glucobate), which promises a diabetes cure. The sites are littered with fake customer and medical professional endorsements to show just how people can spot a false testimonial in future. With the government spotlight on catching out any firms making fake claims, it would be foolish to try getting away with this.

Another trap to avoid is using the pictures of celebrities in your advert without their permission. The racing driver Eddie Irvine won damages after it was proved that radio station Talksport had used an image of him in its advert without permission. Although the radio station may well have legitimately bought the picture, the judge ruled that by using the image of Irvine, this suggested the driver endorsed the station. So avoid messy legal difficulties by steering clear of using anything where the person involved hasn't given overt permission and don't ever consider faking anything in your marketing materials.

You can avoid such problems if you make sure that you do everything above board. For instance:

✔ **Don't pay for your testimonials.** Get only genuine quotes from happy customers or others who are expressing their honest opinions for free.

✔ **Make sure that any quotes say things that are patently obvious, that reflect the truth and are statements that you can easily substantiate.** Customer opinions about the quality of your service are easy to prove if you have the letter on file. But don't ask your customer to give you a testimonial saying, '100 per cent of leading doctors say that using this product will make you immortal.' In other words, be reasonable in what you claim or ask others to claim.

✔ **Let them express their own opinions instead of having them state facts.** For example, if a man says that he believes your weight-loss product is the best one he's tried and he has encouraged friends and family to do so, that's his opinion. But if you get a man to claim that he's used your product and it's undoubtedly the best on the market, you may run into difficulties. Make sure that you are always clearly showing your customers' views to be their opinions, and you shouldn't have anyone challenge that.

Another legal issue concerns the provider's rights to his or her quote. If a person says or writes something, he may have legal rights to it under copyright law. So you need to make sure that you get permission to use the quotes in your marketing. *In writing.* And keep a record of your request as well as the customer's reply, so that it's clear that you're using his quote as you said you would and as he said you could. A nicely maintained file of your correspondence is good protection. And so is good legal advice – from a lawyer, not just a couple of authors of a marketing book, like us.

BROOKLANDS COLLEGE LIBRARY WEYBRIDGE. SURREY KT13 8TT

The best way to have full, clear and accurate information about the source of a testimonial is to ask the person to fill in a short form when you ask for permission (see the preceding section 'Seeking permission to use the testimonial'). Ask for the source's name, position or title, and employer (if relevant). Include the phrase 'as the source wishes this information to appear in your marketing materials' on the form to make sure that the source has given you permission not only for the quote, but also for the identifying information.

You really have no limits to how you can use these quotes. We like them sprinkled in ads, brochures and catalogues. They add a lot of credibility to direct-mail offers, and you may even consider putting some on the outside of your envelope to increase the likelihood of potential customers opening it.

Testimonials can appear on web pages to good effect. (Using quotes is vital if your customers often use your website to research their purchases or browse your product selection.) If you have enough material, create a button on your site labelled 'Customer Testimonials' and allow viewers to click through to an entire page or more of such quotes. If you have some longer case-history type customer stories, don't just stick to quotes but add a tab or button called 'Customer Case Histories'. Write these stories in the third-person point of view, as if in a newspaper, or in first person, as if the customers are telling it. And, of course, get written permission for your quotes and keep the permissions on file.

Using Customer Videos and Photos

Candid customer comments or reactions on video or audiotape have many of the same virtues and uses as written testimonials. You can use them to create effective radio or television ads, and you can use them in a promotional video you distribute to prospects if you do business-to-business marketing. Some private schools and colleges now hand out videos to prospective students, and these videos are a great medium for some candid reactions as well as for testimonials from students and alumni.

We also encourage you to consider using customer footage on your website if your product is particularly visual or has an effect on customer appearances. The technology exists to put short (keep it short, please!) clips of video or audio recordings on sites and to make them available at the click of a button. People love watching TV, and they gladly sit and watch short videos on your website if they're interesting or relevant. Videos pull people into a site, increase the amount of time that they spend there and also increase the credibility of your marketing claims.

Photos of customers combined with their quotes or comments are also powerful marketing tools. This tactic helps build up the image of the recommending customer in other prospects' minds and makes it appear more believable. You can include them on a web page, in a catalogue, in print ads and even on a product's packaging.

Get written permission from people you show in a photo or video. Make up a release form in advance that explains what you intend to do with their photograph or recording and that makes clear that they're allowing you to use the product for that purpose (see the later section 'Don't forget to ask permission!'). If someone objects, stop using the image or recording. But usually people are happy to be included.

Photographing endorsers

We like the idea of using a customer's photo, perhaps with a short quote in his own words. You see this technique in some print advertising for consumer products, although when major advertisers do it, the presentation is so slick that you're never sure whether the person is a real customer or a paid model, which reduces its effectiveness. The best photos are honest, genuine ones. They show a real person, hopefully a reasonably attractive and friendly one, but not some smooth-skinned model who looks like all the other models in the fashion magazines.

If one or more customers agree to be photographed for your ad, catalogue, web page or other marketing communication, remember that you have to do all the work involved. You must hire a professional photographer who routinely does portrait work outside the studio. You want the photographer to take portraits of your customer, so make sure that you find a photographer with plenty of comparable work in his portfolio. Then arrange a time for the photographer to visit the subject at home (if the ad is for a retail product or service) or at work (if the ad is for a business-to-business product or service). Assume that the photographer needs about an hour to get a decent shot and that the session is going to cost you anywhere from £100 to £500, depending on the photographer.

We think that digital cameras make everyone a photographer because you can see the image right at the moment and take more if you didn't capture just what you need. We suggest you invest in a corporate digital camera that everyone is allowed to borrow so that you're sure to get an ongoing archival and promotional file to assist in marketing. Photocopy a pile of permission forms that employees take along with the camera to make it easy to obtain releases from the subjects of the photos.

Make sure that you get the subject to give you written permission to use his image in your marketing. Having a lawyer draw up a simple release form for your subject to sign may also be wise.

A word about video quality

Make sure that you use high-quality video cameras to record customers' candid reactions. The average home video camera doesn't produce as fine an image as you'd probably like to use, even for local television advertising or a business promotional video. If you have access to professional-quality digital cameras, they're obviously the best idea. Or, if you have a big enough business that you can afford to use a professional production studio, just turn the filming over to them and tell them to get high-quality, usable footage of customers or you won't pay them for their work.

Keep in mind the importance of good lighting, whether you make the video yourself or hire a crew to do it. Basically, all cameras, including digital video cameras, take better pictures when *more light* is available. If you can shoot under bright indoor lights or outdoors on a bright day, you're likely to get a video that looks good. If

you film in a dim interior room or at night, the video footage doesn't look good. Bright light not only gives a good sharp image, but also permits greater *depth of field* (in other words, the depth is in focus). In dim light, the camera has to adjust itself (or someone has to adjust it) by opening up its *aperture* (the hole that lets light come in). And the wider the aperture, the more shallow the area that's in focus. So the foreground and background of a scene are blurry when the light is dim, but increase the lighting, and everything jumps into sharper focus.

If you want to use sound (such as the customer's voice), plug a good quality microphone into the camera and hold the mike near the sound source. Don't count on built-in camera mikes; they aren't good enough for most marketing uses. Sound should be clear and crisp enough to match the clear, crisp visuals from that good camera you're using in bright light.

Making candid customer videos

TV commercials using customer testimonials are among the most effective ads. Not flashy, but effective. They don't win design awards in the advertising industry, but they do win high believability ratings from viewers – especially when they use candid testimonials.

A *candid testimonial* is what a customer says and does before you tell him that you're recording. For instance, a car dealership may have a hidden video camera on the floor of its showroom aimed at a centrally placed new model that looks really great. An employee can monitor the camera's view from a nearby office or a hiding place on the showroom floor and when a shopper approaches the new model, the employee turns the camera on and hopes for a good reaction. Perhaps the shopper does a double-take upon opening the driver's door and says, 'Wow! I've got to have one of these!' and then jumps right in. And the video camera captures it all. Think how much more effective a commercial would be if it had a few candid reactions praising a new model instead of a fast-talking salesman in a cheap suit!

You can also create more heavily managed situations designed to increase the chances of usable responses. For instance, you can set up a booth in a shopping centre where you display samples of a retail product and invite people to interact with it. You can even have someone who knows where the camera is to engage these people in conversations, asking them what they think, to make sure they deliver some lines in the right place – facing the hidden camera and/or microphone. Similarly, you can demonstrate a business-to-business product or service at a trade show in a booth that's set up for recording. Getting some footage of candid customer reactions to a product or service isn't too hard if you do some advance planning.

Don't forget to ask permission!

The key is obviously to ask whomever you quote or photograph for permission for whatever use you have in mind. Be specific and clear about what you want to do. Ask in writing and get a written response, preferably with the person's signature (email is a little less solid from a legal perspective). And when you're going to use a photo or video – in other words, the person's likeness – you need to be extra careful about getting appropriate permission. In the paperwork, make it clear that you're using his likeness. Also, consider getting legal advice, especially if your organisation makes enough money to be an attractive deep pocket target for legal actions.

After you record a candid customer reaction, look at it immediately and see whether the result is any good. If it's inadequate, just plan to discard it and don't trouble the customer for permission. If it may be usable, however, immediately speak to the subject.

Explain that you're doing a candid camera operation and that you caught the person's reaction on video. If possible, keep the video rolling as you explain so that you can record his reaction to supplement his written permission. Thank him and treat him kindly. Try to encourage his natural tendency to be amused and pleasantly surprised. If he's angry, apologise and promise that you're going to discard the footage. Then go on to the next subject. But if he doesn't seem to mind, secure his permission right away to use the video. Ask him if you can use the tape in future marketing communications. Get his 'yes' on tape, and then have him sign a permission form and make sure that everything is clear.

He may want to see a copy of the finished ad or whatever the product will be. This request is certainly reasonable, and you should promise to send a copy to him as soon as it's finished.

If you're going to describe the person providing the testimonial as being affili-ated with an organisation, make sure that the person has the authority to give you permission to mention the organisation's name, too. A senior executive obviously has this authority, but if you interview a mailroom clerk at a big company and plan to run a quote from him in which you describe him as an employee of that company, you'd better check with the firm's publicity depart-ment first. The company may have a policy against endorsing products or ser-vices, and you don't want to find out about it after you've printed a thousand brochures. After all, nothing's worse than receiving a blow to your testimonials!

And Now for an Easy Alternative

You may want to harness the power of customer testimonials without actu-ally securing any. That's impossible. But you can do some next-best things that work pretty well. The best alternative to getting customer testimonials is to create a plausible fictional situation in which you create a customer char-acter or characters. Then you tell a story, perhaps using dialogue or quotes, which conveys an accurate picture of what makes your product or service great.

Basically, what you do is substitute fiction for non-fiction. Many consumer ads use fictional scenes and characters to make their points. Simply turn on a TV or radio and take in a few dozen ads, and you come across at least a few of this type.

You can also create dialogue between fictional characters. Radio ads in which two people talk about a product are fairly common and can work well. These ads often attempt to be humorous, and sometimes even are, but don't have to be. As long as the characters personify the feelings of the listener, the listeners may identify with them just as strongly as they would identify with real customers.

Selling Services with Customer Stories

Services are intangible. You can't take them for a test drive or kick their wheels. You have to imagine them. When people shop for services, they often have difficulty deciding whether what they imagine is really appropriate and whether it will have sufficient quality to meet their needs.

For example, how do you know that a bank can handle your business current account well? You don't. You just assume that a bank with a well-known name and a well-built branch is able to provide basic banking services. You're using two symbolic indicators of the quality of the bank's service to aid your imagination: its brand name and its facility. Other indicators of the quality of the bank's service, such as how professional the tellers appear and how nice the chequebooks are, also may influence you.

Whenever people shop for a service, they rely significantly on such indicators of service quality. For this reason, service marketers are supposed to manage the evidence, which means making sure that your lobby, brochure, staff and other visible elements are professional and appealing. And that's good advice. But we like to add another strategy, which is to let the people who actually *know* how good your service is give evidence to customers who want to find out.

Customer stories and testimonials are especially powerful when you're marketing services. Some consulting firms use them to good effect by including brief case histories of past client work in their brochures or presentation folders. The Jack Morton Company, a specialist in marketing events and promotions, uses this strategy very effectively. Some years ago, the company went to some of its best customers and obtained permission to write descriptions of specific projects that it did for those clients. The Jack Morton Company printed each project description on a single sheet of glossy paper and included a colour photo to illustrate it. The clients agreed to let the company use their names and stories in these marketing devices. When future clients want to get a better idea of how this company's services work, they can simply read actual real-life stories from past clients. Powerful evidence indeed.

Files on the CD

Check out the following files on the CD-ROM:

- ✔ **File 15-1:** Script for soliciting a testimonial
- ✔ **File 15-2:** Follow-up letter script

Part V
Sales and Service Success

'And as they move so slowly, people can actually read the message.'

In this part . . .

It all comes down to sales in the end. Are they up or
down? Did you land the new account or not? Did the
customer reorder or switch to a competitor? Did the leads
from the trade show convert to sales or just end up wasting your time? The answers to these vital questions are
often written in the details of how you select, approach
and interact with your prospects. Even the best marketing
programmes too often struggle on the shores of sales
errors and mistakes.

In this part, we share techniques and processes for managing customer interactions and for closing important
sales. We also show you how managing your attitude can,
and does, drive sales success – or lack thereof.

Chapter 16

Mastering the Sales Process

· ·

· ·

*T*his chapter focuses on ways of making a sale in person. Salespeople interact with customers to help them find what they want and to make them feel good about making a purchase. Building contractors discuss a project with the prospective customer and then prepare and present a proposal they hope wins them the job. Business-to-business marketers contact prospects in person, and by email and telephone, to generate business.

Even businesses that don't seem to use personal selling often have occasional need for the skill. For example, the owner of a web-based business may need to make a sales pitch to a bank loan officer or investor in order to fund an expansion plan.

Personal selling is an incredibly important part of marketing. This chapter looks at how the sales process works and how you can maximise its effectiveness in your business.

Walking through the Sales Process

Every expert has a different model of the sales process. Some models are simple. Many are highly elaborate. And, to be honest, few of them really give you much help in improving your sales success because they're rarely realistic or prescriptive.

We favour a model that reflects the reality that you need to do some work to figure out what the prospect needs, and then you present your offerings to meet that need (what we call a *need-driven* sales process). We also favour a model that suggests what to do and how and when to do it to optimise your sales efficiency. Sometimes, for example, you may have to abandon a sales call and go on another – something few sales models or trainers are willing to promote.

The following is the sales process model we generally prefer when we train salespeople or work on the sales and marketing process.

- ✔ **Step 1: Contact.** This first step involves identifying prospects through lead-generation systems, cold calls, referrals and any other methods you can think of to recruit potential buyers. As the name of this step implies, the point is to create the context for prolonged contact with prospects so that you can attempt to make the sale. Speak (by phone or in person) or write (via email or letter) to prospects to ask for a chance to see them. Set up appointments or find a way to drop by and catch them at an available moment. Plan and make that vital contact that opens the door to the sales process.

- ✔ **Step 2: Need-discovery.** This step focuses on gaining a sufficient under-standing of the prospect and her situation so that you can propose a purchase that makes sense for her. Use brief interactions or the begin-ning of a longer sales meeting to ask confirming and exploring ques-tions in order to discover more about the prospect's requirements. The knowledge and insight you gain in this phase helps you present a proposal that's customised to the needs of the prospect. The later sec-tion 'Exploring need-discovery techniques' contains more details on this step.

- ✔ **Step 3: Proposal(s).** In this step, present your offerings to your prospect – show what you have to sell. But because you've done some discovery in the previous step, you adapt your presentation to the needs and wants of the prospect. You may describe certain services or products and not others. You may emphasise price to one prospect, quality to another and speed to a third. And where possible, show spe-cifically how your products and/or services can help the prospect over-come constraints and achieve her goals.

- ✔ **Step 4: Attempted closes.** In this step, you ask the prospect for busi-ness. You initiate the process of making an actual sale and see how she reacts. If the prospect is reluctant, you can cycle back to Step 3 or even to Step 2, based on your judgement of the situation. Then, make another attempt to close the deal later on.

In general, we suggest trying at least three times to close before you conclude that the prospect is truly unwilling to make a purchase at the moment. After that, you need to do a reality check to make sure that you have an appropriate prospect. If attempts to close go poorly, you may decide that this prospect is the wrong one for you, or just the wrong time to be making a sale. Maybe she just isn't ready to buy yet, or maybe she wants to but can't afford to. If you discover a problem that prevents the sale from going through, back off gracefully and quickly look for another prospect. No use wasting time on improbabilities when the world is full of new possibilities waiting for you to discover.

✔ **Step 5: Follow-up.** In this step, you contact the prospect after the sales meeting to thank her for her time (and for the order, if you closed), to reinforce any key points and to prepare the prospect for the next contact. If your attempts to close failed, explore the reasons why and seek a future opportunity to re-contact the prospect and initiate another sales effort. If the close succeeded, confirm the purchase and prepare the prospect for the next step.

✔ **Step 6: Service.** In this step, you build upon the initial sale. You seek future sales, and you continue to explore needs and propose solutions in an ongoing effort to form a consultative selling partnership with the prospect. Excellent customer service and follow-through on all promises are vital now. You may need to monitor the service and keep up good relations for a long time after the initial sales meeting ends.

Figure 16-1 illustrates this sales process, showing several options for moving through it depending on how the prospect reacts. The sales process may not flow smoothly from step to step. Sometimes, you need to revisit earlier steps. Other times, you need to abandon all hope and write off the prospect, moving on to another prospect and sales attempt, at least for the time being. (Lost causes sap your time and enthusiasm, so please avoid them!)

Getting the Most out of Your Contacts

You need to identify and then establish contact with any prospects before you can hope to make a sale to them. In this section, we present a few of the strategies you can use to reach out and identify prospects and cue them up for a sales contact. We also present ideas on how to make the most of any incoming sales calls. Finally, we explain the importance of need-discovery techniques in building a successful relationship with your contact.

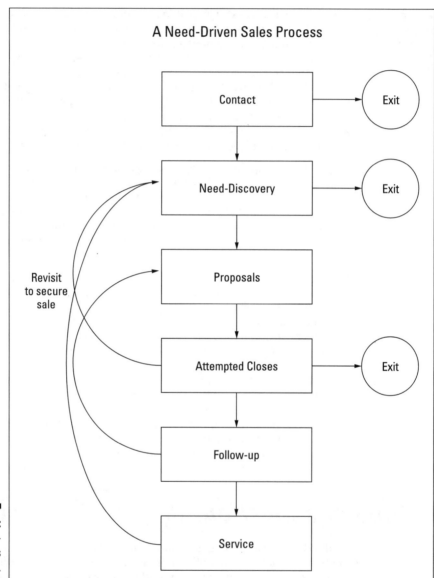

A Need-Driven Sales Process

Figure 16-1:
A need-driven sales process.

Gaining contacts

Here are some ways of generating *leads* (names and contact information of likely prospects):

✓ Attend or display at a trade show, convention or other event that attracts prospects. Make sure that you find ways to interact with prospects and collect information about them for later follow-ups. One thing is for sure: if you don't attend, you're surely invisible to potential clients.

✓ Buy mailing lists from list compilers, brokers, membership organisations or subscription-based publications. Send letters, postcards, fliers or other mail solicitations inviting prospects to return something by mail, visit your website or call if they're interested in more information. Use telephone sales or personal sales calls to follow up with the ones who respond.

✓ Buy email lists and use them just as you would a mailing list.

✓ Network with friends and customers to find new prospects.

✓ Speak at industry or community events to let people know the work you do and to share your expertise. Collect leads after the event.

✓ Run a small display ad in an appropriate magazine or newspaper and include your telephone number, website details and/or address. Use the ad to generate inquiries from interested prospects.

✓ Develop a telephone sales script and have an employee, temp worker or telemarketing firm (for larger lists) make calls to generate leads or try closing some sales for you.

✓ Write and post a weekly blog full of tips and ideas that prospective customers are likely to appreciate. Include ways for readers to get in touch with you if they're interested in more information.

✓ Include a 'Join Our Mailing List' or 'Sign Up for Our Newsletter' button on your web page to attract interested prospects. When they fill out a form with their contact information, send them your newsletter and other mailings, and also put them on your call list for future contact.

✓ Send an email newsletter to interested prospects (who have opted-in to receive information from your business), sharing useful information and positioning yourself or your business as a source of expertise. In the newsletter, include marketing messages designed to bring prospects your way, by phone or through a supporting website.

Utilising your incoming sales calls

Many businesses list a freephone number and web address in directories, marketing materials and ads, and then wait for calls or web orders. When calls come in, they're typically from prospects expecting to talk to someone who may be able to help them make a purchase. So the salesperson answering the phone is in an enviable position and simply needs to help callers figure out what they need and then write up the orders. But is it that simple?

If you have non-salespeople answering the phones and taking orders, you're missing a great chance to do some selling. Anyone who responds to a marketing communication and makes the effort to call you is a serious prospect and deserves serious sales attention. Whoever handles that call needs to be knowledgeable and skilled in soft-sell sales methods because, in addition to simply writing up the prospect's order, the salesperson can conceivably pursue a number of other marketing objectives, such as:

- Gathering useful information about the caller for your database (and for use in future marketing initiatives aimed at the caller).
- Cross-selling other products/services to the caller.
- Helping the caller make a tough decision.
- Diagnosing the caller's situation and suggesting solutions (involving your products/services if possible, of course!).
- Projecting a positive, helpful, interested image for your business that brings the prospect back again and stimulates positive word of mouth.
- Handling any complaints or concerns with sensitivity, recovering the caller and preventing her from hanging up with a negative feeling toward your business.
- Gathering useful suggestions and ideas from the caller for use in refining the marketing programme, product offerings or other elements of your business process.

Many businesses put people to work answering their phones without giving them enough training and support to pursue such objectives. In fact, few operators or telephone salespeople are ever given a list to think about. They don't even know they should aim for these objectives, let alone know how to achieve them! Make sure that you don't ignore the above list of valuable objectives.

Exploring need-discovery techniques

The better you understand customers' needs and how they prefer fulfilling those needs, the better you can position yourself and your products or services to get a good sale. Large-company marketing programmes use extensive marketing research to explore customer needs. In smaller organisations, individual one-on-one discussions with customers and occasional do-it-yourself surveys can work just as well. In all organisations in which individuals interact face-to-face with prospects and customers, you can gather a great deal of information using need-discovery techniques.

Need-discovery techniques were developed for use in consultative selling, where the salesperson acts as a problem-solver for the customer and tries to become part of the customer's business team. Like a business consultant, the salesperson uses a combination of research and exploratory questions to diagnose the client's situation. (Check out 'Asking exploring questions', later in this chapter, for more on questioning.) This need-discovery process puts the salesperson in a position to generate and propose helpful solutions to the customer's problems. Often, those solutions involve the products and services of the salesperson's business.

Over time, the customer comes to trust and rely on the consultative salesperson. The customer shares more details so that the salesperson can discover more needs and offer more solutions. The result of this process is a collaborative business partnership that is beneficial to both parties. Because collaboration provides many intangible benefits, consultative selling often shifts the focus away from price.

Customers value businesses that emphasise consultative selling for their superior service, flexibility and willingness to help the customer succeed. The customer who enjoys such benefits isn't as quick to give the business to some new competitor just because the competitor offers a minor price reduction or other incentive.

The following sections look closely at some simple but powerful conversational techniques that help you uncover customer needs and concerns.

Planning your questions

Start by reviewing what you know about your prospects. What are their needs? What are their constraints? What sorts of changes or trends in the news may be affecting them? If you're planning to call on a business, seek out information about the business on the Internet. In addition, review the business's marketing communications and talk to others who work for or do business with the prospect.

From these inquiries, you should find yourself asking questions and generating hypotheses about the prospect. You're then able to come up with some theories about the prospect's needs. If you have trouble clarifying your thoughts about the prospect, fill in the form shown in Figure 16-2 (a template of this form is in File 16-1, so you can print a stack of them and keep them in your customer files).

You may need ten minutes to fill in this form. If you're eager to see as many prospects as possible, you may be tempted to skip it. Why plan when you can just give a canned presentation and trust to luck? Because the planning phase greatly increases the chances of building a consultative relationship and securing a sale. Most salespeople find that ten minutes of planning is well invested and worthwhile.

Prospect Analysis Sheet

Prospect name	
Does prospect make a purchase decision?	___ yes ___ no *If not, who does?*
Who else is involved in purchase decision?	
Past purchase history	
Brand preferences	
Suspected priorities	
Time constraints	
Other contraints, i.e., cost, compatibility	
Prospect's most important problem or challenge	

Figure 16-2:
Prospect
Analysis
Sheet.

Next, you need to pre-plan some questions for the prospect. Doing so takes another five minutes. Again, you may be tempted to skip this step, but the sales calls go much better if you prepare. To pre-plan your questions, review your Prospect Analysis Sheet and simply generate confirming or exploring questions (which we describe in the next two sections).

Asking confirming questions

A *confirming question* is one that checks facts or your understanding or interpretation of the situation. You're wise to use confirming questions to check your assumptions and to update your prospect's profile. You may be amazed how much of the information you think you know about prospects turns out not to be so!

Here are some examples of confirming questions:

- ✔ 'I recall that you said you need to make a purchase decision by the end of March. Is that still the case?'
- ✔ 'Is it true that Bob wants to stick with black and white labels for now?'
- ✔ 'Are you definitely committed to buying only organic produce?'
- ✔ 'Am I right that your top priority is service, followed by price?'

Asking exploring questions

Exploring questions probe to find out more about your prospect's situation. Use exploring questions to fill in missing facts, discover reasons for preferences or unusual requests, and seek to reveal more about the prospect's preferences and needs. When you ask exploring questions, you often find out something surprising and helpful about the prospect.

Here are examples of typical exploring questions:

- ✔ 'Why is it so important for your organisation to get same-day deliveries?'
- ✔ 'Are you the one who's in charge of the final purchase decision?'
- ✔ 'Does the colour have to match your office colour scheme?'
- ✔ 'Do you have any other problems that we may be able to help you with?'
- ✔ 'Why do you do it that way?'
- ✔ 'Why haven't you updated this equipment in recent years?'
- ✔ 'What goals do you hope to accomplish this season?'
- ✔ 'Are you experiencing any service problems or frustrations right now?'
- ✔ 'Are you looking for ways to cut costs?'
- ✔ 'Are you looking for better quality?'

Figure 16-3 shows a form that you can use to pre-plan your questions.

Question Preplanning Form	
Prospect: _____	
Confirming Questions:	Exploring Questions:
1.	1.
2.	2.
3.	3.
4.	4.
5.	5.
Other comments or notes:	

Figure 16-3:
Question
preplanning
form.

Now that you've done all this planning, you're bound to have some good insights and questions as you approach the prospect. Basically, the idea is to use your insights from the need-discovery stage to make your presentation interactive and consultative instead of just forcing your information down the prospect's throat.

File 16-2 has a printable version of the question pre-planning form.

Making the Presentation

Presenting your offer is clearly a crucial part of the sales process. You don't want to go to the trouble of finding a prospect and setting up an opportunity for contact, only to blow it at this stage! So, you probably already know what you want to say. Or do you?

Before you present your products or services to the prospect, ask yourself what you found out about the prospect during the need-discovery process (as we describe in the preceding section). Then focus on how you can help meet your prospect's needs. The idea is to adapt your presentation to fit the specific needs and wants of each prospect. Be flexible. Emphasise different ideas. Offer different approaches or select different items to present.

When you make your sales presentation (whether verbally or in writing), make sure to recap your understanding of the prospect's situation and needs. As you do so, ask whether your understanding is correct. Make clear that you're trying to appreciate and address the person's specific needs.

If you've used the sales process and asked enough questions to understand the prospect's position, taking a flexible approach to presenting your offerings should feel natural. All you need to do is translate your extensive knowledge of the product or service into a clear, compelling presentation. You did say you were an expert in the ins and outs of your product, didn't you? If not, you'd better work on it.

Don't forget: *in the end, everything and anything you do or show is part of your presentation*. You need to have impeccable manners, clean and attractive clothing and a nice smile. You also need to have good, attractive reference materials about the product at your fingertips. The chapters on writing and designing good marketing materials come to bear here in the presentation phase of the sales process. Sometimes (like when you send a sales letter) you or another salesperson aren't in front of the prospect, so all the work presenting your offering and asking for business is left up to your marketing materials. Please make sure that you present yourself and your marketing materials in a highly effective manner.

Asking for the Business

You contacted the prospect, explored her needs and presented your offerings as the most natural and appropriate solution. You think she likes you and your product or service, and you believe the timing is right. Now what?

You have to ask her to do business with you. You have to try closing the sale. Sure, some customers may volunteer their orders and make the sale easy for you. In retail stores, especially, you can easily fall into a passive role and wait for people to step up with a desired purchase. But this technique is always a mistake. You need to manage the close, whether subtly or overtly. And in our minds, nothing's as challenging and interesting in sales as the close. (That's why we cover closing in more detail in Chapter 17.)

Think about what you're going to say to ask for the business. The best sales-people know that the art of closing is finding a polite way to ask the prospect for the sale. Here are a few ways to ask for the business (flip to Chapter 17 for more options):

- ✔ 'If I've answered all your questions, may I put together an agreement?'
- ✔ 'Based on everything we've discussed, are you ready to go forward in our partnership?'
- ✔ 'I'll call you in the morning between 9.00 and 9.15 to answer any remaining questions that you may think about tonight, and then I'll send over an agreement so we can go forward. Does that time work for you?'

In the right context, an assertive effort to close can get the prospect beyond the natural indecisiveness many people feel before making a purchase. Practise different closes and make a note of any that seem to work well for you and your customers.

If your assertive efforts to close the sale are a failure, don't give up on the prospect. Ask yourself whether the timing may have been wrong. People buy some things quite often, but buy many other things infrequently. People buy food every day, toothpaste every month, new laptops every year or two and new cars every few years. Businesses also buy big-ticket items infrequently. If you're trying to get someone to switch to a new brand or service, and they only buy every now and then to start with, a long time may pass before they're truly ready to make a switch.

Don't throw the contact information away. Set it aside and try again later.

Files on the CD

Check out the following items on the CD-ROM:

- ✔ **File 16-1:** Prospect Analysis Sheet
- ✔ **File 16-2:** Question Pre-planning Form

Chapter 17

Closing the Sale

· ·

In This Chapter

▶ Using sales closes in all your marketing materials and methods

▶ Investigating the many ways to seal the deal

▶ Passing the prospect's smell test

· ·

You have your foot in the door. The prospect agreed to meet with you. You presented your products or services. You answered his questions. The prospect seems interested, and you think you have something that he needs. Now what? How do you turn that interest into immediate action? Can you actually secure an order before you leave?

To find out, you have to ask for the business by trying to close the deal. In fact, in many cases, you may have to try to close it more than once. Some salespeople say you can't accept a 'No' until you've tried to close the deal at least three times. Others say you never accept a 'No' when you sense an opportunity for a 'Yes'. We think the truth lies somewhere in between these two options. We also think that if you make a careful study of closing techniques, you're certain to find yourself having to accept far fewer rejections, because *how* you ask for the business often determines whether you get the business and how much business you get. In this chapter, we discuss some strategies for closing the deal.

Relying on Practice, Not Talent, to Close the Sale

We want to address what we consider to be the biggest myth in marketing, which is the belief that top-performing salespeople are born, not made. Because people assume that peak sales results are reserved for the naturally talented, marketers excuse themselves when they don't close a sale, and they also hesitate to go out and pound the pavement.

The truth (according to numerous studies of sales force recruiting and performance) is that training and motivation are more important than talent. For example, here's a quote from a research paper published in the *Journal of Marketing* in January 1989: 'Whom one recruits is not as important as what one does with the recruits after they have been hired.' Big companies get good results when they train and support their sales forces. If you train and support yourself, you can also be a high-performing salesperson. And discovering and practising closing techniques is, in our opinion, the most important thing you can do to boost your sales performance.

Realising That Closes Aren't Only for Salespeople

Few people realise that the challenges of personal selling and marketing are very much the same. Marketing simply sells from a distance. Its ultimate goal is to make the sale, just as in personal selling, so every marketing programme needs to have some good closes built into it, whether salespeople deliver them or not.

At the point of purchase, your marketing programme can ask for the business by presenting a tempting product with a price tag, warranty information, usage instructions, shipping options or other indications that you expect the prospect to purchase it. Or the marketing materials themselves can incorporate the close. After all, many calls, letters, faxes and emails to prospects are simply long-distance sales calls. Finally, less personal forms of marketing communication, such as a direct-mail pieces or catalogues, also need to incorporate multiple efforts to close the deal.

 Because every marketing programme needs to include multiple efforts to close, you can often improve the effectiveness of marketing materials by using classic sales closing techniques in the materials rather than in a personal presentation. For example, in a direct-mail letter or mailed catalogue, you can incorporate a number of trial closes that say something like:

> *You'll find that our order form is detachable in case you want to check off possible purchases on it as you read the catalogue.*
>
> *If you're serious about solving your problems, you'll no doubt be making regular use of our service, which means you'll want to have our contact information handy. So why not get a head start by popping out the perforated Rolodex card on the bottom of this page and filing it under 'O' for our name right now?*

By presenting hypothetical situations relating to future use of your product or service, such *trial closes* help move the catalogue reader toward a real close and a big fat order for your business (see the later section 'The trial close' for details). You can incorporate trial closes into any and all marketing materials with a little imagination and some basic knowledge of the salesperson's array of closing techniques.

Mastering Closing Techniques

We've collected a variety of closing techniques from super salespeople who we've interviewed over the years and from the sales training programmes of a variety of companies. Based on these various sources, we've compiled a master list of different closes that you can try out in your own sales and marketing efforts. In this section, we discuss each of the items on this list.

The direct close

The *direct close* simply involves asking prospects to place an order or to sign a contract now. You generally want to ask for the business in a specific manner by saying what you'd like them to do, how much you'd like them to buy or when you'd like them to start accepting deliveries. The direct close is the most basic technique, so you may as well start with it. If you're lucky, it works, and you don't have to try anything harder.

The idea behind the direct close is to propose a business relationship and see what the prospect says. He may just say, 'Fine, let's get started. Can you draw up a contract?' or 'Do you need a purchase order from me?'

More often, he begins to negotiate the specifics of doing business, which is also a positive result because it means you're probably going to close the deal after a little haggling. For example, the prospect may say, 'Not so fast. I'd like to hire you, but we need to find a way to do this project for less money than what you suggested, and I need to have some guarantees of performance.' Great! The direct-close approach has opened the door to a serious business discussion. If you negotiate in good faith, you should be able to walk away with a deal.

When you're selling products, the direct close should generally include the suggestion that the prospect purchases whatever amount of product is usual or appropriate. You can't expect a store buyer to commit to six months' inventory of your product. Asking the prospect to put in a two-week supply may be just about right, if that's conventional in the category or industry in question.

If you're designing a brochure, catalogue or ad, make sure that you incorporate direct-close requests. For example, include an order form or a message such as, 'To place your order, call . . .' On your website, ask for business by including a 'Proceed to Checkout' prompt or having a section or tab labelled 'To Place an Order' or 'To Request a Quote'.

Here are some examples of direct-close scripts:

- ✔ 'Shall I write up an order for XYZ product now?'
- ✔ 'Would an order for x amount be appropriate right now?'
- ✔ 'It sounds like it may make sense for us to try working together. Would you be willing to sign a contract for – let's say x units – if I get one prepared for you and fax it over later today?'
- ✔ 'I sent you a detailed proposal for the consulting work we discussed. Did you receive it? Okay, good. I'm calling to see whether you have any questions about it and if you want to move ahead with the project.'
- ✔ 'Based on what you've told me, it sounds like you really can use the XYZ product right now. I can start processing your order tomorrow, if you want to give me a purchase order number for it before I go.'

Sometimes the direct-close technique just doesn't work. The prospect ducks the question, refusing to give you an immediate yes or no. Often, people avoid responding to a direct close by raising questions or objections that require your detailed response. Respond to their questions fully. Don't be put off by their unwillingness to close a deal. They aren't going to say yes until they're ready. Customers don't care if you're ready. Bide your time, keep the conversation going, if possible, and try another type of close the next time they give you a chance to talk to them.

The trial close

The *trial close* is a good technique to use casually throughout a sales presentation or discussion as a way of seeing how ready to buy the prospect is. A trial close does *not* directly ask for business, but it does test the waters by asking the prospect hypothetical questions.

To come up with appropriate hypothetical questions, ask yourself what the prospect would know or do if he were really going to order from you. Then ask him questions about those topics. If the prospect's answers are specific and thoughtful, the prospect is thinking the same way you are and may be ready for you to escalate to a real close by using the direct-close technique (discussed in the preceding section).

For example, imagine that you're selling leases on office equipment, and you've just given an impressive presentation of a new copier that includes some desktop-publishing features. To test the waters with a trial close, you may ask hypothetical questions such as, 'If you lease this machine, would you get rid of one or more of your older machines?' or 'Do you think this machine would permit you to do some things in-house that you currently have to pay to have done by graphic artists or printers?'

If the prospect answers these questions with ease, you know that he's thinking in a detailed manner about what leasing your equipment would be like. Your trial close tells you the time is right to work toward a real closing effort. You may go on to say something such as, 'Well, it sounds like you've thought this through pretty carefully already. Are you ready to sign a contract right now?'

Here are some sample trial close scripts:

- ✔ 'If you start carrying our brand, will you drop another brand to make room for it?'
- ✔ 'If you decide to use our delivery service, what sort of volume would we need to be able to handle for you on a weekly basis?'
- ✔ 'If you decide to switch to us, when do you think would be a good time to make the transition?'
- ✔ 'Do you have a date in mind for when this consulting project would start?'
- ✔ 'Do you have a specific project in mind so we can develop a proposal for you?'
- ✔ 'How much have you budgeted for this purchase, and what kind of payment schedule are you thinking of?'

You can also use trial closes in sales letters, websites, brochures or other arms-length marketing communications. Incorporate questions such as, 'Are you in need of specific supplies right now?' When prospects read these questions, some may be spurred to action. And a Shopping Cart area in which website visitors can inventory a list of possible purchases is also a great way to offer hypothetical purchase options.

Your attempt at a trial close may not generate the response you hoped for. If that happens, no harm's been done. The prospect who answers a trial-close question with an 'I don't know' or 'I haven't really had time to think about it' isn't ready for a close yet. Go back to probing for insights into his needs and wants and to communicating information about your offerings. Then try another trial close later on. Sometimes you have to try three or four times before you get a positive response. Using trial closes often is okay, as long as you read the body language and verbal responses of your prospect and avoid irritating him.

The wrap-up close

The *wrap-up close*, also called the *summary close* or the *scripted close* by some salespeople, signals to the prospect that the time has come to make a decision. This technique works especially well if you've given some kind of presentation or reviewed information about your offering and the prospect's needs and wants.

You perform the wrap-up close by summarising the main points of the meeting or presentation. Try to recap not only the main points you made, but also the points that the prospect made. In many cases, you can ask the prospect to clarify any information you didn't understand or ask you any final questions. When you sense that the wrap-up is close to completion, you can naturally move on to the question of whether and how much the prospect wants to buy. Your closing technique at the end of the wrap-up should generally involve a direct close.

Here are some sample wrap-up close scripts:

- ✔ 'If I may just take a minute to summarise the main concerns I think you've raised . . .'

- ✔ 'To wrap up my presentation, I'd like to reiterate our commitment to meeting or exceeding all your specifications. Specifically, we can . . . and . . . and . . .'

- ✔ 'I appreciate all the time you've made for me today, but I'm sure that you have other appointments, too. Would this be a good time to wrap up our discussion and see where we stand?'

- ✔ 'I think I'm beginning to get a clear picture of what you're looking for. As I understand it, you need . . . Does that sound about right?'

In a wrap-up close, use language signalling that you've reached a natural ending point and that you're ready to move on to the next stage. Also, use body language to signal that you're attempting to wrap up the proceedings. For example, if you're sitting, sit up straight and look the prospect in the eye. These body movements traditionally signal an intention to depart, so they help set the stage for a wrap-up.

If you're standing during the presentation, move away from the podium or screen (if there is one) and toward the prospects. Face the decision-maker (the prospect with the most seniority or power) directly as you deliver your wrap-up close. Then pause and let him have an opportunity to reply with a question or a decision to order.

If you're communicating in a brochure or letter, use a heading, such as 'In Conclusion' or 'Now It's Your Turn', to signal the start of a wrap-up close.

On a website, use a summary of the order or a check-the-numbers form that allows the prospect to see what an order would cost – with the option of converting the data into a real order.

The process close

If you use a *process close* (also called an *action close*, a *contract close* or an *order-form close*), you simply start a closing process and see how far into it the prospect is willing to go. We recommend this technique when the prospect seems reasonably certain to order. For example, the process close usually works when writing a reorder. The process close is also appropriate when a new prospect asks for an appointment or otherwise indicates interest in making a purchase.

To make a process close work, you need to have a multi-step purchase process in which the prospect is likely to go along with the first few steps. For example, you may start prospects off by completing a spec sheet with them. Or you may enter them into your database of national accounts so that they qualify for a discount. After you get them to take an initial step, move on to the next step of the close. That step may be to write down detailed information about their order or project and then read it back to them as if you're checking a formal order.

Here are some sample process close scripts:

- ✔ 'Okay, let's get started on this order form. Do you use the same billing and shipping addresses?'

- ✔ 'To qualify for credit terms, we need to make sure that your company is in our customer database. Can I go through what we've got in the computer right now and make sure that it's complete?'

- ✔ 'Assuming that you do end up making this purchase, we need to have a completed order form. I can get that process started now. What kind of quantities are you thinking about?'

- ✔ 'The next step is usually for us to prepare a detailed proposal. To do that, I need to clarify a few points. Can we go over those now so I can send you a proposal in the next day or two?'

In some businesses, the deal closes when money changes hands. In others, the deal closes when prospects sign a contract or initial an order form. Whatever that last step is for you, your process close should move you and the buyer nearer to it. And the nearer you get, the more committed the buyer must be to stick with your process. The process usually ends with a direct request to 'sign the order form', 'provide your credit-card number' or otherwise complete the process and formalise the sale.

Weeding out the unwilling

In most businesses where we work with salespeople, we find that they spend a lot of their time (15 to 50 per cent, depending on the industry) talking with prospects who seem interested but who drag their heels and then don't make a purchase. Shopping is a lot easier than buying, and we're not surprised that a lot of apparently interested prospects end up dropping out before the purchase stage of the sales process. But they certainly do waste your time! What can you do to reclaim some of this wasted time?

Don't be afraid to ask for the business. Try to close as soon as possible. If the prospect balks, work with him a little more and then try again. After a few tries, you have a better idea of how serious he is. If he's just shopping around, he pulls back as soon as you begin talking about

closing a deal, and continues backing off when you probe for objections and try to close again. Your testing of him indicates that he just isn't ready to buy right now. You can ask directly whether he's ready. If not, thank him for his interest, explain that you're ready to talk later if he decides he wants to buy and then get out of there. A new prospect awaits, so don't waste time on one who won't close.

If walking away from a potential sale sounds counter-intuitive to you, think about it this way: while you're trying to convince someone to buy who doesn't really want to, can't afford it or is just fishing for free information, your competitor is probably with a customer who needs what you have and is ready to buy.

In addition to securing business quite quickly, the process close also weeds out prospects who are just shopping around and aren't ready to close the deal. These prospects get more and more resistant and uncomfortable as you try to move them through the process. They may bail out by saying something like, 'I'm just not ready to sign anything right now' or 'I don't think we need to go into all this right now'. If they don't appear ready to close, keep them alive as prospects, continue trying to find out more about their needs and wants, tell them more about your offerings and then try a different close next time.

The analytical close

The *analytical close* is a guided decision-making process in which you help the prospect compare options and weigh alternatives. You can frame the analysis however you think best fits the situation. Sometimes the key question in the prospect's mind is whether or not to buy. Other times, the question is which of the competing alternatives to try. More rarely, the prospect may be wrestling over which of your offerings to purchase or how much to buy. The analytical close helps the prospect think through his decision, because until he assesses the decision from all angles, he won't be ready to close.

As part of an analytical close, you can use *consultative selling* – a popular buzz-word and a useful technique to use, but only when the purchase process is difficult. The essence of consultative selling is to ask lots of questions that allow you to develop a specific understanding of the prospect's unique or individual needs and then propose a customised solution. If the prospect faces complex and/or technical decisions (as is the case for someone purchasing a home remodel or a business information system), consultative selling is helpful. The analytical close is a consultative selling technique. Whenever you think the prospect seems unclear or confused about what to buy, switch to a consultative approach and help them analyse their options.

The analytical close works well for fairly complicated purchase decisions, especially when the prospects are careful, thoughtful and highly involved in the purchase decision. Use the analytical close when selling an expensive new car to someone who's shopping around to compare models. Use it when someone's deciding what sort of new camera to buy or which insurance policy makes the most sense. Also, use it in many business-to-business sales situations, because when people make purchases on behalf of their businesses, they generally take a fairly analytical approach.

Here are some sample analytical close scripts:

- 'You sound as if you're having a little bit of trouble thinking this decision through in all its complexity. Why don't we analyse your options and see what really makes the most sense?'

- 'We've explored quite a few different issues as we discussed the idea of a possible purchase. In fact, I'm feeling a little confused by all the details. Would you mind if I did a simple pro/con analysis of the decision you're facing right now so that I can see the issues more clearly?'

- 'I gather you're seriously considering several alternatives right now. I'd like to help you analyse each of these alternatives, because it helps me see whether my offering makes sense. And it should help you make a better decision, too. Do you mind if we spend a few minutes thinking each of these options through to see how they're going to affect you in the long run?'

Presenting the pros and cons

Perhaps the easiest way to conduct an analytical close is to help someone think through the options and reach a comfortable decision by presenting the pros and cons of each alternative. You can present verbally or on paper, depending on the physical environment and the prospect's openness to various alternatives.

To present the pros and cons of making a purchase right now, you can divide a sheet of paper or flip chart into two columns or do the same thing on a PowerPoint slide. Label the left column 'Pros' and the right column 'Cons'.

Don't feel, however, as if you have to complete the table in that order. You don't want to end your analysis with the cons of the purchase. So start by skipping over the Pros column and asking the prospect to help you identify cons – anything that he may think is negative about the purchase. For example, you may suggest that the purchase will, of course, cost some money.

Now go on to the Pros side, listing as many good qualities about the purchase as you can. Frame the qualities in terms of their effect on the buyer. Keep the list personal and specific. You find that the Pros column naturally grows considerably longer than the Cons column because you can more easily list benefits of a purchase than negative consequences.

When you finish the analysis, you can ask the prospect how it balances out in his mind. Say something like, 'So, what do you think? Do the benefits outweigh the costs in your eyes?' Hopefully, your offer is good enough and is targeted to someone who really would benefit from it so that the analysis clearly favours a decision to purchase. But if not, don't give up. Just keep the lines of communication open and try another type of close later on.

Offering multiple scenarios

Another way to approach the analytical close is to offer multiple scenarios and work out in detail how each impacts the prospect. One scenario may be for the prospect to do nothing right now. Another may be for him to purchase from some alternative vendor that the prospect is obviously considering. And, of course, you have to include at least one alternative in which the prospect buys from you. Then you try to engage him as you analyse each of his alternatives.

Your goal is to show the prospect what happens over time and how each scenario affects him. Hopefully, the prospect finds the scenario you construct around the purchase of your product or service the most appealing, and your analysis helps him make the decision to buy.

Printed marketing materials also lend themselves to analytical closes. Use tables, charts, diagrams or statistics to prove the value of your offering.

The sales promotion close

The *sales promotion close* uses an incentive to encourage prospects to take immediate action. The incentive may be a special discount offer that expires soon, an offer to bundle additional products or services into the sale, or any promotion you can dream up, as long as it's likely to interest the prospect and not wipe out your entire profit margin.

Giving new customers a gift is often a great device for securing an immediate close. Companies such as Reader's Digest or pension plan sellers have used this technique for many years. They buy large numbers of inexpensive but reasonably nice gifts – pens, portable radios, alarm clocks, DVD players and so on – and offer to send you a gift for free if you subscribe or buy their products by a certain deadline.

Gifts can work especially well for business-to-business sales, where the margins are often large enough that you can afford something nice. But remember not to make the gift overly expensive; otherwise, you're entering the realm of bribery. A good rule is that you don't want to offer buyers any gift so lavish that they'd be embarrassed to openly display it in their office or home. And remember that some companies and most government entities restrict employees from accepting any personal gift (to avoid the risk of bribery), so your offer has to be for the benefit of the business, not the individual employee, in those cases.

If you're uncomfortable with personal gifts when selling to businesses, consider making a modest donation in the individual's name to a charity of his choice. You can call it your 'Sales for Society Programme' or whatever you like. The prospect may find it quite exciting to select a charity and fill out a donor form. (Have some nice cards made up for this purpose.) This novel inducement feels good, not only because it does some good for society, but also because it helps you accomplish your goal of getting the prospect in the right frame of mind to close the deal now rather than next week.

The relationship-building close

The idea behind this strategy is to focus on building a natural relationship with the prospective buyer and let the closes happen in their own good time. It's sort of the Zen approach to closing: don't worry about the closing, and it will take care of itself!

To put this strategy into action, take note of the prospect's needs, concerns and interests. Send the prospect an email with a useful link, give him a referral to someone who can help him or drop off an informative book or useful tool. In a low-key way, show him that you've been paying attention and are a helpful resource. This way, he's likely to turn to you (rather than your competitors) when he's ready to make a purchase.

Also, make sure that you keep your promises. If you say you're going to send the prospect some information, do it right away; don't keep him waiting. If he asks you to call him later in the week, put it on your calendar and make sure that you do! You may not realise it, but the prospect judges your character from how well you follow through on your commitments. Show that you're reliable, and you may find that the prospect initiates a sales close for you!

Something Stinks! Passing the Prospect's Smell Test

No matter what you sell, and no matter when, where or how customers buy your product, you risk losing customers at the last moment unless everything you do seems professional and appropriate. All customers use what we call the *smell test* when they buy – although they often use it quite unconsciously.

When did a person, product or business last fail your smell test? Here's a recent example from our own shopping experience: we were looking to buy a new car recently and had done extensive research online to find out which model we wanted. When we'd decided on a model, we then checked out the websites of local dealers until we found one that had the model we wanted and at the price that we liked.

We spoke to the dealer on the phone, who was polite and friendly and made an appointment to attend his showroom to take the car for a test drive. However, when we arrived at the dealership the senior salesperson we spoke to on the phone wasn't there, and a junior colleague took us on our test drive instead. He was unable to answer any of our questions about the car, its warranty or its history. We went from being sure that we wanted to buy the car before we arrived, to leaving it and trying other dealerships who we felt knew more about the product and were able to give us the information we wanted.

We bet you can think of plenty of similar experiences. Do you want to buy a product from the supermarket when the package looks dirty or dented? Do you want to do business at a bank where the tellers are sloppily dressed and seem disorganised or confused? Of course not!

At the last moment before purchase, even a small problem can spook your prospects and cause them to hesitate and look for alternatives. So make sure that your presentation is professional – all the way through the close. Don't let any minor problems derail a good sale. Dress well. Spell-check your proposals, emails and letters. Spell the prospect's and the business's name correctly. (Yes, misspellings are one of the most common errors salespeople make, and they can lose you the sale.)

In personal selling, avoid body odour, overpowering colognes or perfumes, and bad breath; people can be amazingly sensitive to these smells, so avoid flunking their literal smell tests, too.

Professionalism is ten times more important at the close than at any other time during a sale, so make sure that you give the close ten times as much care and attention.

Chapter 18

The Sales Success Workshop

. . . .

In This Chapter

▶ Increasing worthwhile leads

▶ Understanding the importance of great sales collateral

▶ Being flexible in your sales approach

▶ Staying positive when failure strikes

. . . .

*I*n this chapter we show you some great ways to improve your sales success at all stages of the process, from getting quality leads (that actually lead somewhere!) to creating a positive, professional impression and maintaining a healthy attitude to success and failure.

The secret recipe for sales success is a bit like baking a great-tasting cake – you need to have all the best ingredients at your disposal, the right tools to work with and plenty of patience.

In this chapter we give you the ingredients you need to create your own sales success. Mixing them in the right proportion is up to you, but we do our best to provide the recipe and some handy tools too.

We also look at the importance of creating the right type of sales collateral and give you some tips on different sales approaches. We even show you the art of staying upbeat when your best efforts are met with a negative – remember, cooking up sales success isn't always an exact science, but get the right recipe and you'll taste great success.

Improving the Flow of High-Quality Leads

Most salespeople and marketers are held back by a lack of high-quality leads. If you don't have enough good leads, you're forced to work extra hard to try to close a high percentage of the leads you do have – and that's not a healthy pressure to impose on your sales efforts.

Who is *your* best lead? When you ask yourself this question, you're on the road to figuring out what sort of leads you want most, which in turn helps you generate more of those high-quality leads. When many people ask themselves what kind of leads they want most, the answer usually sounds something like:

> *I want leads who are actively considering a purchase and who want to talk to me to find out more about my offerings.*

Leads who are ready to explore purchase options and want your information are ideal. You just need to get the timing right. At the right moment in their purchase-and-use cycle, prospects *want* to hear your information. They may even approach you, instead of you having to go and find them. And that's much more efficient and easier for you! So how do you generate these ideal leads?

Beefing up your marketing programme

To generate great leads, make sure that you have an active, multifaceted marketing programme working to bring you good leads. Here are some ways to bring in good leads, which you should consider doing if you don't already:

- ✔ **Obtain and publicise a freephone telephone number with someone polite, friendly, knowledgeable and always available to answer it.** If the person answering the phone doesn't know the answer, have a system for getting a response back to the customer within 24 hours. Lately, websites have begun to be as important as telephone leads, but the telephone is always an important source of leads. Don't overlook it.

- ✔ **Make your website work for you.** For most businesses, the Internet is one of the primary sales lead generators. Give your website lots of appeal and rich information for comparison shoppers to use. Ensure that your site includes multiple ways to contact you – from email and phone calls to chat-room options and e-commerce purchasing capabilities, if appropriate for your business.

✔ **Advertise an offer for a free catalogue.** You can choose to advertise in print, on the Internet or in postcards or letters sent to mailing lists. If you want to increase the response rate a bit, add a one-time discount or deal that readers can redeem if they order from the catalogue. Or just mail out your catalogue or a brochure version of it (a smaller catalogue of highlights is good for testing new lists inexpensively).

To get the timing right, send out your catalogue at least once a quarter. Last quarter's uninterested consumer may now be eager to buy! But don't overdo it; nobody wants to be seen as a forest burner, constantly sending out unwanted catalogues and brochures. Regularly check with your customers to see whether they still want to receive a catalogue – those that don't will say so.

✔ **Offer free trial-size samples (or the service equivalent) in ads, emails or letters.** Often, people come forward and identify themselves as good leads when you give them a chance to try something for free. Car dealerships use this technique by offering test drives – a great way to attract interested leads.

In many businesses, a freephone telephone number is a good way to bring in leads. Even in the modern Internet era, many prospects prefer talking to someone on the phone to contacting someone in any other way. So make sure that you publicise your phone number widely by including it in and on every communication you send – from ads to bills. And please make sure that you have well-trained, polite people (not machines!) ready to answer those calls. Give them a good form or a computerised database to record information about each caller and train them how to use it.

We know that most businesses have switched to interactive computer-answering systems, but we believe that these lose some of your leads and that a human being is still the best way to go. We recently called our local van hire company, and even though we hadn't hired anything from them for a couple of years, the employee who took our call quickly sourced our records using our phone number and was ready to do business without us having to spell our name five times for him. The telephone should be a cornerstone of your sales and marketing programme!

Getting creative when you still need more leads

If you aren't getting enough high-quality leads, the following fixes often help:

- ✔ Offer free samples or consultations in exchange for contact information at your industry's regional or national trade shows and on your website.

- ✔ Put a special offer on your website, such as a free month of service or a free special product, for the customer who purchases or makes an appointment with a salesperson within the month.

- ✔ Mail, call or email the people on your customer list from the past three years to ask whether they need anything else and to let them know about all the products you sell. (They may not realise that you can provide additional products and services beyond what they've already purchased.)

- ✔ Run a direct-response ad in an appropriate magazine or newspaper (see Chapters 5 and 6 in Part II for tips on planning and designing your ads).

- ✔ Buy a list of 1,000 names of people who fit the profile of your better customers (for example, people who own homes with gardens in high-income areas or managers of businesses with 50 or more employees). Send an introductory letter inviting them to find out more about your products or services by setting up an appointment, visiting your website or calling for more information. Follow the mailing with a telephone call to see whether you can set up an appointment.

- ✔ Send out a press release and generate positive publicity about an interesting product or service you offer. Sometimes media coverage produces a flood of leads (see Chapter 11 for all about using publicity).

Make sure that your leads are high quality. If you don't have enough leads so that you can afford to chuck the poor ones and solely focus on eager-to-buy prospects, work on your lead-generation methods until you do. Everything else in the field of marketing can and should work to support sales by producing a rich flow of leads!

According to MarketingSherpa (www.marketingsherpa.com), a typical sales-lead database can be broken down as follows:

- ✔ **7 per cent:** Sales ready; buy within 90 days.

- ✔ **9 per cent:** Duds; competitors, perpetual window-shoppers.

- ✔ **84 per cent:** Mid- to long-range prospects.

If you're focused on sales, you're most likely to go after those 7 per cent ready to buy now and neglect the 84 per cent of longer-term prospects. However, the statistics show that 80 per cent of these will buy your product or service – from you or someone else – within 24 months.

Don't neglect the bulk of the people on your list who aren't actively shopping right now. Continue to contact them by email, mail, phone or in person and also make sure that they're exposed to any publicity and advertising you're doing.

When you remember to communicate with your entire list, you invest in the next 7 per cent of ready-to-buy customers. This cream-of-the-crop group turns over every month, so you have to be forward-looking in order to have active buyers in the future.

 Set leads aside if the prospect really doesn't seem interested. But don't throw away the lead. Instead, cue it up for next month. Often the timing is off and if you try again later, you get a better response.

Using Sales Collateral to Help Win 'Em Over

One secret of superior selling performance is to make a good impression. You can impress your customers by using *sales collateral* – an umbrella term that covers anything designed and supplied to help salespeople achieve success. We're using a broad definition because we want you to turn your marketing imagination loose and see if you can come up with better sales collateral.

Sticking with good collateral

Make a dream list of everything you may need throughout the sales process. Good support ensures success! Here are some ideas to get you started:

- **Impressive stationery and fax forms.** Order your business's paper in multiple sizes for advance letters and other correspondence.

- **Matching business cards, preferably with information about the firm/ product and all the correct contact options.** Consider special paper or unusual designs for cards. If they're noticeably special and interesting, they're going to generate calls.

- ✔ **Clear, appealing specification sheets.** Your spec sheets need to describe the facts of each and every product or service accurately so that all your prospects' possible factual questions are answered.

- ✔ **Samples, demos and/or catalogues.** These marketing materials make showing and telling your prospects about your products and services much easier.

- ✔ **Cases, stories, testimonials and other evidence from happy customers.** Only a few per cent of salespeople have any collateral of this type, and yet it's the most powerful form of sales collateral!

- ✔ **Attractive, valuable premium items.** Such premium items include a pen, mug, cap or box of sweets, marked subtly with your business's name and contact information. Prospects appreciate these leave-behinds when they're good quality. These tokens remind prospects that your firm exists and that you value their business. Your leave-behinds don't need to be expensive, but prospects should see them as valuable enough to keep.

Avoiding bad collateral

The sales collateral is a vital part of the packaging of the salesperson. If the sales collateral looks bad, the salesperson and product looks bad, too. The effects of poor collateral on the prospect are subtle and often unconscious, but they're *extremely* powerful. So make sure that everything your salespeople carry and/or distribute is polished and impressive. Sales collateral is a very good place to spend your design and printing budget.

Don't use collateral that hurts sales. Any materials, such as brochures or product literature, that don't look professional and appealing are going to hurt your sales.

In choosing your sales collateral, avoid the following:

- ✔ **Plastic.** Cheap plastic folders, clear plastic page protectors or big, ugly plastic sample cases all say 'tacky' and 'cheap' to prospects. Use high-quality papers and good quality folders where possible.

- ✔ **Amateur designs and layouts.** Sure, anyone can design sales and marketing materials in this era of desktop publishing, but most people shouldn't. Amateurs often create poor-looking, confusing layouts. Their work just doesn't have that special look that characterises fine design – and this can scare off some good prospects. If you have a talent for designing marketing communications, go ahead and do your own, but plan to give the project the time and care needed to produce excellent materials.

Perception is reality

What's the difference between a nice premium item and a cheap one? A box of truffles in gold foil, stamped with your business name and 'We appreciate your business', is nice. A plastic mug stamped with your business logo, filled with boiled sweets and wrapped in cellophane and a ribbon, is tacky. The items probably cost about the same, but customers perceive them quite differently. Matching the promotion gift to what you do makes sense. If your business fixes computers, offer a mouse pad or laser mouse with your name and emergency number. If you're a dentist, offer a toothbrush with your name and phone number on it. But whatever item you choose, make sure that customers think it's valuable, not tacky.

✔ **Errors.** An amazing number of factual and spelling errors exist in sales collateral. Salespeople perpetually have to make corrections or explain errors in front of prospects, which is like saying 'We can't even type a spec sheet accurately, but I'm sure we can muddle through your order somehow.'

✔ **Omissions.** Most salespeople go on calls without all the collateral materials and information they need to do a great job. They don't have a good brochure. Their business cards don't have the current address or the firm's fax number and website. The price list is out of date. Their order form is a cheap pad bought at the local stationery store. Make sure that you or whoever is doing the selling is well equipped.

Overcoming Sales Setbacks

Consider this startling statistic: the best way to predict how much a salesperson is going to sell is to measure her – no, not I.Q., not product knowledge, not connections or experience, but yes – her *level of optimism*. Psychology has shown that how you manage your own attitude really does have a powerful effect on how you sell. It's not a myth; the link between attitude and performance is real and powerful, especially in sales, where the high amount of negative feedback can cause attitudes to easily deteriorate.

Sometimes people refuse your sales pitch. Sometimes they aren't ready, don't like the product or just aren't in a good mood. In sales and marketing, rejections and failures always exist, and it can be hard to persist. How well do you handle rejection and failure?

A good sales or marketing programme is more efficient and suffers fewer wasted calls than a poor programme. Although you can improve your success rates and reduce your rejection rates significantly, you can *never* achieve perfection. Marketing is not a precise science. In fact, finding yourself dealing with prospects that always say 'yes' is a sign that you need to push your programme a bit. Try asking more people or raising your prices. Unless some people say 'no', you're not really stretching yourself. So, failures are a natural and important part of healthy sales and marketing.

Coming back for more: The bounce-back factor

How successful you are has a great deal to do with how well you handle failures:

- ✔ If you bounce back from each rejection with an optimistic outlook, failure can't hold you back. You keep trying rather than giving up. In fact, you may even try harder.

- ✔ If you gain insight from each rejection, you can reduce the failure rate in the future and improve your odds of success over time.

Both points are closely related. Your ability to bounce back – to stay positive and motivated – has everything to do with how you explain each failure to yourself. If you maintain a positive attitude, attributing failures to appropriate, accurate causes over which you can exercise some control, you're going to be resilient. Failures don't upset you or slow you down. In fact, they give you renewed energy because you discover something from each failure that should help you with the next try.

So, listen to how you talk to yourself when you're trying to make a sale or grow a business. Normally, people don't attend carefully to their internal explanations, but to achieve higher-than-average success, you need to begin to manage normally unconscious or automatic self-talk.

To be a successful marketer or salesperson – or to be successful at achieving your goals in general – you need to take credit for success and avoid blaming yourself for failure (Martin Seligman's book, *Learned Optimism*, published by Vintage Books, explains the extensive research behind this conclusion if you want to find out more).

Generalising success

Attribute successes to aspects of your own personality, talents and behaviour. Giving yourself at least a share of the credit for each success builds the essential positive attitude needed to maintain motivation and build momentum. People who explain away their successes as simply good luck are encouraging a feeling of helplessness.

Generalising from a success is helpful, too. Avoid narrow, meaningless ways of giving yourself credit. Don't say something demeaning to yourself like, 'Oh, I guess I was responsible for closing that sale, but it was only because I happened to know that prospect personally.' Explaining such a success is more productive as follows: 'I closed that sale easily with an old acquaintance, which proves that I can present this product effectively. I should be able to close sales with other people, too.' Generalising that from one accomplishment you have an ability to achieve others is important as you build the attitudes needed to pursue success.

Getting specific about failure

Attributing failures to factors outside your own personality and abilities is very important. Many people question themselves when they receive a rejection or 'no' answer. Instead, you should consider many other external factors that are within your control and are easy to adjust. These factors include the wrong list of prospects, the wrong closing technique, the wrong timing, the wrong way of presenting the product or even the wrong product. When you look at specific, controllable factors, you can take a philosophical attitude toward failure.

Notice that when you blame specific, controllable factors for your failures, you avoid generalisations. You can easily make sweeping generalisations when you encounter a sales rejection or marketing failure. Big mistake. Big, big mistake. When you allow yourself to generalise about failures, you come to see them as unavoidable. The cards appear to be stacked against you, which discourages you from playing in the future. We've heard many managers and marketers say things like:

> *We don't advertise. We tried it once or twice, and it just doesn't work for our business.*

> *We can't do direct mail. Our products don't have high enough prices to work, given the typical low response rates for mailings.*

> *Websites are fine for communicating information about our business, but it doesn't work to try to close actual sales on the Internet. We take a low-key approach to our site. It's really just an online brochure.*

> *I can't sell. I'm just no good at it. Believe me, I've tried! That's why I subcontract all our sales out to independent sales reps.*

REAL WORLD

Top salespeople manage themselves well

If you know some people who are master marketers or salespeople, we recommend taking them out for a cup of coffee and quizzing them on their approach. Often, you're surprised by what they have to say. Allow us to tell you about a certain acquaintance of ours.

John is affiliated with a big life insurance underwriter but is basically an entrepreneur and must take full responsibility for earning his own commission. As you may know, many people try their hand at this work, but only very few manage to turn it into a lucrative and successful career. John is very disciplined about his work and has managed to write an amazing number of insurance policies over the years.

He once told us about a unique system that he uses to keep track of his prospects. He makes a series of ticks in his appointment book, each one representing a prospect he had phoned, and other markings for the number of sales visits he actually went on during the course of the day.

When we asked him why he kept those tallies, he explained that he found that the easiest way to get more business was simply to go on more sales visits, and the easiest way to do that was to make more phone calls each morning. The more people he called, the more meetings he was able to set up. So, by tracking the number of prospecting calls, he reminded himself of his goal of calling a certain number each week. And by tracking the number of meetings, he was able to see the positive results of his efforts.

Then he explained that he had a story behind his system. Back in his early business days, he and another salesman had been complaining and saying that they really wanted to double their income by making twice as many sales. John pointed out that all they needed to do was make twice as many sales calls, but sitting at the phone trying to set up appointments wasn't much fun, which is why they usually quit phoning and went out selling as soon as they had a few calls lined up.

So John challenged his friend: they both agreed to keep an accurate tally of how many prospecting calls they made by phone each day and agreed to pay the other a pre-arranged sum if at the end of the month they hadn't made twice as many calls as usual. John met his friend at the end of the month, and they both opened their books and counted up their phone calls. John had made his quota of calls, but his friend was just a tad under. So, the friend got his cheque book out to settle his bet on the spot.

You may think the story ends there, but not so. Even though he was out of pocket from the bet, John's friend said he wanted to try the challenge again next month. Apparently, he had made enough extra calls that his income almost doubled, and the loss of the bet was trivial compared to his gain.

After several months of making twice as many calls and reaching their goals, the practice became a habit for both men. In fact, they never stopped using this technique because they were both so pleased to find that they were bringing in twice as much revenue as before. And although John doesn't need the stimulus of a contest any longer to make those calls, he still keeps up with his simple information system. It serves to remind him of his goal, and with it, he always makes his targets.

These phrases come from business people who we've encountered over the years. Each quote reflects a belief that prevents the speaker from ever trying something again. And each quote is a broad, absolute conclusion based on a very narrow set of unsuccessful experiences. For example, the person who said, 'We can't do direct mail,' works for a business that can certainly profit from direct mail. We know that several of the company's direct competitors use mailings quite effectively. But the man's defeatist attitude, based on a few early failures, prevents his business from profiting in this arena. And the person who told us that the Internet can't sell her services is creating a self-fulfilling prophecy by failing to develop a website good enough to support e-commerce.

So you can see that allowing yourself to make broad, pessimistic generalisations from failures is very dangerous. Such behaviour narrows your view of the future and shortens your strategic horizons; it turns off your marketing imagination and drains you of motivation and self-confidence. How you think about and explain those failures has everything to do with whether you bounce back from them, wiser and more motivated than before, or whether you curl up in a ball and refuse to try again.

Retraining for success

Only that small group of people who instinctively take to sales and have a natural flair for entrepreneurship truly possess healthy, positive explanatory styles. And that's bad news, because we guess that, like us, you weren't born with the positive attitude toward success and failure that you need to be a high-achiever in sales and marketing.

Now for the good news: you can easily change your style and adopt more positive approaches to success and failure. When you retrain those old, unhelpful mental habits, you find yourself coping with failures far more productively and positively. And you discover that your new, healthier attitudes naturally lead to greater success in sales and marketing, as well as in life in general.

So what steps can you take to train yourself so that you have the most helpful attitudes toward success and failure? Glad you asked:

1. Use the Attitudes of Success Profile that we include on the CD (File 18-1) to develop a profile of your own attitudes.

2. Follow the instructions for interpreting your profile. Where your profile deviates from the profile associated with the highest levels of success in sales and marketing, you can find pointers to simple, easy exercises and tips to help you shift your attitudes.

Taking a Flexible Approach

In Chapter 2, we talk about finding your *marketing zone*, defined as the set of formulas that work well for your business. Similarly, of course, a *sales zone* also exists – it's the specific approach to selecting leads and making sales pitches that produces a profitable result and helps your business grow. If you're frustrated by sales and find it difficult, you're not yet in your sales zone and need to keep experimenting. Try new approaches. Question all your assumptions. Anyone who's not getting complete sales success needs to try new approaches.

One way to be flexible in your sales strategy is to experiment with different closes until you find one or two that seem to work reliably for most of your customers. Chapter 17 offers a selection of closes you can experiment with.

Another way to be flexible is to use a consultative approach. Instead of telling prospects about your product or service, ask them about their needs. When you've asked several questions, you can begin to offer information. The consultative approach is solution-oriented, meaning that you don't tell customers what you have to sell; you tell them how you can solve their problem or meet their objectives. Again, we cover this in more detail in Chapter 17.

A third way to be flexible is to take lessons from failure. At least once a week, take the time to go over each lost sale and look for patterns. Some prospects just weren't right for a sale, so don't worry about those. However, if you think that you lost potential sales, examine these failures closely. Ask yourself what you could have done differently. Then try a different approach next time you encounter a similar situation.

In general, salespeople (and, in fact, all marketers) do best when they're open to new ideas and willing to adjust their approach.

Files on the CD

Check out the following item included on the CD-ROM:

▮ ✔ **File 18-1:** Attitudes of Success Profile

Chapter 19

Dealing with Different Customer Personalities

. . . .

In This Chapter

▶ Adapting to the customer's style

▶ Assessing style discrepancies between you and your customers

▶ Determining the style of your marketing communications

. . . .

*T*he world is full of difficult prospects and customers: people who complain loudly and make unreasonable demands; people who walk away
and take their business with them just because they don't think they can
communicate with you; and those who are difficult to sell to because they're
hard to get along with or don't seem to like you.

You can eliminate the occasional crazy customers determined to make not
only their own lives miserable, but also yours as well. These few worst cases
should be cut from your customer list as soon as possible. But, with the right
treatment on your part, the remaining 90 per cent of so-called difficult people
can become some of your best and most loyal customers.

So what makes customers seem difficult? Sometimes a critical incident upsets
or angers a customer or prospect, and you need to deal with the situation
carefully. Most problems, however, arise because of communication issues.
So, the best overall strategy for dealing with difficult customers is to focus on
how to better communicate with them.

In this chapter, we show you how to figure out which communication style
works better than the one you're currently using. We give you a simple but
powerful tool (the Difficult Customer Diagnostic) for diagnosing style-related
communication problems that can help you to tailor your interpersonal style,
and we provide the advanced skills you need to adapt your communication
style so as to please the customer or prospect. By focusing your efforts on a
specific relationship that you identify as troubling or difficult, you can make
the results relevant and important in your daily working life.

Flexing Your Style to Be Customer Oriented

Good salespeople know that they do best when they communicate in the style the customer prefers. They adapt their communication techniques because different customers have different interpersonal styles. *Flexing your style* means changing to the most comfortable style for the other person or, in other words, doing it their way.

Most organisations know that to be customer-oriented, they have to offer the products and services that customers need and want. By adapting their offerings to the customer's needs, organisations can focus on the *substance* of what the customer needs. But good salespeople know they must also focus on the *style* the customer prefers.

Experienced salespeople, service providers and marketers already accept the fact that style is as important as substance. Yet they're still likely to encounter some customers who are difficult because of style conflicts. Style is often far harder to get right than substance because human personalities are subtle and difficult to diagnose. Consider the following facts:

- The majority of salespeople sell to people who are most like them in terms of personality profiles and communication styles. They don't close many sales with people who have different interpersonal styles, which means they may run into problems with 50 to 60 per cent of prospects.

- Even the most experienced and skilled salespeople encounter some customers with interpersonal style needs they can't meet, and therefore have trouble with 10 to 15 per cent of customers.

- Top-performing salespeople are very good at flexing their interpersonal styles; therefore they encounter even fewer people whose style needs they can't meet. They may have style problems with 1 to 5 per cent of prospects and customers.

No matter where you, your associates or your employees fall in this spectrum of experience and interpersonal skills, some business is still left on the table; business that you're unable to obtain because you lack additional interpersonal skills.

Sorry, Sinatra, I did it their way . . .

In order to flex your style, you must make small changes in your behaviour. The sorts of changes you need to make depend on the style differences between you and your customer.

Accommodating the introverted customer

If you're dealing with a very private, introverted customer and you have an extroverted, social style, the person may be put off by your more outgoing style. To make him feel comfortable, you need to do the following:

✔ Cut back your sales presentation so as to talk much less than you usually do.

✔ Give your customer plenty of personal space; don't crowd him!

✔ Don't ask too many personal questions.

✔ Speak more quietly than usual.

✔ Ask for his permission to talk about his purchase decision instead of assuming that he wants to talk about it.

✔ Schedule meetings and telephone conversations at his convenience, giving him control over when he talks with you.

✔ Use arm's-length channels of communication more fully. Write him notes and send emails and faxes. Prepare a written report to present your suggested solution to his problem rather than presenting it in person.

In general, your understanding of this customer's need for privacy helps you make sure that he's comfortable around you. You give more personal space, you're careful not to overstay your welcome and you make a point of listening more and leaving more gaps in the conversation to let him think about what you've said. You can solve most of your communication problems just by realising that his greater preference for privacy is at the root of these problems.

Many salespeople and marketers are social by nature and tend to use an extroverted style, which puts off introverted customers. By flexing your own style, you – the public extroverted salesperson – cool down your style significantly. The introverted customer feels more comfortable and at ease in future interactions. He is less likely to form a negative opinion of you and, in fact, probably grows to like you. You seem respectful and polite, and you appear to be a good listener who's more interested in and aware of your customer's preferences and feelings.

Fitting in with the logical customer

Some marketers are very creative, offering lots of creative solutions to problems in a first meeting. This approach confuses some people. A logical person likes to hear one clear plan, with a series of well-defined steps. You do best with logical customers when you do your creative thinking on your own time and then present them with three options and keep your mouth shut while they decide which they like best.

To help them decide, you can also prepare a table listing the pros and cons of each of their options. If you get more ideas in the meeting, write them down and think about them later, on your own time. You have to curb your enthusiasm for creativity when presenting a proposal to a logical customer, so as not to confuse and upset them.

If you tend to be creative, you may also need to be careful to package your ideas and work into clear, logical presentations and sequential plans. Bear in mind that your customer may be a logical person. Clues to a logical, sequential temperament include the following:

✔ Neat desk

✔ Punctuality

✔ Tendency to stay on one topic during conversation

✔ Use of date books, file cabinets and other organising tools

If you're a creative multi-tasker (meaning you tend to skip from topic to topic as you make creative associations), your natural style is going to irritate logical, organised customers. Remember to flex to their style when interacting with them. Organise in advance, stick to the agenda and avoid appearing disorganised.

Adjusting to the creative, free-wheeling customer

Sometimes the sales or marketing person is the organised, logical one and the customer is more free and easy. When your customer is less organised than you, seems forgetful and changes his mind about what he wants at the last minute, you may find yourself uncomfortable with the lack of structure. If so, you need to recognise that your customer's style is more free-wheeling than yours, and that your need for structure may not suit this customer.

When you have a customer who doesn't like to be structured, back off. Let the customer change the topic or jump from one possible purchase to another. Have faith that in his own creative way, this customer is still going to manage to make a purchase decision, even if it's not the one he said he was considering when you first talked about it.

However, sometimes when dealing with very disorganised customers or clients, you do have to provide the structure. If they keep switching from one idea to another but never actually finalise a purchase, you may need to try a wrap-up close, in which you summarise what you think their needs are and suggest a solution (flip to Chapter 17 for details on the wrap-up close and other ways of closing a sale).

Web communication with style

Even when people communicate over the Internet, they want customised treatment in order to feel like their communication needs are being met. But have you ever tried to get help from company employees over the Internet? Emailing them from their website is usually a disaster. Most companies send the same message to every query. And that message is rarely helpful.

Here's a simple way to handle email and website inquiries from customers: ask competent sales or service staff to read every email received from a legitimate customer or prospect. Instruct them to email back immediately with a full reply or a request for more information. Also instruct them to ask how the person would like to proceed. Switch to phone? Stick with email? Get detailed information in the mail? See a salesperson? Visit a location of the business? In other words, get the communication going, and give customers the options so that you can find out their style preferences.

If they reject your effort to narrow them down to one solution, try giving them a choice of three options. Free-wheeling customers like to have options, so it may be easier for them if you give them three ways to close the sale and let them choose which one they like.

Oh, but a word of warning! Your free-wheeling, creative customer may choose none of the options. In this case, be prepared to respond by customising a solution that's a combination of two or three of the options.

What exactly is my way?

Now we want to take a look at your own style. Profiling your own style is critical to understanding how your style compares to your customer's (or distributor's, associate's or anyone else's that you want to work better with in the future).

To complete a style profile, you answer some simple agree/disagree questions, which you can find in the Difficult Customer Diagnostic (see the following section 'Using the Difficult Customer Diagnostic'). These questions give you eight separate scores, which you can plot on a simple graph in order to draw your own style profile and compare it with your customer's. The first four sets of questions address thinking style. The next four sets of questions address interpersonal style. Together, they determine how you work with customers and how your customers prefer you to work with them.

When you look at all this information about yourself and an apparently difficult customer, you almost always find that you and the customer have some significant points of difference. When you adjust your style to accommodate the customer's profile, you can overcome those differences.

Using the Difficult Customer Diagnostic

Some customers can appear to be more difficult than others. When salespeople or account representatives have difficulties dealing with a particular customer or prospect, in spite of multiple efforts to get along or close the sale, the problem is often one of style, not substance.

Often a salesperson has something of legitimate value to offer the customer but can't make the sale because of a mismatch in their styles. Many instances also occur in which an ongoing sales or service relationship seems to be less productive and more difficult than it should be. Again, style issues may be at fault.

In the modern workplace, employees now commonly receive training in how to flex their styles in order to co-operate more effectively with team members or other co-workers. But this simple principle is rarely applied to sales relationships. In the training activity we provide later in this section, salespeople (or customer service representatives) have the chance to do the following:

- ✔ Discover that they have significantly different style profiles than most of their difficult customers.

- ✔ Pick out some simple ideas about how to communicate more effectively with a difficult customer.

- ✔ Find out how to improve their ability to communicate with difficult customers in general by adapting their style to suit the customer's preferences.

By knowing how to communicate in the customer's preferred style, the salesperson truly becomes customer-oriented.

The method we explain is very simple, but it works only when you have the information necessary to analyse profiles correctly. People are often unable to recognise that these key style differences exist until they use a formal diagnostic tool and gain some experience with it. Have a go at filling in the Difficult Customer Diagnostic form in the next section 'Answering the questions' or you can print a clean copy from File 19-1.

Answering the questions

Rate each of the following statements based on how well they fit your own style and the style of a specific customer you have in mind. If a statement fits very well, circle 5. If it doesn't fit at all, circle 1. Or circle a number between these two extremes. Here's the scale:

1 = Not at all

2 = Not really

3 = Maybe, maybe not

4 = Usually

5 = Definitely

When you finish answering the questions, calculate your scores by adding each set of five questions and entering the totals in the Total sections. You get eight scores for yourself and eight scores for your customer. Each score should be somewhere between 5 and 25.

1. Ra Scores

You	How Well Does Statement Fit?	Customer
1 2 3 4 5	Throws self into project without a plan	1 2 3 4 5
1 2 3 4 5	Takes unstructured approach	1 2 3 4 5
1 2 3 4 5	Does not like to follow instructions	1 2 3 4 5
1 2 3 4 5	Likes to work on many things at once	1 2 3 4 5
1 2 3 4 5	Does things out of order	1 2 3 4 5
Your total = ___	Ra scores	Customer's total = ___

2. Se Scores

You	How Well Does Statement Fit?	Customer
1 2 3 4 5	Likes detailed plans	1 2 3 4 5
1 2 3 4 5	Stays focused on a single goal	1 2 3 4 5
1 2 3 4 5	Does things in proper order	1 2 3 4 5
1 2 3 4 5	Follows instructions	1 2 3 4 5
1 2 3 4 5	Is analytical, not intuitive	1 2 3 4 5
Your total = ___	Se scores	Customer's total = ___

3. Di Scores

You	How Well Does Statement Fit?	Customer
1 2 3 4 5	Seeks options and alternatives	1 2 3 4 5
1 2 3 4 5	Seeks new combinations	1 2 3 4 5
1 2 3 4 5	Has many ideas	1 2 3 4 5
1 2 3 4 5	Gets excited about each new thing	1 2 3 4 5
1 2 3 4 5	Asks unusual questions	1 2 3 4 5
Your total = ___	Di scores	Customer's total = ___

4. Co Scores

You	How Well Does Statement Fit?	Customer
1 2 3 4 5	Narrows down the choices	1 2 3 4 5
1 2 3 4 5	Organises projects well	1 2 3 4 5
1 2 3 4 5	Combines projects to get them done	1 2 3 4 5
1 2 3 4 5	Good at finishing things	1 2 3 4 5
1 2 3 4 5	Finds common ground in arguments	1 2 3 4 5
Your total = ___	Co scores	Customer's total = ___

5. Pr Scores

You	How Well Does Statement Fit?	Customer
1 2 3 4 5	Likes to work alone	1 2 3 4 5
1 2 3 4 5	Not very social	1 2 3 4 5
1 2 3 4 5	Finds collaboration difficult	1 2 3 4 5
1 2 3 4 5	Distracted by too many people	1 2 3 4 5
1 2 3 4 5	Keeps thoughts to self	1 2 3 4 5
Your total = ___	Pr scores	Customer's total = ___

6. Pu Scores

You	How Well Does Statement Fit?	Customer
1 2 3 4 5	Enjoys working with others	1 2 3 4 5
1 2 3 4 5	Very social	1 2 3 4 5
1 2 3 4 5	Contributes to groups with confidence	1 2 3 4 5
1 2 3 4 5	Stimulated by other people	1 2 3 4 5
1 2 3 4 5	Likes to share ideas with others	1 2 3 4 5
Your total = ___	Pu scores	Customer's total = ___

7. Re Scores

You	How Well Does Statement Fit?	Customer
1 2 3 4 5	Attracts people who want to talk	1 2 3 4 5
1 2 3 4 5	Good at sensing how others feel	1 2 3 4 5
1 2 3 4 5	Open-minded	1 2 3 4 5
1 2 3 4 5	Asks lots of questions	1 2 3 4 5
1 2 3 4 5	Appreciates advice and suggestions	1 2 3 4 5
Your total = ___	Re scores	Customer's total = ___

8. Ex Scores

You	How Well Does Statement Fit?	Customer
1 2 3 4 5	Shares ideas with others	1 2 3 4 5
1 2 3 4 5	Expresses feelings well	1 2 3 4 5
1 2 3 4 5	Has strong opinions	1 2 3 4 5
1 2 3 4 5	Not afraid to disagree	1 2 3 4 5
1 2 3 4 5	Champions own ideas	1 2 3 4 5
Your total = ___	Ex scores	Customer's total = ___

Interpreting your scores

Using File 19-2, transfer your scores to each bar of the scoring sheet; just circle the appropriate numbers on each side of the black square on the first half of the profile sheet. Then, on each bar, darken the area between your two scores to see what your style looks like. Is the bar centred or biased towards one side? (Usually, people have a clear bias.) And is the bar short, indicating a lack of flexibility, or is it long, indicating that you can use both styles? (Usually, bars are fairly short.)

Next, transfer your customer's scores to the second half of the profile sheet. Darken the areas between scores to draw the customer's bars, just as you did for your own.

Your profile

Random   Sequential

25 23 21 19 15 13 11 9 7 5 ■ 5 7 9 11 13 15 19 21 23 25

How do you think?

Divergent   Convergent

25 23 21 19 15 13 11 9 7 5 ■ 5 7 9 11 13 15 19 21 23 25

What do you think about?

Private   Public

25 23 21 19 15 13 11 9 7 5 ■ 5 7 9 11 13 15 19 21 23 25

Do others use up or give you energy?

Receptive   Expressive

25 23 21 19 15 13 11 9 7 5 ■ 5 7 9 11 13 15 19 21 23 25

Do you tend to listen or talk more?

Your customer's profile

Random   Sequential

25 23 21 19 15 13 11 9 7 5 ■ 5 7 9 11 13 15 19 21 23 25

How does your customer think?

Divergent   Convergent

25 23 21 19 15 13 11 9 7 5 ■ 5 7 9 11 13 15 19 21 23 25

What does your customer think about?

Private   Public

25 23 21 19 15 13 11 9 7 5 ■ 5 7 9 11 13 15 19 21 23 25

Do others use up or give your customer energy?

Receptive   Expressive

25 23 21 19 15 13 11 9 7 5 ■ 5 7 9 11 13 15 19 21 23 25

Does your customer tend to listen or talk more?

Comparing your profile to your customer's

Now that you've plotted your own profile and your difficult customer's profile, you simply need to compare the two and see where the biggest difference lies. On one or more of the bars, your score is probably quite different from the customer's. Your shaded area is centred toward one side, while his is centred toward the other side. Right?

We knew it. Otherwise, he probably wouldn't be a difficult customer! Make a note of which dimensions you differ on so that you can use the advice we give you in the next section. For instance, are you more of a divergent thinker, whereas he's a strongly convergent thinker? (The second line of the profiles shows this dimension.)

Make a note of the one or more dimensions in which your profile is clearly different from your customer's profile. These differences are most likely the root of your difficulties.

You can use the Interpretation Key for the Difficult Customer Diagnosis (in File 19-3) to analyse your results in more detail. This file includes an interpretation key that gives you detailed descriptions and examples illustrating what each of the style names means. See whether your style profile rings true when you look up the styles that dominate your profile.

Prescribing the cure

Now you need to work out how to adapt your style to your customer's style. For instance, if you're more of a divergent thinker and your customer is strongly convergent, you need to adapt the way you think and talk about business with this customer to accommodate his need for a convergent style. For example, convergent thinkers like to focus narrowly and want to move towards closure. They don't want to keep hearing about more complexities or options. They want a neat, orderly directional process that gets them to their end goal efficiently. And you can give them that. You can easily accommodate this style need when you understand it.

The preceding example is only one of thousands. To find out how to deal with your difficult customer, simply locate the appropriate section in the table that appears on the CD as File 19-4.

If you plan to flex your sales style to work well with a difficult customer, you need to prepare by reviewing File 19-4 before you interact with the customer. If you fear that you may have difficulty sticking to the guidelines in a meeting or telephone conversation, make some notes to use during the interaction so that you don't forget your game plan for taming the difficult customer.

Adjusting your service style

Customer service is integral to good marketing because it builds profitable long-term relationships. Just as in sales, the Difficult Customer Diagnostic works well in handling customer service problems and complaints when you have trouble soothing the customer. Some customers just don't like your style. They get increasingly irritated when you try to calm them down. Or they demand to speak to someone else. Some customers become chronic complainers who never seem satisfied. Often the roots of these service difficulties are the differences in your interpersonal styles, which the Difficult Customer Diagnostic measures.

When you flex your service style to make sure that you communicate well with all your customers, everything goes much more smoothly. You acquire loyal customers who like your style and feel that they have good, open communication with you. You're also more likely to hear about any problems early on so you can move to fix them.

In File 19-5, the Difficult Customer Diagnostic is interpreted for use in ongoing service interactions (or perhaps when coping with an escalating customer problem). The principles are the same as in the sales interactions in File 19-4, but the application is a little different, so this more service-oriented table is useful to have, too.

Making Sure Your Ads Hit the Target

A really helpful extension of the profiling exercise is to profile the style of your marketing communications. In other words, use an ad, brochure or website (or several of them) to fill in the 'you' side of the Difficult Customer Diagnostic.

Ask yourself how well each statement describes the style that your marketing communications use. Then ask yourself how well the statements describe your customers in general. Or, if you have the time and resources, turn the diagnostic into a customer survey (just block out the right-hand answer column) and collect data from 50 or more customers about their own styles.

Does a pattern exist? Which style profile is most common among customers? Does it clash with the style of your ad or website? If so, rework your marketing communications to match the dominant customer-style needs so you don't turn customers off with incompatible marketing materials.

Most copywriters and designers who develop marketing materials have unusual style profiles that clash with the average customer. Designers are more random and divergent, and their work is sometimes more public or in your face than customers want. You can use the prescriptions of the Difficult Customer Diagnostic to help shift designers' styles to be more compatible with customers' preferences – making it easier for your marketing messages to connect with customers.

You can profit from your knowledge of your own style profile by seeking out customers who particularly like your style and sharing your profile with them. After all, doing business with people like you is always easier. You can use an ad, website, sales-letter or newsletter to call for people with profiles like your own. Make sure that the messages are an extreme example of your profile. For instance, if you're sequential, make the copy follow a 1-2-3 outline format. Those who share your sequential style are going to enjoy reading it and are going to love your style!

Files on the CD

Check out the following items on the CD-ROM:

- ✔ **File 19-1:** Difficult Customer Diagnostic
- ✔ **File 19-2:** Interpreting Your Score
- ✔ **File 19-3:** Interpretation Keys for the Difficult Customer Diagnostic
- ✔ **File 19-4:** How to Adapt Your Sales Style for a Difficult Customer
- ✔ **File 19-5:** How to Adapt Your Service Style for a Difficult Customer

Part VI
The Part of Tens

'It was a marketing company's suggestion and it's also a great help to the school finances.'

In this part . . .

We give you 30 quick tips and suggestions for boosting your sales and making your marketing more effective and profitable. This part offers ideas that can save you money, maximise your marketing impact, boost results from your website and stimulate new and creative ways of landing new business.

Chapter 20

Ten Great Marketing Strategies

*I*n this chapter, we summarise a range of strategies that have boosted sales and built businesses for other marketers. See whether one of them is a good fit for your marketing programme right now.

Going for Market Share Now – and Worrying about Raising Profits Later

Businesses with the greatest market share do best, and that's a fact – they make more profits and have an easier time growing their sales. That's why computer manufacturer Dell slashed prices as it introduced significantly improved servers and computers in 2008, at a time when its market share had been eaten into by Hewlett-Packard and other competitors. Dell's marketing strategy was to increase market share now, so as to ensure better profits later.

Ask yourself whether you're already the clear leader in your market. Even if that market is local or a narrow niche compared to Dell's global arena, the relationship between market share and profits is likely to apply. If you aren't the clear leader, can you grow your market share significantly while operating at least at break-even? If so, it may be worth taking the losses on the chin for a year or two in order to reposition yourself for longer term profitability and market dominance.

Be careful to protect your pricing while growing your market share. Don't slash your prices. Instead, invest in marketing that promotes your image, reaches out to new customers and strengthens your sales process.

This strategy can be risky, and you must ensure that you're not gaining market share at the expense of important factors such as a workable business plan, robust profit and loss or a price premium. Remember that a strong marketing programme isn't employed to the detriment of other parts of the business in the long run.

Sponsoring a Community Event

Nike is a global sports clothes manufacturer, well known for glitzy and expensive brand advertising campaigns – usually featuring some famous sports stars. However, the brand is also a master at creating and supporting local community or grass roots initiatives that offer something to the local community and foster positive sentiment towards the Nike brand.

A great example of this is the brand's 10K run in London. This grass roots running event, also known as Nike Run London, encourages people to train towards a community 10-kilometre run in the capital. The brand provides a host of online tools to help people to train, from websites where you can plot your favourite runs on a map and then share them with friends, to more detailed information about sports equipment and advice from experts.

The initiative culminates in the event itself, but it lives online perpetually through these other elements, ensuring that the brand is synonymous with sports and achievement.

We're not suggesting that you try and create your own event, unless you have a great idea, but take time to find an event that you can be associated with and to which you can bring real value, in the same way Nike does to its Run London event.

You want to sponsor an event that's good for your image and that attracts large numbers of your prospective customers, but also one with which you have a natural fit – so don't just put your name to anything, do a little legwork to see what works for you. If you're a building business for example, you can get involved in community building projects by supplying your services or if you're a hairdresser, you can become a sponsor of the local theatre group's annual pantomime – again offering your skills.

Finding the Right Trade Show

Have you ever gone into a number of different department stores, boutiques and specialist shops and seen the same wonderful 'unique and unusual' porcelain figures that your grandmother just has to have? Do you wonder how the maker of these figures, who fires them in her own garden kiln, manages to be so effectively on the map as a supplier to upscale gift stores? The answer is likely that she simply attends one trade show each year where she rents a booth, shows her work and collects orders. The show attracts buyers from gift stores and galleries far and wide, and they place their orders at the show and then reorder by phone during the year if the products sell well.

Picking the right trade show – and focusing all your resources on getting there and presenting you and your products well – is often the best way to build a wholesale business.

If you aren't already familiar with the trade show, attend it as an individual guest the first time around and make sure that it attracts lots of your prospective customers. Also, check out the marketing support the trade show gives its exhibitors. Some shows are great about support, sending lots of promotional materials prior to the show. Others are more oriented toward a conference or other associated event and don't seem to be as focused on helping you market your wares. Favour the shows that really get it and are on the same marketing page you are.

Updating the Benefits You Emphasise in Your Marketing Communications

The needs of customers change. Periodically ask yourself what your customers' biggest priorities are today.

A simple example is provided by prospective car purchasers. When the price of petrol spikes, mileage rises to the top of the list of priorities. When petrol is cheap and the economy is booming, fashion and status are dominant. But when customers have babies, safety and carrying capacity may come to the fore. Seasonally, priorities can change, too. A cold winter with lots of snow pushes handling and winter road performance to the top of the list, along with remote starting and the quality of the heating and defrosting systems.

You get the idea: customer priorities aren't stable. If you keep your ear to the ground and adjust your marketing message accordingly, you're more in step with current concerns and priorities than most marketers.

As well as reacting promptly to changing customer priorities, a similar, useful strategy is to keep your customers' attention by applying innovative thinking to your product range or services menu.

Fairgrounds and other amusement parks market themselves on what's new, as well as what's traditional, and you can try doing the same thing.

Use your imagination and product development skills to come up with new ideas that can be launched every three months. The 90-day cycle maximises the chances of getting good editorial coverage, which, of course, is free marketing. We like free marketing. How about you? (See Chapter 11 for details of how to publicise your new attraction.)

Rewarding Large Purchasers

Many retailers use a strategy that encourages customers to buy more than they normally would in order to get a free gift. This gift sometimes takes the form of vouchers – 'Spend £100 in store today and receive a £10 voucher to spend on our website' – or it can take the form of physical goods – 'Spend over £50 on cosmetics today and you receive this free travel make-up bag'.

If you're going to adopt this strategy, you should try and make it work as hard as possible for you. Too often marketers offer deals that aren't linked to the size of purchase. Thus, businesses tend to reward many small customers. But in most businesses, the fewer big customers are the most valuable. Why not target your promotions to them? Here's one way to go about it:

1. **Calculate your average purchase size.**

2. **Multiply it by 1.5.**

3. **Offer an incentive (free product, special gift, reward or extra service) to anyone who buys more than that amount.**

   The incentive can also be a 10 to 15 per cent discount on a future purchase.

Telling Your Customers How You're Saving Energy and Materials

A so-called *green marketing strategy* is simply an effort to reduce waste by using recycled materials, reducing energy usage and doing other things that benefit both your bottom line and the environment. Most businesses are doing some of these things already, but fail to tell their customers about their green initiatives. We recommend telling them more, and using the simple and non-intimidating term *Green Initiatives* or *Sustainable Initiatives* to describe these activities.

Put a bulleted list of your green endeavours in your catalogue or on your website and on your packaging or envelopes. If you have even three items for the list, go ahead and use it. Over time, you're likely to get good feedback and start adding more initiatives.

Green marketing is becoming more important as consumers become more interested in the provenance of goods and services and their impact on the world. This trend is set to continue as younger generations, who have been brought up aware of the impact of their lives on the planet, grow up and become the consumers of tomorrow – and so starting your green efforts now, rather than later, is worthwhile.

Allowing Customers to Access You Easily

Nobody likes call centres. Although providing your customers with contact points is good, even better is giving them contact details that can really help them. If you aren't a massive business, why not try giving customers your personal phone or mobile number? They aren't going to use it very often, but when they do, they'll have an important question and be glad when you can take their call and solve their issues.

Introducing Products or Services at a High Price and Then Cutting Price with Volume

This strategy is a favourite at high-tech companies. Witness the launch of any new TV, DVD, MP3 player or mobile phone and you can see this strategy in action. When the product is hot and new, the retailer charges a premium for it – therefore creating a certain level of desirability for the product, which, being so expensive, is obviously going to be good! However, a few months later that same product will no doubt be much cheaper as initial demand has dropped off or other competing products have come on the market.

Often when you introduce something new, you're unsure of how big the market is going to be or what the ultimate price should be. You may not even be sure yet of your own costs. A safer bet, therefore, is to introduce a new product at a fairly high price, see what happens and then adjust downward as needed. If you find you've got a bestseller (as Apple did when it introduced the iPhone), you can cut prices aggressively. If not, your margin is protected at lower volume by the high introductory price.

Letting Prospects Test You

Do you think that your product is superior? Let prospects find out by offering them a free trial. Apple used this technique successfully with its 'test drive a Macintosh' promotion, and the practice is traditional among retailers of intangible goods (such as computer software and online services) who are sure that when a customer tries their product, which doesn't cost them anything to arrange, they are sure to go on and buy it.

Getting Everyone Talking about You

With a little creativity, any business or salesperson can take advantage of the outrageousness strategy. For example, mobile phone company Orange recently dumped a giant popcorn box on Londoners to celebrate the anniversary of its Orange Wednesdays 2-4-1 cinema ticket offer. The event received considerable press coverage due to its unusual nature – not to mention the great photo opportunities that it created.

You don't have to be a massive mobile phone company to arrange this sort of event; it can be as simple as hiring a snake handler to bring her pet python to your bookstore to celebrate the launch of a new nature book. With a little imagination, the possibilities are endless.

Chapter 21

Ten Ways to Make Marketing Pay

Marketing needs to be bottom-line oriented. You can't treat it as a black hole into which you toss money after funding the annual payroll. Marketing is an essential part of a growing, successful organisation, and you must approach it as a vital business discipline at all times. This chapter offers tips to help you make marketing a productive and financially-sound part of your business.

Printing Advertising Material Yourself

Traditionally, marketers have been heavy users of printing and copying services, and the printing bills tend to get out of control in a hurry. Today you can purchase colour laser printers that handle multiple types of job, from large square sheets to long banners.

For example, we sometimes use our office printers to crank out everything from colour catalogue pages, fliers, product sheets, rate cards and numerous other marketing materials. The cost per sheet is very low for small batches, compared to the cost of using a professional printer. And bear in mind that if you don't need to run off printed materials in their tens or hundreds of thousands, this printing method can be cost effective.

If you're going to print your own marketing materials, remember that quality matters and make sure that you use appealing, professional graphic design and a good quality paper. A little extra care in the design of your piece doesn't add costs but does increase effectiveness.

Doing More Publicity

If anything you do or say may be newsworthy, make sure that you tell the media about it early and often. You need to send a press release at least every quarter, if not every month. Just make sure that you work out what news value your business can offer to the media instead of pitching something that interests you or your business's executives. Publicity is free advertising, and it ought to be a large part of your marketing.

Using More Distributors

We haven't seen any firm that can't sell through other businesses in one way or another. Creatively using distributors (call them sales partners, if you like) is a great way to expand your marketing footprint using someone else's budget.

For example, in our businesses, someone has the responsibility of seeking and courting distributors, and the goal is to try to add a new one each month. The sales through distributors have grown from zero a few years ago to about 20 per cent of our total sales now. That's a lot of business that our firms wouldn't have found left to their own devices.

Giving More Product Away

The more you give away, the more you make, and the more economical your marketing programme is. This paradox is true because, in general, the best advertisement for a product is the product itself (and we use the word 'product' broadly here, to include services or whatever you want to sell).

So please, find more ways to give prospects an opportunity to sample your wares or experience your service. Doing so cuts out a lot of expensive marketing by giving your prospects the real thing instead of having to spend your time and money trying to tell them about it. Some of the best consulting jobs we've ever seen in marketing involved simply figuring out how to get the client's free samples, test drives or other giveaways to good prospects so that the product sells itself. Nothing is more powerful in all marketing.

Editing Your Marketing Material

As writers and marketers, we often notice that marketing materials, websites and so on are out of control. Sometimes you can save money and produce better results by simply cutting down and cleaning up all your written materials.

We guarantee that you can punch up the impact and cut costs if you edit all your materials with the goal of cutting the total number of marketing pages in half. Give it a try.

Eating out More

Many businesses have a formal marketing programme, and then the real programme, networking – where the good customers actually come from. More often than not, customers really come from word of mouth – from the personal contacts and networks of key people in the business.

If this generalisation is true for your business, consider cutting the formal marketing stuff (ads, catalogues and so on) back by 15 per cent and putting that money into networking instead. Go to more events and conferences. Take more customers and industry experts out for lunch. If your personal contacts can produce good leads, you ought to be eating out every day. Become the best entertainer in your industry – just make sure that you can afford to pay the bill!

Slashing Unproductive Programmes

Every business has a few marketing activities or expenses that don't pull their weight. Usually they exist because they're traditional, and nobody thinks to question having them. Well, we think that the time is right to sacrifice these sacred cows. If you never seem to get any sales from those expensive ads in your industry's premiere trade magazine, try cutting them out of the budget and see whether anything bad happens.

Investing More in Your Stars

The 80:20 rule usually applies to marketing: 80 per cent of the results come from 20 per cent of the marketing activities. So figure out what your best marketing activities are and shift funding toward them. For example, in many businesses today, the return on investment for web-based marketing is considerably higher than for print advertising, yet print still gets a bigger share of the budget.

Increasing your return on investment from marketing is easy – you simply shift your spending into the highest-return activities that you have. Focusing on the one or two most effective marketing activities is the essence of our advice in Chapter 2 about finding your marketing zone. Keep experimenting until you have a pyramid-shaped programme with most of your marketing budget going to effective primary and secondary marketing methods.

Maintaining Your Profile through Events

Events like industry breakfasts and how-to seminars for customers and prospects are powerful ways to make connections and establish your identity as a leading expert in your field. But events take planning and organisation, which intimidates many marketers who therefore never use them.

Your business should stage at least one high-profile event each quarter. They're surprisingly economical ways to build visibility and attract or retain top customers. (See *Marketing For Dummies 2nd Edition*, also written by us and published by Wiley, for how-to information.)

But keep those events modest in scope, making sure to invite only those prospects who fit your profile for good customers. You don't want to waste time and money entertaining people who aren't ever going to make a big purchase.

Controlling Product Costs

The cost of purchasing or producing your product is a hidden driver of your marketing and sales efficiency. Given a big enough margin, you can afford to market anything. Too often, however, we find that businesses are trying to make their marketing programme sell something on a razor-thin margin. With a tight profit margin, nothing is left to spend on sales and marketing. This common problem may be misdiagnosed: it gives the illusion that the marketing programme is to blame when profits are poor.

Instead of blaming the marketing, try cutting costs and improving the margin on the product. A good general rule in many businesses is that you want at least a five-fold difference between basic production or purchase cost and the list price at which you sell the product. Spend time and imagination seeking ways to reduce your product costs so that you can market with a big margin. Then you can afford to do good marketing and build a following for your product.

Chapter 22

Ten Effective Ways to Market on the Web

In This Chapter

▶ Determining your website's purpose

▶ Taking advantage of web marketing

*T*he Internet is obviously a hot marketing medium, and it's one of the most affordable and effective ways to get your message across. So don't be afraid of experimenting with it. This chapter details winning ideas for marketing on the web.

Experimenting with Virtual Brochures and Catalogues

Whether you decide to go the whole hog and launch an e-commerce business or just dabble in web marketing, you need to be aware of the Internet's many valuable contributions to marketing. Here are a few options that are working well for many businesses:

- ✔ Creating interactive, interesting and/or informational *virtual brochures* on websites for customers and prospects: such sites often generate good leads.

- ✔ Searching for prospects by sending emails or buying banner ads.

- ✔ Building relationships with prospects by producing email newsletters.

- ✔ Running a *virtual store* or *virtual catalogue* where people can go to examine your wares and place orders.

- ✔ Maintaining a site that fulfils the service needs of your customers – for example, by giving them up-to-date information about their orders.

Having a Well-Defined Objective

No matter how you choose to use your website, you must have a clear marketing objective. When you do so, you can see what each web-marketing option is supposed to do for you and why it may appeal to your prospects. The basic rule to marketing on the Internet is: *always design your web marketing with a specific, well-defined marketing objective in mind.*

Building a badly thought-out website is a waste of time, money and effort; it only makes your business look unprofessional. You don't help your business by spending time or money simply creating a presence on the Internet. Know what you're accomplishing and why the Internet is a good way to accomplish it. Then, and only then, are you ready to discover how to take advantage of this complex environment's many possibilities.

One of the best objectives is to use the Internet to generate leads. Another good objective is to try switching your customers from person-to-person to web-based ordering. Whatever your aim, be clear about it and design your website to achieve it.

Using a Power Name

When you know what you want your website to accomplish, pick and register a name for it. (If you have a website that doesn't get enough traffic, consider improving the domain name.) Check with your Internet Service Provider (ISP) or any number of registration services that advertise on the Internet to find out how to register the name of your choice. (You can use various services, such as Nominet and NetNames.) And don't be disappointed if the first name you try is already taken. Just try a variant of it.

The best names meet three simple criteria:

- They're relevant to the site's purpose.
- They're easy to remember and spell.
- They're unique, meaning that they're not easily confused with competitors.

So, for example, www.airtravel.com is a great name for a site that brokers aeroplane tickets and holidays involving an aeroplane flight: it's relevant, easy and nobody is likely to spell it wrong. People tend to remember an obvious and intuitive name. Domain names like this one have real marketing potential, and you should keep thinking until you have a power name for your Internet business. (In fact, we see that a business is using that name to broker Caribbean holidays. More power to them!)

Acting outrageously

An interesting alternative to a power name is to choose an outrageous moniker that sticks in everyone's minds.

Bookseller `Amazon.co.uk` is a good example of the effectiveness of this strategy. The name sounds like the business has something to do with travel in Brazil or the preservation of rain forests. But that's not a problem for `Amazon.co.uk` because it received so much press coverage that it taught everyone to associate this name with its products.

Maybe you should use this strategy, too. For example, if you market quality cuts of meat on the Internet, see whether `www.karatechop.com` is available and create a high-powered site that uses lots of exciting martial arts images to promote your product.

Maintaining clarity

When choosing a domain name, avoid words that can be spelled more than one way. Often people give out web addresses verbally over the phone, in conversation, or on the radio in an interview or in an ad. You don't want to have to spell a name or explain that the user has to type an underline symbol to separate two words.

For example, if you're a sail maker, you may choose the address `www.sail.com`. But this address is ambiguous because people may think that you're saying *sale* rather than *sail*. Better to lengthen it enough to make the name unambiguous. `www.sailmakers.com` works better.

If you're set on picking a name that may be misspelled or spelled in more than one way, buy the other domain as well and point it directly to your main site; this is also a good way to ensure that your rivals can't buy up these misspellings and use them to steal away business meant for you.

Going global

If you're marketing in a non-English-speaking country, consider creating more than one domain name: one in the local language and one in English. English seems to be emerging as the dominant language of the Internet, at least for businesses. And your ISP can easily route visitors from more than one address to the same site.

Giving Away Great Content

People don't surf the Internet to read sales pitches and lengthy bragging about how great a business is. The number one reason people return to a site is the quality of the content.

To attract and retain high-quality visitors, you need to create and post valuable content, which is a real challenge. Are you up to it? If not, consider hiring a writer to create some good content.

Also, see whether you can give away some technical information or advice that people value. Your site needs to be a modern-day encyclopaedia, a place where prospective customers go for help. The more information you give away, the more you sell.

Take a look at the website for food-stock brand Knorr. Now, what makes people visit a site about stock cubes? Well, probably most people simply use the website at first to find out where to buy them. But because the site has so many information-heavy and entertaining elements, they may stick around to see the recipes, tips and videos, and an email newsletter from celebrity chef Marco Pierre White.

The end result of visiting the Knorr website is that people probably spend a lot more time there than they expect and end up looking at the recipes and other products in the range. Then they may decide to try some of the recipes or other products; as a result of its online content, Knorr has managed to sell more than the visitor initially intended to buy.

Most businesses have lots of raw content just gathering dust. Search your file cabinets and hard drives for how-to lists, old press releases, catalogues, brochures and even old customer proposals or reports. You can create lots of useful pages by editing these source materials into case studies (always ask for permission!) and tips or advice.

Minimising Your Load Time

When people have to wait for a table, their interest in a restaurant declines. The same is true for a website. No matter how much great information you give away or how many useful products you sell at incredible prices, your site may not be appealing unless people can get to it in a hurry.

What's a hurry? One approach is to compare your site's load time to the load times of some of the most popular e-commerce sites:

Site	Average Load Time (Seconds)
www.amazon.co.uk	3.2
www.borders.co.uk	4.4
www.hmv.co.uk	4.0
www.johnlewis.co.uk	2.1

We wonder whether the fact that Amazon.co.uk does a lot more business than competitor Borders and just happens to have a shorter load time is a coincidence.

If your load time isn't virtually instantaneous, you're going to lose a lot of potential visitors. Those big, expensive sites are investing a lot in fast load times, and they're setting the pace for anyone who wants to market on the Internet. Also, recognise that a trade-off exists between fancy content and load time. Keep in mind that Flash files and large graphics and files slow down load time. A good way to avoid this problem is to keep large graphic and video files off the home page and allow visitors to elect to open them after the page has loaded.

Creating a Sense of Community

Encourage interaction among your visitors, for example, through the use of bulletin boards, discussion forums and chat rooms. (The latter only work well, though, if you have high traffic; otherwise you may simply appear unpopular if people aren't interested in taking part in a conversation on your site.)

When consumers make meaningful connections on your site, traffic grows, and you generate more interest, leads and sales. And the sense of community you build helps ensure that visitors keep coming back.

Holding Contests

Stimulate interest through the use of contests for visitors. Pick something that's participatory (why don't you get visitors to submit something of their own?) and give prizes or announce winners fairly frequently. You can have a 'best spoof ad' of the month or 'craziest place the product turns up' contest each week.

Post submissions on the website, if possible, to encourage people to spend time examining them. (For example, a florist may invite people to submit photos of floral arrangements and pick the best arrangement every two weeks.) Or even ask visitors to your site to vote for their favourites.

You may have to do some publicity to let people know about your contest, but the ongoing results can be well worth the time!

Adding a News Feature

Provide new content regularly. You can do so in a What's New section or page or in a regularly updated News and Views section, guest column or Headline News section summarising the latest developments in your industry.

In essence, this technique is what people now like to call *blogging*, but really, it's just creating an interesting column that you update as often as possible – daily is best, if you have the time.

Taking Advantage of Links

Use links to create lots of easy paths back to your site. Often people don't return to a website because they simply don't recall it. But if they run into a link and remember that your site was great, they're likely to come back.

How do you create links? The general strategy is to ask other people with websites to add your URL to their pages. Usually they want a reciprocal agreement, which is fine. Also, try adding a Link to Us page on your site with linking images that other site managers can copy and use on their sites.

Bidding on Key Terms

A helpful technique is to play in the great game of search terms. Google offers easy-to-use, effective paid listings to go along with their search engines. We like the way you can adjust your selection of terms, message and bid amount as often as you want. This way, you can control your web-ad spending and keep experimenting until you find a combination that generates lots of business.

If you're not already using *paid-for links* (where you run a short ad next to the Google search results that appears when someone searches for a term linked to whatever product or service you're marketing) paid listings or search terms, go online right now and explore the options. Set up an account. Start discovering how to place your link where people are going to see it when they're searching for your product or service.

All good web marketing plans use this method – and savvy marketers check their search-term ad performance and adjust it weekly or daily.

Avoid terms that have millions of hits a day such as 'CD' or 'book'. These are very expensive because many people want to use them. Narrow your field by bidding on more specific terms or combinations of terms. For example, if you produce books about cooking, bid on the term 'cooking books' or 'chef books'. The more specific you can be the better; try 'Italian cooking books' or 'Tuscan cooking books'. This technique reduces your costs and improves effectiveness.

Appendix

About the CD

· ·

· ·

*T*he CD-ROM that accompanies this book is a treasure trove of do-it-yourself files for you to use when putting your marketing plan together. Here, we give you a few tips on how to use the CD, what you'll find on it and what to do if you have any problems.

System Requirements

Make sure that your computer meets the minimum system requirements shown in the following list. If your computer doesn't match up to most of these requirements, you may have problems using the software and files on the CD. For the latest and greatest information, please refer to the ReadMe file located at the root of the CD-ROM.

- ✔ A PC running Microsoft Windows or Linux with kernel 2.4 or later
- ✔ A Macintosh running Apple OS X or later
- ✔ An Internet connection
- ✔ A CD-ROM drive

If you need more information on the basics, check out these books published by Wiley: *PCs For Dummies,* by Dan Gookin; *Macs For Dummies,* by Edward C. Baig; *iMacs For Dummies* by Mark L. Chambers; *Windows XP For Dummies* and *Windows Vista For Dummies,* both by Andy Rathbone.

Using the CD

To access the items on the CD, follow these steps.

1. **Insert the CD into your computer's CD-ROM drive.**

   The license agreement appears.

   Note to Windows users: The interface won't launch if you have autorun disabled. In that case, choose Start➪Run. (For Windows Vista, choose Start➪All Programs➪Accessories➪Run.) In the dialog box that appears, type *D*:**\Start.exe**. (Replace *D* with the proper letter if your CD drive uses a different letter. If you don't know the letter, see how your CD drive is listed under My Computer.) Click OK.

   Note for Mac Users: When the CD icon appears on your desktop, double-click the icon to open the CD and double-click the 'Start' icon.

2. **Read through the license agreement and then click the Accept button if you want to use the CD.**

   The CD interface appears. The interface allows you to browse the contents and/or install them on your computer with just a click of a button (or two).

What You'll Find on the CD

The following sections provide a summary of the files and software you'll find on the CD. If you need help with accessing the items provided on the CD, refer to the instructions in the preceding section.

Files

All of the marketing files referred to in the book are included on the CD-ROM. You can automatically copy all of the files to your hard drive by clicking on the 'Copy Files to Local Drive' button within the interface. This takes you to a screen with directions on how to copy the files to your local hard drive.

The files come as Microsoft Word and Excel files which you can modify and use to your best advantage, and Adobe Reader (PDF) files, which you can't modify, but if you have Adobe Reader, you can view and print them. Adobe Reader for Mac and Windows is included on the CD-ROM.

Table A-1	Files at a Glance
File Number	*File Name*
File 2-1	Your Five Minute Marketing Plan
File 2-2	Your Marketing Zone Programme Worksheet
File 2-3	Your Marketing Zone Planning Pyramid
File 3-1	Marketing Audit
File 3-2	Audit Score Form
File 3-3	Marketing Agenda
File 3-4	Marketing Plan Template
File 3-5	Marketing Budget Worksheet
File 3-6	Sales Projection Worksheet
File 4-1	Tips for Boosting Sales
File 4-2	The Message Pyramid
File 5-1	Budgeting for Advertising A Practical Approach
File 5-2	Annual Advertising Budget and Plan
File 5-3	Advertising Objectives Worksheet
File 5-4	Monthly and Annual Advertising Budget Templates
File 6-1	An image ad template
File 6-2	Informative ad template
File 6-3	Informative ad template
File 6-4	Call-to-action ad template
File 6-5	Call-to-action ad template
File 6-6	Insurance company ad
File 6-7	Postcard design sample
File 6-8	Postcard front and back templates
File 7-1	Four standard business card designs
File 7-2	Business card sheet for printing
File 7-3	Colourful business card made from a free HP template
File 7-4:	Sample letterhead design with strong visual appeal
File 7-5:	Editable Word version of sample letterhead design
File 8-1	Product Offerings brochure template in Word
File 8-2	Brochure template with photographic design elements
File 8-3	Illustration of bitmapped versus vector line art options
File 9-1	Coupon Profitability Analysis

(continued)

Table A-1 *(continued)*

File Number	File Name
File 9-2	Excel spreadsheet for doing your own coupon profitability analysis
File 10-1	A newsletter marked to show how modular design is used
File 10-2	Seasonal newsletter Word template
File 10-3	What's New four-page Word newsletter template
File 11-1	A well-done press release
File 12-1	Customer Debriefing Form (template)
File 12-2	7 x 7 Customer Satisfaction Survey
File 12-3	Customer Service Audit (template)
File 13-1	Creative Roles Analysis
File 14-1	Evaluation Form 1
File 14-2	Two Dimensions of Your Appeal
File 14-3	Evaluation Form 2
File 14-4	Press release about new Xerox logo
File 15-1	Script for soliciting a testimonial
File 15-2	Follow up letter script
File 16-1	Prospect Analysis Sheet
File 16-2	Question Preplanning Form
File 18-1	Attitudes of Success Profile
File 19-1	Difficult Customer Diagnostic
File 19-2	Interpreting Your Score
File 19-3	Interpretation Keys for the Difficult Customer Diagnostic
File 19-4	How to Adapt Your Sales Style for a Difficult Customer
File 19-5	How to Adapt Your Service Style for a Difficult Customer

Other software

We've included the freeware software Adobe Reader from Adobe Systems for Mac OS and Windows on the CD-ROM. This programme enables you to view and print Portable Document Format (PDF) files.

Freeware programs are free, copyrighted games, applications, and utilities. You can copy them to as many computers as you like – for free – but they offer no technical support. *Shareware programs* are fully functional, free, trial versions of copyrighted programs. If you like particular programs, register with their authors for a nominal fee and receive licenses, enhanced versions, and technical support. *GNU software* is governed by its own license, which is included inside the folder of the GNU software. There are no restrictions on distribution of GNU software. See the GNU license at the root of the CD for more details. *Trial*, *demo* or *evaluation* versions of software are usually limited either by time or functionality (such as not letting you save a project after you create it).

Troubleshooting

Hopefully, you won't encounter any problems using the CD. In the unlikely event that you do, two possible problems are that you don't have enough memory (RAM) or you have other programmes running that are affecting installation or running of a programme. If you get an error message such as Not enough memory or Setup cannot continue, try one or more of the following suggestions and then try using the software again:

- **Turn off any antivirus software running on your computer.** Installation programmes sometimes mimic virus activity and may make your computer incorrectly believe that it's being infected by a virus.

- **Close all running programmes.** The more programmes you have running, the less memory is available to other programmes. Installation programmes typically update files and programmes; so if you keep other programmes running, installation may not work properly.

- **Ask your local computer shop to add more RAM to your computer.** This is, admittedly, a drastic and somewhat expensive step. However, adding more memory can really help the speed of your computer and allow more programmes to run at the same time.

Customer Care

If you have trouble with the CD-ROM, contact Wiley Product Technical Support at http://support.wiley.com. Wiley Publishing will provide technical support only for installation and other general quality control items. For technical support on the applications themselves, consult the program's vendor or author.

Index

BROOKLANDS COLLEGE LIBRARY
WEYBRIDGE, SURREY KT13 8TT

FOR DUMMIES®

Making Everything Easier!™

UK editions

BUSINESS

978-0-470-51806-9

978-0-470-74381-2

978-0-470-71382-2

FINANCE

978-0-470-99280-7

978-0-470-71432-4

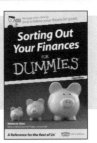

978-0-470-69515-9

HOBBIES

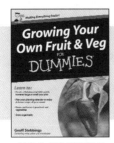

978-0-470-69960-7

978-0-470-74535-9

978-0-470-75857-1

British Sign Language
For Dummies
978-0-470-69477-0

Business NLP For Dummies
978-0-470-69757-3

Competitive Strategy For Dummies
978-0-470-77930-9

Cricket For Dummies
978-0-470-03454-5

CVs For Dummies, 2nd Edition
978-0-470-74491-8

Digital Marketing For Dummies
978-0-470-05793-3

Divorce For Dummies, 2nd Edition
978-0-470-74128-3

eBay.co.uk Business All-in-One
For Dummies
978-0-470-72125-4

Emotional Freedom Technique For
Dummies
978-0-470-75876-2

English Grammar For Dummies
978-0-470-05752-0

Flirting For Dummies
978-0-470-74259-4

Golf For Dummies
978-0-470-01811-8

Green Living For Dummies
978-0-470-06038-4

Hypnotherapy For Dummies
978-0-470-01930-6

IBS For Dummies
978-0-470-51737-6

Lean Six Sigma For Dummies
978-0-470-75626-3

**Available wherever books are sold. For more information or to order direct go to www.wiley.com
or call +44 (0) 1243 843291**

8041_p1

FOR DUMMIES®

A world of resources to help you grow

UK editions

SELF-HELP

978-0-470-01838-5

978-0-7645-7028-5

978-0-470-74193-1

Motivation For Dummies
978-0-470-76035-2

Overcoming Depression For Dummies
978-0-470-69430-5

Personal Development All-In-One For
Dummies
978-0-470-51501-3

Positive Psychology For Dummies
978-0-470-72136-0

PRINCE2 For Dummies
978-0-470-51919-6

Psychometric Tests For Dummies
978-0-470-75366-8

Raising Happy Children
For Dummies
978-0-470-05978-4

Sage 50 Accounts For Dummies
978-0-470-71558-1

Succeeding at Assessment Centres For
Dummies
978-0-470-72101-8

Sudoku For Dummies
978-0-470-01892-7

Teaching English as a Foreign
Language For Dummies
978-0-470-74576-2

Teaching Skills For Dummies
978-0-470-74084-2

Time Management For Dummies
978-0-470-77765-7

Understanding and Paying Less
Property Tax For Dummies
978-0-470-75872-4

Work-Life Balance For Dummies
978-0-470-71380-8

STUDENTS

978-0-470-74047-7

978-0-470-74711-7

978-0-470-74290-7

HISTORY

978-0-470-99468-9

978-0-470-51015-5

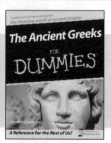

978-0-470-98787-2

**Available wherever books are sold. For more information or to order direct go to www.wiley.com
or call +44 (0) 1243 843291**